Lecture Notes in
Computer Science

Edited by G. Goos and J. Hartmanis

381

J. Dassow J. Kelemen (Eds.)

Machines, Languages, and Complexity

5th International Meeting of Young Computer Scientists
Smolenice, Czechoslovakia, November 14–18, 1988
Selected Contributions

Springer-Verlag
Berlin Heidelberg New York London Paris Tokyo Hong Kong

Volume Editors

Jürgen Dassow
Sektion Mathematik, Technische Universität Magdeburg
Postfach 124, DDR–3010 Magdeburg, GDR

Jozef Kelemen
Institute of Computer Science, Comenius University
Mlynská dolina, 842 43 Bratislava, Czechoslovakia

CR Subject Classification (1987): D.2.8, F.1–2, F.4.1–3, I.2.6

ISBN 3-540-51516-X Springer-Verlag Berlin Heidelberg New York
ISBN 0-387-51516-X Springer-Verlag New York Berlin Heidelberg

Printing and binding: Druckhaus Beltz, Hemsbach/Bergstr.
2145/3140-543210 – Printed on acid-free paper

Foreword

The International Meetings of Young Computer Scientists are organized biannually by the Association of Slovak Mathematicians and Physicists in cooperation with the Institute of Computer Science of the Comenius University, Bratislava, and the Computer and Automation Institute of the Hungarian Academy of Sciences, Budapest. The aim of the meetings is threefold: (1) to inform on new and actual trends, results, techniques, and problems in theoretical computer science and related fields by a tutorial and by a relatively large number of invited lectures, (2) to present and to discuss the results of the participants themselves, and (3) to create an opportunity for establishing first professional relations among the participants.

This volume contains the written versions of selected contributions from the scientific programme of the **Fifth International Meeting of Young Computer Scientists** held at Smolenice Castle (Czechoslovakia), November 14-18, 1988. We include the text of the IMYCS tutorial, the texts of all invited lectures as well as some of the communications presented during the meeting's sessions and informal evening sessions.

The volume is divided into five chapters approaching from different perspectives the three crucial notions of the contemporary theoretical computer science -- **machines**, **languages**, and **complexity**.

The first chapter contains the contributions on the theory of formal languages. The contributions are by F. Hinz, G. Jirásková, K.-J. Lange, M. Latteux, and B. Reichel.

The papers dealing with abstract machines are included in the second chapter. These are the contributions by Z. Ésik, K. Inoue, A. Ito, I. Takanami, and A. Slobodová.

The contributions in the third chapter are covered by the common label of algorithmics. They are written by D. Cortolezzis, C. Gaibisso, M. Křivánek, M. Loebl, J. Nešetřil, K. Unger, and D. Wood.

The contributions by F. van Harmelen and K. P. Jantke dealing with important theoretical problems of artificial intelligence form the fourth chapter.

The chapter devoted to cryptography closes the volume. It contains the communication by J. Kari and the IMYCS'88 tutorial by A. Salomaa.

We are indebted to all contributors for their cooperation. We should also like to express our gratitude to the members of the IMYCS'88 programme committee, namely to E. Csuhaj-Varjú, S. K. Dulin, J. Karhumäki, A. Kelemenová, J. Sakarovitch, and M. Szijártó for their valuable work. We highly appreciate the support of the Mathematical Institute of the Slovak Academy of Sciences, and last but not least the willingness of Springer-Verlag to publish this selection.

Magdeburg and Bratislava
May 1989

Jürgen Dassow
Jozef Kelemen

Contents

Chapter 3: **Algorithmics**

Chapter 4: **Artificial Intelligence**

Chapter 5: **Cryptography**

Chapter 1

Languages

QUESTIONS OF DECIDABILITY FOR CONTEXT-FREE CHAIN CODE PICTURE LANGUAGES

Friedheld Hinz
RWTH Aachen, Lehrstuhl für Informatik II
Templergraben 55, 5100 Aachen, FRG

The research was done during the author's stay at IIG,
Institutes for Information Processing,
Graz University of Technology,
Schießstattgasse 4a, A-8010 Graz, Austria

To the glory of God, who gave wisdom to man

Abstract. A picture description is a word over the alphabet {u,d,r,l,↑,↓} with the following interpretation: "move one unit line up (down, right, left, resp.) from the current point" for letter u (d,r,l, resp.) and "lift (sink) the pen" for ↑ (↓) . The set of unit lines traversed with sunk pen is the picture described. A set of pictures given by a set of picture descriptions generated by a context-free grammar is called a context-free (chain code) picture language.

We show that the membership problem and the superpicture problem are undecidable for context-free and for linear context-free picture languages, while the subpicture problem is decidable. This result is in contrast to the situation for *regular* picture languages and for context-free picture languages generated without using a "lift the pen"-symbol. For these classes all three problems are known to be decidable, and the subpicture problem is harder than the superpicture problem (NP-complete instead of polynomial time).

1. INTRODUCTION

There are various approaches to questions of picture description and pattern recognition that apply the knowledge of formal language and automata theory. Acceptor concepts for array picture languages are investigated in [1]. A close connection between string language theory and picture language theory can be established following a suggestion of [7] to interpret a string as a traversal of a picture through its subpatterns. The concept of chain code introduced in [2] can be viewed as an interesting special case thereof. Basically it allows to traverse a picture in the plane using eight directions as shown in Fig. 1.1a. Additional features allow to lift the pen to take it to a new position and sink it again. Subsequent papers simplify the concept using only an alphabet of four letters, {u,d,r,l} , corresponding to the four directions up, down, right, left. For example, the word "urrrddurrldl" describes the picture shown in Fig. 1.1b.

Fig. 1.1a

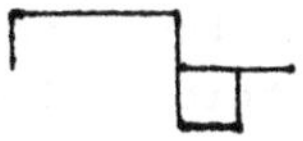

Fig. 1.1b urrrddurrldl

A hierarchy of picture languages analogous to the classical Chomsky hierarchy is established in [4]. The membership problem is shown to be NP-complete by [8] and [3] for regular and context-free chain code picture languages (i.e. sets of pictures described by words in regular resp. context-free string languages). The subpicture problem and the superpicture problem (decide for a picture and a language, whether the picture is subpicture resp. superpicture of a picture described in the language) are shown to be decidable for context-free languages in [4].

The investigation of the class of general picture languages that allow "invisible lines", i.e. that are generated by grammars over {u,d,r,l,↑,↓} , is started in [9]. It is proven that the membership and the subpicture problem are NP-complete for regular picture languages both in the restricted and in the general concept, and that the superpicture problem is solvable in polynomial time. For the restricted concept the superpicture problem of context-free picture languages is also solvable in polynomial time by an algorithm in [6], but for the general concept we will show that the superpicture problem is undecidable. Even for a linear context-free picture language the membership and the superpicture problem will turn out to be undecidable. In contrast to this we will see that the subpicture problem is decidable for all context-free picture languages.

We will first give some basic definitions and show decidability of the subpicture problem for all context-free chain code picture languages (Section 2). In Section 3 we simulate a two-counter-machine by a linear grammar and a set of pictures. Thereby we show that the membership and the superpicture problem are undecidable for linear context-free picture languages. Finally (Section 4) we add some remarks concerning possible variants of the description concept.

2. BASIC DEFINITIONS AND ELEMENTARY PROPERTIES

Let Z be the set of integers and N the set of nonnegative integers. We adopt the basic definitions of formal language theory. A *vertex* is an element of Z^2. A *unit line* is an unordered pair of neighboring vertices $\{(m,n),(m,n+1)\}$ or $\{(m,n),(m+1,n)\}$. An *attached picture* is a finite set of unit lines. An (unattached basic) *picture* is an equivalence class of attached pictures, where two attached pictures are equivalent if they differ only by their relative position in Z^2, but the shape is the same. (We will later give a precise definition of this equivalence relation.) We will say p is a *subpicture* of p' or p' is a *superpicture* of p, if there are representatives $\underline{p}$ of p and $\underline{p'}$ of p' such that $\underline{p} \subseteq \underline{p'}$. When we want to fix a start point and an end point of a picture, we will attach the picture such that the origin $(0,0)$ is the (implicit) initial vertex and use the notion of a *drawn picture*, which is a pair (p,v) consisting of an attached picture p and a (final) vertex v.

The best investigated picture description alphabet so far is the set of unit vectors $\pi = \{u,d,r,l\}$, where $u = (0,1)$, $d = (0,-1)$, $r = (1,0)$, $l = (-1,0)$. However, it can be used to describe connected pictures only. To describe possibly disconnected pictures one may join the set of states $\{\uparrow,\downarrow\}$ to the alphabet, where $\uparrow$ indicates lifting the pen and $\downarrow$ indicates sinking the pen. Intuitively speaking, a state-letter occurring in a word specifies the state of the sequence of moves indicated by the subsequent vector-letters. For example in the word "ur↑ll↓dl" the moves indicated by the subword "ll" are executed with lifted pen and the other with sunk pen, see Fig. 2.1.

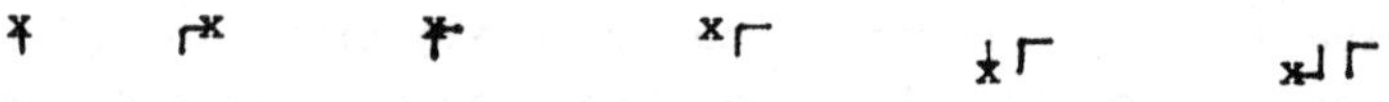

u ur ur↑l ur↑ll ur↑ll↓d ur↑ll↓dl

Fig. 2.1 "x" indicates the current position of the pen

So we consider words over the alphabet $\pi_0 := \pi \cup \{\uparrow,\downarrow\}$. At the end of a word w the pen will be in lifted mode if the last state letter occurring in w is $\uparrow$. The drawn picture described by a word is defined inductively by

$\mathrm{dpic}(\lambda) = (\emptyset,(0,0))$

If $\mathrm{dpic}(w) = (p,v)$, then for every state $s \in \{\uparrow,\downarrow\}$ we set

dpic(ws) = (p,v) and for every vector $b \in \pi$ we set
dpic(wb) = (p,v+b) for $w \in \pi_o^*\{\uparrow\}\pi^*$ and
dpic(wb) = $(p \cup \{v,v+b\}, v+b)$ for $w \notin \pi_o^*\{\uparrow\}\pi^*$

To move the cursor from the origin (0,0) without drawing any lines one can use a "translation word", i.e. an element of $\{\uparrow\}\pi^*\{\downarrow\}$. Two attached pictures p,p′ are equivalent, if there are vertices $v,v' \in Z^2$, a translation word $x \in \{\uparrow\}\pi^*\{\downarrow\}$, and a word $y \in \pi_o^*$ such that dpic(y) = (p,v) and dpic(xy) = (p′,v′) . The equivalence class of p (which is the picture represented by p) is then called the picture described by y and is denoted by pic(y) . Any grammar G (regular, linear, context-free, etc.) generates its string language L(G) , its drawn picture language Dpic(G) := {dpic(w) | $w \in L(G)$} , and its picture language Pic(G) := {pic(w) | $w \in L(G)$} (then also called regular, linear, context-free, etc.). We define the language of all superpictures with respect to G as Super(G) := {p′| p′ is superpicture of some $p \in$ Pic(G)} and the language of all subpictures as Sub(G) := {p′| p′ is subpicture of some $p \in$ Pic(G)} .

Maurer, Rozenberg, and Welzl [4] show that the subpicture problem is decidable for context-free picture languages over π . To transfer this result to languages over π_o we may use a homomorphism h that enlarges the shape of a picture and a generalized sequential machine VIS that is designed to make "unvisible" lines "visible" as shown in the following figure.

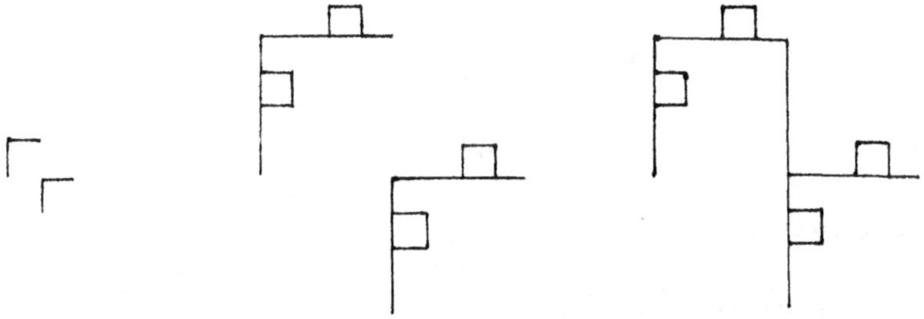

Fig. 2.2 ur↑dr↓ld h(ur↑dr↓ld) VIS(ur↑dr↓ld)

We define h by h(b) = **bburdlbb** for $b \in \pi$ and h(s) = s for $s \in \{\uparrow,\downarrow\}$. The machine VIS consists of the set of states Q = $\{\uparrow,\downarrow\}$, start state $\downarrow$, transition function δ given by

$\delta(q,s) = s$ for $q \in Q$, $s \in \{\uparrow,\downarrow\}$
$\delta(q,b) = q$ for $q \in Q$, $b \in \pi$,

output function pr given by

$pr(q,s) = \lambda$ for $q \in Q$, $s \in \{\uparrow,\downarrow\}$
$pr(\uparrow,b) = bbbb$ for $b \in \pi$
$pr(\downarrow,b) = h(b)$ for $b \in \pi$.

Clearly, pic(h(w)) depends on pic(w) only, so the function h can be extended to pictures. Then it is easy to see that a picture p is subpicture of a context-free language L if and only if h(p) is subpicture of VIS(L) . Since VIS(L) is a context-free language over π , the subpicture problem of VIS(L) is decidable according to [4, Theorem 5.3]. So we have the following

2.1 <u>Theorem</u> The subpicture problem is decidable for context-free chain code picture languages.

It will be shown in a forthcoming paper [10], that moreover the subpicture problem is NP-complete for context-free chain code picture languages.

Intuitively speaking, drawing a picture according to a derivation in a *linear* grammar can be done using *two* cursors: The first one works according to the letters left of the variable and the second one according to the letters right of the variable, in opposite direction. For an example see the following figure:

S

⇒ rAu

⇒ rurrBlrru

⇒ rurrdrrArrdlrru

⇒ rurrdrrrrrrdlrru

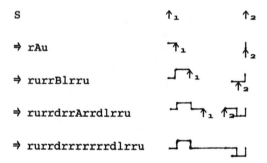

3. SIMULATING A TWO-COUNTER-MACHINE

In this section we introduce the notion of a two-counter-machine. From Minsky [5] we know how to simulate a Turing machine by a two-counter-machine. We present an idea to simulate a two-counter-machine by a linear grammar and a set of pictures. This allows to transfer results about Turing machines to linear picture languages, specifically we obtain that the membership problem and the superpicture problem are undecidable.

A two-counter-machine (tcm) works with two integer counters and a finite memory. Each of the counters may be incremented or decremented or tested for zero, so the set of elementary commands is C = {inc1, inc2, dec1, dec2, if1, if2} . To be precise, C is the set of partial functions from Z^2 to Z^2 given by inc1(m,n)=(m+1,n), dec1(m,n)=(m-1,n), if1(0,n)=(0,n) and if1(m,n) is undefined for $m \neq 0$; the other commands work analogously on the second component. A tcm is a tuple M = (Q,q_0,δ,F) , where Q is a finite set of control states, $q_0 \in Q$ is the initial state, $F \subseteq Q$ is the set of final states, and the transition relation δ is a subset of $Q \times C \times Q$. Intuitively speaking, a triple $(q,c,q') \in \delta$ indicates that for control state q the tcm may carry out command c and change control to the state q' . The single-step-relation $\vdash$ is defined as the smallest subset of $Q \times Z^2$ that contains $(q,(m,n)) \vdash (q',c(m,n))$ for every $(q,c,q') \in \delta$ and $(m,n) \in Z^2$ such that c(m,n) exists. We define the mapping of M as $f_M : Z^2 \to Pot(Z^2)$ given by $f_M(m,n) = \{(m',n') \mid$ there is a $q' \in F$ such that $(q_0,(m,n)) \vdash^* (q',(m',n'))\}$. For example to multiply with 2 we need a machine DUP with $f_{DUP}(m,0) = \{(2m,0)\}$ for every $m \in N$. A solution of this problem is the tcm DUP = $(\{q_0,q_1,\ldots,q_5\},q_0,\delta,\{q_5\})$ with δ given by

$(q_0,dec1,q_1)$ $(q_1,inc2,q_2)$ $(q_2,inc2,q_0)$	$(q_0,(m,0)) \vdash^* (q_0,(0,2m))$ (shift the value of the first counter to the second and duplicate it)
$(q_0,if1,q_3)$	$(q_0,(0,2m)) \vdash (q_3,(0,2m))$ (assure that the above operation is finished)
$(q_3,dec2,q_4)$ $(q_4,inc1,q_3)$	$(q_3,(0,2m)) \vdash^* (q_3,(2m,0))$ (shift the value of the second counter to the first one)
$(q_3,if2,q_5)$	$(q_3,(2m,0)) \vdash (q_5,(2m,0))$ (assure that the above operation is finished)

In an analogous way one can construct a machine that multiplies with an arbitrary fixed integer instead of 2 or divides by an arbitrary fixed integer. Combining such multiplication machines and division machines Minsky [5] builds a tcm to simulate a Turing machine. The concept of Minski is different from our concept, as he allows nonnegative integers for the counters only, i.e. a dec-command is defined for positive value of its counter only. Note that with this change of meaning we still have $f_{DUP}(m,0) = \{(2m,0)\}$ for every $m \in N$. The functions computed by the multiplication machines and division machines of [5] are not affected within the relevant range either. Therefore, we can carry over [5, Theorem 1] to our machine concept and obtain the following

3.1 Proposition Every Turing machine T over the alphabet {0,1} is represented by a tcm M in the following sense: If and only if T, started at the x-th square of its tape with the binary number k as input, may reach a final state at the y-th square with the binary number n as output on its tape, then $(2^n 3^{2^y},0) \in f_M((2^k 3^{2^x},0))$.

It is well-known that for pushdown automata different accepting conditions ("final state", "empty stack", "final state + empty stack") are equivalent. Since we are not interested in the function computed by M, but only in the domain of f_M, we could also use different accepting conditions like "empty counters" or "final state + empty counters". It is not too difficult to see that all these conditions are equivalent. Yet we restrict ourselves to presenting the following

3.2 Lemma For every tcm M there exists a tcm M' such that for every $(m,n) \in Z^2$ we have the following assertion: If $f_M(m,n) \neq \emptyset$ then $f_{M'}(m,n) = \{(0,0)\}$ else $f_{M'}(m,n) = \emptyset$.

Proof Let $M = (Q,q_0,\delta,F)$. We define $M' = (Q \cup \{q_1,q_2,q_3\}, q_0, \delta', \{q_3\})$, where $q_1,q_2,q_3 \notin Q$, by $\delta' := \delta \cup \{(q,\text{inc1},q_1) \mid q \in F\} \cup \{(q_1,\text{dec1},q_1), (q_1,\text{dec2},q_1), (q_1,\text{if1},q_2), (q_2,\text{if2},q_3)\}$. Clearly, M' fulfills the claim. @

3.3 Theorem For every tcm M there are linear grammars G and G' such that for every $m \in N$ the following assertions are equivalent:

(i) $f_M(m,0) \neq \emptyset$

(ii) $\text{dpic}(\uparrow 1^m \downarrow 1r) \in \text{Dpic}(G)$

(iii) $\text{pic}(1\uparrow 1^{3m} \downarrow 11) \in \text{Pic}(G')$

(iv) $\text{pic}(1\uparrow 1^{3m} \downarrow 11) \in \text{Super}(G')$

Proof This proof consists of four parts: At first we construct G; in the second part we show that (i) implies (ii) and in the third we prove that (ii) implies (i). At last we will construct G' and prove the equivalence of (ii), (iii), and (iv).

Part I Construction of G

According to (3.2) we may assume without loss of generality that for $f_M(m,0) \neq \emptyset$ we have $f_M(m,0) = \{(0,0)\}$. Let $p = \text{dpic}(\uparrow 1^m \downarrow 1r)$. The only line in p is called the zero-mark and will be drawn by the grammar G using the word $z := \downarrow 1r$ as often as there is a test for zero in a corresponding computation of M. Recall that drawing a picture according to a derivation in a linear grammar can be understood as drawing it with two cursors. The main idea of the proof is to represent the values of the counters of M as positions of the cursors relative to the zero-mark and will be explained in the following. For $M = (Q, q_0, \delta, F)$ we choose the set Q as set of variables for G , q_0 as start symbol, and the following set of productions:

$q \to \uparrow rq'$	for $(q,inc1,q')\in\delta$	$q \to q'\uparrow l$	for $(q,inc2,q')\in\delta$
$q \to \uparrow lq'$	for $(q,dec1,q')\in\delta$	$q \to q'\uparrow r$	for $(q,dec2,q')\in\delta$
$q \to zq'$	for $(q,if1,q')\in\delta$	$q \to q'z$	for $(q,if2,q')\in\delta$
$q \to z$	for $q\in F$ (final rules)		

<u>Part II</u> (i) implies (ii)

Given a successful computation of M on input (m,0) we construct a derivation in G as follows: In the i-th step apply the rule corresponding to the i-th step of the computation for $i\in\{1,\ldots,n\}$, (where n is the length of the computation,) and in the (n+1)-st step finish with a rule of the form $q\to z$. Since the computation ends in a final state, a suitable rule of the form $q\to z$ must exist. A final rule of this form means that both cursors used to draw the picture according to the derivation meet in the same vertex in the last step, namely at the zero-mark. Remember that M accepts with value zero in both counters. Then it is easily seen by induction that in every step the values of the counters are the same as the positions of the cursors. This has three consequences:

1) A rule of the form $q\to zq'$ can be applied only when the first cursor is at vertex zero, since a triple (q,if1,q') can be applied in a successful computation only when the first counter holds value zero. So an application of that rule always means redrawing the zero-mark, but never adding further lines to the picture drawn in the derivation.
2) By a similar reason a rule of the form $q\to q'z$ can be applied only when the second cursor is at vertex zero and no new lines are added to the picture. The remaining rules use penup-mode only, so the whole derivation draws only one line (the zero-mark).
3) The first step of the derivation finds the cursors in positions m and 0 , so the picture p is drawn.

<u>Part III</u> (ii) implies (i)

Now, on the other hand, let an arbitrary derivation in G of a description of p be given. By construction of G the last and only the last step is an application of a final rule . Omitting this step we can construct a computation of M according to the above table. We have to show that this is a successful computation on input (m,0) .

By definition of the final rules one line is drawn in the last step of the derivation, that is, the zero-mark of p . In the same way as above a correspondence between the values of the counters and the positions of the cursors relative to the zero-mark is established for all steps of the computation. An application of a rule of the form q→q'z is allowed only if the second cursor is positioned exactly at the zero-mark, because in any other case a second line different from the zero-mark would be added to the picture. This position of the cursor indicates that the second counter contains the value zero, so in this situation a triple (q,if2,q')∈δ may be used in a computation of M . By an analogous argument, an application of a triple (q,if1,q')∈δ occurs only when the first counter contains value zero. By definition of the final rules of G the computation of M ends in a final state.

Part IV Equivalence of (ii), (iii), and (iv)
To construct G' from G we replace r by rrr and l by lll and z by z':=↓llrr. So far, clearly, (ii) is equivalent to dpic(↑l^{3m}z') ∈ Dpic(G') . We now introduce a new start symbol S and a rule S → lq_0 . Then (ii) is equivalent to (iii). Furthermore, every picture described in G' has at least three lines. So there is no p'∈Pic(G') such that p≠p' and p is superpicture of p'. This implies that (iii) is equivalent to (iv). @

From Proposition (3.1) we know that there is a two-counter-machine M such that emptiness of $f_M(m,0)$ is undecidable. Hence Theorem (3.3) implies the following

3.4 Corollary There is a linear chain code picture language for which the membership problem and the superpicture problem are undecidable.

While the membership problem is decidable for context-free picture languages without invisible lines (over {u,d,r,l} [4, Theorem 5.1]) and even decidable in polynomial time for picture languages over {r,l,d} [11], we have shown that there is a linear picture language over {r,l,↑,↓} for which the membership problem is undecidable. In contrast to this Theorem (2.1) states decidability of the subpicture problem for arbitrary context-free picture languages.

4. DISCUSSION

It is easy to extend our concept of a picture language to more than two dimensions, to add features like colours or diagonal lines, or to switch to a triangle grid instead of the square grid: All such changes have no effect on the presented results. It is more interesting to consider the restricted class of "stripe" picture languages, which are essentially one-dimensional. Regular picture languages consisting of pictures all fitting into a stripe of fixed width are "easy", since they can be simulated by regular string languages [8, Lemma 5.8], so membership problem, subpicture problem, and superpicture problem are decidable for these languages in linear time [9]. But for a strictly one-dimensional picture language generated by a linear grammar we have shown undecidability of the membership and the superpicture problem. Are there any language classes which are significantly "richer" than regular languages such that the membership problem is decidable? For the class of languages accepted by automata with a finite control and *one* counter it is straight forward to prove undecidability in the same manner as in Theorem 3.2 (draw the picture using *one* cursor, its position represents a second counter).

The length of a shortest description of a picture in a regular language is quadratically bounded in the extension of the described picture [9]. A similar result for linear and for context-free languages without penup is known [8], but for linear and for context-free picture languages in general no such bound can exist, since any such bound would immediately give rise to a decision procedure for the membership problem.

REFERENCES

[1] Rosenfeld, A.: Picture Languages - Formal Models of Picture Recognition, Academic Press, London (1979).

[2] Freeman, H.: Computer Processing of Line-Drawing Images, Comput. Surveys 6 (1974), 57-97.

[3] Kim, C. and Sudborough, I.H.: The Membership and Equivalence Problems for Picture Languages, TCS 52 (1987), 177-192.

[4] Maurer, H.A., Rozenberg, G., Welzl, E.: Using String Languages to Describe Picture Languages, Inform. and Contr. 54 (1982), 155-185.

[5] Minsky, M.L.: Recursive Unsolvability of Post's Problem of "Tag" and other topics in Theory of Turing Machines, Annals of Mathematics 74 (1961), 437-455.

[6] Mylopoulus, J.: On the Application of Formal Language and Automata Theory to Pattern Recognition, Pattern Recognition 4 (1972), 37-51.

[7] Shaw, A.C.: A Formal Picture Description Scheme as a Basis for Picture Processing Systems, Inform. and Contr. 14 (1969), 9-52.

[8] Sudborough, I.H. and Welzl, E: Complexity and Decidability for Chain Code Picture Languages, TCS 36 (1985), 175-202.

[9] Hinz, F. and Welzl, E.: Regular Chain Code Picture Languages with Invisible Lines, Graz University of Technology, Institute fuer Informationsverarbeitung, Report 252 (1988).

[10] Hinz, F: doctoral thesis (in German), in preparation.

[11] Kim, C.: Complexity and Decidablility for Restricted Classes of Picture Languages, to appear in TCS.

CHOMSKY HIERARCHY AND COMMUNICATION COMPLEXITY

Galina Jirásková
Mathematical Institute, Slovak Academy of Sciences
Ždanovova 6, 040 01 Košice, Czechoslovakia

Abstract. Chomsky hierarchy is compared with the hierarchy of communication complexity for VLSI. It is shown that only regular languages belong to the same levels of both hierarchies. There are hard languages according to Chomsky hierarchy that belong to the lowest level in communication complexity hierarchy. On the other hand there is a deterministic linear language that requires the highest (linear) communication complexity. This is the main result because it implies that VLSI circuits need $\Omega(n)$ area and $\Omega(n^2)$ area.(time)^2 complexity to recognize deterministic context-free languages which solves an open problem of Hromkovič [7].

1. Introduction

The communication complexity for VLSI is a powerful tool for proving lower bounds on VLSI circuits. It is well-known that the communication complexity of any language L provides direct lower bound on the area complexity of VLSI circuits recognizing L, and that communication complexity squared provides direct lower bound on the complexity measure area.(time)^2 of VLSI circuits.

Originally, the communication complexity was defined in Papadimitriou and Sipser [10] and investigated in several papers [2, 3, 5-9, 11]. Informally, it can be defined in the following way. Suppose a language $L \subseteq (\{0, 1\}^2)^*$ has to be recognized by two distant computers. Each computer receives half of the input bits, and computation proceeds using some protocol for communication between the two computers. The minimal number of bits that has to be exchanged in order to successfully recognize $L \cap \{0, 1\}^{2n}$, minimized over all partitions of the input bits into two equal parts, and considered as a function of n, is called the communication complexity of L.

An improvement of the communication complexity model was suggested in Aho at al. [1] and formally defined and investigated as so called S-communication complexity in Hromkovič [4]. Since the model of S-communication complexity provides useful lower bounds on A and AT^2 of VLSI circuits in many cases in which the original communication complexity provides no reasonable lower bounds (see [4] for details) we study the S-communication complexity in this paper.

The relation between communication complexity hierarchy and Chomsky hierarchy was studied in [7]. S-communication complexity differs essentially from the communication complexity in the sense that the results from [7] cannot be directly transformed in order to obtain the relation between S-communication complexity hierarchy and Chomsky hierarchy. In this paper we show that all regular languages are recognizable within constant S-communication complexity but, for any constant c, there is a regular language which cannot be recognized within S-communication complexity less than c. Next we show that there are hard languages according to the Chomsky hierarchy (e.g. outside the class of recursively enumerable languages) which can be recognized within one bit S-communication complexity. The main result is the linear lower bound on S-communication complexity of a deterministic linear language. It implies that VLSI circuits need $\Omega(n)$ area and $\Omega(n^2)$ area.(time)^2 complexity to recognize deterministic context-free languages which solves an open problem of Hromkovič [7].

The structure of the paper is as follows. In Section 2 definitions and notations are given. The relation between the Chomsky hierarchy and the S-communication complexity hierarchy is studied in Section 3.

2. Definitions and notations

Now, let us formally define the S-communication complexity in the same way as in [4]. In the paper N denotes the set of all natural numbers (positive integers). For $n \in N$, let $[n] = \{1, 2, \ldots, n\}$ and let $|A|$, for a finite set A, denotes the number of elements in A.

Let Y be a subset of $[n]$ such that $|Y| = 2m$, for some m. A partition of $[n]$ according to Y is a pair $\pi = (S_I, S_{II})$, where $S_I \cap S_{II} = \emptyset$, $S_I \cup S_{II} = [n]$ and $|S_I \cap Y| = |S_{II} \cap Y| = m$. We denote by x_I (x_{II}) the input word x from $\{0, 1\}^n$ restricted to the set S_I (S_{II}), and we write

$x = \pi^{-1}(x_I, x_{II})$.

A <u>protocol</u> on n inputs is a triniply $D_n = (Y, \pi, \Phi)$, where

(a) Y is a subset of [n] and $|Y| = 2m$, for some m,

(b) $\pi = (S_I, S_{II})$ is a partition of [n] according to Y (which corresponds to the partition of the input bits for two computers),

(c) Φ is a function from $(\{0, 1\}^{|S_I|} \cup \{0, 1\}^{|S_{II}|}) \times \{0, 1, \$\}^*$ to $\{0, 1\}^* \cup \{\text{accept, reject}\}$ which has the following <u>prefix-freeness property:</u> for a given string $c \in \{0, 1, \$\}^*$ and two different $y, y' \in \{0, 1\}^{|S_I|}$ $(\{0, 1\}^{|S_{II}|})$ $\Phi(y, c)$ is not a proper prefix of $\Phi(y', c)$. (Intuitively, Φ describes the communication between the two computers.)

A <u>computation</u> of D_n on input word x in $\{0, 1\}^n$ is a string $c = c_1\$c_2\$\ldots c_k\$c_{k+1}$, where $k \geq 0$, $c_1, \ldots, c_k \in \{0, 1\}^*$, $c_{k+1} \in \{\text{accept, reject}\}$, and such that for each integer j, $0 \leq j \leq k$, we have

(1) if j is even, then $c_{j+1} = \Phi(x_I, c_1\$c_2\$\ldots\$c_j)$, and

(2) if j is odd, then $c_{j+1} = \Phi(x_{II}, c_1\$c_2\$\ldots\$c_j)$.

The computation $c = c_1\$c_2\$\ldots\$c_{k+1}$ is called <u>accepting</u> if c_{k+1} = accept and the <u>length</u> of this computation is the total length of all messages c_j, $1 \leq j \leq k$ (ignoring \$'s and final accept/reject).

The <u>S-communication complexity of D_n</u> = (Y, π, Φ), shortly $SC(Y, \pi, \Phi)$ is the maximum of the lengths of all computations of D_n.

We say that D_n <u>computes</u> a Boolean function $h: \{0, 1\}^n \to \{0, 1\}$ (within S-communication complexity c) if, for each $x \in \{0, 1\}^n$, there exists a computation of D_n (of length at most c) on the input word x, and it is accepting iff $h(x) = 1$.

The <u>S-communication complexity of h according to Y</u> is defined as $SC(h, Y) = \min\{SC(Y, \pi, \Phi) \mid \text{the protocol } (Y, \pi, \Phi) \text{ computes } h\}$, and the <u>S-communication complexity of h</u> as $SC(h) = \max\{SC(h, Y) \mid Y \subseteq [n]$ and $|Y| = 2m$, for some $m\}$. Obviously, for each Boolean function $h: \{0, 1\}^n \to \{0, 1\}$, $SC(h) \leq n/2$ holds (in fact, the first computer can send all its input bits to the second one).

Let $L \subseteq \{0, 1\}^*$ be a language. The <u>S-communication complexity of L</u> is defined as a function SC_L from N to nonnegative integers such that $SC_L(n) = SC(h_{L,n})$, where $h_{L,n}: \{0, 1\}^n \to \{0, 1\}$, and $h_{L,n}(x) = 1$ iff $x \in L \cap \{0, 1\}^n$.

Let f be a real function defined on natural numbers. We say that L is <u>recognizable within S-communication complexity f(n)</u>, shortly $L \in SCOMM(f(n))$, if $SC_L(n) \leq f(n)$ holds for any natural n. Obviously, each language is recognizable within S-communication complexity n/2. In [4] it is shown that, for all functions f: $N \rightarrow N$ such that $1 \leq f(n) \leq n/2$, $SCOMM(f(n)-1) \subsetneq SCOMM(f(n))$. So, the hierarchy of languages according to S-communication complexity is obtained.

Before starting our study, we introduce some notation. For a word w, $\#_a(w)$ denotes the number of occurences of the symbol a in w, for a real number x, $\lfloor x \rfloor$ ($\lceil x \rceil$) is the floor (ceiling) of x, and for a nonnegative integer i, $BIN_j(i)$ is the binary code of i on j bits (e.g. $BIN_4(5)$ = 0101).

3. Chomsky hierarchy and S-communication complexity

First, we study the S-communication complexity of regular languages.

Theorem 1. For each regular language $L \subseteq \{0, 1\}^*$ there exists a constant c such that L belongs to SCOMM(c).

Proof. Let $L \subseteq \{0, 1\}^*$ be a regular language. Then there exists a deterministic finite automaton A recognizing L and having s states q_0, q_1, ..., q_{s-1}, for some s. We show that $L \in SCOMM(c)$, where $c = \lceil \log_2 s \rceil$.

Let n be a natural number and let $Y = \{i_1, i_2, \ldots, i_{2m}\}$, where $i_1 < i_2 < \ldots < i_{2m}$, be a subset of $[n]$. We consider the protocol D_n = (Y, π, Φ), where $\pi = (S_I, S_{II})$ is the partition of $[n]$ according to Y such that $S_I = [i_m]$ and for all x in $\{0, 1\}^{i_m}$, y in $\{0, 1\}^{n-i_m}$, j in $\{0, 1, \ldots, s-1\}$

$\Phi(x, \varepsilon) = BIN_c(i)$ iff A computihg on x ends in the state q_i,

$\Phi(y, BIN_c(j))$ = accept (reject) iff A beginning to compute on y in the state q_j ends the computation in an accepting (unaccepting) state.

It is easy to see that the protocol $D_n = (Y, \pi, \Phi)$ computes function $h_{L,n}$ within S-communication complexity c. □

Theorem 2. For all natural c there exists a regular language L such that L does not belong to SCOMM(c).

Proof. Let c be a natural number and let us consider the regular language $L = \{x \in \{0, 1\}^* \mid \#_1(x) = 2^{c+1}\}$. We prove by contradiction that, for $n = 2^{c+2}$ and $\bar{Y} = [n]$, $SC(h_{L,n}, \bar{Y}) > c$ holds, which is sufficed to prove the assertion.

Let there exists the protocol $D_n = (\bar{Y}, \pi, \Phi)$, $\pi = (S_I, S_{II})$, $n = 2^{c+2}$, computing $h_{L,n}$ within S-communication complexity c. Then the number of all accepting computations of D_n is at most 2^{c+1} (because of the prefix-freeness property of Φ). Consider $2^{c+1}+1$ disjoint nonempty classes $L_i = \{x \in \{0, 1\}^n \mid \#_1(x_I) = i$ and $\#_1(x_{II}) = 2^{c+1} - i\}$, $i = 0, 1, \ldots, 2^{c+1}$, of the words from L. There exist two input words x in L_i and y in L_j, $i \neq j$, having the same accepting computation. Then the computation of D_n on the input word $z = \pi^{-1}(x_I, y_{II})$ is the same, i.e. accepting, although z does not belong to L. So, we have a contradiction. □

We obtained that all regular languages can be recognized within constant S-communication complexity but there is no constant c such that the family of all regular languages is included in SCOMM(c). Next theorem shows that much more languages belong to SCOMM(1).

Theorem 3. Each language $L \subseteq \{0, 1\}^*$ such that L involves at most one word of length n, for all n, belongs to SCOMM(1).

Proof. Let $L \cap \{0, 1\}^n$ involves the word $\bar{x}$. For any $Y \subseteq [n]$, $|Y| = 2m$, and a partition (S_I, S_{II}) of $[n]$ according to Y, we can informally describe the function Φ as follows. The first computer rejects in the case that its input $x \in \{0, 1\}^{|S_I|}$ disagrees with $\bar{x}_I$. If the input x agrees with $\bar{x}_I$, it sends the message 1 to the second computer which accepts (rejects) if its input agrees (disagrees) with $\bar{x}_{II}$. □

Corollary 1. Each language $L \subseteq \{0\}^*$ ($\{1\}^*$) belongs to SCOMM(1). □

Corollary 2. There exists a language which is not recursively enumerable and belongs to SCOMM(1). □

Considering Theorem 3 and its corollaries we obtain that there are hard languages according to the Chomsky hierarchy which are recognizable within S-communication complexity 1. Further, we solve an open problem of Hromkovič [7] proving a linear lower bound on the S-communication complexity of a deterministic linear language.

Theorem 4. There exists a deterministic linear language L such that $SC_L(n) \geq n/32 - 1/2$, for all sufficiently large natural numbers n.

Proof. Let us consider the following deterministic context-free language

$$L = \{0w_1 0w_2 0 \ldots 0w_{a-1} 0w_a 1^b 0w_a 0w_{a-1} 0 \ldots 0w_2 0w_1 1^c \mid a, b, c \geq 1, \\ w_i \in \{0, 1\} \text{ for } i = 1, 2, \ldots, a\}.$$

It is not difficult to see that the language L is generated by the following linear grammar $G = (\{S, A, B, C\}, \{0, 1\}, S, \{S \to A1, A \to A1, A \to 00B00, A \to 01B01, B \to 00B00, B \to 01B01, B \to C, C \to C1, C \to 1\})$ and so, it is even linear.

Let n be a sufficiently large natural number, let r be even one of the numbers $\lfloor n/8 \rfloor$, $\lfloor n/8 \rfloor - 1$ (i.e. $8r \leq n$) and let $\bar{Y}$ denote the set $\{2, 4, 6, \ldots, 2r\}$ of size r. A set $\{i, j\}$, $i, j \in [n]$, $i \neq j$, is said to be divided by a partition $\pi = (S_I, S_{II})$ of $[n]$ iff neither S_I nor S_{II} involves both i and j. First, we will formulate a Lemma, then considering this assertion we will prove Theorem 4, and finally the Lemma will be proved.

Lemma. For any partition π of $[n]$ according to $\bar{Y}$ there exists a natural number m, $2r < m < 6r$, such that at least $r/4$ of the sets $\{2i, m+2r-2i+2\}$, $i = 1, 2, \ldots, r$, are divided by the partition π.

Now, we show by contradiction that the S-communication complexity of each protocol $D_n = (\bar{Y}, \pi, \Phi)$ computing $h_{L,n}$ is at least $r/4$, which proves Theorem 4 ($r/4 \geq n/32 - 1/2$). So, let $D_n = (\bar{Y}, \pi, \Phi)$ be a protocol computing $h_{L,n}$ within S-communication complexity $k - 1 < r/4$, $k \in N$. Then there exist at most $2^k - 1$ accepting computations of this protocol on the input words $x \in \{0, 1\}^n$. According to Lemma there exists m, $2r < m < 6r$, and there exist $i_1, i_2, \ldots, i_k$ such that, for all $j = 1, 2, \ldots, k$, i_j is even, $2 \leq i_j \leq 2r$ and the set $\{i_j, m+2r-i_j+2\}$ is divided by π.

Let $z^s = z_1^s z_2^s \ldots z_k^s$, for $s = 1, 2, \ldots, 2^k$, be all words from $\{0, 1\}^k$. For each s in $[2^k]$ the following word $y^s = y_1^s y_2^s \ldots y_n^s$ belongs to L

$y_{i_j}^s = y_{m+2r-i_j+2}^s = z_j^s$, for all $j = 1, 2, \ldots, k$,

$y_t^s = 1$, for all natural t such that $2r < t \leq m$ or $m+2r < t \leq n$,

$y_t^s = 0$, otherwise.

There exist s and $\bar{s}$, $s \neq \bar{s}$, such that y^s and $y^{\bar{s}}$ have the same accepting computation of D_n and so, the computation of D_n on the word $\pi^{-1}(y_I^s, y_{II}^{\bar{s}})$ is also accepting. It is not difficult to see that this word does not belong to L.

Proof of Lemma. Let π be a partition of $[n]$ according to $\bar{Y}$. Let us consider the $r \times r$ matrix $A = \| a_{ij} \|$ such that, for all $i, j = 1, 2, \ldots, r$, $a_{ij} = 1$ (0) iff the set $\{2i, 6r-2j+2\}$ is (not) divided by π. We note that exactly $r/2$ elements from $\{2, 4, 6, \ldots, 2r\} = \bar{Y}$ belong to S_I (S_{II}) and so, exactly $r^2/2$ elements of the matrix A are equal to 1. Consider the partition of the elements of A into $2r - 1$ following sets

$A_q = \{a_{ii+q} \mid i \in [r-q]\}$, for all $q = 0, 1, \ldots, r-1$,

$A_q = \{a_{ii+q} \mid i \in \{1-q, 2-q, \ldots, r\}\}$, for all $q = -1, -2, \ldots, -(r-1)$.

There must exist an integer p, $-(r-1) \leq p \leq r-1$, such that at least $r/4$ elements from A_p are equal to 1, i.e. there exist at least $r/4$ subscripts i from [r] such that the set $\{2i, 6r-2p-2i+2\}$ is divided by π. Thus, we can take $m = 4r - 2p$. □

Corollary. There is a deterministic linear language requiring linear area and $AT^2 = \Omega(n^2)$ to be recognized on any VLSI circuit. □

We conclude this paper with the note that there are the hard (simple) languages according to the Chomsky hierarchy which are simple (hard) according to the S-communication complexity hierarchy and so, there is no substantial coherence between these hierarchies of languages.

Acknowledgement

I would like to thank Juraj Hromkovič for his comments concerning this work.

References

[1] A.V.Aho, J.D.Ullman and M.Yannakakis, On notions of information transfer in VLSI circuits. Proc. 15th Ann. ACM Symp. on Theory of Computing (1983) 133-139.
[2] P.Ďuriš, Z.Galil and G.Schnitger, Lower bounds on communication complexity. Inform. and Comput. 73, 1(1987) 1-22.
[3] S.Hornick and M.Sarrafzatch, On problems transformability in VLSI. Algorithmica 1(1987) 97-112.
[4] J.Hromkovič, The advantages of a new approach to defining the communication complexity for VLSI. Theoret. Comput. Sci. 57(1988) 97-111.
[5] J.Hromkovič, Communication complexity hierarchy. Theoret. Comput. Sci. 48(1986) 109-115.
[6] J.Hromkovič, Lower bound techniques for VLSI algorithms. Proc. IMYCS´86, Hungarian Academy of Sciences (1986) 9-19.
[7] J.Hromkovič, Relation between Chomsky hierarchy and communication complexity hierarchy. Acta Math. Univ.Comenian. 48-49(1986) 311-317.
[8] J.Ja´Ja and V.K.Prasanna Kumar, Information transfer in distributed computing with applications to VLSI. J. Assoc. Comput. Mach. 31(1984) 150-162.
[9] J.Ja´Ja, V.K.Prasanna Kumar and J.Simon, Information transfer under different sets of protocols. SIAM J. Comput. 13(1984) 840-849.
[10] Ch.Papadimitriou and M.Sipser, Communication complexity. Proc. 14th Ann. ACM Symp. on Theory of Computing (1982) 196-200.
[11] A.C.Yao, The entropic limitations of VLSI computations, Proc. 13th Ann. ACM Symp. on Theory of Computing (1981) 308-311.

Complexity Theory and Formal Languages

Klaus–Jörn Lange

Institut für Informatik
Technische Universität München
Arcisstr. 21
D-8000 München 2

1 Introduction

This lecture contains a collection of results relating and connecting formal languages with complexity theory. It is one aim of this work to show, how complexity theory serves as a unifying framework integrating many approaches and results which seem to be unrelated at first sight. Thus we are interested in exploring and crossing the border between the theory of formal languages and complexity theory as presented in [47]. (We do not deal here with algorithms, communication complexity, *VLSI* systems, or relativizations.)

We assume the reader to be familiar with the basic notions of formal languages and complexity theory as contained in [22]. A very detailed survey of complexity theory is given in the excellent book [67] of Wagner and Wechsung in 1986. In particular, we will use without explanation the following formalisms:

- off–line, multitape turing machines and their complexity measures;
- determinism, nondeterminism, and alternation;
- the Chomsky hierarchy, OL systems, macro–languages, and stack automata;
- the $o(\ )$ and $O(\ )$ notation.

Just to avoid confusions, we specify the notation $|v|$ for the length of a word v and λ for the empty word.

This paper is divided into four parts. The first section is this introduction. Part 2 contains some aspects of sequential complexity theory. Section 3, the main part of this work, describes some connections between formal languages and complexity theory. Finally Part 4 collects some recent results concerning parallel complexity theory.

2 Sequential complexity

The beginning of complexity theory can be determined by the discovery of arbitrary hard sets; that is for every computable function f there exists a set $\mathbf{L}$ such that every algorithm $\mathbf{A}$ solving the word problem of $\mathbf{L}$ takes at least time $f(|v|)$ for infinitely many v. This approach, to say $\mathbf{L} \in \mathbf{DTIME}(f(n))$ if $\mathbf{L}$ is recognizable within $f(|v|)$ steps for almost all inputs v by some algorithms for $\mathbf{L}$, is called the worst case approach and is the most frequently used method of complexity theory compared with average case analysis or generally stochastic methods.

In this way there was a phase of complexity theory, in which one tried to determine the absolute complexity of a problem, i.e. given a problem $\mathbf{P}$, find a time bound f such that $\mathbf{P} \in \mathbf{DTIME}(f)$ and $\mathbf{P} \notin \mathbf{DTIME}(g)$ for any $g \in o(f)$. A statement of the type $\mathbf{P} \in \mathbf{DTIME}(f)$ gives an upper bound for the running time necessary to solve p and is usually proved by exhibiting an algorithm for $\mathbf{P}$ running in time f. The problem is to prove lower bounds, i.e. statements of the type $\mathbf{P} \notin \mathbf{DTIME}(g)$. Until now there is no general theory or systematic method to obtain lower bounds. There exist some single results which pertain to special sets, under more or less restricting assumptions with a more or less restricted machine model.

A way to cope with this situation is to compare the complexity of problems by using reducibilities and completeness.

We call a mapping $f : X^* \to Y^*$, where X and Y are finite alphabets, computable within logarithmic space (resp. polynomial time), if there is a Turing–Machine M which, started with some $v \in X^*$ on its read only input tape, computes and prints $f(v)$ on its write only output tape, consuming no more than $O(\log(|v|))$ space on its working tapes (resp. performing no more than $p(|v|)$ steps for some polynomial p).

A set $\mathbf{L} \subseteq X^*$ is many–one 'LOG–reducible' to a set $M \subseteq Y^*$, denoted by $\mathbf{L} \leq^{\mathbf{L}}_{\mathrm{m}} M$, if there exists a mapping $f : X^* \to Y^*$ computable within logarithmic space such that $v \in \mathbf{L}$ if and only if $f(v) \in M$ holds for all $v \in X^*$. If we require f to be computable within polynomial time, instead, we get 'POL–reducibility' denoted by $\mathbf{L} \leq^{\mathbf{P}}_{\mathrm{m}} M$. If not otherwise stated we will use in the following LOG–reducibilities. The 'LOG–closure' of a class of languages $\mathbf{A}$ is denoted by $\mathrm{LOG}(A) := \{\mathbf{L} \mid \exists M \in \mathbf{A} : \mathbf{L} \leq^{\mathbf{L}}_{\mathrm{m}} M\}$.

Proposition 2.1 *For every class* $\mathbf{A}$ *we have* $\mathrm{LOG}(\mathbf{Co\text{-}A}) := \mathbf{Co\text{-}}\mathrm{LOG}(\mathbf{A})$ *and* $\mathrm{LOG}(\mathrm{LOG}(\mathbf{A})) = \mathrm{LOG}(\mathbf{A})$. *Here* $\mathbf{Co\text{-}A} := \{X^* \setminus \mathbf{L} \mid \exists \mathbf{L}, X : \mathbf{L} \subseteq X^*, \mathbf{L} \in \mathbf{A}\}$.

Thus we try to determine the 'relative complexity' of a problem, i.e. given a problem $\mathbf{P}$ find a class $\mathbf{A}$ such that $\mathbf{P} \in \mathbf{A}$ and $\mathbf{P}$ is $\mathbf{A}$–complete. Here $\mathbf{P} \in \mathbf{A}$ is a 'relative upper bound' and the $\mathbf{A}$–completeness of $\mathbf{P}$ is a 'relative lower bound' for the complexity of $\mathbf{P}$. A motivation for analyzing relative complexities is that a relative lower bound becomes an absolute one, as soon as the corresponding comparison of complexity classes is solved: if a problem $\mathbf{P}$ is complete for a class $\mathbf{A}$ and if $\mathbf{A}$ is not contained in $\mathbf{DTIME}(f(n))$, then for some $c < 0$ $\mathbf{P} \notin \mathbf{DTIME}(f(n^c))$. Unfortunately, the status of very many important class inclusions is unknown. Even worse, 'relativization result' (essentially this means considering time or tape–bounded Turing reducibilities instead of complexity classes) indicate that nearly all known proof methods cannot answer these questions ([7]). Nevertheless, completeness results are a valuable tool to characterize complexities of problems by infering class properties to complete problems.

Typical classes in complexity theory are $\mathbf{PSPACE} := \bigcup_{k \geq 1} : \mathbf{DSPACE}(n^k)$, $\mathbf{NP} := \bigcup_{k \geq 1} : \mathbf{NTIME}(n^k)$, $\mathbf{P} := \bigcup_{k \geq 1} : \mathbf{DTIME}(n^k)$, $\mathbf{NL} := \mathbf{NSPACE}(\log n)$, and $\mathbf{L} := \mathbf{DSPACE}(\log n$
These classes form a hierarchy:

$\mathbf{L} \subseteq \mathbf{NL} \subseteq \mathbf{P} \subseteq \mathbf{NP} \subseteq \mathbf{PSPACE}$. Although most researchers believe this hierarchy to be proper, i.e. that all inclusions are strict, $\mathbf{NL} \neq \mathbf{PSPACE}$ is the only known inequality here. Hence, equalities like $\mathbf{L} = \mathbf{NP}$ or $\mathbf{P} = \mathbf{PSPACE}$ still may hold. All these classes are closed under LOG–reduciblity, i.e. $\mathrm{LOG}(\mathbf{PSPACE}) = \mathbf{PSPACE}, \ldots, \mathrm{LOG}(\mathbf{L}) = \mathbf{L}$ and possess well known complete sets:

- **True quantified boolean formulae:** the set $TQBF$ of all true quantified boolean formulae is **PSPACE**–complete ([59]),
- **Satisfiability:** the set SAT of all satisfiable (= true existentially quantified) boolean formulae is **NP**–complete ([13]),
- **Circuit value problem:** the set CVP of all pairs of a boolean circuit and an input assignement such that a designated output yields the value true is **P**–complete ([33]),
- **Graph–accessability problem:** the set GAP of all directed graphs with designated source and sink such that there exists a path from source to sink is **NL**–complete ([55]), and
- the trivial set $\{1\}$ is **L**–complete.

An important research topic of complexity theory is the polynomial hierarchy as defined in [45] by oracle machines. It can be characterized by bounded quantification and by alternating Turing machines (see [10], [59], [69]): A set $\mathbf{L}$ is an element or the k–th level of the polynomial hierarchy, denoted by $\Sigma_n^{\mathbf{P}}$, if there exists a set $M \in \mathbf{P}$ and a polynomial p such that $\mathbf{L} = \{v \mid \exists_{x_1}, |x_1| \leq p(|v|) : \forall_{x_2}, |x_2| \leq p(|v|) : \ldots Qx_k, |x_k| \leq (|v|) : (v, x_1, \ldots, x_k) \in M\}$, where Q denoted $\exists$ for odd k, and $\forall$ otherwise. Further on, set $\Pi_k^{\mathbf{P}} := \mathbf{Co}\text{-}\Sigma_k^{\mathbf{P}}$. The classes $\Sigma_k^{\mathbf{P}}$ and $\Pi_k^{\mathbf{P}}$ are closed under LOG–reducibility and possess complete sets, which are related to $TQBF$ (see [69]). It is an open question whether the polynomial hierarchy is proper, i.e. infinite, which is assumed by most researchers.

As an attempt to construct an $\mathbf{L}$ analogy, Chandra et al, defined in [10] the logarithmic alternation hierarchy with the help of alternating Turing machines. To put a space bound on oracle machines or bounded quantification is not obvious and led at first back to the polynomial hierarchy (see [35], [59], [39]). Later on, a logarithmic quantification hierarchy and a logarithmic oracle hierarchy were found. But while the former coincides with the logarithmic alternation hierarchy ([40]), the later contains the whole logarithmic alternation hierarchy in its second level ([53]). Again, the common believe assumed these hierarchies to be proper, at least until 1986. But since then things changed dramatically: in October 1986 the logarithmic alternation hierarchy collapsed to its second level ([42]). Then in April 1987 this result was improved by Schöning and Wagner in [56]. They showed that the second levels of the logarithmic alternation hierarchy and the logarithmic oracle hierarchy coincide, thereby collapsing the logarithmic oracle hierarchy to its second level. Finally, in July 1987 Immerman showed the closure under complement of nondeterministic space classes ([26])! Hence the hierarchies mentioned above all collapse to their first level $\mathbf{NL} = \mathbf{Co}\text{-}\mathbf{NL}$. Surprisingly, this result was found independently in April 1987 by R. Sczelepcsényi ([57]) from Bratislava, but get not public before late 1987.

3 Formal Languages

This section contains a collection of results from the interface between formal language theory and complexity. (More details and related results concerning this topic may be found [47] or [67]). Out of the huge abundance of formal languages we selected the Chomsky–languages, the context–free families of Lindenmayer languages, the index and macro languages, and some classes of stack languages. The complexities of several dedidable problems for these families have been characterized by showing these problems to be complete for well–known complexity classes. In this way complexity theory serves as a unifying framework and related different families of formal alnguages thereby giving new insights and a better understanding of formal language theory.

This section is divided into three parts. First of all, we consider the membership problem for classes of languages. We do not consider the general membership problem, i.e. the case that the language generating grammar is not fixed, but part of the input. Very often it is equivalent to the emptiness problem, which is investigated in the second part of this section. Finally, we consider shortly the complexities of operations on formal languages.

3.1 The membership problem

In the following the families of the context–sensitive, deterministic context–sensitive, context–free, linear, and regular languages are denoted by **CS**, **DLBA**, **CF**, **DCF**, **LIN** and **REG**, respectively. The type 0 languages, i.e. the recursive enumerable languages, are not considered, since they strictly contain the decidable languages, which in turn are a proper superset for any somplexity class.

Since linear bounded automata correspond to linear space bounded turing machines we have **CS** = **NSPACE**(n) and **DLBA** = **DSPACE**(n). Applying reducibilities of the type $f(v) = v\#^{p(|v|)}$, where p is a polynomial, we get

Proposition 3.1 LOG(**CS**) = LOG(**DLBA**) = **PSPACE**.

Concerning context–free languages we know by [70] **CF** $\subseteq$ **DTIME**(n^3). Hence

Proposition 3.2 LOG(**CF**) $\subseteq$ **P**.

Now let **DAPDA**$(\log n)$ (resp. **NAPDA**$(\log n)$) be the class of languages accepted by deterministic (resp. nondeterministic) push–down automata with a two–way input tape augmented with a logarithmically space bounded working tape. The following result of Cook implies proposition 3.2.

Theorem 3.3 ([12]) **DAPDA**$(\log n)$ = **NAPDA**$(\log n)$ = **P**.

Sudborough characterized the difference between LOG(**CF**) and **P** by putting a polynomial bound on the running time of augmented push–down automata, defining the classes **DAPDA**$_{\mathrm{PT}}(\log n)$ and **NAPDA**$_{\mathrm{PT}}(\log n)$:

Theorem 3.4 ([63]) LOG(**DCF**) = $\mathbf{DAPDA}_{\mathrm{PT}}(\log n)$ and LOG(**CF**) = $\mathbf{NAPDA}_{\mathrm{PT}}(\log n)$.

The best space bound for recognition of context–free languages is still given by the algorithm of Lewis, Stearns, and Hartmanis:

Theorem 3.5 ([44]) LOG(**CF**) ⊆ **DSPACE**($\log^2 n$).

Since **P** and **DSPACE**($\log^2 n$) seem to be incomparable, **CF** should not be expected to be complete either for **P** or **DSPACE**($\log^2 n$). Concerning simultaneous resource bounds, Cook showed

Theorem 3.6 ([14]) LOG(**DCF**) ⊆ **DTIMESPACE**($\mathit{POL}, \log^2 n$),

Here **DTIMESPACE**(f, g) (resp. **NTIMESPACE**(f, g)) denotes the class of all languages recognizable be a deterministic (resp. nondeterministic) Turingmachines with g–bounded workingtapes and a time bounded by f and POL means the union over all polynomials. For context–free languages only LOG(**CF**) ⊆ **NTIMESPACE**($\mathit{POL}, \log^2 n$) is known.

The families of the deterministic context–free languages and of the linear languages are incomparable and the same seems to hold for their LOG–closures, since Sudborough was able to show

Theorem 3.7 ([61]) LOG(**LIN**) = **NL**.

Some remarks:

i) The same result holds true for the family of nondeterministic one–counter languages.

ii) Theorems 3.7 and 3.5 imply the famous result of Savitch **NSPACE**(f) ⊂ **DSPACE**(f^2) for $\log(n) \in O(f(n))$ ([55]). It is remarkable that the algorithm of Lewis, Stearns, and Hartmanis is considerably older than that of Savitch.

iii) The result of Immerman–Sczelepcsényi implies with the help of proposition 2.1: LOG(**Co-LIN**) = LOG(**LIN**).

Finally, we have LOG(**REG**) = **L**, because of **REG** ⊆ **L**.

The results of this part are summarized in the figure 3.1 below.

We see that Chomsky languages fit in nicely in the existing framework of complexity classes. The same holds true for the many types of Lindenmayer Languages. Among their wide variety we cite result characterizing the complexities of languages generated by the following classes of context–free L–systems. **ETOL, EOL, EDTOL**, and **EDOL**. (The definitions of these families of languages may be found e.g. in ([50]).

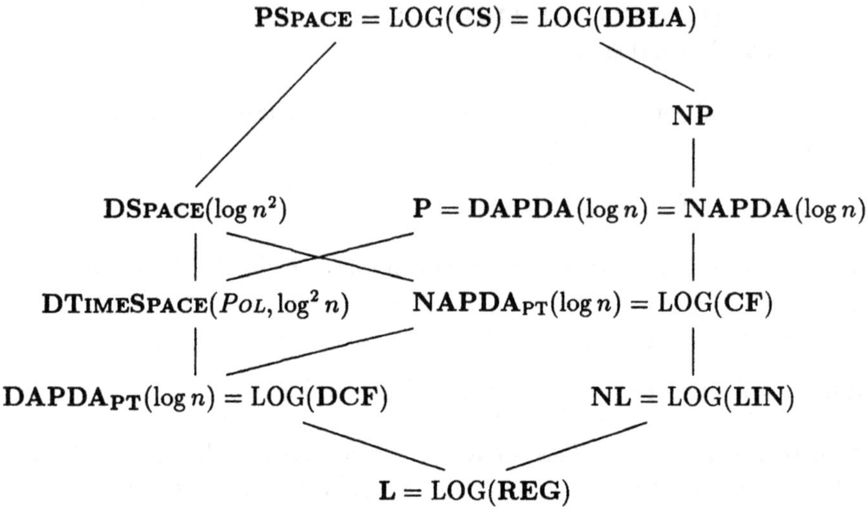

Figure 1:

Theorem 3.8 **([64],[62],[31])**

a) LOG(**ETOL**) = **NP**

b) LOG(**EOL**) = LOG(**CF**)

c) LOG(**EDTOL**) = **NL**, and

d) LOG(**EDOL**) = **L**

Remark: i) although **EOL** and **EDTOL** are incomparable, Theorem 3.8 indicates that EOL languages might have more difficult parsing problems than EDTOL languages. This relation turns, if we consider the trio's, i.e. the closure under nonerasing homomorphisms, inverse homomorphisms, and intersections with regular sets, M(**EOL**) and M(**EDTOL**) generated by **EOL** resp. **EDTOL**. We then have LOG(M(**EOL**)) = LOG(**CF**) and LOG(M(**EDTOL**)) = **NP** (see [38]). Note that both **EOL** and **EDTOL** are closed under homomorphisms and intersections with regular sets.

ii) There are a lot of results examining the complexity of controlled **L** systems and more general parallel rewriting mechanisms (see e.g. [4], [5], or [37]).

The family **INDEX** of indexed languages by Aho ([1]) was shown by Fischer to coincide with the family **OI** of outside in macro languages ([17]). Fischer also defined the inside–out macro languages, constituting the family **IO**, and showed these two classes to be incomparable. Complexity results indicate that **OI** seems to have harder membership problems than **IO**.

Theorem 3.9 ([6])

a) LOG(**OI**) = **NP**

b) LOG(**IO**) = LOG(**CF**)

Finally, we consider the families of languages accepted by nondeterministic nestedstack automata, nondeterministic stack automata, nondeterministic nonerasing stack automata, nondeterministic checking stack automata, deterministic stack automata, deterministic nonerasing stack automata, and deterministic checking stack automata (all restricted to have a one–way input tape), dentoed by **1-NNSTSA**, **1-NSA**, **1-NNESA**, **1-NCSA**, **1-DSA**, **1-DNESA**, and **1-DCSA** as defined in [2], [20], [19]. Obviously these classes fulfill **1-DX** ⊆ **1-NX** for $X \in \{\mathbf{SA}, \mathbf{NESA}, \mathbf{CSA}\}$ and **1-XCSA** ⊆ **1-XNESA** ⊆ **1-XSA** for $X \in \{D, N\}$, as well as **1-NSA** ⊆ **1-NNSTSA**.

By **1-NNSTSA** = **INDEX** and the existence of **NP**–complete sets in **1-NCSA** we get

Theorem 3.10 ([2],[58]) LOG(**1-NCSA**) = LOG(**1-NNESA**) = LOG(**1-NSA**) = LOG(**1-NNSTSA**) = **NP**

and for the deterministic case

Theorem 3.11 ([24])

a) LOG(**1-DNESA**) = LOG(**1-DSA**) = **P**

b) LOG(**1-DCSA**) = **L**.

Remarks: i) for the automata types occuring in this subsection also alternating versions exist (see e.g. [10], [28], [34], [36]).

ii) Since all the families of formal languages occuring in this subsection are contained in **NP**, a natural question to ask is: are there any 'reasonable' families of formal languages with a decidable emptiness problem and membership problems which are likely to lie outside of **NP**. (An 'unreasonable' familiy of this type ould be **HFIL**, the class of all homomorphic images of languages generated by IL systems with a finite, possible empty set of axioms: On the one hand the emptiness problem of **HFIL** is simple, since we only have to ckeck the set of axioms for emptiness, while on the other hand **HFIL** coincides with the set or all recursively enumberable languages!).

3.2 The emptiness problem

For a class **X** of languages given by some language generating devices of type **X** we denote by **∅-X** the nonemptiness problem of this class: given an object A of type **X** determine whether A generate does not the empty set. There might be difficulties if **X** is represented by several mechanisms with different properties (see e.g. remark ii) at the end of the first subsection). But in our case this only affects the class **X** = **REG**, where we assume that recular sets are given by (non)deterministic finite automata and not by regular expressions, i.e. the types of language generating devices are **DFA** and **NFA**.

In these emptiness problems all occuring automata are assumed to have an input tape with one one–way reading head. (Two–way or two–head automata in nearly all cases have an undecidable emptiness problem. There is a very interesting connection between the complexities of the emptiness problem for one–way automata and the membership problem of two–way automata (as already noted by Hunt in [23]) in that the complexity of the emptiness problem for one–way automata of type **X** very often coincides with the complexity of languages accepted by two–way automata of type **X**. This transition from the one–way to the two–way case forms an important bridge between the theory of formal languages and complexity theory.

Since we are interested in LOG–closures of language classes it is reasonable to investigate two–way automata equipped with additional memory of logarithmic size (or equivalently two–way multi–head automata). Thus we consider classes $\mathbf{NAX}(\log n)$ and $\mathbf{DAX}(\log n)$ denoting the families of languages accepted by nondeterministic resp. deterministic two–way automata of type **X** augmented with a logarithmically bounded working tape (see [12]).

These classes are closed under LOG–reducibilities, i.e.
$\mathrm{LOG}(\mathbf{NAX}(\log n) = \mathbf{NAX}(\log n))$ and $\mathrm{LOG}(\mathbf{DAX}(\log n)) = \mathbf{DAX}(\log n)$.

The context–free languages are a good examples for the mentioned connection between emptiness problems and membership in two–way languages.

Theorem 3.12 **([30],[12])**

a) $\mathrm{LOG}(\emptyset\text{-}\mathbf{CF}) = \mathrm{LOG}(\emptyset\text{-}\mathbf{DCF}) = \mathbf{P}$,

b) $\mathrm{NAPDA}(\log n) = \mathrm{DAPDA}(\log n) = \mathbf{P}$.

Theorem 3.13 **([29],[25])**

a) $\mathrm{LOG}(\emptyset\text{-}\mathbf{LIN}) = \mathrm{LOG}(\emptyset\text{-}\mathbf{NFA}) = \mathrm{LOG}(\emptyset\text{-}\mathbf{DFA}) = \mathbf{NL}$,

b) $\mathbf{NAPDA}_{\text{1-turn}}(\log n) = \mathbf{NL}$,

c) $\mathbf{NAFA}(\log n) = \mathbf{NL}$ and $\mathbf{DAFA}(\log n) = \mathbf{L}$ (obvious).

Here $\mathbf{PDA}_{\text{1-turn}}$ denotes push–down automata, which make at most one reversal on their push–down. This (one–way) device exactly recognizes the linear languages.

Concerning OL systems we remark that **ETOL** (resp. **EOL**) coincides with the class of languages recignized by **CSPD** (resp. **RPAC**) automata ([65] resp. [49]). We then have

Theorem 3.14 **([32],[65][43])**

a) $\mathrm{LOG}(\emptyset\text{-}\mathbf{ETOL}) = \mathrm{LOG}(\emptyset\text{-}\mathbf{EDTOL}) = \mathbf{NACSPD}(\log n) = \mathbf{PSPACE}$

b) $\mathbf{NP} \subseteq \mathrm{LOG}(\emptyset\text{-}\mathbf{EOL}) = \mathbf{NARPAC}(\log n) \subseteq \mathbf{PSPACE}$,

c) $\text{LOG}(\emptyset\textbf{-EDOL}) = \textbf{NP}$.

Open question: is it possible to locate **∅-EOL** in the polynomial hierarchy?

Theorem 3.15 **([23])** $\text{LOG}(\emptyset\textbf{-OI}) = \textbf{EXPolyTime} := \bigcup_{k>0} : \textbf{DTime}(2^{n^k})$.

Remark: The algorithm to solve **∅-IO** in [17] and [1] runs in polynomial time (as mentioned in [23]) but is not correct. Else Theorem 3.14 would imply **P** = **PSpace**. A correct algorithm may be found in [3]. **∅-IO** should be **EXPolyTime**–complete, too.

All types of stack automata but the checking stack show the close connection between emptiness and two–way membership mentioned above.

Theorem 3.16 **([8],[24],[23])**

a) LOG(**∅-NNStSA**) = LOG(**∅-NSA**) = LOG(**∅-DSA**) = **EXPolyTime** ([23]),

b) **NANStSA**($\log n$) = **NASA**($\log n$) = **DASA**($\log n$) = **EXPolyTime**,

c) LOG(**∅-NNeSA**) = LOG(**∅-DNeSA**) = **PSpace**,

d) **NANeSA**($\log n$) = **DANeSA**($\log n$) = **PSpace**,

e) **NACSA**($\log n$) = **PSpace**,

f) **DACSA**($\log n$) = **L**.

g) LOG(**∅-DCSA**) = LOG(**∅-NCSA**) = **PSpace**

Remark: The checking stack automata is one of the few models in complexity theory, where determinism and nondeterminism are provably in equivalent.

3.3 Operation on formal languages

This subsection gives a short survey on results, characterizing complexity classes by formal language operators. We consider the following operations on families of formal languages:

i) Kleene closure: $\mathbf{A}^* := \{L^* \mid L \in \mathbf{A}\}$,

ii) nonerasing homomorphisms: $H(\mathbf{A}) := \{h(L) \mid L \in \mathbf{A}$, h is a nonerasing homomorphism $\}$,

iii) iterated shuffle (see e.g. [27]): $\mathbf{A}^\dagger := \{L^\dagger \mid L \in \mathbf{A}\}$.

Further on, let **1-L** be the set of all languages accepted by logarithmically space–bounded Turing machines with an one–way input tape.

Theorem 3.17 ([18], [39], [46], [68])

i) $\mathbf{NL} = \mathrm{LOG}(\mathbf{L}^*)$,

ii) $\mathbf{NL} = \mathrm{LOG}(H(\mathbf{1\text{-}L}))$,

iii) $\mathbf{NP} = \mathrm{LOG}(H(\mathbf{L}))$,

iv) $\mathbf{NP} = \mathrm{LOG}(\mathbf{L}^\dagger)$.

Remarks:

i) **NL** and **NP** are characterized by these operations since **NL** closed under * and **NP** in addition under H_λ and †.

ii) For arbitrary homomorphisms $H_\lambda(\mathbf{L})$ concides with the class all recursively enumerable languages, which in turn is closed under λ.

Theorem 3.17 suggest the question for language operations characterizing complexity classes like **P**, **PSPACE**, **EXPOLYTIME** etc. This question seems to be related to the search for families of formal languages, which are complete for this complexity classes. Concerning the complexity class LOG(**CF**), a modification of iterated insertion yields an operation ^{B} (just as iterated concatenation yields Kleene's *–operation) fulfilling

Theorem 3.18 ([41]) $\mathrm{LOG}(\mathbf{CF}) = \mathrm{LOG}(\mathbf{L}^B)$ and $\mathrm{LOG}(\mathbf{CF})^B \subseteq \mathrm{LOG}(\mathbf{CF})$.

Theorem 3.17 and 3.18 relativize and give interesting characterization of different types of relativization. We state these result without explaining the details, but refer to [39] instead.

Theorem 3.19 ([39], [41]) For arbitrary oracle **A** we have

i) $\mathbf{NP}(\mathbf{A}) = \mathrm{LOG}(H(\mathbf{L}(\mathbf{A})))$

ii) (Ladner–Lynch relativization): $\mathbf{NL}(\mathbf{A}) = \mathrm{LOG}(H(\mathbf{1\text{-}L}(\mathbf{A})^*)$

iii) (Ruzzo–Simon–Tompa relativization): $\mathbf{NL}\langle\mathbf{A}\rangle = \mathrm{LOG}(\mathbf{L}(\mathbf{A})^*)$

iv) $\mathrm{LOG}(\mathbf{CF})^{\langle A\rangle} = \mathrm{LOG}(\mathbf{L}(\mathbf{A})^B)$

Remark: These results hold for other types of reducibilities, too.

4 Parallel Complexity

A very fast growing area of complexity theory is the field of synchronous parallel computations. ([15] gives a very good summary of this topic). This section is to give some of those results which concern formal languages.

In spite of the many different models of complexity theory for describing parallel computations, there occurs as a rule the phenomenon of parallel time bounded complexity classes being polynominally related to sequential space bounded complexity classes. This led to the declaration of the *Parallel Computation Thesis*, that every reasonable model of parallel computation shows this behaviour (see [59] and [21]).

In the following we consider three main models of parallel complexity theory:

- parallel random access machines with several ways of settling read and write conflicts. In particular we are interested in CRCW–, CREW–, and CROW–PRAM's (see [16]).
- Boolean circuits with bounded, semi–unbounded, or unbounded fan–in (see [15], [66]).
- Alternating Turing machines ([10]) bounded in time, space or depth of alternation.

The close relation between these apparently different devices can be seen by the three characterizations of the class AC^1 (see [15]) by

i) alternating logarithmically space–bounded Turing machines the alternation depth of which is logarithmically bounded,

ii) unbounded fan–in circuits of logarithmic depth, and

iii) logarithmically time–bounded CRCW–PRAM's

or by Ruzzos characterization of NC^k, which is defined by uniform bounded fan–in circuits of polynomial size and $\log^k$ depth, through alternating logarithmically space–bounded Turing machines with a $\log^k$ time–bound.

We state this as

Theorem 4.1 **([11], [15], [60], [52])**

a) $AC^1 :=$ **ALTERNATIONDEPTHSPACE**$(\log, \log) =$ **UNBOUNDED_FAN-INDEPTHSIZE**$(\log, Pol) =$ **CRCW-TIME#PROC**$(\log, Pol)$

b) $NC^k =$ **BOUNDED_FAN-INDEPTHSIZE**$(\log^k, Pol) =$ **ATIMESPACE**$(\log^k, \log)$ for $k \geq 2$

Here Pol again denotes the union over all polynomials. (Actually, instead of $\log n$ often it should read $\bigcup_{c>0} : c \cdot \log n$).

By Venkateswaran ([66]) LOG(**CF**) coincides with the class of all languages recognizable by uniform semi–unbounded circuits of polynomial size and logarithmic depth. (Here semi–unbounded means that the fan–in of all and–Gates is bounded by some constant):

Theorem 4.2 ([66]) LOG(**CF**) = **SEMI-UNBOUNDED_FAN-INDEPTHSIZE**(log, *POL*).

This reproves the known fact **CF** $\subseteq AC^1$, i.e. that context–free languages can be recognized in logarithmic time on a CRCW–PRAM, which is a consequence of the following results of Ruzzo, which relate time–bounded nondeterministic auxiliary pushdown automata with alternating logarithmically space–bounded Turing machines of bounded 'tree–size'.

Theorem 4.3 ([51], [52]) For $k \geq 1$ we have

a) **NAPDATIMESPACE**$(2^{\log^k}, \log)$ = **ATREESIZESPACE**$(2^{\log^k}, \log)$

b) **ATREESIZESPACE**$(2^{\log^k}, \log) \subseteq$ **ALTERNATIONDEPTHSPACE**$(\log^k, \log)$

c) $AC^k \subseteq NC^{k+1}$

Remark: LOG(**CF**) = **NAPDATIMESPACE**(*POL*, log)(= $\mathbf{NAPDA}_{\mathrm{PT}}(\log n)$).

Following the ideas of Immermann–Sczelepcsényi and using Theorem 4.2 Borodin et. al. succeeded in showing the closure of LOG(**CF**) under complement.

Theorem 4.4 ([9]) Co-LOG(**CF**) = LOG(**CF**).

Remark: It is possible to show this result directly without using Boolean circuits (see e.g. [41]).

The family **UCF** of unambiguous context–free language can be recognized in logarithmic time on a CREW–PRAM.

Theorem 4.5 ([54]) LOG(**UCF**) $\subseteq$ **CREW-TIME#PROC**(log, *POL*).

Here the following questions seem to be interesting:

- Is LOG(**UCF**) closed under complement?
- Can these classes be characterized in terms of Boolean circuits or sequential automata?

That polynomial time bounded **DAPDA**$(\log n)$'s are not an answer to the last question, is indicated by the following surprising equality:

Theorem 4.6 ([16]) LOG(**DCF**) = **CROW-TIME#PROC**(log, *POL*).

It should be remarked, that Theorem 3.6 can be phrased in terms of parallel complexity, since **DTIMESPACE**$(POL, \log^2 n)$ = **BOUNDED_FAN-INSIZEWIDTH**$(POL, \log^2 n)$ ([48]).

Question: Are there similar parallel representations of the order formal languages mentioned in subsection 2?

Some of these results are summarized in Diagram 2.

	APDA		P-RAM		ALTERNATION		(UNIFORM)CIRCUIT
							B = BOUNDED_FAN-IN UB = UNBOUNDED_FAN-IN SUB = SEMI-UNBOUNDED
NC^{k+1}							
AC^k			CRCW-TIME#PROC($\log^k$, POL)	=	ALT.DEPTHSPACE($\log^k$, log)	=	UB-DEPTHSIZE($\log^k$, POL)
CF^k	NTISP($2^{\log^k}$, log)			=	TREESIZESPACE($2^{\log^k}$, log)	=	SUB-DEPTHSIZE($\log^k$, POL)
–			CREW-TIME#PROC($\log^k$, POL)				
DCF^k	DTISP($2^{\log^k}$, log)	=	CROW-TIME#PROC($\log^k$, POL)				
NC^k					TIMESPACE($\log^k$, log)	=	B-DEPTHSIZE($\log^k$, POL)

The validity of the last line for $k = 1$ depends on the type of uniformity condition we choose (see [52])

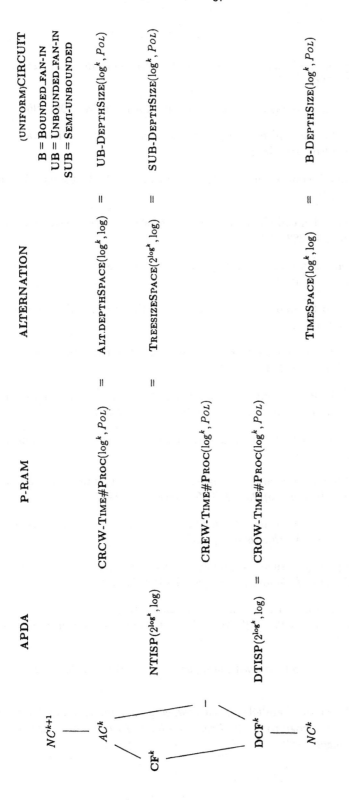

References

[1] A. Aho. Indexed grammars – an extension of context-free-grammars. *J. Assoc. Comp. Mach.*, 15:647–671, 1968.

[2] A. Aho. Nested stack automata. *J. Assoc. Comp. Mach.*, 16:383–406, 1969.

[3] J. Albert. Über indizierte und m-Block-indizierte Grammatiken. Dissertation, Universität Karlsruhe, 1976. (in German).

[4] P. Asveld. Iterated context-independent rewriting. Ph.d. thesis, Technische Hogeschool Twente, 1978.

[5] P. Asveld. Space-bounded complexity classes and iterated deterministic substitutions. *Inform. and Control*, 44:282–299, 1980.

[6] P. Asveld. Time and space complexity of inside-out macro languages. *Internat. J. Comput. Math.*, 10:3–14, 1981.

[7] T. Baker, J. Gill, and R. Solovay. Relativizations of the P = ? NP question. *SIAM J. Comp.*, 4:431–442, 1975.

[8] C. Beeri. Two-way nested stack automata are equivalent to two-way stack automata. *J. Comp. System Sci.*, 10:317–339, 1975.

[9] A. Borodin, S. Cook, P. Dymond, W. Ruzzo, and M. Tompa. Two applications of complementation via inductive counting. In *Proc. of 3rd StCT*, 1988.

[10] A. Chandra, D. Kozen, and L. Stockmeyer. Alternation. *J. Assoc. Comp. Mach.*, 28:114–133, 1981.

[11] A. Chandra, L. Stockmeyer, and U. Vishkin. Complexity theory for unbounded FAN-IN parallelism. In *Proc. of 23rd FOCS*, pages 1–13, 1982.

[12] S. Cook. Characterizations of pushdown machines in terms of time-bounded computers. *J. Assoc. Comp. Mach.*, 18:4–18, 1971.

[13] S. Cook. The complexity of theorem proving procedures. In *Proc. of the 3rd Annual ACM Symp. on Theory of Computing*, pages 151–158, 1971.

[14] S. Cook. Deterministic cfl's are accepted simultaneously in polynomial time and log squared space. In *Proc. on the 11th Annual ACM Symp. on Theory of Computing*, pages 338–345, 1979.

[15] S. Cook. A taxonomy of problems with fast parallel algorithms. *Inform. and Control*, 64:2–22, 1985.

[16] P. Dymond and W. Ruzzo. Parallel rms with owned global memory and deterministic context-free language recoginition. In *Proc. of 13th ICALP*, number 233 in LNCS, pages 95–104. Springer, 1987.

[17] M.J. Fischer. Grammars with macro-like production. Ph.d. thesis, Harvard Univ., 1968.

[18] P. Flajolet and J. Steyaert. Complexity of classes of languages and operators. Rap. de Recherche 92, IRIA Laboria, Nov. 1974.

[19] S. Ginsburg, S. Greibach, and M. Harrison. One-way stack automata. *JACM*, 14:389–418, 1967.

[20] S. Ginsburg, S. Greibach, and M. Harrison. Stack automata and compiling. *J. Assoc. Comp. Mach.*, 14:172–201, 1967.

[21] J.-W. Hong. On similarity and duality of computation. *Inform. and Control*, 62:109–128, 1984.

[22] J. Hopcroft and J. Ullman. *Introduction to Automata Theory, Language, and Computation.* Addison-Wesley, Reading Mass., 1979.

[23] H. Hunt. On the complexity of finite, pushdown, and stack automata. *Math. Systems Theory*, 10:33–52, 1976.

[24] O. Ibarra. Characterizations of some tape and time complexity classes of turingmachines in terms of multihead and auxiliary stack automata. *J. Comp. System Sci.*, 5:88–117, 1971.

[25] O. Ibarra, S. Kim, and L. Rosier. Space and time efficient simulations and characterizations of some restricted classes of pdas. In *Proc. of 11th ICALP*, number 172 in LNCS, pages 247–259. Springer, 1984.

[26] N. Immerman. Nondeterministic space is closed under complement. Technical Report 552, Yale University, 1987.

[27] M. Jantzen. The power of synchronizing operations on strings. *Theoret. Comput. Sci.*, 14:127–154, 1981.

[28] B.J. Jenner and B. Kirsig. Characterizing the polynomial hierarchy by alternating auxiliary pushdown automata. In *Proc. of 5th STACS*, number 294 in LNCS, pages 118–125. Springer, 1988.

[29] N. Jones. Space-bounded reducibility among combinatorial problems. *J. Comp. System Sci.*, 11:68–85, 1975.

[30] N. Jones and W. Laaser. Complete problems for deterministic polynomial time. *Theoret. Comput. Sci.*, 3:105–117, 1977.

[31] N. Jones and S. Skyum. Recognition of deterministic etol languages in logarithmic space. *Inform. and Control*, 35:177–181, 1977.

[32] N. Jones and S. Skyum. Complexity of some problems concerning L systems. *Math. Systems Theory*, 13:29–43, 1979.

[33] R. Ladner. The circuit value problem is log space complete for p. *SIGACT NEWS*, 7:18–20, 1975.

[34] R. Ladner, R. Lipton, and L. Stockmeyer. Alternating pushdown and stack automata. *SIAM J. Comp.*, 13:135–155, 1984.

[35] R. Ladner and N. Lynch. Relativization of questions about log space computability. *Math. Systems Theory*, 10:19–32, 1976.

[36] R. Ladner, L. Stockmeyer, and R. Lipton. Alternation bounded auxiliary pushdown automata. *Inform. and Control*, 62:93–108, 1984.

[37] K.-J. Lange. Context-free controlled etol systems. In *Proc. of 9th ICALP*, number 154 in LNCS, pages 723–733. Springer, 1983.

[38] K.-J. Lange. L systems and nlog-reductions. In G. Rozenberg and A. Salomaar, editors, *The book of L*, pages 245–252, Berlin, 1986. Springer.

[39] K.-J. Lange. Nichtdeterministische Reduktionen und logarithmische Hierarchien. Technical Report 119, Fachbereich Informatik, Universität Hamburg, 1986. (in German).

[40] K.-J. Lange. Two characterizations of the logarithmic alternation hierarchy. In *Proc. of MFCS*, number 233 in LNCS, pages 518–526. Springer, 1986.

[41] K.-J. Lange. On the complexity of iterated insertion. In preperation, 1988.

[42] K.-J. Lange, B. Jenner, and B. Kirsig. The logarithmic alternation hierarchy collapses':$A\Sigma^L = A\Pi^{L'}$. In *Proc. of 14th ICALP*, number 267 in LNCS, pages 531–541. Springer, 1987.

[43] K.-J. Lange and M. Schudy. A further link between formal languages and complexity theory. *EATCS Bull.*, 33:67–71, 1987.

[44] P. Lewis, R. Stearns, and J. Hartmanis. Memory bounds for recognition of context-free and context-sensitive languages. In *Proc. 6th Annual IEEE Symp. on Switching Circuit Theory and Logical Design*, pages 191–209, 1965.

[45] A. Meyer and L. Stockmeyer. The equivalence problem for regular expressions with squaring requires exponential space. In *Proc. of the 13th Annual IEEE Symposium on Switching and Automata Theory*, pages 125–129, 1972.

[46] B. Monien. About the deterministic simulation of nondeterministic $(\log n)$-tape bounded turing machines. In *2-te TI Fachtagung Automatentheorie und Formale Sprachen*, number 33 in LNCS, pages 118–126. Springer, 1975.

[47] B. Monien and I. Sudborough. The interface between language theory and complexity theory. In R. Book, editor, *Formal Languages – Perspectives and Open Problems*, pages 287–324, New York, 1980. Academic Press.

[48] N. Pippinger. On simultaneous resource bounds. In *Proc. of 20th FOCS*, pages 307–311, 1979.

[49] G. Rozenberg. On a family of acceptors for some classes of develpmental languages. *Internat. J. Comput. Math.*, 4:199–228, 1974.

[50] G. Rozenberg and A. Salomaar. *The Mathematical Theory of L Systems.* Academic Press, New York, 1980.

[51] W. Ruzzo. Tree-size bounded alternation. *J. Comp. System Sci.*, 21:218–235, 1980.

[52] W. Ruzzo. On uniform circuit complexity. *J. Comp. System Sci.*, 22:365–338, 1981.

[53] W. Ruzzo, J. Simon, and M. Tompa. Space – bounded hierarchies and probabilistic computations. *J. Comp. System Sci.*, 28:216–230, 1984.

[54] W. Rytter. Parallel time. o(log n) recognition of unambiguous context-free languages. *Inform. and Control*, 73:75–86, 1987.

[55] W. Savitch. Relationships between nondeterministic and deterministic tape complexities. *J. Comp. System Sci.*, 4:177–192, 1970.

[56] U. Schöning and K. Wagner. Collapsing oracle hierarchies, census functions and logarithmically many queries. In *Proc. of 5th STACS*, number 294 in LNCS, pages 91–97. Springer, 1988.

[57] R. Sczelepcsényi. The method of forcing for nondeterministic automata. *EATCS-Bull.*, 33:96–100, 1987.

[58] E. Shamir and C. Beeri. Checking stacks and context-free programmed grammars accept p-complete languages. In *Proc. of 2nd ICALP*, number 14 in LNCS, pages 277–283. Springer, 1974.

[59] L. Stockmeyer and A. Meyer. Word problems requiring exponential time: preliminary report. In *Proc. of the 5th Annual ACM Symposium on Theory of Computing*, pages 1–9, 1973.

[60] L. Stockmeyer and C. Vishkin. Simulation of random access machines by circuits. *SIAM J. Comp.*, 13:409–422, 1984.

[61] I. Sudborough. A note on tape-bounded complexity classes and linear context-free languages. *J. Assoc. Comp. Mach.*, 22:499–500, 1975.

[62] I. Sudborough. The complexity of the membership problem for some extensions of context-free languages. *Internat. J. Comput. Math. SECT A*, 6:191–215, 1977.

[63] I. Sudborough. On the tape complexity of deterministic context-free languages. *J. Assoc. Comp. Mach.*, 25:405–414, 1978.

[64] J. van Leeuwen. The membership question for etol languages is polynomially complete. *Information Processing Letters*, 3:138–143, 1975.

[65] J. van Leeuwen. Variations of a new machine model. In *Proc. of 17th FOCS*, pages 228–235, 1976.

[66] H. Venkateswaran. Properties that characterize logcfl. In *Proc. of 19th STOC*, pages 141–150, 1987.

[67] K. Wagner and G. Wechsung. *Computational complexity.* VEB Deutscher Verlag der Wissenschaften, Berlin, 1986.

[68] M. Warmuth and D. Haussler. On the complexity of iterated shuffle. *J. Comp. System Sci.*, 28:345–358, 1984.

[69] C. Wrathall. Complete sets of the polynomial hierarchie. *Theoret. Comput. Sci.*, 3:23–33, 1976.

[70] D. Young. Recognition and parsing of context-free languages in time n^3. *Inform. and Control*, 10:189–208, 1967.

RATIONAL CONES and COMMUTATIONS†

Michel Latteux
LIFL,CNRS UA 369
University of Lille Flandres Artois.
F-59655 Villeneuve d'Ascq

ABSTRACT *This survey presents some results concerning total commutations, partial commutations and semi-commutations in connection with the families of rational and algebraic languages and more generaly with (faithful) rational cones..*

INTRODUCTION

The study of free partially commutative monoids has been initiated by Cartier and Foata [11]. It happened that words on partially commutative alphabets became of interest to computer scientists studying problems of concurrency control. Thus, traces languages, which are subsets of a free partially commutative monoid, have been proposed by Mazurkiewicz [44] as a tool for describing the behaviour of concurrent program schemes. Recently several surveys deal with partially commutative monoids (Aalbersberg and Rozenberg [1], Berstel and Sakarovitch [7], Cori [19], Mazurkiewicz [45], Perrin [51]). Other results on this subject can be found in [21,22,23,24,48]. We shall focus here on (partial) commutations which are unary operations on languages associated with partially commutative alphabets. We shall examine also the semi-commutation operation which is a useful and natural extension of the partial commutation operation.

A partially commutative alphabet is a couple (A,θ) where A is an alphabet and θ, the commutation relation, is a symmetric and irreflexive binary relation over A. Associated to the commutation relation θ, one can define a mapping $f_\theta : 2^{A^*} \to 2^{A^*}$ by : for each language L over the alphabet A, $f_\theta(L)$ is the set of words equivalent to some word in L for the congruence generated by θ. Thus f_θ is a unary operation on languages, called the partial commutation associated to θ. It seems useful to study this operation in

†This work has been partially supported by the Programme de Recherche Coordonnée "Mathématiques et Informatique" du Ministère de la Recherche et de la Technologie.

transduction, shuffle and intersection(see [6,28] for precise definitions of these operations).

Since partial commutations generalize total commutations, we shall start this study by recalling in section I the main results concerning total commutations. For each of these results it is quite natural to wonder whether it remains true for partial commutations. On one hand, this can raise new questions, on the other hand this points out important differences between partial and total commutations. The results presented in this section concern mainly rational and algebraic (or context-free) commutative languages, rational cones generated by commutative languages and commutatively closed rational cones.

Section II is devoted to semi-commutations. If θ is an irreflexive binary relation over an alphabet A, one can consider the semi-Thue system whose the set of rules is $\{yx \rightarrow xy / (y,x) \in \theta\}$. For $L \subset A^*$, $f_\theta(L)$ denotes the set of words which can be derived in the semi-Thue system from some word of L. For instance, if $A=\{a,b\}$, $\theta=\{(b,a)\}$ and $L=(ab)^*$, then $f_\theta(L)$ is the semi-Dyck language, a language which often appears for describing synchronization processes. It is important to note that here for u in A^*, $f_\theta(u)$ is not an equivalent class. However, several results proved originally for partial commutations remain true for semi-commutations.

In section III we shall present the main results on partial commutations which cannot be extended to semi-commutations. In particular, two nice characterizations of the family of rational languages closed under θ-commutations will be enonced. The first one, due to Ochmanski [49] uses operations which preserve this family. The second one, due to Zielonka [61] deals with asynchronous automata, a new type of finite automaton.

I. TOTAL COMMUTATIONS

We shall first examine commutative languages, that is; languages closed under total commutations. Commutative rational languages admit simple characterizations. In particular rational unary languages have been studied by Salomaa [58] :

Proposition *Let R be a language over the alphabet A={a}.Then the following properties are equivalent:*

i) R is rational,

ii) R is a finite union of languages of the form xy^* with x,y in a^*,

iii)$R=F \cup Gz^*$ where z is in a^* and F,G are finite subsets of a^*.

For instance the language $a^2 + a^3 + a(a^3)^* + a^5(a^2)^*$ which is a finite union of languages of the form $a^i(a^j)^*$ is also represented by the rational expression $a^2 + (a+a^3+a^4+a^5)(a^6)^*$.

Now, if $F \subset a^*$ is a finite language. Let $k = \gcd(F)$ be the greatest common divisor of the lengths of the words of F. It is clear that F^* is included in $(a^k)^*$. Conversely it can be shown that there exists an integer i such that $a^{ik}(a^k)^*$ is included in F^*. That implies:

Proposition *Let $F \subset a^*$ be any finite unary language. Then $F^* = G \cup z^i z^*$ for some $i \in \mathbb{N}$, $z \in a^*$ and $G \subset z^* - z^i z^*$.*

Let us take for instance $F = a^4 + a^6 + a^9$. Then $\gcd(F) = 1$ and the least integer i such that $a^i a^*$ is included in F^* is 12. It can be verified that $G = a^4 + a^6 + a^8 + a^9 + a^{10}$ and $F^* = (a^4 + a^6 + a^8 + a^9 + a^{10}) + a^{12}a^*$.

Now let us consider an arbitrary unary language L. Clearly it contains a finite language F such that $\gcd(F) = \gcd(L) = k$. From the previous proposition we get $a^{ik}(a^k) \subset F^* \subset L^* \subset (a^k)^*$ for some integer i. Thus $L^* - F^*$ is finite, which implies:

Proposition *Each unary monoid is finitely generated. Hence it is rational.*

Example: $\{ a^{1+n^2} / n \geq 2 \}^* = (a^5 + a^{17} + a^{26})^*$

Similarly, for $L \subset a^*$ and $z \in a^+$, Lz^* is rational since it is a finite union of languages of the form $a^i z^*$. If $F = z_1 + z_2 + \cdots + z_t$ is a nonempty set then $LF^* = L(z_1)^*(z_2)^* \cdots (z_t)^*$ is also rational and the above proposition can be generalized:

Proposition *Let L_1, L_2 be nonempty subsets of a^+. Then $L_1(L_2)^* = F_1(F_2)^*$ for some finite sets $F_1 \subset L_1$ and $F_2 \subset L_2$.*

Let us consider now the alphabet $A=\{a_1, a_2, \ldots, a_n\}$ and a commutative rational language $R \subset A^*$. Then, $R = \mathrm{Com}(K)$ is the commutative closure of the rational language $K = R \cap a_1^* a_2^* \ldots a_n^*$

which is a finite union of languages of the form $R_1R_2 \cdots R_n$ where $\forall\, i \in \{1,..,n\}$, R_i is a rational language included in a_i^*. It follows that R is a finite union of languages of the form $Com(x_1y_1^* .. x_ny_n^*)$ where $\forall\, i \in \{1,..,n\}$, $x_i, y_i \in a_i^*$. But, for commutative languages L, M, Com(LM) is equal to $L ⧢ M$, the shuffle of L and M. This implies the following characterization of commutative rational languages:

Proposition *For each $R \subset A^*$ the following three statements are equivalent:*
i) R is a commutative rational language,
ii) R is a finite union of languages of the form

$$x_1y_1^* ⧢ \ldots ⧢ x_ny_n^* \qquad \text{where } x_i, y_i \in a_i^*,$$

iii) R is a finite union of languages of the form $Com(xP^*)$ where $x \in A^*$ and $P \subset a_1^* + a_2^* + \ldots + a_n^*$ is a finite set.

The links between commutative rational languages and bounded rational languages are very strong as shown by the following proposition:

Proposition *Let $L \subset A^*$ be a commutative language. Then L is rational if and only if $L \cap a_1^* a_2^* .. a_n^*$ is rational.*

Some of the above results concerning unary languages can be generalized to commutative languages. Indeed one can state:

Proposition *Let $F, P \subset A^*$ be finite sets. Then $Com(FP^*)$ is rational if and only if $\forall a \in alph(P)$, $P \cap a^+ \neq \emptyset$.*

Proposition *Let $P \subset A^*$ be a language such that $\forall a \in A$, $P \cap a^+ \neq \emptyset$. Then for each $L \subset A^*$ $Com(LP^*)$ is rational.*

Example: $Com(\{ a^{n^2}b^{n^3} / n \geq 1 \}(\{a^nb^n / n \geq 2 \} \cup \{a^2, b^3\})^*) =$

$Com((ab + a^4b^8)(a^2b^2 + a^3b^3 + a^2 + b^3)^*) =$

$Com((ab + a^3b^3 + a^4b^4 + a^5b^5 + a^4b^8)(a^2 + b^3)^*) =$

$Com(ab + a^3b^3 + a^4b^4 + a^5b^5 + a^4b^8) ⧢ (a^2)^* ⧢ (b^3)^*.$

These results can be deduced from the following proposition which gives a necessary and sufficient condition for the rationality of commutative languages [41]:

Proposition *Let $R \subset A^*$ be a commutative language. Then R is rational if and only if $\exists K \in \mathbb{N}\ \ \forall u \in R, a \in A, (|u|_a \geq K \Rightarrow u(a^K)^* \subset R)$.*

By using the pumping lemma for linear languages, it is easy to find again that each commutative linear language is rational[25]. We get a similar result for the the family of commutative restricted one-counter languages, that is the rational cone generated by the semi-Dyck language over one pair of parentheses[41]:

Proposition *Every commutative restricted one counter language is rational.*

Let R be a rational language. By looking at its syntactic monoid it is easy to determine whether R is a commutative language (more generally, it permits to find the largest semi-commutation θ such that $f_\theta(R) = R$). On the other hand, it is undecidable to determine whether an algebraic language is commutative[12]. More difficult is to determine whether Com(R) remains rational. However, Ginsburg and Spanier[29], and Gohon[31] have proved the decidability of this problem. If we consider partial commutations instead of the total commutation this problem is yet open (see [56]), even if $R = F^*$ for some finite language F. Conversely, it could be interesting to have a simple characterization of commutative languages of the form F^* with F a finite language. A necessary condition is that $u^{-1}F^* = (A^t)^*$ for some u in F^* and some integer t [42], but this condition is not sufficient. In connection with this problem, note that a language L^* is commutative if and only if $Com(L \cup L^2) \subset L^*$ (more generally L^* is closed under a semi-commutation θ if and only if $f_\theta(L \cup L^2) \subset L^*$).

Let us consider now the family of algebraic languages. Parikh's theorem asserts that Com(**Alg**)=Com(**Rat**), that is, for each algebraic language L there exists a rational language R such that Com(L)=Com(R):

Parikh's Theorem *Com(**Alg**) = Com(**Rat**). That is if $L \in$ **Alg** then Com(L) is a finite union of languages of the form Com(FP^*) with F, P finite languages.*

In particular this implies that unary algebraic languages are rational. Clearly in the statement of the Parikh's theorem it cannot be assumed that the rational language is included in the algebraic language.

Blattner and Latteux[9] have proved that one can find a bounded language included in L with the same commutative image (see[32] for a proof of this property in a larger family):

Proposition *The algebraic languages are Parikh-bounded. That is, for each algebraic language L there exist words* $y_1, \ldots, y_n$ *such that* $Com(L) = Com(L \cap y_1^* \ldots y_n^*)$.

For instance for the algebraic language E generated by the grammar $S \to aSbSc + \varepsilon$, we get $Com(E) = Com((abc)^*) = Com(\{(ab)^n c^n / n \geq 0\})$.
Contrarily to the structure of commutative rational languages which is very simple, the structure of commutative algebraic languages is quite mysterious. Since bounded algebraic languages are well known it should be interesting to find some links between these two families. This is done in the following proposition for languages over a three letters alphabet[43, 50, 52]:

Proposition *Let* $L \subset \{a, b, c\}^*$ *be a commutative language. Then* $L \in$ ***Alg*** *if and only if* $L \cap a^*b^*c^* \in$ ***Alg***.

However this result is no longer true if the alphabet contains more than three letters. If $L = Com(M)$ with $M = \{a^n b^n / n \geq 0\}\{c^n d^n / n \geq 0\}$, then $L \cap a^*b^*c^*d^* = M \in$ **Alg** but $L \notin$ **Alg** since $L \cap a^*c^*b^*d^* = \{a^n c^i b^n d^i / i,n \geq 0\} \notin$ **Alg.** Thus one can define a new class of languages:

Definition $L \subset A^*$ *is said to be a* ***B-CF language*** *if for each permutation* σ *of* $\{1, \ldots, n\}$, $L \cap a_{\sigma(1)}^* a_{\sigma(2)}^* \ldots\ldots a_{\sigma(n)}^* \in$ ***Alg.***

Then **Fliess conjecture**(1970) (see [3,53])can be stated very simply: Each commutative B-CF language is algebraic.
The above proposition shows that this conjecture holds for languages over a three letters alphabet. Recently, Beauquier, Blattner and Latteux[5] have proved this conjecture in a particular case:

Proposition *Let* $F, P \subset A^*$ *be finite sets. Then* $Com(FP^*) \in$ ***Alg*** *if and only if it is a B-CF language.*

The proof of this proposition is based on the existence of two properties **P1**) and **P2**) such that:

$Com(FP^*)$ is B-CF $\Rightarrow$ **P1**) and **P2**) hold $\Rightarrow$ $Com(FP^*) \in$ **Alg**.

In order to define **P1**) and **P2**) we need some notations:

$Q = \{ u \in P / u \in (x + y)^* \text{ for some } x, y \in A \}$ and $Q_{i,j} = P \cap (a_i^+ \sqcup\!\sqcup a_j^+)$

P1) $\forall u \in P$, $u^+ \cap Com(Q^*) \neq \emptyset$

P2) $\forall u \in Q_{i,j}$, $v \in Q_{s,t}$, either $(uv)^+ \cap Com(Q-Q_{i,j})^* \neq \emptyset$
or $(uv)^+ \cap Com(Q-Q_{s,t})^* \neq \emptyset$.

Examples:

$P = a_1a_2a_3 + a_1^2a_2 + a_1a_4^3 + a_2a_3^2 + a_3a_4^3$

$-(a_1a_2a_3)^2 \in Com((a_1^2a_2)(a_2a_3^2)) \subset Com(Q^*)$

$-(a_1^2a_2a_3a_4^3)^2 \in Com((a_1^2a_2)(a_1a_4^3)^2(a_2a_3^2)) \subset Com(Q - Q_{3,4})^*$

$-(a_1a_4^3a_2a_3^2)^2 \in Com((a_1^2a_2)(a_3a_4^3)^2(a_2a_3^2)) \subset Com(Q - Q_{1,4})^*$

Then $Com(P^*) \in$ **Alg**.

$P = a_1a_2^2 + a_1a_3 + a_2a_3 + a_2a_4 + a_1^2a_2 + a_3^2a_4$

$-a_1a_2^2a_3^2a_4,\ a_1^2a_2a_3^2a_4 \in Com(Q - Q_{1,2})^*$ but:

$-(a_1a_3a_2a_4)^+ \cap Com(Q - Q_{1,3})^* = \emptyset$

$-(a_1a_3a_2a_4)^+ \cap Com(Q - Q_{2,4})^* = \emptyset$

Then $Com(P^*) \notin$ **Alg**.

Since **P1**) and **P2**) are decidable properties it follows:

Proposition *It is decidable to determine whether $Com(FP^*)$ is algebraic.*

Recently, Kortelainen [36] has disproved the Fliess conjecture:

Proposition *There exists a commutative B-CF language that is not algebraic.*

This language is the union of the commutative algebraic language $L_0 = \{u \,/\, |u|_{a_1} \neq |u|_{a_2} + |u|_{a_3} + |u|_{a_4}\}$ with $Com((a_1^3a_2a_3a_4)^*)$.

Then $K_0 = \text{Com}((a_1^3 a_2 a_3 a_4)^*) \cup L_0$ can also be written as $\text{Com}((a_1^3 a_2)^*(a_3 a_4)^*) \cup L_0$ or as $\text{Com}((a_1^3 a_3)^*(a_2 a_4)^*) \cup L_0$. So it can be verified that K_0 is a B-CF language. But K_0 is not algebraic. Indeed there exist three words $x = a_1a_2$, $y = a_1a_3$ and $z = a_1a_4$ such that $K_0 \cap x^*y^*z^* = \{x^n y^n z^n / n \geq 0\}$ is not algebraic.

In this example $\mathcal{C}(K_0)$, the rational cone generated by K_0 contains a non algebraic bounded language. Hence it can be conjectured that each non algebraic commutative language dominates by rational transduction a non algebraic bounded language. Since $\mathcal{C}(\text{Com})$, the rational cone generated by commutative languages contains only Parikh-bounded languages one can show that this conjecture is equivalent to:

Conjecture *A commutative language L is algebraic if and only if for all words* $y_1, \ldots, y_n$ $L \cap y_1^* \ldots y_n^*$ *is algebraic.*

We have seen that a language Com(P*) with P finite is algebraic if and only if it is a B-CF language. It seems that the finiteness of P is not mandatory:

Conjecture *A commutative star language L* is algebraic if and only if it is a B-CF language.*

The best known example of algebraic commutative language is the language $D_1^* = \text{Com}((ab)^*)$. This language is not of finite index or equivalently it is not a quasi-rational language and it is quite natural to wonder if there exist non rational algebraic commutative languages of finite index. More generally, one can try to determine those subfamilies of Alg for which commutativity implies rationality. It has been seen above that each commutative restricted one-counter language is rational and that each commutative linear language is also rational. This last result is now extended to the family of quasi-rational languages. In order to prove that each algebraic commutative language of finite index is rational[35], Kortelainen has proved an important property of the family Com(**Rat**). This family has a minimal language for rational transduction, namely the language $\bar{D}_1^* = (a+b)^* - D_1^*$:

Proposition *If L is a non rational language in Com(**Rat**), then* $\bar{D}_1^* \in \mathcal{C}(L)$.

Since the family of algebraic languages of finite index is a rational cone and that the language $\bar{D}_1^*$ is of infinite index[40], it follows:

Proposition *Each algebraic commutative language of finite index is rational.*

The above results show that a lot of algebraic languages do not dominate any non rational commutative language. Conversely, it is shown in [38] that several algebraic languages do not belong to $\mathcal{C}$(**Com**), the rational cone generated by the family of arbitrary commutative languages. For instance, the families of linear languages and of restricted one-counter languages are not included in $\mathcal{C}$(**Com**). Thus **Alg** does not posses any commutative generator (a commutative language L such that $\mathcal{C}$(L) = **Alg**). However it could happen that there exists an algebraic commutative language which dominates each algebraic commutative language by rational transductions. So $\mathcal{C}(D_1^*)$ contains each algebraic commutative language over a two letters alphabet[37] but the algebraic language $Com((ab)^*(ac)^*(bc)^*) \notin \mathcal{C}(D_1^*)$ [38] and the following conjecture is enonced in [39]:

Conjecture *The rational cone generated by the family of algebraic commutative languages is not principal.*

Ginsburg and Spanier have enounced in[30] the same conjecture for the rational cone generated by Com(**Rat**),the family of the commutative closures of rational languages. This have been solved positively in [37] where it was proved that $\mathcal{C}$(Com(**Rat**)) is equal to $\mathcal{C}_\cap(D_1^*)$, the intersection closed rational cone generated by the language D_1^*. But $D_1^* = C_1 ш \hat{C}_1$ with $C_1=\{a^nb^n/n\geq 0\}$ and $\hat{C}_1= \{b^na^n/n\geq 0\}$[37]. Then $\mathcal{C}$(Com(**Rat**)) is also equal to $\mathcal{C}_\cap(C_1)$, the intersection closed rational cone generated by the language C_1. Since an intersection closed rational cone $\mathcal{L}$ is commutatively closed (i.e. $Com(\mathcal{L}) \subset \mathcal{L}$) if and only if $C_1 \in \mathcal{L}$ [37] , it follows that $\mathcal{C}$(Com(**Rat**)) is the smallest commutatively closed rational cone. Moreover we have the equality $\mathcal{C}$(Com(**Rat**)) = $\mathcal{H}$sa(Com(**Rat**) $\wedge$ **Rat**), that is every language in $\mathcal{C}$(Com(**Rat**)) is the image by a strictly alphabetic (i.e. length preserving) homomorphism of the intersection of a language in Com(**Rat**) with a rational language. If we consider $\mathbf{Rat}_n$, the family of rational languages defined on n letters alphabets, Com($\mathbf{Rat}_n$) is a principal rational cone[34]. More precisely, $\mathrm{Com}((a_1a_2..a_n)^*)$ and $\mathrm{Com}((a_2b_2)^*..(a_nb_n)^*)$ are two generators of $\mathcal{C}(\mathrm{Com}(\mathbf{Rat}_n))$.

Let us consider now $\mathcal{C}(\mathbf{Com})$, the rational cone generated by **Com** the family of arbitrary commutative languages. Then $\mathcal{C}(\mathbf{Com}) = \mathcal{H}sa(\mathbf{Com} \wedge \mathbf{Rat})$ is a non principal rational cone[37]. Moreover $\mathcal{C}(\mathbf{Com}) = \mathcal{C}_\cap(\mathbf{Un})$, the intersection closed rational cone generated by **Un**, the family of unary languages (languages defined on a one letter alphabet)[33]. The intersection is mandatory since each algebraic commutative language in $\mathcal{C}(\mathbf{Un})$ is rational, but $\mathcal{C}(\mathbf{Un})$ contains a non rational algebraic language [4]. In [34], it is shown that **Rat** is the single AFL included in $\mathcal{C}(\mathbf{Com})$. Lastly, Turakainen has proved that each language in $\mathbf{Com}_{re}$, the family of recursively enumerable commutative languages can be obtained from the language $SQE=\{a^nb^{n^2}/n>0\}$ by intersection and rational transductions [60] hence the equality $\mathcal{C}(\mathbf{Com}_{re}) = \mathcal{C}_\cap(SQE)$.

II. SEMI-COMMUTATIONS

Semi-commutations which have been introduced by Clerbout in her thesis[12] (see also [15,16,59]) correspond to particular rewriting systems on words. In such systems, the rules are of the form $yx \to xy$ where x and y are two different letters.

For instance, if the commutation relation θ is equal to $\{(b,a),(b,c),(c,a)\}$ over the alphabet $A=\{a,b,c\}$, the rules are $ba \to ab$, $bc \to cb$, $ca \to ac$. The language $L=f_\theta((cba)^*) \notin \mathbf{Alg}$ since $L \cap a^*c^*b^*=\{a^nc^nb^n /n \geq 0\}$. Indeed $(cba)^t \overset{*}{\Rightarrow} a^t(cb)^t \overset{*}{\Rightarrow} a^tc^tb^t$. On the contrary, if we consider $\theta=\{(a,b),(b,c),(c,a)\}$, the rules are $ab \to ba$, $bc \to cb$, $ca \to ac$. Then $f_\theta((cba)^*) = (cba)^*$ and $f_\theta((abc)^*)$ is rational. More generally, $f_\theta(u^*) \in$ **Rat** for each word u such that alph(u) = A and $f_\theta(R) \in \mathbf{Alg}$ for each rational set R. This can be deduced from more general results stated in the sequel.

But first let us enonce two useful "derivation" lemmas. The first one due to Clerbout [12] states that the image of a word by a semi-commutation can be reconstructed from the images by this semi-commutation of the projections of this word on the two letters subalphabets. Let us consider a semi-commutation f_θ on the alphabet A. For a,b in A, $\pi_{a,b}$ denotes the projection on the alphabet $\{a,b\}$.

Projection Lemma *Let f_θ be a semi-commutation on an alphabet A. For $u,v \in A^*$, $v \in f_\theta(u)$ if and only if $\forall$ a, b$\in$A, $\pi_{a,b}(v) \in f_\theta(\pi_{a,b}(u))$.*

It is often useful to consider words which do not contain two occurrences of the same letter. For that, we can use a gsm which numerotes the different occurrences of the same letter[55]. More precisely, if we define:

- The alphabet $A_k = A \times \{1,...,k\}$, where k is a positive integer,
- The commutation relation $\theta_k = \{((a,i),(b,j)) \in A_k \times A_k \,/\, (a,b) \in \theta\}$,
- The gsm num_k by: $\forall\, u \in A^*$, $a \in A$, $num_k(ua) = num_k(u)(a,s)$ with $s = inf(k, |ua|_a)$,

then, we can enonce:

Numerotation Lemma *Let f_θ be a semi-commutation on an alphabet A. For $u,v \in A^*$, $v \in f_\theta(u)$ if and only if $num_k(v) \in f_{\theta_k}(num_k(u))$.*

In particular, if $k \geq |u|$, $num_k(u)$ do not contain two occurrences of the same letter. Now, by using the two previous lemmas it is easy to find again other useful results. For instance, in[46], it is shown that if $xy \in f_\theta(uv)$, there exist $x_1,x_2,y_1,y_2 \in A^*$ such that $x_1y_1 \in f_\theta(u)$, $x_2y_2 \in f_\theta(v)$, $x \in f_\theta(x_1x_2)$, $y \in f_\theta(y_1y_2)$ and for each letter $a \in alph(y_1)$ (the set of the letters occuring in y_1), and for every letter $b \in alph(x_2)$, $(a,b) \in \theta$. In [18], it is proved that if uv and u'v' $\in f_\theta(w)$, with Com(u) = Com(u'), then there exist $t,z \in A^*$ such that $tz \in f_\theta(w)$, $u,u' \in f_\theta(t)$, $v,v' \in f_\theta(z)$. Hence, uv' and u'v belong to $f_\theta(w)$.

Two subcases of semi-commutations are particularly interesting. When the relation θ is symmetric, we get partial commutations which are linked with the theory of trace languages. If moreover $\overline{\theta} = A \times A - \theta$ is an equivalence relation corresponding to a partition $\{A_1,...,A_k\}$ of A, we get partitionned commutations (see [14]). Then, for each $u \in A^*$, $f_\theta(u) = \pi_1(u) \sqcup\!\sqcup \ldots \sqcup\!\sqcup \pi_k(u)$, where π_i is the projection on the subalphabet A_i. The composition of partitionned commutations have been studied in[13,55] and several problems remain open on this subject.

For a language family $\mathcal{L}$, SC($\mathcal{L}$) (resp. PC($\mathcal{L}$), P($\mathcal{L}$)) denotes the family of the languages of the form $f_\theta(L)$ where $L \in \mathcal{L}$ and f_θ is a semi-commutation (resp. a partial commutation, a partitionned commutation). Then, infinite hierarchies are obtained from the family of rational languages[12]. Indeed if for $k \in \mathbb{N}$, $P^{k+1}(\mathbf{Rat})$ is, defined as $P(P^k(\mathbf{Rat}))$, it has been proved[12]:

Proposition *For each positive integer k, $P^{k+1}(\mathbf{Rat}) - SC^k(\mathbf{Rat}) \neq \emptyset$*

However, each (faithful) rational cone closed under partitionned commutations is also closed under semi-commutations[14]. This is a consequence of the following result[12]:

Proposition *Each semi-commutation can be obtained as a composition of partitionned commutations, morphisms and inverse morphisms.*

For (faithful) rational cones the relationship between semi-commutations and intersection is given by the proposition[14]:

Proposition *An intersection closed (faithful) rational cone is closed under semi-commutations if and only if it contains the language Copy* $= \{uu \,/\, u \in (a+b)^*\}$.

Since it is easy to verify that $\mathcal{C}^f(P(\mathbf{Rat}))$ is closed under intersection, we get that $\mathcal{C}^f_\cap(\text{Copy})$, known as the family MULTI-RESET[10], is the smallest faithful rational cone closed under semi-commutations[14]. More precisely:

Proposition *The family MULTI-RESET* $= \mathcal{C}^f_\cap(Copy)$ *is equal to* $\mathcal{H}sa(P(\mathbf{Rat}) \wedge \mathbf{Rat})$. *Hence, MULTI-RESET is the smallest faithful rational cone closed under semi-commutation.*

Since $\mathcal{C}_\cap(\text{Copy})$ is equal to r.e., the family of recursively enumerable languages, we can deduce that r.e.= $\mathcal{H}a(P(\mathbf{Rat}) \wedge \mathbf{Rat})$ is the smallest rational cone closed under semi-commutation[14].

Let us consider, now, θ-closed rational languages $R_1, R_2 \subset A^*$ ($f_\theta(R_i) = R_i$ for i= 1,2). Then, $f_\theta(R_1 \cup R_2) = f_\theta(R_1) \cup f_\theta(R_2) \in \mathbf{Rat}$, and $f_\theta(R_1R_2)$ is also a rational language[16]. In order to obtain a sufficient condition for the rationality of $f_\theta(R_1)$, we need the notion of **non-commutation graph** of θ, noted $(A,\bar{\theta})$. The vertices of $(A,\bar{\theta})$ are the letters of A and (b,a) is an edge if $(b,a) \in \bar{\theta}$. If, for each u in R_1, $(\text{alph}(u), \bar{\theta})$, the partial subgraph of $(A,\bar{\theta})$, corresponding to the letters occurring in the word u, is strongly connected, then $f_\theta(R_1^*)$ is a rational language[16]. More generaly, Metivier[46] has established the following result:

Proposition *Let $R \subset A^*$ be a rational language such that for each iterating factor u of R, the partial subgraph (alph(u), θ) is strongly connected. Then $f_\theta(R)$ is a rational language.*

The non-commutation graph of θ permits also to characterize the words u such that $f_\theta(u^*)$ is a rational language or an algebraic language[16,18]:

Proposition *Let u in A^* and k, the number of strongly connected components of the partial subgraph (alph(u), $\bar{\theta}$). Then the language $f_\theta(u^*)$ is rational if and only if k = 1 and algebraic if and only if $k \leq 2$.*

Of particular interest are the algebrico-rational semi-commutations which, by definition, transform rational languages in algebraic languages. These semi-commutations admit the following characterization[17] which implies in particular that each semi-commutation defined on a two letters alphabet is algebrico-rational :

Proposition *The semi-commutation f_θ is algebrico-rational if and only if for each $(a,b) \in \theta$ there do not exist c, d $\in$ A-{a,b} such that (a,c) and $(d,b) \in \theta$.*

III. PARTIAL COMMUTATIONS

In this section, we shall mention several important results concerning partial commutations which do not exist for semi-commutations. Firstly, the "embedding lemma" due to Clerbout and Latteux[14](see also [51]) shows that partitionned commutations, defined in [12], play a central role for studying partial commutations:

Embedding Lemma *Let f_θ be a partial commutation over the alphabet A. Then, there exist a partitionned commutation $f_{\theta'}$ over the alphabet B = A xA and a morphism g: $A^* \to B^*$ such that: $\forall$ u, v $\in A^*$, v $\in f_\theta(u)$ if and only if $g(v) \in f_{\theta'}(g(u))$.*

Let $a_1, a_2, . . , a_n$ be an ordering of the alphabet A. In the first section it is stated that a commutative language L is rational if and only if $L \cap a_1^* a_2^* . . . a_n^*$ is rational. The language $K = a_1^* a_2^* . . . a_n^*$ is the set of minimal words for the total commutation in the sense that a word u is in K if u is the smallest element of Com(u) for the lexicographical ordering of A^*. Now, if f_θ is a partial commutation, one says that a word u is θ-minimal if it is the smallest element of $f_\theta(u)$ for the lexicographical ordering of A^*. Then $Min(A^*)$ denotes the set of θ-minimal words. Clearly, $Min(A^*)$ is a rational language since its complement is equal to the union for all $(a_i,a_j) \in \theta$ and $i<j$ of the languages $A^*a_jA_i^*a_iA^*$ where $A_i = \{ a_s \in A \mid (a_i,a_s) \in \theta\}$. Then, for each rational language $R \subset A^*$, $Min(R) = Min(A^*) \cap R$ is rational. Ochmanski has proved in [49] that the converse is true for θ-closed languages:

Proposition *Let f_θ be a partial commutation over the alphabet A and $R \subset A^*$ a θ-closed language . Then R is rational if and only if Min(R) is rational.*

This proposition is useful for the proof of the characterization theorem of Ochmanski[49] which asserts that the family of θ-closed rational languages over the alphabet A is the closure of the family of elementary languages(languages included in $A \cup \{\varepsilon\}$) under some operations on languages. These operations are the union, the θ-product which, for $R, R' \subset A^*$ yields $f_\theta(RR')$ and a new operation, the **asynchronous star operation** that we define here. For u in A^*, let us take $A_1,\ldots,A_s$, the maximal cliques of the graph $(A,\bar{\theta})$, that is maximal subalphabets of alph(u) such that the graphs $(A_i,\bar{\theta})$ are strongly connected. Then AS(u) denotes the set $\{\pi_1(u),\ldots,\pi_s(u)\}$ where for i in $\{1,\ldots,s\}$, $\pi_i(u)$ is the projection of u on the alphabet A_i. For $R \subset A^*$, $AS(R) = \{v \in AS(u) \mid u \in R \}$ and the asynchronous star of R is equal to $f_\theta(AS(R)^*)$.

Proposition *The family of θ-closed rational languages is the smallest family of languages containing the family of elementary languages and closed under union, θ-product and the asynchronous star operation.*

Now, if we consider the family $f_\theta(\mathbf{Rat}(A^*))$, that is $\{f_\theta(R) \mid R$ rational, $R \subset A^*\}$. This family is closed under union but, generally, it is not closed under complement. However, if θ is the total commutation, $f_\theta(\mathbf{Rat}(A^*)) = Com(\mathbf{Rat}(A^*))$ is closed under the boolean operations[26,27]. Partial commutations for which this property holds have been characterized in[2,8,57]:

Proposition *Let f_θ be a partial commutation over the alphabet A. Then $f_\theta(\mathbf{Rat}(A^*))$ is closed under the boolean operations if and only if $\theta \cup \{(a,a) \mid a \in A\}$ is an equivalence relation.*

An important characterization of θ-closed rational languages has been given by Zielonka in terms of asynchronous automata, a special type of finite deterministic automaton[61]. A θ-asynchronous automaton is such that if $(a,b) \in \theta$, then for every state q, the state reached by reading ab from q is necessarily the same that the state reached by reading ba from q. Hence, the language recognized by a θ-asynchronous automaton is surely a θ-closed rational language. Roughly, in such an automaton, the states are n-tuples, each letter of the alphabet A can only rise to a given subset of the components of the states and two permutting letters cannot rise to the same component. Let us give a precise definition of this type of automaton:

A **θ-asynchronous automaton** is a couple $(\mathcal{A}, \gamma)$, where $\mathcal{A} = (A,Q,q_0,*,F)$ is a finite deterministic automaton with $Q = Q_1 x ... x Q_n$ and γ is a mapping from A into the family of subsets of $\{1,...,n\}$ such that:

-θ is equal to $\{(a,b) \in A \times A \mid \gamma(a) \cap \gamma(b) = \emptyset\}$,

-$\forall a \in A, q \in Q$ and $i \notin \gamma(a)$, the ith component of $q*a$, noted $[q*a]_i$, is equal to $[q]_i$,

-$\forall a \in A, q, q' \in Q$, if $\forall i \in \gamma(a)$, $[q]_i = [q']_i$, then $\forall i \in \gamma(a)$, $[q*a]_i = [q'*a]_i$.

The difficult part of of Zielonka's theorem consists in the construction of a θ-asynchronous automaton for a given θ-closed rational language[61]:

Proposition *The family of θ-closed rational languages is the family of languages recognized by θ-asynchronous automata.*

Since, several attempts have been made to give simpler proofs for this result[47,56]. The main lesson of these attempts is to show the intrinsic difficulty of this theorem. In the construction given in [61] the sets $\gamma^{-1}(i)$ are the maximal cliques of the graph (A,θ). In particular, if the commutation relation θ is empty one gets states with a single component, that is a normal finite deterministic automaton. However, in[20] it is proved that each rational language can be recognized by a ∅-asynchronous automaton $(\mathcal{A}, \gamma)$ in which $\gamma^{-1}(i)$ contains at most two elements. More generally, a θ - asynchronous automaton $(\mathcal{A}, \gamma)$ in which $\gamma^{-1}(i)$ contains at most two elements is said a **distributed** θ - asynchronous automaton . In [20] it is shown that distributed θ - asynchronous automaton have exactly the same power than θ - asynchronous automaton:

Proposition *Each θ-closed rational language can be recognized by a distributed θ-asynchronous automaton.*

At last, the notion of virtually asynchronous automaton is introduced in [54]: a finite deterministic automaton is virtually θ-asynchronous if it can be transformed into a θ-asynchronous one only by renaming its states. A simple algorithm is then given to determine whether a finite deterministic automaton is virtually θ-asynchronous and if the answer is positive, the corresponding θ-asynchronous automaton is easily built.

REFERENCES

[1] IJ.J.Aalbersberg and G.Rozenberg, Theory of traces, Tech.Rep., University of Leiden, 1986.

[2] IJ.J.Aalbersberg and E.Welzl, Trace languages defined by regular string languages, RAIRO Inform.Theor. **20**(1986) 103-119.

[3] J.M.Autebert, J.Beauquier, L.Boasson and M.Latteux, Very small families of languages, in R.V.Book,ed., Formal Language Theory, Perspective and Open Problems (Academic Press, New York,198O) 89-107.

[4] J.M.Autebert, J.Beauquier, L.Boasson and M.Latteux, Langages algébriques dominés par des langages unaires, Information and Control **48**(1981) 49-53.

[5] J.Beauquier, M.Blattner and M.Latteux, On commutative context-free languages, J.of Comput. and Syst.Sc. **35**(1987).

[6] J.Berstel,Transductions and Context-Free Languages (Teubner,1979).

[7] J.Berstel and J.Sakarovich, Recent results in the theory of rational sets, Lect.Notes in Comp.Sci. **233**(1986) 15-28.

[8] A.Bertoni, G.Mauri and N.Sabadini, Unambiguous regular trace languages, in J.Demetrovics, G.Katona and A.Salomaa, eds., Algebra, Combinatorics and Logic in Computer Science (North Holland, 1985).

[9] M.Blattner and M.Latteux, Parikh-bounded languages, Lect.Notes in Comp.Sci. **115**(1981) 316-323.

[10] R.V.Book, S.Greibach and C.Wrathall, Reset machines, J.of Comput. and Syst.Sc. **19**(1979) 256-276.

[11] P.Cartier and D.Foata, Problèmes combinatoires de commutations et réarrangements, Lect. Notes in Math. **85**(1969).

[12] M.Clerbout, Commutations partielles et familles de langages, Thesis, University of Lille, 1984.

[13] M.Clerbout, Compositions de fonctions de commutation partielle, to appear in RAIRO Inform.Theor. , 1986.

[14] M.Clerbout and M.Latteux, Partial commutations and faithful rational transductions, Theoretical Computer Science **34**(1984) 241-254.

[15] M.Clerbout and M.Latteux, On a generalization of partial commutations, in: M.Arato, I.Katai, L.Varga, eds, Proc.Fourth Hung. Computer Sci.Conf. (1985) 15-24.

[16] M.Clerbout and M.Latteux, Semi-commutations, Information and Computation **73**(1987) 59-74.

[17] M.Clerbout and Y.Roos, Semi-commutations algebrico-rationnelles, Tech. Rep. n^0 126-88, University of Lille, 1988.
[18] M.Clerbout and Y.Roos, Semi-commutations et langages algébriques, Tech.Rep. n^0 129-88, University of Lille, 1988.
[19] R.Cori, Partially abelian monoids, Invited lecture, STACS, Orsay, 1986.
[20] R.Cori, M.Latteux, Y.Roos and E.Sopena, 2-asynchronous automata, to appear in Theoretical Computer Science, 1987.
[21] R.Cori and Y.Metivier, Recognizable subsets of partially abelian monoids, Theoretical Computer Science **38**(1985) 179-189.
[22] R.Cori and D.Perrin, Automates et commutations partielles, RAIRO Inform.Theor. **19**(1985) 21-32.
[23] C.Duboc, Some properties of commutation in free partially commutative monoids, Inform.Proc.Letters **20**(1985) 1-4.
[24] C.Duboc, Commutations dans les monoïdes libres: un cadre théorique pour l'étude du parallélisme, Thesis, University of Rouen, 1986.
[25] A.Ehrenfeucht, D.Haussler and G.Rozenberg, Conditions enforcing regularity of context-free languages, Lect.Notes in Comp.Sci. **140**(1982) 187-191.
[26] S.Eilenberg and M.P.Schützenberger, Rational sets in commutative monoids, J. of Algebra **13**(1969) 344-353.
[27] S.Ginsburg, The Mathematical Theory of Context-Free Languages (McGraw-Hill, New York,1966).
[28] S.Ginsburg, Algebraic and Automata-Theoretic Properties of Formal Languages (North Holland, Amsterdam, 1975).
[29] S.Ginsburg and E.H.Spanier, Semigroups, Preburger formulas and languages, Pacif.J.Math. **16**(1966) 285-296.
[30] S.Ginsburg and E.H.Spanier, AFL with the semilinear property, J.of Comput. and Syst.Sc. **5**(1971) 365-396.
[31] Ph.Gohon, An algorithm to decide whether a rational subset of N^k is recognizable, Theoretical Computer Science **41**(1985) 51-59.
[32] A.K.Joshi and T.Yokomori, Semi-linearity,Parikh-boundedness and tree adjunct languages, Inform.Proc.Letters **17**(1983) 137-143.
[33] J. Kortelainen, On language families generated by commutative languages, Ph.D. Thesis, University of Oulu, 1982.
[34] J. Kortelainen, A result concerning the trio generated by commutative slip-languages, Discrete Applied Mathematics **4**(1982) 233_236.
[35] J.Kortelainen, Every commutative quasirational language is regular, RAIRO Inform.Theor. **20**(1986) 319-337.
[36] J.Kortelainen, The conjecture of Fliess on commutative context-free languages,to appear, 1988.
[37] M. Latteux, Cones rationnels commutativement clos, RAIRO Inform.Theor.**11**(1977) 29-51.
[38] M. Latteux, Cones rationnels commutatifs, J.of Comput. and Syst.Sc. **18**(1979) 307-333.
[39] M. Latteux, Langages commutatifs, transductions rationnelles et intersection, in M.Blab ed., Actes de l'école de printemps de théorie des langages (Tech.Rep.82-14, LITP, 1982) 235-242.
[40] M. Latteux and J.Leguy, On the usefulness of bifaifhful rational cones, Math.Systems Theory **18**(1985) 19-32.
[41] M. Latteux and G. Rozenberg, Commutative one-couter languages are regular, J.of Comput. and Syst.Sc. **29**(1984) 54-57.

[42] M.Latteux and G.Thierrin, Codes and commutative star languages, Soochow J.of Math. **10**(1984) 61-71.
[43] H.A.Maurer, The solution of a problem by Ginsburg, Inform.Process.Lett. **1**(1971) 7-10.
[44] A.Mazurkiewicz, Concurrent program schemes and their interpretations, DAIMI PB 78, University of Aarhus, 1977.
[45] A.Mazurkiewicz, Traces, histories and graphs: instances of process monoids, Lect.Notes in Comp.Sci. **176**(1984) 115-133.
[46] Y.Metivier, Semi commutations dans le monoïde libre,Tech. Rep. n^0 I-8606, University of Bordeaux, 1986.
[47] Y.Metivier, Contribution à l'étude des monoïdes de commutations,Thèse d'état,University of Bordeaux, 1987.
[48] Y.Metivier, On recognizable subsets of free partially commutative monoids, Lect.Notes in Comp.Sci. **226**(1986) 254-264.
[49] E.Ochmanski, Regular behaviour of concurrent systems, Bulletin of EATCS **27**(1985) 56-67.
[50] T.Oshiba, On permutting letters of words in context-free languages, Information and Control **20**(1972) 405-409.
[51] D.Perrin, Words over a partially commutative alphabet, NATO ASI Series F12,Springer (1985) 329-340.
[52] J.F.Perrot, Sur la fermeture commutative des C-langages, C.R.Acad.Sci.Paris **265**(1967) 597-600.
[53] A.Restivo and C.Reutenauer, Rational languages and the Burnside problem, Theoretical Computer Science **40**(1985) 13-30.
[54] Y.Roos, Virtually asynchronous automata, Conference on Automata, Languages and Programming Systems, Salgotarjan, 1988.
[55] Y.Roos, Contribution à l'étude des fonctions de commutation partielle, Thesis, University of Lille , 1989.
[56] B.Rozoy, Un modèle de parallélisme: le monoïde distribué, Thèse d'état, University of Caen, 1987.
[57] J.Sakarovitch, On regular trace languages, to appear in RAIRO Inform.Theor.
[58] A.Salomaa, Theory of Automata, (Pergamon Press, Oxford, 1969).
[59] M.Szijarto, The closure of languages on a binary relation, IMYCS Conference, Smolenice,1982.
[60] P.Turakainen, On some bounded semiAFLs and AFLs, Inform.Sci. **23**(1981) 31-48.
[61] W. Zielonka, Notes on asynchronous automata, RAIRO Inform.Theor. **21**(1987) 99-135.

A REMARK ON SOME CLASSIFICATIONS OF INDIAN PARALLEL LANGUAGES

Bernd Reichel
Department of Mathematics, Technological University
P.O.Box 124, Magdeburg, DDR - 3010, German Democratic Republic

A b s t r a c t. We discuss the descriptional complexity measures number of nonterminals, number of productions, and number of symbols of Indian parallel grammars and Indian parallel languages.

1. INTRODUCTION AND PRELIMINARIES

A good review about the theory of descriptional complexity of context-free languages is given in [6]. It is stated that the knowledge about descriptional complexity of other families of languages is very small in relation to the situation of context-free languages. Therefore, in this paper we study some classifications of Indian parallel languages. Indian parallel grammars (IPG) and Indian parallel languages (IPL) were first investigated in [9] and [10].

It is assumed that the reader is familiar with basic concepts concerning formal language theory. We refer, for instance, to [7].

An Indian parallel grammar G is a 4-tuple (N,T,P,S) where N is the alphabet of nonterminals, T is the alphabet of terminals, $N \cap T = \emptyset$, $N \cup T = V$, P is the set of productions, and $S \in N$ is the initial nonterminal. A word w_1 over V generates a word w_2 ($w_1 \Rightarrow_G w_2$) if and only if

i) $w_1 = x_0Ax_1A\ldots Ax_n$ where $A \in N$, $x_i \in (V\setminus\{A\})^*$ for $i = 0,1,\ldots,n$,

ii) $w_2 = x_0wx_1w\ldots wx_n$, and

iii) $A \to w$ is in P.

The Indian parallel language generated by the Indian parallel grammar G is defined by $L(G) = \{w \in T^* \mid S \overset{*}{\Rightarrow}_G w\}$ where $\overset{*}{\Rightarrow}_G$ denotes the reflexive and transitive closure of the direct derivation $\Rightarrow_G$. For $\Rightarrow_G$ and $\overset{*}{\Rightarrow}_G$ we write $\Rightarrow$ and $\overset{*}{\Rightarrow}$, respectively, if there is no danger of misunderstanding.

By IP we denote the family of Indian parallel grammars. $\mathcal{L}(IP)$ is the family of languages generated by Indian parallel grammars. If it is not stated otherwise, then grammar and language stand for Indian parallel grammar and Indian parallel language, respectively.

A grammatical complexity measure K_{IP} is a mapping from the set of IPG into the set of natural numbers. Let further $K_{IP}(L) = \min \{K_{IP}(G) \mid G \in IP,\ L(G) = L\}$ be a mapping from $\mathcal{L}(IP)$ into the set of natural numbers. In this paper we investigate some complexity measures with respect to the size of an IPG. For an IPG $G = (N,T,P,S)$ we denote by $Var_{IP}(G)$ the number of its nonterminals and by $Prod_{IP}(G)$ the number of its productions. $Symb_{IP}(G)$ is the number of symbols, i.e. $Symb_{IP}(G) = \sum_{A \to w \in P} (|w|+2)$.
We shall show that the defined measures are connected, i.e., for each natural number n, there is an IPL L such that $K_{IP}(L) = n$. In the second part we shall discuss some decision problems for the complexity measures of IPL. The results of section 2 have been already given in [8], in which one can also find the complete proofs of these results and further results concerning the defined complexity measures.

2. CONNECTIVITY

In this section, we shall investigate the defined complexity measures of Indian parallel languages concerning connectivity, i.e., whether, for every positive integer n, there exists an IPL L such that $K_{IP}(L) = n$. But first we shall prove an useful lemma.

Lemma 2.1. Let p be a prime number and $L_p = \{a^{p^i} \mid i \geq 0\}$. Then $Symb_{IP}(L_p) = p+5$.

Proof. Let $G_p = (N,T,P,S)$ be a reduced IPG generating L_p with $Symb_{IP}(L_p) = Symb_{IP}(G_p)$. Since L_p is a language over an one-letter-alphabet, we do not have to give due regard to the order of letters in a word $w \in V^+$. Therefore, without loss of generality, we write $A_1 \overset{*}{\Rightarrow} a^{i_0} A_1^{i_1} A_2^{i_2} \ldots A_n^{i_n}$ for a derivation $A_1 \overset{*}{\Rightarrow} w$ where $\#_a(w) = i_0$ and $\#_{A_j}(w) = i_j$ for $j = 1,\ldots,n$.
Since L_p is not a CFL, there must be a nonterminal $A \in N$ such that there are derivations $S \overset{*}{\Rightarrow} a^{k_0} A^{k_1}$ where $k_0 \geq 0$, $k_1 \geq 1$, and $A \overset{*}{\Rightarrow} a^{m_0} A^{m_1}$ where $m_0 \geq 0$, $m_1 \geq 1$ (if $m_0 = 0$, then $m_1 \geq 2$). Let further $\{a^n\} \subseteq G(A)$ for some $n \geq 1$. Then the following derivations are possible:

$$
\begin{array}{llll}
S \overset{*}{\Rightarrow} a^{k_0} A^{k_1} & & \overset{*}{\Rightarrow} a^{k_0} (a^n)^{k_1} & = a^{p^{s_0}} \\
S \overset{*}{\Rightarrow} a^{k_0} A^{k_1} & \overset{*}{\Rightarrow} a^{k_0} (a^{m_0} A^{m_1})^{k_1} & \overset{*}{\Rightarrow} a^{k_0} (a^{m_0} a^{m_1 n})^{k_1} & = a^{p^{s_1}} \\
\vdots & \vdots & & \vdots \\
S \overset{*}{\Rightarrow} a^{k_0} A^{k_1} & \overset{*}{\Rightarrow} a^{k_0} (a^{m_0} a^{m_0 m_1} \ldots a^{m_0 m_1^{i-1}} A^{m_1^i})^{k_1} \overset{*}{\Rightarrow} & & \\
 & \overset{*}{\Rightarrow} a^{k_0} (a^{m_0} a^{m_0 m_1} \ldots a^{m_0 m_1^{i-1}} a^{m_1^i n})^{k_1} & & = a^{p^{s_i}}
\end{array}
$$

where $s_j < s_{j+1}$ for $j \geq 0$. If we consider the terminal words of above derivations, we get for s_j, $j \geq 0$, the following equalities:

$$\begin{aligned} k_0 &+ k_1 n && = p^{s_0} \\ k_0 &+ k_1(m_0 + m_1 n) && = p^{s_1} \\ &\vdots && \vdots \\ k_0 &+ k_1(m_0 + m_0 m_1 + \ldots + m_0 m_1^{i-1} + m_1^i n) && = p^{s_i} \end{aligned}$$

From this $p^{s_{i+1}} - p^{s_i} = k_1 m_1^i(m_0 + m_1 n - n)$ and with $p^{s_1} - p^{s_0} = k_1(m_0 + m_1 n - n)$ finally

$$p^{s_{i+1}} - p^{s_i} = m_1^i(p^{s_1} - p^{s_0}) \qquad (1)$$

follows. Especially for i=1, we get $p^{s_2} - p^{s_1} = m_1(p^{s_1} - p^{s_0})$. Because of $s_0 < s_1 < s_2$ then $p^{s_2-s_0} - p^{s_1-s_0} = m_1(p^{s_1-s_0} - 1)$ and further $p^{s_2-s_0} + m_1 = (m_1 + 1)p^{s_1-s_0}$. Since $p^{s_1-s_0}$ clearly divides $p^{s_2-s_0}$, $p^{s_1-s_0}$ must divide m_1, too. Therefore, $m_1 = p^m$ for some $m \geq 0$. From (1) then $p^{s_{i+1}} - p^{s_i} = p^{im}(p^{s_1} - p^{s_0})$ and further $p^{s_{i+1}-im} - p^{s_i-im} = $ $= p^{s_1} - p^{s_0}$. But then $p^{s_{i+1}-im} = p^{s_1}$ and $p^{s_i-im} = p^{s_0}$ must hold and we finally get $p^{s_i} = (p^m)^i p^{s_0}$. Because of $s_i > s_0$ $m \geq 1$ must hold. We have shown now that for all derivations of G_p of the structure $A \overset{*}{\Rightarrow} a^{m_0}A^{m_1}$ $m_1 = p^m$ for some $m \geq 1$ must hold.

In the second part we shall show that for the derivation $A \overset{*}{\Rightarrow} a^{m_0}A^{p^m}$, $m \geq 1$, a production $B \rightarrow w$, where $|w| \geq p$, is necessary and can not be deleted. We consider the derivation $A = w_0 \Rightarrow w_1 \Rightarrow \ldots \Rightarrow w_n = a^{m_0}A^{p^m}$ where for all $i = 1,\ldots,n-1$, $w_i \neq a^{j_1}A^{p^{j_2}}$ for some $j_1 \geq 0$, $j_2 \geq 1$ (otherwise we consider the derivation $A \overset{*}{\Rightarrow} w_i$). In order to get a contradiction, we assume that only rules $B \rightarrow w$ with $|w| < p$ are used for the above derivation. From this it follows that there is an i_0, $1 \leq i_0 \leq n-1$, such that in w_{i_0} at least two different nonterminals appear (otherwise we cannot generate A^{p^m} by Indian parallelism). Then we can consider two cases:

Case 1. In w_{n-1} two different nonterminals appear, then one of these must be A. Let $w_{n-1} = a^{b_1}A^{b_2}B^{b_3}$ where $B \neq A$, $b_1 \geq 0$, $b_2 \geq 1$, $b_3 \geq 1$. Then we have $A \overset{*}{\Rightarrow} a^{b_1}A^{b_2}B^{b_3} \Rightarrow a^{m_0}A^{p^m}$ with $B \rightarrow a^{b_4}A^{b_5} \in P$. From this we get the condition

$$b_2 + b_3 b_5 = p^m \qquad (2).$$

Let us assume that no production $B \rightarrow w$, $w \in V^+$, is used in the above derivation up to w_{n-2} (otherwise we consider $B \overset{*}{\Rightarrow} a^{m_0'}B^{p^{m'}}$ for some $m' \geq 1$). Then we construct the derivation $A \overset{*}{\Rightarrow} a^{b_1}A^{b_2}B^{b_3} \overset{*}{\Rightarrow}$ $\overset{*}{\Rightarrow} a^{b_1}(a^{b_1}A^{b_2}B^{b_3})^{b_2}B^{b_3} \overset{*}{\Rightarrow} a^{b_1+b_1b_2+b_4(b_2b_3+b_3)}A^{b_2b_2+b_5(b_2b_3+b_3)}$. Then the following equality for some $m' > 1$ must hold: $b_2b_2 + b_5b_3 + b_5b_2b_3 = p^{m'}$ or $b_2(b_2 + b_3b_5) + b_3b_5 = p^{m'}$. With (2) we get $b_2p^m + b_3b_5 = p^{m'}$. Because of $m' > m$ p^m must divide b_3b_5. If $m'' \geq 1$ and $p^{m''}$ divides b_5, then we have $B \rightarrow a^{b_4}A^{g_1 p^{m''}} \in P$ for some $g_1 \geq 1$, a contradiction to our assumption. Therefore, we have to assume $b_5 = 1$. Hence $b_3 = g_2p^m$ for some $g_2 \geq 1$. But then from (2) it follows that $g_2=1$ and $b_2=0$, a contradiction.

Case 2. In w_{n-1} only one nonterminal appears, say B. Obviously, $B \neq A$. Let $w_{n-1} = a^{c_1}B^{c_2}$ be, then we have $A \overset{*}{\Rightarrow} a^{c_1}B^{c_2} \Rightarrow a^{m_0}A^{p^m}$. From this $c_2 = p^m$ and $B \rightarrow a^{c_3}A \in P$ follow. But then we can consider the derivation $B \Rightarrow a^{c_3}A \overset{*}{\Rightarrow} a^{c_3+c_1}B^{p^m}$.

We have proved now, if $G_p = (N,T,P,S)$ generates L_p, then there is at least one production $B \rightarrow w$ with $|w|>p$ in P. Therefore, $G_p = (\{S\},\{a\},\{S \rightarrow S^p, S \rightarrow a\},S)$ is minimal for L_p with respect to $Symb_{IP}$. Hence $Symb_{IP}(L_p) = p+5$. □

Remark. From this lemma it follows that there are IPL which have no IPG in CHOMSKY-Normalform (canonical two form, binary standard form, m-standard form for given m).

Lemma 2.2. For every integer $n \geq 1$, there exists an IPL L_n such that $Var_{IP}(L_n) = n$.

Proof. The lemma trivially holds for $n=1$. For $n \geq 2$, we set $L_n = \{ba^{p_1^{i_1}}ba^{p_2^{i_2}}b \ldots ba^{p_{n-1}^{i_{n-1}}}b \mid p_i$, for $i = 1,\ldots,n-1$, are different prime numbers, $i_j \geq 0$, $j = 1,\ldots,n-1\}$. Let $G = (N,T,P,S)$ an IPG generating L_n. Obviously, L_n is not a CFL and, hence, there must be a "real Indian parallel" derivation for some word of L_n. Since L_n is infinite, there must be some nonterminal $A \in N$ for which $A \overset{*}{\Rightarrow} uAv$, $u,v \in V^*$, exists. But then u and v clearly contain no b (because the occurence of b's in $w \in L_n$ is bounded). Hence, there must be the following derivation $S \overset{*}{\Rightarrow} uba^{k_1}A^{k_2}bv \overset{*}{\Rightarrow} u'ba^{p_i^{i_j}}bv'$ where $u,v,u',v' \in V^*$, k_1,k_2,i_j are integers and p_i is a prime number, for $i = 1,\ldots,n-1$.

Using the proof of lemma 2.1 we can show now that there must be productions $A_i \rightarrow a^{n_i}A_i^{p_i^{m_i}}$ in P, $m_i \geq 1$, for $i = 1,\ldots,n-1$. Finally we get that such productions must exist for different nonterminals A_i. Indeed, otherwise, we can generate a word $uba^{p_i^{i_1}p_j^{j_1}}bv$ where $p_i \neq p_j$ and $i_1, j_1 \geq 2$ which is not an element of L_n. Since we have n-1 different prime numbers, we need including the initial nonterminal at least n different variables to generate L_n.

The Indian parallel grammar $G = (N,\{a\},P,S)$ where $N = \{S\} \cup \{A_i \mid i=1,\ldots,n-1\}$, $P = \{S \rightarrow bA_1bA_2b\ldots bA_{n-1}b\} \cup \cup \{A_i \rightarrow A_i^{p_i}, A_i \rightarrow a \mid i = 1,\ldots,n-1\}$ completes the proof. □

Lemma 2.3. For every integer $n \geq 1$, there exists an IPL L_n such that $Prod_{IP}(L_n) = n$.

Proof. Here we only give a sketch of the proof. A complete proof one can find in [6].

For $n=1$ the lemma trivially holds. For $n>1$ we use the Indian

parallel language $L_n = \{aba^2b\dots a^ib \mid 1 \leq i \leq n\}$ to show the lemma. Obviously $Prod_{IP}(L_n) \leq n$. Let $G_n = (N, \{a,b\}, P, S)$ be a reduced IPG such that $L(G_n) = L_n$ and $Prod_{IP}(G_n) = Prod_{IP}(L_n)$. If $A \neq S$ is a nonterminal in G_n, then $|G(A)| \geq 2$. Otherwise, there would exist a grammar G_n' for L_n having fewer productions than G_n. It is easy to see that there exists no derivation $A \overset{*}{\Rightarrow} xAy$ where $xy \in V^+$.
First one can prove by quite technical and numerical investigations that there exists no nonterminal $A \neq S$ such that there is a derivation $S \overset{*}{\Rightarrow} x$ where $\#_A(x) \geq 2$.
In the second part, by similar consideration, one can show that the grammar G_n must be linear.
Finally, by similar quite technical investigations one can show that G_n contains only productions of the form $S \rightarrow w$, $w \in T^*$, which would complete the proof. □

Lemma 2.4. For every integer $n \geq 2$, there is an IPL $L_n \subseteq \{a\}^*$ such that $Symb_{IP}(L_n) = n$.

Proof. The proof of theorem 1 in [4] for the complexity measure $Symb_{CF}$ can be used in the same manner for $Symb_{IP}$. □

In [8] one can find another proof of lemma 2.4, which is a constructive one.

Finally we can give here the result of this section, which immediately follows from the lemmas 2.2, 2.3, and 2.4.

Theorem 2.5. The complexity measures Var_{IP}, $Prod_{IP}$, and $Symb_{IP}$ are connected for each alphabet T, $|T| \geq 2$ (for $Symb_{IP}$ even for each one-letter-alphabet). □

3. DECISION PROBLEMS

In [4] some basic complexity problems for context-free grammars and context-free languages are formulated. In analogy to these questions the following basic decision problems concerning complexity measures of Indian parallel grammars and languages arise:

P1. Is there an algorithm to determine a complexity measure $K_{IP}(G)$ for an arbitrary IPG G ?

P2. Is there an algorithm to determine $K_{IP}(L(G))$ for an arbitrary IPG G ?

P3. Is it decidable, for a positive integer n and an arbitrary IPG G, whether or not $K_{IP}(L(G)) = n$?

P4. Is it decidable, for an arbitrary IPG G, whether or not $K_{IP}(G) = K_{IP}(L(G))$? (That is, whether G is the simplest grammar for $L(G)$ with respect to K_{IP}.)

P5. Is there an algorithm to construct to an arbitrary IPG G an IPG G' such that L(G) = L(G') and $K_{IP}(G') = K_{IP}(L(G))$? (In other words, whether there exists an algorithm to construct the simplest grammar for L(G).)

Then it is easy to see that for the defined complexity measures Var, Prod, and Symb of Indian parallel grammars the answer to the problem P1 is yes. On the other hand, for an arbitrary complexity measure K, a positive answer to P1 and a negative answer to P3 imply negative answers to P2 and P5. That means, in order to show for the complexity measures Var_{IP}, $Prod_{IP}$, and $Symb_{IP}$ the negative answers to P2 - P5, we have only to show the negative answers to P3 and P4.
Since the considered complexity measures of Indian parallel grammars are defined in the same way as of context-free grammars and we ask the same questions as in context-free case, the proofs of undecidability will be based on proofs of analogous results for the context-free case in [4] and [5].
The proofs of undecidability will be realized by using the POST Correspondence Problem. Therefore, we use the following notation (see [4]).
Let $x = (x_1, x_2, \dots, x_n)$ and $y = (y_1, y_2, \dots, y_n)$ are n-tuples of nonempty words over the alphabet {a,b}. Further, P(x,y) is a predicate which holds if and only if there exists a sequence $i_1, i_2, \dots, i_k$ $(1 \le i_j \le n)$ such that $x_{i_1} x_{i_2} \dots x_{i_k} = y_{i_1} y_{i_2} \dots y_{i_k}$.
Then (Theorem of POST) it is undecidable, for arbitrary n-tuples x and y, whether or not P(x,y) holds.
Let x and y be n-tuples of nonempty words over {a,b}. We define the following languages, where c and d are not in the alphabet {a,b}:

$$L(x) = \{ba^{i_1}ba^{i_2}\dots ba^{i_k}cx_{i_k}\dots x_{i_2}x_{i_1} \mid 1 \le i_j \le n\},$$

$$L(x,y) = L(x)cL^R(y), \text{ and}$$

$$L_s = \{w_1cw_2cw_2^Rcw_1^R \mid w_1, w_2 \in \{a,b\}^*\}$$

where w^R is the reverse of w and $L^R = \{w^R \mid w \in L\}$.

<u>Lemma 3.1.</u> For every integer n≥1, it is undecidable, for an arbitrary IPG G, whether or not $Var_{IP}(L(G)) = n$.

Proof. Let x and y be n-tuples over {a,b}. Then we define the language $L_{x,y} = \{a,b,c\}^* \cdot \{d\} \setminus (L(x,y)\cdot\{d\} \cap L_s\cdot\{d\})$. Using the proof of lemma 4.2.4 and 4.2.6 in [1], for given n-tuples x and y, a linear grammar $G_{x,y}$, i.e. $G_{x,y}$ is an IPG, too, generating $L_{x,y}$ can be constructed. For this language we are able to show that

$$Var_{IP}(L_{x,y}) = 1 \text{ if and only if } L(x,y)\cdot\{d\} \cap L_s\cdot\{d\} = \emptyset \quad (1).$$

We know that $L(x,y)\cdot\{d\} \cap L_s\cdot\{d\} = \emptyset$ holds if and only if P(x,y) does not hold. Therefore, from (1) using POST's theorem the lemma would follow for n=1.

For $n=2$ we define the Indian parallel language $L_2 = L_{x,y} \cup \{e\}$ and, for $n\geq3$, we define the Indian parallel language $L_n = L_{x,y} \cup \{fe^{p_1^{i_1}}fe^{p_2^{i_2}}\dots fe^{p_{n-2}^{i_{n-2}}}f \mid i_j\geq0,\ j = 1,2,\dots,n-2\}$ where p_i for $i = 1,2,\dots,n-2$ are different prime numbers. By lemma 2.2 we get $\mathrm{Var}_{IP}(L_n \setminus L_{x,y}) = n-1$ for $n\geq3$. It is easy to see that then, for $n\geq2$, from (1) the equivalence $\mathrm{Var}_{IP}(L_n) = n$ if and only if $L(x,y)\cdot\{d\} \cap L_s\cdot\{d\} = \emptyset$ follows. Therefore, using POST's theorem, from (1) it follows that the theorem is true for $n\geq1$.

It is left to prove the equivalence (1). If $L(x,y)\cdot\{d\} \cap L_s\cdot\{d\} = \emptyset$, then $\mathrm{Var}_{IP}(L_{x,y}) = 1$ immediately follows. Now let us suppose that $L(x,y)\cdot\{d\} \cap L_s\cdot\{d\} \neq \emptyset$. Then there is a sequence $i_1,i_2,\dots,i_k$ $(1 \leq i_j \leq n)$ such that $x_{i_1}x_{i_2}\dots x_{i_k} = y_{i_1}y_{i_2}\dots y_{i_k}$. If we denote $I = ba^{i_1}ba^{i_2}b\dots ba^{i_k}$, $X = x_{i_k}\dots x_{i_2}x_{i_1}$, $J = I^R$, $Y = X^R$, then $I^rcX^rcY^rcJ^rd$ for no $r\geq1$ is an element of $L_{x,y}$. We want to show by contradiction that then $\mathrm{Var}_{IP}(L_{x,y}) > 1$ follows. We suppose that the IPG G generating $L_{x,y}$ has only one variable, say S. Then there has to be a production $S \to ud$ for some $u \in V^+$. But this means that G must be a linear grammar, otherwise there are terminal words containing more than one d. And much more, G must be a right linear grammar, otherwise there would exist terminal words of the form ydz with $z \neq \varepsilon$. Thus, in G there are only rules of the form $S \to y_1S$ or $S \to y_2d$ for some $y_1,y_2 \in T^*$. Now we can use the same idea of the proof of lemma 3.2 in [4] to construct a contradiction.

For some $i > \mathrm{Rul}(G)$, where Rul(G) denotes the maximal length of the right sides of the rules of an IPG G, the word $I^icX^{i+1}cY^{i+1}cJ^{i+1}d$ is obviously an element of $L_{x,y}$. Hence, there must be an $\alpha \neq \varepsilon$ such that $S \to \alpha S \overset{*}{\Rightarrow} \alpha w_0 d = I^icX^{i+1}cY^{i+1}cJ^{i+1}d$. Because of $i > \mathrm{Rul}(G)$ α contains no c. Then there must exist words z_0 and z_1 such that $I = z_0z_1$ and $\alpha = I^{i_0}z_0$ for some $i_0 \leq i$. This implies $\alpha z_1z_0w_0d \notin L_{x,y}$.

Because of the regular structure of the words which are not in $L_{x,y}$ and the fact that $\alpha \neq \varepsilon$ we get $z_1z_0w_0d \in L_{x,y}$. Then a derivation $S \overset{*}{\Rightarrow} z_1z_0w_0d$ must exist. But then we get $S \to \alpha S \overset{*}{\Rightarrow} \alpha z_1z_0w_0d \in L_{x,y}$, a contradiction. □

<u>Lemma 3.2.</u> It is undecidable, for a given integer $n\geq3$ and for an arbitrary IPG G, whether or not $\mathrm{Prod}_{IP}(L(G)) = n$.

Proof. The proof is based on the proof of theorem 2 in [5]. We construct a homomorphism φ on $\{a,b,c\}^*$ by $\varphi(a) = ab$, $\varphi(b) = aabb$, and $\varphi(c) = aaabbb$. Using the proofs of lemma 4.2.4 and 4.2.6 in [1], we can effectively construct, for given x and y, an IPG $G_{x,y}$ generating the language $L_{x,y} = \{a,b,c\}^* \setminus (L(x,y) \cap L_s)$. This implies that, for given x and y, an IPG $G'_{x,y}$ can be effectively constructed, too such that $L(G'_{x,y}) = \{a,b\}^* \setminus \varphi(L(x,y) \cap L_s)$.

Obviously, $\mathrm{Prod}_{IP}(L(G'_{x,y})) = 3$ if and only if $L(x,y) \cap L_s = \emptyset$. But $L(x,y) \cap L_s = \emptyset$ holds if and only if the POST Correspondence Problem, for given x and y, has a solution. Hence, from the undecidability of the POST Correspondence Problem the lemma for $n=3$ follows.
For $n>3$, we construct the language $L_n = L(G'_{x,y}) \cup \cup \{ded^2e...ed^ie \mid 1 \leq i \leq n-3\}$. Then from lemma 2.3 it follows that $\mathrm{Prod}_{IP}(L_n) = n$ if and only if $L(x,y) \cap L_s = \emptyset$. Hence, by POST's theorem the proof is complete. □

Remark. Obviously, for $n=1$ it is decidable, for an arbitrary IPG G, whether or not $\mathrm{Prod}_{IP}(L(G)) = n$. But for $n=2$ the problem is open.

Lemma 3.3. It is decidable (undecidable), for given $n\leq 5$ $(n\geq 10)$ and for an arbitrary IPG G, whether or not $\mathrm{Symb}_{IP}(L(G)) = n$.

Proof. $\mathrm{Symb}_{IP}(L(G)) \leq 5$ if and only if $L(G) = \emptyset$, $\{w_1\}$, or $\{\varepsilon, w_2\}$ where $w_1, w_2 \in T^*$ with $|w_1| \leq 3$ and $|w_2| = 1$. Therefore, the decision problem is decidable for $n\leq 5$.
In order to prove the theorem for $n\geq 10$, we use the proof of theorem 4 in [5]. We consider the language $L(G'_{x,y})$ constructed in the proof of lemma 3.2. Obviously, $\mathrm{Symb}_{IP}(L(G'_{x,y})) = 10$ if and only if $L(x,y) \cap L_s = \emptyset$. Hence the lemma for $n=10$ follows from the undecidability of POST's theorem. Now we consider homomorphisms φ_1, φ_2, and φ_3 defined by $\varphi_1(a) = \varphi_2(a) = a$, $\varphi_1(b) = bb$, $\varphi_2(b) = bbb$, $\varphi_3(a) = aa$, $\varphi_3(b) = bbb$. Then we get, for $i = 1,2,3$, $\mathrm{Symb}_{IP}(\varphi_i(L(G'_{x,y}))) = 10+i$ if and only if $L(x,y) \cap L_s = \emptyset$. That means the lemma is true for $n = 11,12,13$.
For $n>13$, we proceed as follows. By lemma 2.4, there exists an IPL $L_{n-11} = \{d^{i_0}\}$ for some $i_0 \geq 1$ such that $\mathrm{Symb}_{IP}(L_{n-11}) = n-11$. Then, obviously, $\mathrm{Symb}_{IP}(L_{n-11} \cdot L(G'_{x,y})) = n$ if and only if $L(x,y) \cap L_s = \emptyset$. Finally, using POST's theorem this completes the proof of the lemma for $n\geq 10$. □

Remark. For $6 \leq n \leq 9$, it is an open problem, whether it is decidable or not, for a given integer n and an arbitrary IPG G, whether or not $\mathrm{Symb}_{IP}(L(G)) = n$.

Lemma 3.4. It is undecidable, for an arbitrary IPG G, whether or not $\mathrm{Symb}_{IP}(G) = \mathrm{Symb}_{IP}(L(G))$.

Proof. The proof of theorem 7, which is an analogous result for context-free lanuages, in [5] can be used in the same manner to show this lemma. □

Now we can summarize the results of this section and get the following theorem.

Theorem 3.5.

(i) For the classification $Symb_{IP}$ the answer to the problem P1 is positive and the answers to the problems P2 - P5 are negative.

(ii) For the classifications Var_{IP} and $Prod_{IP}$ the answer to the problem P1 is positive and the answers to the problems P2, P3, and P5 are negative. □

Remark. For the complexity measures Var_{IP} and $Prod_{IP}$ the problem P4 is open.

Acknowledgement. I wish to thank J. Dassow for many useful discussions.

REFERENCES

[1] S. Ginsburg, The Mathematical Theory of Context-Free Languages (McGraw-Hill, New York, 1966).

[2] J. Gruska, On a classifikation of context-free languages, Kybernetika 3 (1967) 22-29.

[3] J. Gruska, Some classifications of context-free languages, Information and Control 14 (1969) 152-179.

[4] J. Gruska, Complexity and unambiguity of context-free grammars and languages, Information and Control 18 (1971) 502-512.

[5] J. Gruska, On the size of context-free grammars, Kybernetika 8 (1972) 213-218.

[6] J. Gruska, Descriptional complexity of context-free languages, in: Proc. MFCS'73 High Tatras (1973) 71-83.

[7] M.A. Harrison, Introduction to Formal Language Theory (Addison-Wesley P.C., Reading Massachusetts, 1978)

[8] B. Reichel, Some classifications of Indian parallel languages, submitted for publication.

[9] R. Siromoney and K. Krithivasan, Parallel context-free languages, Information and Control 24 (1974) 155-162.

[10] S. Skyum, Parallel context-free languages, Information and Control 26 (1974) 280-285.

Chapter 2

Machines

An Extension of the Krohn-Rhodes Decomposition of Automata

Zoltán Esik*
Bolyai Institute, A. József University
Aradi v. tere 1, Szeged, 6720, Hungary

Abstract

The notion of an irreducible semigroup has been fundamental to the Krohn-Rhodes decomposition. In this paper we study a similar concept and point out its equivalence with the Krohn-Rhodes irreducibility. We then use the new aspect of irreducible semigroups to provide cascade decompositions of automata in a situation when a strict letter-to-letter replacement is essential. The results are stated in terms of completeness theorems. Our terminology follows [10], so that the cascade composition is referred to as the α_0-product.

1. Basic Notions

For a finite nonempty set X, let X^* denote the free monoid of all *words* over X, including the *empty word* λ. We set $X^+ = X^* - \{\lambda\}$ and $X^\lambda = X \cup \{\lambda\}$.

An *automaton* is a triple $\mathbf{A} = (A, X, \delta)$ with finite nonempty sets A (*states*), X (*input letters*) and *transition* $\delta : A \times X \to A$. The function δ extends to a map $A \times X^* \to A$ as usual. Given a word $u \in X^*$, define the mapping $u_\mathbf{A} : A \to A$ by $au_\mathbf{A} = \delta(a, u)$, for all $a \in A$. We set $S_1(\mathbf{A}) = \{u_\mathbf{A} : u \in X^*\}$ and $S(\mathbf{A}) = \{u_\mathbf{A} : u \in X^+\}$. $S_1(\mathbf{A})$ is called the *characteristic monoid* of $\mathbf{A}$, while $S(\mathbf{A})$ is the *characteristic semigroup* of $\mathbf{A}$.

Our fundamental notion is the α_0-product of automata. Let $\mathbf{A}_t = (A_t, X_t, \delta_t)$, $t = 1, \ldots n, n \geq 0$, be automata. For each t, let $\phi_t : A_1 \times \ldots \times A_{t-1} \times X \to X_t^*$ be a (*feedback*) function, where X is a new finite nonempty set. The α_0^*-*product* $\mathbf{A} = \mathbf{A}_1 \times \ldots \times \mathbf{A}_n(X, \phi)$ is defined to be the automaton (A, X, δ), where $A = A_1 \times \ldots \times A_n$ and

$$\delta((a_1, \ldots, a_n), x) = (\delta_1(a_1, u_1), \ldots, \delta_n(a_n, u_n)),$$

$$u_t = \phi_t(a_1, \ldots, a_{t-1}, x), t = 1, \ldots, n,$$

for all $(a_1, \ldots, a_n) \in A$ and $x \in X$. In the special case that each ϕ_t maps into $X_t^+(X_t^\lambda, X_t)$, we obtain the notion of the α_0^+-*product* (α_0^λ-*product*, α_0-*product*). Let $\mathcal{K}$ be any class of automata. We define:

$\mathbf{P}_0^*(\mathcal{K}) :=$ all α_0^*-products of automata from $\mathcal{K}$,
$\mathbf{H}(\mathcal{K}) :=$ all homomorphic images of automata from $\mathcal{K}$,
$\mathbf{S}(\mathcal{K}) :=$ all subautomata of automata from $\mathcal{K}$.

The operators $\mathbf{P}_0^+, \mathbf{P}_0^\lambda$ are defined likewise and correspond to the formations of α_0^+-products, α_0^λ-products and α_0-products. In this paper the main object of study is the combination **HSP**, where **P** is any of the above product operators.

As defined here, the α_0-product is obtained as a special case of each of the following: α_0^*-product, α_0^+-product and α_0^λ-product. Moreover, any α_0^+-product or α_0^λ-product is an α_0^*-product.

* This paper has been completed with the assistance of the Alexander von Humboldt Foundation

It is however important to note that the converse also holds. For an automaton $\mathbf{A} = (A, X, \delta)$, define $\mathbf{A}^* = (A, S_1(\mathbf{A}), \delta^*)$ with $\delta^*(a, u_{\mathbf{A}}) = au_{\mathbf{A}}$, for all $a \in A$ and $u \in X^*$. Similarly, let $\mathbf{A}^+ = (A, S(\mathbf{A}), \delta^+)$ and $\mathbf{A}^\lambda = (A, \{x_{\mathbf{A}} : x \in X^\lambda\}, \delta^\lambda)$, where $\delta^+(a, u_{\mathbf{A}}) = \delta(a, u)$ and $\delta^\lambda(a, x_{\mathbf{A}}) = \delta(a, x)$ for every $a \in A$, $u \in X^+$ and $x \in X^\lambda$. If $\mathcal{K}$ is a class of automata and z is any modifier $*$, $+$ or λ, then we have $\mathbf{P}_0^z(\mathcal{K}) = \mathbf{P}_0(\mathcal{K}^z)$, so that the α_0^z-product can be defined in terms of the α_0-products.

The α_0-product is equivalent to either one of the following:*loop-free product* [12], *series-parallel composition* [1], *cascade composition* [1,11]. Our terminology follows [10]. The index 0 indicates that the α_0-product is the bottom of a hierarchy connecting the loop-free product to the *Glushkov-type product.* The hierarchy of α_i-products is the subject of [10]. The automaton $\mathbf{A}^*$ corresponds to the *transformation monoid* of an automaton $\mathbf{A}$ and $\mathbf{A}^+$ is just the *transformation semigroup* of $\mathbf{A}$. The operators $\mathbf{P}_0^*$ and $\mathbf{P}_0^+$ thus correspond to the *wreath product* of transformation semigroups and/or monoids, see [5].

2. Completeness

The Krohn-Rhodes Decomposition Theorem, that we recall below, is a basis for studying the α_0-product. But first we need some definitions.

Let S and T be (finite) semigroups. It is said that S *divides* T, written $S < T$, if and only if S is a homomorphic image of a subsemigroup of T. Following [1], a semigroup S is called *irreducible*, if for every nonempty class $\mathcal{K}$ and automaton $\mathbf{A} \in \mathbf{HSP}_0(\mathcal{K})$, the condition $S < S(\mathbf{A})$ implies that $S < S(\mathbf{B})$ for some $\mathbf{B} \in \mathcal{K}$. As in [1], by U_3 we denote the monoid with two right zero elements. The divisors of U_3 are the trivial semigroup U_0, the two element right zero semigroup U_1, and the two-element monoid with a right zero U_2 . The semigroups U_i, $i = 0, 1, 2, 3$, are called *units*. Recall that a group G is *simple* if it has no nontrivial proper normal subgroup.

Let S be a semigroup and S^1 the smallest monoid containing S as a subsemigroup. We define $Aut(S) = (S^1, S, \delta)$ with $\delta(s, t) = st$, for all $s \in S^1$ and $t \in S$. If $\mathcal{S}$ is a class of semigroups then let $Aut(\mathcal{S}) = \{Aut(S) : S \in \mathcal{S}\}$.

A *permutation automaton* is an automaton $\mathbf{A}$ such that $S_1(\mathbf{A})$ is a group. Equivalently, $\mathbf{A} = (A, X, \delta)$ is a permutation automaton if and only if $x_{\mathbf{A}}$ is a permutation for each $x \in X$. A *discrete automaton* is an automaton as above with $x_{\mathbf{A}}$ the identical mapping $A \to A$ for each $x \in X$.

Theorem 1. *Krohn-Rhodes Decomposition Theorem.* (i) Let $\mathbf{A}$ be an automaton and $\mathcal{G}$ the class of those simple groups G with $G < S(\mathbf{A})$. Then $\mathbf{A} \in \mathbf{HSP}_0(Aut(\mathcal{G} \cup \{U_3\}))$. If $\mathbf{A}$ is a permutation automaton which is not discrete, then $\mathbf{A} \in \mathbf{HSP}_0(Aut(\mathcal{G}))$.

(ii) The irreducible semigroups are the simple groups and the units.

Let $\mathcal{K}$ and $\mathcal{K}_0$ be two classes of automata and take any variant of the α_0-product. Let $\mathbf{P}$ be the corresponding product operator. We say that $\mathcal{K}_0$ is α_0-*complete* (α_0^*-*complete*, ...) for $\mathcal{K}$ if $\mathcal{K} \subseteq \mathbf{HSP}(\mathcal{K}_0)$. In particular, an α_0-complete (α_0^*-complete, ...) class for the class of all automata is called an α_0-complete (α_0^*-complete, ...) class.

Let $\mathcal{G}$ be a nonempty class of simple groups. For $i = 0, 1, 2, 3$, define $\mathcal{K}_i(\mathcal{G}) = \mathbf{HSP}_0(Aut(\mathcal{G} \cup \{U_i\}))$ and $\mathcal{K}_{1,2}(\mathcal{G}) = \mathbf{HSP}_0(\mathcal{G} \cup \{U_1, U_2\}))$. To avoid trivial situations, when writing $\mathcal{K}_0(\mathcal{G})$, we shall always assume that $\mathcal{G}$ contains a nontrivial simple group.

Corollary 2. A class $\mathcal{K}$ of automata is α_0^+-complete (α_0^*-complete) for $\mathcal{K}_i(\mathcal{G})$, $i = 0, 1, 2, 3$, if and only if the following hold:

(i) For every $G \in \mathcal{G}$ there is $\mathbf{A} \in \mathcal{K}$ wiht $\mathcal{G} < S(\mathbf{A})(G < S_1(\mathbf{A}))$.
(ii) There is an automaton $\mathbf{A} \in \mathcal{K}$ with $U_i < S(\mathbf{A})(G < S_1(\mathbf{A}))$.

$\mathcal{K}$ is α_0^+-complete (α_0^*-complete) for $\mathcal{K}_{1,2}(\mathcal{G})$ if and only if $\mathcal{K}$ safisfies (i) and (ii) with $i = 1, 2$.

Notice that the conditions $G < S(\mathbf{A})$ and $G < S_1(\mathbf{A})$ are equivalent for any group G and automaton $\mathbf{A}$. For various formalizations and proofs of the Krohn-Rhodes Decomposition Theorem and Corollary 2, see [1,5,10,11,13]. By the Krohn-Rhodes Decomposition Theorem, an automaton $\mathbf{A}$ belongs to $\mathcal{K}_3(\mathcal{G})$ if and only if, for every simple group G with $G < S(\mathbf{A})$ we have $G < H$ for some $H \in \mathcal{G}$. The class $\mathcal{K}_0(\mathcal{G})$ consists of all permutation automata in $\mathcal{K}_3(\mathcal{G})$. For further characterizations, see [5], the references contained in [5], as well as [14,15].

When $\mathcal{G}$ is the class of all simple groups, $\mathcal{K}_3(\mathcal{G})$ is the class of all automata.

Corollary 3. A class $\mathcal{K}$ is α_0^+-complete (α_0^*-complete) if and only if the following hold:
(i) For every (simple) group G there is $\mathbf{A} \in \mathcal{K}$ with $G < S(\mathbf{A})$.
(ii) There is $\mathbf{A} \in \mathcal{K}$ with $U_3 < S(\mathbf{A}) (U_3 < S_1(\mathbf{A}))$.

The conditions involved in Corollaries 2 and 3 are only necessary for α_0-completeness. For some particular cases, necessary and sufficient conditions were obtained in [4,7,8]. The following concept was first suggested in [6] and further examined in [3,7]. Let S be a semigroup and $\mathbf{A} = (A, X, \delta)$ and automaton. Put $S \mid^{(n)} S(\mathbf{A})$ for an integer $n \geq 1$ if and only if there exist a subsemigroup T of $S(\mathbf{A})$ and an onto homomorphism $\psi : T \to S$ such that $\psi^{-1}(s) \cap \{u_\mathbf{A} : u \in X^n\} \neq \emptyset$, for all $s \in S$. Here X^n denotes the set of all words over X with lenght n. We say that S *divides* $S(\mathbf{A})$ *in equal lenghts*, denoted $S \mid S(\mathbf{A})$, if and only if, $S \mid^{(n)} S(\mathbf{A})$ for some n.

The $|$-irreucible semigroups are now defined in the same way as irreucible semigroups. A semigroup S is said to be ***|-irreducible*** if and only if, for every nonempty $\mathcal{K}$ and $\mathbf{A} \in \mathbf{HSP}_0(\mathcal{K}), S \mid S(\mathbf{A})$ implies the existence of an automaton $\mathbf{B} \in \mathcal{K}$ with $S \mid S(\mathbf{B})$.

Theorem 4. [7] A semigroup is $|$-irreducible if and only if it is irreducible.

By a *counter* we mean an automaton $\mathbf{C}_n = (\{a_0, \ldots, a_{n-1}\}, \{x\}, \delta)$, where $n \geq 1$ and $\delta(a_i, x) = a_{i+1 \bmod n}$.

Theorem 5. [3] If $S \mid^{(n)} S(\mathbf{A})$ then $Aut(S) \in \mathbf{HSP}_0(\{\mathbf{C}_n, Aut(U_1), \mathbf{A}\})$.

An automaton $\mathbf{A} = (A, X, \delta)$ is called ***strongly connected*** if for each pair of states $a, b \in A$ there is a word $u \in X^*$ with $\delta(a, u) = b$. Moreover, $\mathbf{A}$ is ***unambigous*** if and only if $\delta(a, x) = \delta(a, y)$ for all $a \in A$ and $x, y \in X$. Otherwise $\mathbf{A}$ is called ***ambigous***. Using Theorem 4 and 5, the following results can be proved.

Theorem 6. [7] Let $\mathcal{G}$ be a nonempty class of simple groups and $\mathcal{K}$ a class of automata such that $\mathbf{HSP}_0(\mathcal{K})$ contains the counters. Assume the following, where $i = 1$ or $i = 3$:

(i) For every $G \in \mathcal{G}$ there is $\mathbf{A} \in \mathcal{K}$ with $G \mid S(\mathbf{A})$.
(ii) There is $\mathbf{A} \in \mathcal{K}$ with $U_i \mid S(\mathbf{A})$.
(iii) $\mathbf{HSP}_0(\mathcal{K})$ contains a strongly connected ambigous automaton.

Then $\mathcal{K}$ is α_0-complete for $\mathcal{K}_i(\mathcal{G})$. Assuming (i), (iii) and (ii) for $i = 1$ and $i = 2$, it follows that $\mathcal{K}$ is α_0-complete for $\mathcal{K}_{1,2}(\mathcal{G})$.

If $\mathcal{G}$ contains the abelian simple groups, then the presence of the counters in $\mathbf{HSP}_0(\mathcal{K})$ is already necessary. Thus we can turn Theorem 6 into a necessary and sufficient condition.

Theorem 7. [7] Let $\mathcal{G}$ be a class of simple groups that contains the groups of prime order. A class $\mathcal{K}$ is α_0-complete for $\mathcal{K}_i(\mathcal{G}), i = 1, 3$, if and only if the three conditions below hold:

(i) For every $G \in \mathcal{G}$ there is $\mathbf{A} \in \mathcal{K}$ with $G \mid S(\mathbf{A})$.
(ii) There is $\mathbf{A} \in \mathcal{K}$ with $U_i \mid S(\mathbf{A})$.
(iii) $\mathbf{HSP}_0(\mathcal{K})$ contains the counters and at least one strongly connected ambigous automaton.

Moreover, $\mathcal{K}$ is α_0-complete for $\mathcal{K}_{1,2}(\mathcal{G})$ if and only if each of (i), (ii) with $i = 1, 2$ and (iii) holds.

It should be noted that for a nonabelian simple group G and automaton $\mathbf{A}$, the two conditions $G < S(\mathbf{A})$ and $G \mid S(\mathbf{A})$ are equivalent, see Theorem 9 below. Thus, (i) of Theorem 6 or 7 can be devided into two parts: (i_1) For every nonabelian $G \in \mathcal{G}$ there is $\mathbf{A} \in \mathcal{K}$ with $G < S(\mathbf{A})$; (i_2) For every abelian $G \in \mathcal{G}$ there is $\mathbf{A} \in \mathcal{K}$ with $G \mid S(\mathbf{A})$. On the other hand, by Proposition 10, it is obvious that $U_i < S(\mathbf{A})$ if and only if $U_i \mid S(\mathbf{A})$, for each unit semigroup and automaton. Thus we can replace the condition $U_i \mid S(\mathbf{A})$ by $U_i < S(\mathbf{A})$ in Theorems 6 and 7.

Corollary 8. [3] A class $\mathcal{K}$ is α_0-complete if and only if the following are true:
(i) For every (simple) group G there is $\mathbf{A} \in \mathcal{K}$ with $G < S(\mathbf{A})$.
(ii) There is $\mathbf{A} \in \mathcal{K}$ with $U_3 < S(\mathbf{A})$.
(iii) $\mathbf{HSP}_0(\mathcal{K})$ contains the counters and at least one strongly connected ambigous automaton.

It would be interesting to know what are those semigroups S with the property that $S < S(\mathbf{A})$ always implies $S \mid S(\mathbf{A})$. Some results along this line are contained in [7]. Here we recall only the group case and the case of semigroups that are generated by idempotents. The commutator subgroup of a group G is denoted G'.

Theorem 9. [7] The following two conditions are equivalent for a group G:
(i) For every automaton $\mathbf{A}$, $G < S(\mathbf{A})$ implies $G \mid S(\mathbf{A})$;
(ii) $G = G'$.

Proposition 10. [7] Let S be a semigroup generated by idempotents and let $\mathbf{A}$ be any automaton. If $S < S(\mathbf{A})$ then $S \mid S(\mathbf{A})$.

It should be noted that Theorem 9 follows from a strong result of [2] whose only known proof uses the Feit-Thompson theorem. For a direct, in fact elementary proof, see [7].

Theorem 7 and Corollary 8 are in a sense the best possible results. Here we point out this fact only for Corollary 8, for Theorem 7, see [7]. Let us call a class $\mathcal{K}_0$ *critical* if for every $\mathcal{K}$, (i) and (ii) of Corollary 8 together with the stipulation $\mathcal{K}_0 \subseteq \mathbf{HSP}(\mathcal{K})$ imply that $\mathcal{K}$ is α_0-complete.

Theorem 11. [4] A class $\mathcal{K}_0$ is critical if and only if $\mathbf{HSP}(\mathcal{K}_0)$ contains the counters and at least one stronly connected ambigous automaton.

We now turn our attention to the α_0^λ-product. Note that $\mathcal{K}_1(\mathcal{G}) \subseteq \mathbf{HSP}_0^\lambda(\mathcal{K})$ if and only if $\mathcal{K}_3(\mathcal{G}) \subseteq \mathbf{HSP}_0^\lambda(\mathcal{K})$.

Theorem 12. [9] Let $\mathcal{G}$ be a class of simple groups that contains a nontrivial group. Let $\mathcal{K}$ be any class of automata. $\mathcal{K}$ is α_0^λ-complete for $\mathcal{K}_3(\mathcal{G})$ if and only if the following hold:
(i) For every $G \in \mathcal{G}$ there is $\mathbf{A} \in \mathcal{K}$ with $G < S(\mathbf{A})$.
(ii) There is $\mathbf{A} \in \mathcal{K}$ with $U_3 < S_1(\mathbf{A})$.
(iii) $\mathcal{K}$ is not counter-free.

Here the last condition means that $\mathcal{K}$ contains an automaton (A, X, δ), which has at least n distinct states $a_0, \ldots, a_{n-1}, n \geq 2$, and an input letter x with $\delta(a_i, x) = a_{i+1 \ mod \ n}$, for all $i = 0, \ldots, n-1$. It is easily seen that $\mathcal{K}$ is not counter free if and only if there is a nontrivial counter in $\mathbf{HSP}_0(\mathcal{K})$. It should be noted that Corollary 13 below is stated in a somewhat weaker form in [9].

Corollary 13. [9] A class $\mathcal{K}$ is α_0^λ-complete if and only if the following are true:
(i) For every (simple) group G there is $\mathbf{A} \in \mathcal{K}$ with $G < S(\mathbf{A})$.
(ii) There is $\mathbf{A} \in \mathcal{K}$ with $U_3 < S_1(\mathbf{A})$.
(iii) $\mathcal{K}$ is not counter-free.

3. Varieties

Let $\mathcal{K}$ be a class of automata.If $\mathcal{K}$ is closed under the formation of α_0-products, subautomata and homomorphic images, then $\mathcal{K}$ is called an α_0-variety. Similarly, for $z = *, +, \lambda$, an α_0^z-variety is a class $\mathcal{K}$ satisfying $\mathcal{P}_0^z(\mathcal{K}) \subseteq \mathcal{K}$, $\mathcal{S}(\mathcal{K}) \subseteq \mathcal{K}$ and $\mathcal{H}(\mathcal{K}) \subseteq \mathcal{K}$. It is known that for each class $\mathcal{K}$, $\mathbf{HSP}_0(\mathcal{K})$ is the smallest α_0-variety including $\mathcal{K}$. Analogous fact is true for α_0^z-varieties. It follows from our definition that each α_0^*-variety is an α_0^+-variety and also an α_0^λ-variety, furthermore, α_0^+-varieties and α_0^λ-varieties are α_0-varieties. The converse direction fails, yet it holds that every 'large' α_0-variety is an α_0^+-variety. By Z_p, where p is a prime number, we denote a cyclic group of order p.

Theorem 14. [6] Every α_0-variety containing $Aut(U_1)$ and each automaton $Aut(Z_p)$, where p is any prime, is an α_0^+-variety.

The essence of Theorem 14 is that there is a bijective correspondence between 'large' α_0-varieties and 'large' closed classes of transformation semigroups in the sense of [5]. The α_0-variety $\mathcal{V}_0 = \mathbf{HSP}_0(Aut(\{U_1, Z_p : p \text{ is prime }\}))$ is just the class $\mathcal{K}_1(\mathcal{G})$ with $\mathcal{G}$ consisting of the cyclic groups of prime order. Moreover, $\mathcal{V}_0$ is the class of all automata that could be called locally solvable, see [14, 15].

Corollary 15. [6] Every α_0-variety containing the automaton $Aut(U_3)$ and all the automata $Aut(Z_p)$ for prime numbers p is an α_0^*-variety.

Note that each α_0-variety $\mathcal{V}$ with $Aut(U_3) \in \mathcal{V}$ and $Aut(Z_p) \in \mathcal{V}$ for each prime p is of the form $\mathcal{K}_3(\mathcal{G})$ with $\mathcal{G}$ containig at least the abelian simple groups. The smallest such α_0-variety is identified as the class of solvable automata.

Theorem 16. [6] If an α_0^λ-variety contains $Aut(U_3)$ and a nontrivial counter, then it is an α_0^*-variety.

References

[1] Arbib, M.A: (Ed.), Algebraic Theory of Machines, Languages, and Semigroups, with a major contribution by K. Krohn and J.L. Rhodes (Academic Press, New York, 1968).

[2] Dénes, J. and P. Hermann, On the product of all elements in a finite group, Ann. of Discrete Mathematics, 15 (1982), 107-111.

[3] Dömösi, P. and Z. Ésik, On homomorphic realization of automata with α_0-products, Papers on Automata Theory, VIII (1986) 63-97.

[4] Dömösi, P. and Z. Ésik, Critical classes for the α_0-product, Theoret. Comput. Sci., 61 (1988), 17-24.

[5] Eilenberg, S., Automata, Languages, and Machines, vol. B (Academic Press, New York, 1976).

[6] Ésik, Z., Varieties of automata and transformation semigroups, Acta Math. Hung., to appear.

[7] Ésik, Z., Results on homomorphic realization of automata by α_0-products, submitted.

[8] Ésik, Z. and P. Dömösi, Complete classes of automata for the α_0-product, Theoret. Comput. Sci., 47 (1986) 1-14.

[9] Ésik,Z. and J. Virágh, On products of automata with identity, Acta Cybernetica, 7 (1986) 299-311.

[10] Gécseg, F., Products of Automata (Springer-Verlag, Berlin,1986).

[11] Ginzburg, A., Algebraic Theory of Automata (Academic Press, New York, 1968).

[12] Hartmanis, J. and R.E. Stearns, Algebraic Structure Theory of Sequential Machines (Prentice-Hall, Englewood Cliffs, 1966).

[13] Lallement, G., Semigroups and Combinatorial Applications (John Wiley, New York, 1979).

[14] Straubing, H., Finite Semigroup varieties of the form $V * D$, J. of Pure and Appl. Alg., 36 (1985) 53-94.

[15] Thérien, D. and A. Weiss, Graph congurences and wreath products, J. of Pure and Appl. Alg., 36 (1985) 205-215.

A Survey of Two-Dimensional Automata Theory

Katsushi Inoue and Itsuo Takanami
Department of Electronics, Faculty of Engineering
Yamaguchi Univesity, Ube, 755 Japan

Abstract. The main purpose of this paper is to survey several properties of alternating, nondeterministic, and deterministic two-dimensional Turing machines (including two-dimensional finite automata and marker automata), and to briefly survey cellular types of two-dimensional automata.

1. Introduction

During the past thirty years, many investigations about automata on a one-dimensional tape (i.e., string) have been made (for example, see [25]). On the other hand, since Blum and Hewitt [3] studied two-dimensional finite automata and marker automata, several researchers have been investigating a lot of properties about automata on a two-dimensional tape .

The main purpose of this paper is to survey main results of two-dimensional sequential automata obtained since [3], and to give several open problems. Chapter 2 concerns alternating, nondeterministic, and deterministic two-dimensional Turing machines (including finite automata and marker automata). Section 2.1 gives preliminaries necessary for the subsequent discussions. Section 2.2 gives a difference among alternating, nondeterministic, and deterministic machines. Section 2.3 gives a difference between three-way and four-way machines. Section 2.4 states space complexity results of two-dimensional Turing machines. Sections 2.5 and 2.6 states closure properties and decision problems, respectively. Section 2.7 concerns recognition of connected pictures. Section 2.8 states other topics. Chapter 3 briefly surveys cellular types of two-dimensional automata.

2. Alternating, Nondeterministic, and Deterministic Turing Machines

This chapter concerns alternating, nondeterministic, and deterministic two-dimensional Turing machines, including two-dimensional finite automata and marker automata.

2.1. Preliminaries

Let Σ be a finite set of symbols. A two-dimensional tape over Σ is a two-dimensional rectangular array of elements of Σ. The set of all two-dimensional tapes over Σ is denoted by $\Sigma^{(2)}$.

For a tape $x \in \Sigma^{(2)}$, we let $\ell_1(x)$ be the number of rows of x and $\ell_2(x)$ be the number of columns of x. If $1 \leq i \leq \ell_1(x)$ and $1 \leq j \leq \ell_2(x)$, we let $x(i,j)$ denote the symbol in x with coordinates (i,j). Furthermore, we define

$$x[(i,j),(i',j')],$$

when $1 \leq i \leq i' \leq \ell_1(x)$ and $1 \leq j \leq j' \leq \ell_2(x)$, as the two-dimensional tape z satisfying the following: (i) $\ell_1(z)=i'-i+1$ and $\ell_2(z)=j'-j+1$, (ii) for each k,r $[1 \leq k \leq \ell_1(z), 1 \leq r \leq \ell_2(z)]$, $z(k,r)=x(k+i-1,r+j-1)$.

We now give some definitions of two-dimensional alternating Turing machines.

Definition 2.1. A two-dimensional alternating Turing machine (ATM) is a seven-tuple $M=(Q,q_0,U,F,\Sigma,\Gamma,\delta)$, where (1) Q is a finite set of states, (2) $q_0 \in Q$ is the initial state, (3) $U \subseteq Q$ is the set of universal states, (4) $F \subseteq Q$ is the set of accepting states, (5) Σ is a finite input alphabet ($\# \notin \Sigma$ is the boundary symbol), (6) Γ is a finite storage tape alphabet ($B \in \Gamma$ is the blank symbol), and (7) $\delta \subseteq (Q \times (\Sigma \cup \{\#\}) \times \Gamma) \times (Q \times (\Gamma - \{B\}) \times \{\text{left,right,up,down,no move}\} \times \{\text{left,right,no move}\})$ is the next move relation.

A state q in Q-U is said to be existential. As shown in Fig.1, the machine M has

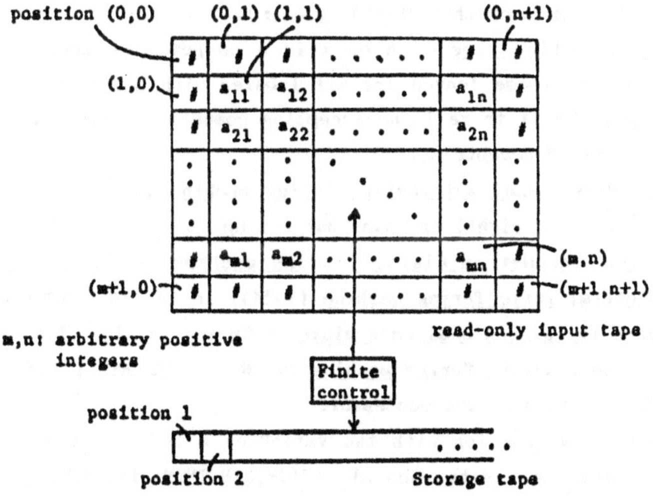

Fig.1. Two-dimensional alternating Turing machine

a read-only rectangular input tape with boundary symbols "#" and one semi-infinite storage tape, initially blank. Of course, M has a finite control, an input head, and a storage tape head. A position is assigned to each cell of the storage tape, as shown in Fig.1. A step of M consists of reading one symbol from each tape, writing a symbol on the storage tape, moving the input and storage heads in specified directions (left,right,up,down,or no move for input head, and left,right, or no move for storage head),and entering a new state, in accordance with the next move relation δ .

A configuration of an ATM $M=(Q,q_0,U,F,\Sigma,\Gamma,\delta)$ is an element of $\Sigma^{(2)}\times(N\cup\{0\})^2 \times S_M$, where $S_M=Q\times(\Gamma-\{B\})^*\times N$, and N denotes the set of all positive integers. The first component x of a configuration $c=(x,(i,j),(q,\alpha,k))$ represents the input to M. The second component (i,j) of c represents the input head position. The third component (q,α,k) of c represents the state of the finite control, nonblank contents of the storage tape, and the storage-head position. If q is the state associated with configuration c, then c is said to be universal (existential, accepting) configuration if q is a universal (existential, accepting) state. The initial configuration of M on input x is $I_M(x)=(x,(1,1),(q_0,\lambda,1))$, where λ denotes the empty string. We write $c \vdash_M c'$ and say c' is a successor of c if configuration c' follows from configuration c in one step of M, according to the transition rules δ . A computation tree of M is a finite, nonempty labeled tree with the properties,

(1) each node π of the tree is labeled with a configuration $\ell(\pi)$,

(2) if π is an internal node (a nonleaf) of the tree, $\ell(\pi)$ is universal, and $\{c \mid \ell(\pi) \vdash_M c\}=\{c_1,\ldots,c_k\}$, then π has exactly k children $\rho_1,\ldots,\rho_k$ such that $\ell(\rho_i)=c_i$,

(3) if π is an internal node of the tree and $\ell(\pi)$ is existential, then π has exactly one child ρ such that $\ell(\pi) \vdash_M \ell(\rho)$.

An accepting computation tree of M on x is a computation tree whose root is labeled with $I_M(x)$ and whose leaves are all labeled with accepting configurations. We say that M accepts x if there is an accepting computation tree of M on input x. Define $T(M)=\{x\in\Sigma^{(2)} \mid M \text{ accepts } x\}$.

A three-way two-dimensional alternating Turing machine (TATM) is an ATM whose input head can move left, right, or down, but not up.

A two-dimensional nondeterministic Turing machine (NTM) (a three-way two-dimensional nondeterministic Turing machine (TNTM)) is an ATM (TATM) which has no universal state. A two-dimensional deterministic Turing machine (DTM) (a three-way two-dimensional deterministic Turing machine (TDTM)) is an ATM (TATM) whose configurations each have at most one successor.

Let $L(m,n):N^2\to R$ be a function with two variables m and n, where R denotes all non-negative real numbers. With each ATM (TATM,NTM,TNTM,DTM,TDTM) M we associate a space complexity function SPACE which takes configuration $c=(x,(i,j),(q,\alpha,k))$

to natural numbers. Let SPACE(c)=the length of α. We say that M is L(m,n) space-bounded if for all m,n≥1 and for all x with $\ell_1(x)$=m and $\ell_2(x)$=n, if x is accepted by M, then there is an accepting computation tree of M on input x such that, for each node π of the tree, SPACE($\ell(\pi)$)≤ ⌈L(m,n)⌉. By "ATM(L(m,n))" ("TATM(L(m,n))", "NTM(L(m,n))", "TNTM(L(m,n))", "DTM(L(m,n))", "TDTM(L(m,n))") we denote an L(m,n) space bounded ATM (TATM, NTM, TNTM, DTM, TDTM).

We are also interested in two-dimensional Turing machines M whose input tapes are restricted to square ones. Let L(m):N→R be a function with one variable m. We say that M is L(m) space-bounded if for all m≥1 and for all x with $\ell_1(x)=\ell_2(x)$=m, if x is accepted by M, then there is an accepting computation tree of M on x such that, for each node π of the tree, SPACE($\ell(\pi)$)≤L(m). By "ATM^s(L(m))" ("$TATM^s$(L(m))", "NTM^s(L(m))", "$TNTM^s$(L(m))", "DTM^s(L(m))", "$TDTM^s$(L(m))") we denote an L(m) space-bounded ATM (TATM, NTM, TNTM, DTM, TDTM) whose input tapes are restricted to square ones.

For any constant k≥0, a k space-bounded ATM (NTM, DTM) is called a two-dimensional alternating (nondeterministic, deterministic) finite automaton, denoted by "AFA" ("NFA", "DFA"). A three-way AFA (NFA, DFA) is denoted by "TAFA" ("TNFA", "TDFA"). For any positive integer k, a two-dimensional alternating (nondeterministic, deterministic) k-marker automaton, denoted by "AMA(k)" ("NMA(k)", "DMA(k)"), is an AFA (NFA, DFA) which can use k markers on the input tape. By "AFA^s" we denote an AFA whose input tapes are restricted to square ones. NFA^s, DFA^s, etc., have the same meaning. Define

$\mathcal{L}$[ATM(L(m,n))]={T | T=T(M) for some ATM(L(m,n)) M}, and

$\mathcal{L}$[ATM^s(L(m))]={T | T=T(M) for some ATM^s(L(m)) M}.

$\mathcal{L}$[NTM(L(m,n))], $\mathcal{L}$[NTM^s(L(m))], $\mathcal{L}$[AFA], $\mathcal{L}$[AFA^s], etc., have the same meaning.

The following concepts are used in the subsequent discussions.

Definition 2.2. A function L(m):N→R (L(m,n):N^2→R) is called two-dimensionally space constructible if there is a DTM^s (DTM) M such that (i) for each m≥1 (m,n≥1) and for each input tape x with $\ell_1(x)=\ell_2(x)$=m ($\ell_1(x)$=m and $\ell_2(x)$=n), M uses at most ⌈L(m)⌉ (⌈L(m,n)⌉) cells of the storage tape, (ii) for each m≥1 (m,n≥1), there exists some input tape x with $\ell_1(x)=\ell_2(x)$=m ($\ell_1(x)$=m and $\ell_2(x)$=n) on which M halts after its storage head has marked off exactly ⌈L(m)⌉ (⌈L(m,n)⌉) cells of the storage tape, and (iii) for each m≥1 (m,n≥1), when given any input tape x with $\ell_1(x)=\ell_2(x)$=m ($\ell_1(x)$=m and $\ell_2(x)$=n), M never halts without marking off exactly ⌈L(m)⌉ (⌈L(m,n)⌉) cells of the storage tape.

Definition 2.3. A function L(m):N→R (L(m,n):N^2→R) is called two-dimensionally fully space constructible if there exists a DTM^s (DTM) M which, for each m≥1 (m,n≥1) and for each input tape x with $\ell_1(x)=\ell_2(x)$=m ($\ell_1(x)$=m and $\ell_2(x)$=n), makes use of exactly ⌈L(m)⌉ (⌈L(m,n)⌉) cells of the storage tape and halts.

Notation 2.1. Let f(n) and g(n) be any functions with one variable n. We write f(n)<<g(n) when $\lim_{n\to\infty} f(n)/g(n)=0$.

2.2. A Difference among Alternating, Nondeterministic, and Deterministic Machines

This section states a difference among the accepting powers of alternating, nondeterministic, and deterministic machines. For the one-dimensional case, it is well known [11,24,69] that the following theorem holds.

Theorem 2.1. For any function $L(n) \ll \log\log n$, $L(n)$ space-bounded two-way alternating, nondeterministic, and deterministic Turing machines are all equivalent to one-way deterministic finite automata in accepting power.

We first show that a different situation occurs for the two-dimensional case. Let $T_1=\{x\in \{0,1\}^{(2)} \mid \exists m\geq 1[\ \ell_1(x)=\ell_2(x)=m\ \&\ \exists i(1\leq i\leq m-1)[x[(i,1),(i,m)]=x[(m,1),(m,m)]]]\}$ and $T_2=\{x\in \{0,1\}^{(2)} \mid \exists m\geq 0[\ \ell_1(x)=\ell_2(x)=2m+1\ \&\ x(m+1,m+1)=1$ (i.e., the center symbol of x is 1)$]]\}$. It is shown in [58,59] that $T_1\in \mathcal{L}[\text{TAFA}^s]-\mathcal{L}[\text{NTM}^s(L(m))]$ and $T_2\in \mathcal{L}[\text{TNFA}^s]-\mathcal{L}[\text{DTM}^s(L(m))]$ for any function $L(m)\ll\log m$. Thus we have

Theorem 2.2. For any function $L(m)\ll\log m$, (1) $\mathcal{L}[\text{DTM}^s(L(m))]\subsetneq \mathcal{L}[\text{NTM}^s(L(m))]\subsetneq \mathcal{L}[\text{ATM}^s(L(m))]$, and (2) $\mathcal{L}[\text{TDTM}^s(L(m))]\subsetneq \mathcal{L}[\text{TNTM}^s(L(m))]\subsetneq \mathcal{L}[\text{TATM}^s(L(m))]$.

Corollary 2.1 [3,58,59,89]. $\mathcal{L}[\text{DFA}^s]\subsetneq \mathcal{L}[\text{NFA}^s]\subsetneq \mathcal{L}[\text{AFA}^s]$, and $\mathcal{L}[\text{TDFA}^s]\subsetneq \mathcal{L}[\text{TNFA}^s]\subsetneq \mathcal{L}[\text{TAFA}^s]$.

For the three-way case, we can show that the following stronger results hold.

Theorem 2.3. (1) $\mathcal{L}[\text{TDTM}^s(L(m))]\subsetneq \mathcal{L}[\text{TNTM}^s(L(m))]\subsetneq \mathcal{L}[\text{TATM}^s(L(m))]$ for any function $L(m)\ll m^2$, (2) $\mathcal{L}[\text{TDTM}(L(m,n))]\subsetneq \mathcal{L}[\text{TNTM}(L(m,n))]\subsetneq \mathcal{L}[\text{TATM}(L(m,n))]$ for each $L(m,n)\in \{f(m)\times g(n),\ f(m)+g(n)\}$, where $f(m):N\to R$ is a function such that $f(m)\ll m$, and $g(n):N\to R$ is a monotone nondecreasing function which is fully space constructible [25], and (3) $\mathcal{L}[\text{TDTM}(L(m,n))]\subsetneq \mathcal{L}[\text{TNTM}(L(m,n))]\subsetneq \mathcal{L}[\text{TATM}(L(m,n))]$ for each $L(m,n)\in \{f(m)\times g(n),\ f(m)+g(n)\}$, where $f(m):N\to R$ is a function, and $g(n):N\to R$ is a function such that $g(n)\ll n$.

Proof. (1): See [44,58].

(2): In [44], it is shown that $\mathcal{L}[\text{TDTM}(L(m,n))]\subsetneq \mathcal{L}[\text{TNTM}(L(m,n))]$. Below, we show that $\mathcal{L}[\text{TNTM}(L(m,n))]\subsetneq \mathcal{L}[\text{TATM}(L(m,n))]$. Let $T[g]=\{x\in \{0,1\}^{(2)} \mid \exists n\geq 1[\ \ell_1(x)=2\times 2^{\lceil g(n)\rceil}\ \&\ \ell_2(x)=n\ \&$ (the top and bottom halves of x are the same)$]\}$. It is easy to show that $T[g]\in \mathcal{L}[\text{TATM}(g(n))]$. The claim follows from this and from the fact [44] that $T[g]\notin \mathcal{L}[\text{TNTM}(L(m,n))]$ for each $L(m,n)\in \{f(m)\times g(n),\ f(m)+g(n)\}$.

(3): In [44], it is shown that $\mathcal{L}[\text{TDTM}(L(m,n))]\subsetneq \mathcal{L}[\text{TNTM}(L(m,n))]$. Below, we show that $\mathcal{L}[\text{TNTM}(L(m,n))]\subsetneq \mathcal{L}[\text{TATM}(L(m,n))]$. Let $T_3=\{x\in \{0,1\}^{(2)} \mid \ell_1(x)=2\ \&$ (the first and second rows of x are the same)$\}$. It is easy to show that $T_3\in \mathcal{L}[\text{TAFA}]$. The claim follows from this and from the fact [44] that $T_3\notin \mathcal{L}[\text{TNTM}(L(m,n))]$ for each $L(m,n)\in \{f(m)\times g(n),\ f(m)+g(n)\}$.

For four-way Turing machines on nonsquare tapes, we have

Theorem 2.4. (1) $\mathcal{L}[\text{NTM}(L(m,n))]\subsetneq \mathcal{L}[\text{ATM}(L(m,n))]$ for each $L(m,n)\in \{f(m)\times g(n),\ f(m)+g(n)\}$, where $f(m):N\to R$ is a function such that $f(m)\ll\log m$, and $g(n):N\to R$ is a monotone nondecreasing function which is fully space constructible. (2) $\mathcal{L}$

$[NTM(L(m,n))] \subsetneq \mathcal{L}[ATM(L(m,n))]$ for each $L(m,n) \in \{f(m) \times g(n),\ f(m)+g(n)\}$, where $f(m):N \to R$ is a monotone nondecreasing function which is fully space constructible, and $g(n):N \to R$ is a function such that $g(n) \ll \log n$.

Proof. We only prove (1), because the proof of (2) is similar. Let $x \in \{0,1\}^{(2)}$ and $\ell_2(x)=n$ $(n \geq 1)$. When $\ell_1(x)$ is divided by $2^{\lceil g(n) \rceil}$, we call $x[((j-1)2^{\lceil g(n) \rceil}+1,1),(j2^{\lceil g(n) \rceil},n)]$ the j-th g(n)-block of x for each j $(1 \leq j \leq \ell_1(x)/2^{\lceil g(n) \rceil})$. We say that x has exactly k g(n)-blocks if $\ell_2(x)=n$ and $\ell_1(x)=k2^{\lceil g(n) \rceil}$ for some positive integer $k \geq 1$. Let $T(g)=\{x \in \{0,1\}^{(2)} \mid (\exists n \geq 1)(\exists k \geq 2)[(x$ has exactly k g(n)-blocks$)$ & $\exists j(2 \leq j \leq k)[$the first and j-th g(n)-blocks of x are identical$]]\}$. It is easy to show that $T(g) \in \mathcal{L}[ATM(g(n))]$. On the other hand, we can show, by using the same technique as in the proof of Lemma 3.3 in [45], that $T(g) \notin \mathcal{L}[NTM(L(m,n))]$ for each $L(m,n) \in \{f(m) \times g(n),\ f(m)+g(n)\}$. Thus (1) follows.

It is well known [3] that one-dimensional 1-marker automata are equivalent to one-dimensional finite automata. For the two-dimensional case, a different situation occurs. Let T_1 be the set described above. We can show that $T_1 \in \mathcal{L}[DMA(1)]-\mathcal{L}[NFA]$. Let $T_4=\{x \in \{0,1\}^{(2)} \mid \exists m \geq 1[\ell_1(x)=2m$ & $\ell_2(x)=m$ & (the top and bottom halves of x are the same)$]\}$. It is shown in [29,113] that $T_4 \in \mathcal{L}[NMA(1)]-\mathcal{L}[DMA(1)]$. Thus we have

Theorem 2.5. (1) There exists a set in $\mathcal{L}[DMA(1)]$, but not in $\mathcal{L}[NFA]$, and (2) $\mathcal{L}[DMA(1)] \subsetneq \mathcal{L}[NMA(1)]$.

Savitch [91] showed that for any fully space constructible function $L(n) \geq \log n$, L(n) space-bounded one-dimensional nondeterministic Turing machines can be simulated by $L^2(n)$ space-bounded one-dimensional deterministic Turing machines. By using the same technique as in [91], we can show that a similar result also holds for the two-dimensional case.

Theorem 2.6. For any two-dimensionally fully space constructible function $L(m) \geq \log m$ $(L(m,n) \geq \log m + \log n)$, $\mathcal{L}[NTM^s(L(m))] \subseteq \mathcal{L}[DTM^s(L^2(m))]$ $(\mathcal{L}[NTM(L(m,n))] \subseteq \mathcal{L}[DTM(L^2(m,n))])$.

Open problems: (1) For any two-dimensionally fully space constructible function $L(m) \geq \log m$ $(L(m,n) \geq \log m + \log n)$, $\mathcal{L}[DTM^s(L(m))] \subsetneq \mathcal{L}[NTM^s(L(m))] \subsetneq \mathcal{L}[ATM^s(L(m))]$ $(\mathcal{L}[DTM(L(m,n))] \subsetneq \mathcal{L}[NTM(L(m,n))] \subsetneq \mathcal{L}[ATM(L(m,n))])$? (2) Let f(m) and g(n) be the functions described in Theorem 2.4(1) or Theorem 2.4(2). Then $\mathcal{L}[DTM(L(m,n))] \subsetneq \mathcal{L}[NTM(L(m,n))]$ for each $L(m,n) \in \{f(m) \times g(n),\ f(m)+g(n)\}$? (3) Is there a set in $\mathcal{L}[NFA]$, but not in $\mathcal{L}[DMA(1)]$? (4) For any $k \geq 1$, $\mathcal{L}[DMA(k)] \subsetneq \mathcal{L}[NMA(k)] \subsetneq \mathcal{L}[AMA(k)]$?

2.3. Three-way versus Four-way

This section states a relationship between the accepting powers of three-way machines and four-way machines.

As shown in Theorem 2.1, for the one-dimensional case, L(n) space-bounded one-way and two-way Turing machines are equivalent for any L(n)<<loglog n. We shall below show that a different situation occurs for the two-dimensional case. Let $T_5=\{x\in\{0,1\}^{(2)} \mid \exists m\geq 1\ [\ \ell_1(x)=\ell_2(x)=2m\ \&\ (x[(1,1),(1,m)]$ is the reversal of $x[(1,m+1),(1,2m)])]\}$. It is shown in [64] that $T_5\in \mathcal{L}[\mathrm{DFA}^s]-\mathcal{L}[\mathrm{TATM}^s(L(m))]$ for any function L(m)<<log m. On the other hand, as stated in Section 2.2, $T_1\in \mathcal{L}[\mathrm{TAFA}^s]-\mathcal{L}[\mathrm{NTM}^s(L(m))]$ for any L(m)<<log m. From these facts, for example, we have

Theorem 2.7. For any function L(m)<<log m, (1) $\mathcal{L}[\mathrm{TXTM}^s(L(m))]\subsetneq\mathcal{L}[\mathrm{XTM}^s(L(m))]$ for each $X\in\{D,N,A\}$, (2) $\mathcal{L}[\mathrm{DTM}^s(L(m))]$ is incomparable with $\mathcal{L}[\mathrm{TNTM}^s(L(m))]$ and $\mathcal{L}[\mathrm{TATM}^s(L(m))]$, and (3) $\mathcal{L}[\mathrm{NTM}^s(L(m))]$ is incomparable with $\mathcal{L}[\mathrm{TATM}^s(L(m))]$.

Remark 2.1. It is shown in [44] that Theorem 2.7(1) can be strengthened as follows: " $\mathcal{L}[\mathrm{TXTM}^s(L(m))]\subsetneq\mathcal{L}[\mathrm{XTM}^s(L(m))]$ for each $X\in\{D,N\}$ and each function $L(m)<<m^2$." It is obvious that $\mathcal{L}[\mathrm{TXTM}^s(L(m))]=\mathcal{L}[\mathrm{XTM}^s(L(m))]$ for each $L(m)\geq m^2$.

Remark 2.2. By using the same technique as in the proof of the fact [74] that L(n) space-bounded one-way and two-way alternating Turing machines are equivalent for any L(n)≥log n, we can show that $\mathcal{L}[\mathrm{TATM}^s(L(m))]=\mathcal{L}[\mathrm{ATM}^s(L(m))]$ for any function L(m)≥log m.

For nonsquare tapes, we have

Theorem 2.8. (1) $\mathcal{L}[\mathrm{TXTM}(L(m,n))]\subsetneq\mathcal{L}[\mathrm{XTM}(L(m,n))]$ for each $X\in\{D,N\}$ and each $L(m,n)\in\{f(m)\times g(n),\ f(m)+g(n)\}$, where f(m) and g(n) are the functions described in Theorem 2.3(2) or Theorem 2.3(3), (2) $\mathcal{L}[\mathrm{TATM}(L(m,n))]\subsetneq\mathcal{L}[\mathrm{ATM}(L(m,n))]$ for each $L(m,n)\in\{f(m)\times g(n),\ f(m)+g(n)\}$, where $f(m):N\rightarrow R$ is a function such that f(m)<<log m, and $g(n):N\rightarrow R$ is a monotone nondecreasing function which is fully space constructible, and (3) $\mathcal{L}[\mathrm{TATM}(L(m,n))]=\mathcal{L}[\mathrm{ATM}(L(m,n))]$ for any function L(m,n)≥log m.

Proof. See [44] for (1). We leave the proof of (3) to the reader. We below show that (2) holds. Let T(g) be the set described in the proof of Theorem 2.4 (1). As stated in the proof of Theorem 2.4(1), $T(g)\in\mathcal{L}[\mathrm{ATM}(g(n))]$. On the other hand, we can show, by using the same technique as in the proof of Lemma 4.2 in [64], that $T(g)\notin\mathcal{L}[\mathrm{TATM}(L(m,n))]$ for each $L(m,n)\in\{f(m)\times g(n),\ f(m)+g(n)\}$. Thus it follows that (2) holds.

It is natural to ask how much space is required for three-way machines to simulate four-way machines. The following two theorems answer this question.

Theorem 2.9. (1) n log n (n^2) space is necessary and sufficient for TDTM's to simulate DFA's (NFA's) (see [48,83]). (2) n space is necessary and sufficient for TNTM's to simulate DFA's and NFA's (see [57]). (3) $2^{\Theta(n\log n)}$ ($2^{\Theta(n^2)}$) space is necessary and sufficient for TDTM's to simulate DMA(1)'s (NMA(1)'s) (see [67]). (4) n log n (n^2) space is necessary and sufficient for TNTM's to simulate DMA(1)'s (NMA(1)'s) (see [67]). (In this theorem, note that n denotes the number of columns of tapes.)

Open problems: (1) $\mathcal{L}$[AFA]$\subseteq$ $\mathcal{L}$[TNTM(n)] ? (2) $\mathcal{L}$[AMA(1)]$\subseteq$ $\mathcal{L}$[TNTM($2^{O(n)}$)] ?

2.4. Two-Dimensionally Space Constructible Functions and Space Complexity Results

This section concerns two-dimensionally space constructible functions and space complexity hierarchy. We state these subjects only for square tapes. (See [78,80,82] for the case of nonsquare tapes.) It is well known [24] that in the one-dimensional case, there exists no space constructible function which grows more slowly than the order of loglog n, thus no space hierarchy of language acceptability exists below space complexity loglog n. Below, we state that a different situation occurs for the two-dimensional case.

We consider the following three functions:

(i) $\log^{(1)}m=\begin{cases} 0 & (m=0) \\ \lceil \log_2 m \rceil & (m\geq 1) \end{cases}$

$\log^{(k+1)}m=\log^{(1)}(\log^{(k)}m)$

(ii) $\exp^*0=1$, $\exp^*(m+1)=2^{\exp^* m}$

(iii) $\log^* m=\min\{x \mid \exp^* x\geq m\}$.

The following theorem demonstrates that there exist two-dimensionally space constructible functions which grow more slowly than the order of loglog m.

Theorem 2.10 [78,82]. The functions $\log^{(k)}m$ (k: any natural number) and $\log^* m$ are two-dimensionally space constructible.

More generally, we have

Theorem 2.11 [78,82]. Let f(m):N→N be any monotone nondecreasing total recursive function such that $\lim_{m\to\infty} f(m)=\infty$. Then, there exists a two-dimensionally space constructible and monotone nondecreasing function L(m) such that (i) L(m)<f(m) and (ii) $\lim_{m\to\infty} L(m)=\infty$.

It is shown in [105] that there exists no fully space constructible function which grows more slowly than the order of log m. It is unknown whether or not there exists a two-dimensionally fully space constructible function which grows more slowly than the order of log m.

For the one-dimensional case, the following three important theorems concerning space complexity hierarchy of Turing machines are known. (By $\mathcal{L}$[1NTM(L(n))] ($\mathcal{L}$[1DTM(L(n))]) we denote the class of languages accepted by L(n) space-bounded one-dimensional nondeterministic (deterministic) Turing machines [25].)

Theorem 2.12 [102].Let L(n) be a space function. For any constant c>0 and each X $\in$ {D,N}, $\mathcal{L}$[1XTM(L(n))]= $\mathcal{L}$[1XTM($c\cdot$L(n))].

Theorem 2.13 [102]. Let $L_1(n)$ and $L_2(n)$ be any space constructible functions such that $\lim_{i\to\infty} L_1(n_i)/L_2(n_i)=0$ and $L_2(n_i)/\log n_i>k$ $(i=1,2,\cdots)$ for some increasing sequence of natural numbers $\{n_i\}$ and for some constant k>0. Then there exists a language in $\mathcal{L}$[1DTM($L_2(n)$)], but not in $\mathcal{L}$[1DTM($L_1(n)$)].

Theorem 2.14 [24]. Let $L_1(n)$ and $L_2(n)$ be space constructible functions such that $\lim_{i\to\infty} L_1(n_i)/L_2(n_i)=0$ and $L_2(n_i)/\log n_i<1/2$ for some increasing sequence of natural numbers $\{n_i\}$. Then there exists a language in $\mathcal{L}[\mathrm{1DTM}(L_2(n))]$, but not in $\mathcal{L}[\mathrm{1DTM}(L_1(n))]$.

By using the ideas similar to those of the proofs of Theorems 2.12 and Theorem 2.13, we can prove the following two-dimensional analogues to these theorems.

Theorem 2.15. Let $L(m)$ be a space function. For any constant $c>0$ and each $X\in\{D,N,A\}$,

$$\mathcal{L}[\mathrm{XTM}^s(L(m))]=\mathcal{L}[\mathrm{XTM}^s(cL(m))].$$

Theorem 2.16 [78,80]. Let $L_2(m)$ be a two-dimensionally space constructible function. Suppose that $\lim_{i\to\infty} L_1(m_i)/L_2(m_i)=0$ and $L_2(m_i)>k\cdot\log m_i$ $(i=1,2,\cdots)$ for some increasing sequence of natural numbers $\{m_i\}$ and for some constant $k>0$. Then there exists a set in $\mathcal{L}[\mathrm{DTM}^s(L_2(m))]$ but not in $\mathcal{L}[\mathrm{DTM}^s(L_1(m))]$.

Recently, It is shown in [28,103] that for each space constructible function $L(n)\geq\log n$, $\mathcal{L}[\mathrm{1NTM}(L(n))]$ is closed under complementation. This result can be extended to the two-dimensional case. By using these facts, we can extend Theorem 2.13 and Theorem 2.16 to the nondeterministic case [21].

The following theorem, which is a two-dimensional analogue to Theorem 2.14, cannot be proved by the same idea as in the proof of Theorem 2.14.

Theorem 2.17 [78,80]. Let $L_2(m)$ be a two-dimensionally space constructible function. Suppose that $\lim_{i\to\infty} L_1(m_i)/L_2(m_i)=0$, $\lim_{i\to\infty} L_2(m_i)=\infty$, and $L_2(m_i)<k\cdot\log m_i$ $(i=1,2,\cdots)$ for some increasing sequence of natural numbers $\{m_i\}$ and for some constant $k>0$. Then there exists a set in $\mathcal{L}[\mathrm{DTM}^s(L_2(m))]$, but not in $\mathcal{L}[\mathrm{DTM}^s(L_1(m))]$.

The following theorem, which is a nondeterministic version of Theorem 2.17, is proved in [60].

Theorem 2.18 [60]. Let $L_2(m)$ be a two-dimensionally space constructible function such that $L_2(m)\leq\log m$. Suppose that $\lim_{m\to\infty} L_1(m)/L_2(m)=0$. Then there exists a set in $\mathcal{L}[\mathrm{NTM}^s(L_2(m))]$ (in fact, in $\mathcal{L}[\mathrm{DTM}^s(L_2(m))]$) but not in $\mathcal{L}[\mathrm{NTM}^s(L_1(m))]$.

From Theorem 2.10 and Theorem 2.18, we have the following corollary, which implies that in the two-dimensional case, there is an infinite hierarchy of acceptabilities even for space complexity classes below loglog m.

Corollary 2.2. For any constant $c>0$, each $k\in N$, and each $X\in\{D,N\}$,

$$\mathcal{L}[\mathrm{XFA}^s]=\mathcal{L}[\mathrm{XTM}^s(c)]\subsetneq\cdots\subsetneq\mathcal{L}[\mathrm{XTM}^s(\log^{(k+1)}m)]\subsetneq\mathcal{L}[\mathrm{XTM}^s(\log^{(k)}m)]\cdots.$$

Open problem: Do results analogous to Theorems 2.16 and 2.17 hold for ATM^s ?

2.5 Closure properties

This section presents only closure properties of the classes of sets accepted by several types of two-dimensional finite automata. (See [41,44,45,48,106] for closure properties of the classes of sets accepted by space-bounded two-dimensional Turing machines.) It is well known [25] that the class of sets accepted by one-dimensional finite automata is closed under many operations , including Boolean operations. We below demonstrate that a different situation occurs for two-dimensional finite automata. We first define several operations over two-dimensional tapes.

Definition 2.4. Let

$$x=\begin{array}{ccc} a_{11} & \cdots & a_{1n} \\ \vdots & \ddots & \vdots \\ a_{m1} & \cdots & a_{mn} \end{array}, \text{ and } y=\begin{array}{ccc} b_{11} & \cdots & b_{1n'} \\ \vdots & \ddots & \vdots \\ b_{m'1} & \cdots & b_{m'n'} \end{array}.$$

Then the rotation x^R of x and the row reflection x^{RR} of x are given by Fig.2 and Fig.3, respectively. A row cyclic shift of x is any two-dimensional tape of the form of Fig.4 for some $1\leq k\leq m$ (not that for k=m this is x itself), and a column cyclic shift of x is any two-dimensional tape of the form of Fig.5 for some $1\leq k\leq n$ (not that for k=n this is x itself). The row catenation $x\ominus y$ is defined only when n=n' and is given by Fig.6, and the column catenation $x\obar y$ is defined only when m=m' and is given by Fig.7.

Definition 2.5. Let S and S' be two sets of two-dimensional tapes. Then

$S^R=\{x^R \mid x\in S\}$ (rotation of S),

$S^{RR}=\{x^{RR} \mid x\in S\}$ (row reflection of S),

$S^{RC}=\{y \mid y$ is a row cyclic shift of some $x\in S\}$ (row cyclic closure of S),

$S^{CC}=\{y \mid y$ is a column cyclic shift of some $x\in S\}$ (column cyclic closure of S).

$S\ominus S'=\{x\ominus y \mid x$ in S,y in S'$\}$ (row catenation),

S $S'=\{x\obar y \mid x$ in S,y in S'$\}$ (column catenation),

$S_+=\bigcup_{i\geq 1}S_i$ (row closure),

$S^+=\bigcup_{i\geq 1}S^i$ (column closure),

$$\begin{array}{ccc} a_{m1} & \cdots & a_{11} \\ \vdots & \ddots & \vdots \\ a_{mn} & \cdots & a_{1n} \end{array}$$

Fig.2

$$\begin{array}{ccc} a_{m1} & \cdots & a_{mn} \\ \vdots & \ddots & \vdots \\ a_{11} & \cdots & a_{1n} \end{array}$$

Fig.3

$$\begin{array}{cccccc} a_{1,k+1} & \cdots & a_{1n} & a_{11} & \cdots & a_{1k} \\ \vdots & \ddots & \vdots & \vdots & \ddots & \vdots \\ a_{m,k+1} & \cdots & a_{mn} & a_{m1} & \cdots & a_{mk} \end{array}$$

Fig.5

$$\begin{array}{ccc} a_{k+1,1} & \cdots & a_{k+1,n} \\ \vdots & \ddots & \vdots \\ a_{m1} & \cdots & a_{mn} \\ a_{11} & \cdots & a_{1n} \\ \vdots & \ddots & \vdots \\ a_{k1} & \cdots & a_{kn} \end{array}$$

Fig.4

$$\begin{array}{ccc} a_{11} & \cdots & a_{1n} \\ \vdots & \ddots & \vdots \\ a_{m1} & \cdots & a_{mn} \\ b_{11} & \cdots & b_{1n} \\ \vdots & \ddots & \vdots \\ b_{m'1} & \cdots & b_{m'n} \end{array}$$

Fig.6

$$\begin{array}{cccccc} a_{11} & \cdots & a_{1n} & b_{11} & \cdots & b_{1n'} \\ \vdots & \ddots & \vdots & \vdots & \ddots & \vdots \\ a_{m1} & \cdots & a_{mn} & b_{m1} & \cdots & b_{mn'} \end{array}$$

Fig.7

where $S_1=S$, $S_2=S\ominus S,\ldots$, $S_{i+1}=S_i\ominus S$, and $S^1=S$, $S^2=S\oplus S,\ldots$, $S^{i+1}=S^i\oplus S$.

For three-way finite automata, we have

Theorem 2.19. (1) $\mathcal{L}$[TDFA] is not closed under union, intersection, rotation, row reflection, row and column cyclic closures, row and column catenations, or row and column closures [44,45,48,56,106]. (2) $\mathcal{L}$[TNFA] is closed under union, row catenation, and row closure, but not closed under intersection, complementation, rotation, row and column cyclic closures, column catenation, or column closure [44,45,56,106]. (3) $\mathcal{L}$[TAFA] is closed under union and intersection, but not closed under rotation, row reflection, row and column cyclic closures, row and column catenations, or row and column closures [64,68].

Open problems: (1) Are $\mathcal{L}$[TDFA] and $\mathcal{L}$[TAFA] closed under complementation ? (2) Is $\mathcal{L}$[TNFA] closed under row reflection ?

For four-way finite automata, we have

Theorem 2.20. (1) $\mathcal{L}$[DFA] is closed under Boolean operations, rotation and row reflection, but not closed under row and column cyclic closures, row and column catenations, or row and column closures [41,42,51]. (2) $\mathcal{L}$[NFA] is closed under union, intersection, rotation, and row reflection, but not closed under row and column cyclic closures, row and column catenations, or row and column closures [41,51,52]. (3) $\mathcal{L}$[AFA] is closed under union and intersection, rotation, and row reflection.

Remark 2.3. That $\mathcal{L}$[DFA] is closed under Boolean operations can be proved by using the technique in [96].

Open problems: (1) Is $\mathcal{L}$[NFA] closed under complementation ? (2) Is $\mathcal{L}$[AFA] closed under complementation, row and column cyclic closures, row and column catenations, and row and column closures ?

2.6. Decision Problems

This section concerns decision problems of two-dimensional finite automata. It is well known [25] that many decision problems of one-dimensional finite automata are decidable. As suggested by the following theorem, most of decision problems of four-way two-dimensional finite automata are undecidable.

Theorem 2.21 [3,111]. The emptiness and universe problems for DFA's are undecidable even for a one-letter alphabet.

We below state some decision problems of three-way finite automata. For each $X\in\{D,N,A\}$, let TXFA(0) denote a TXFA which operates on two-dimensional tapes over a one-letter alphabet. The following two theorems are all that have been obtained for three-way finite automata by now.

Theorem 2.22 [49]. (1) The emptiness and universe problems for TDFA(0)'s are decidable. (2) The emptiness problem for TNFA(0)'s is decidable. (3) The universe, inclusion, and equivalence problems for TNFA's are undecidable.

Theorem 2.23 [70]. (1) The disjointness, inclusion, and equivalence problems for TDFA(0)'s are decidable. (2) The disjointness and inclusion problems for TDFA's are undecidable.

Open problems: (1) Are the emptiness, universe, and equivalence problems for TDFA's decidable ? (2) Are the universe, inclusion, and equivalence problems for TNFA(0)'s and TAFA(0)'s decidable ? (3) Is the emptiness problem for TAFA(0)'s decidable ?

2.7. Recognizability of Connected Pictures

Let T_c be the set of all two-dimensional connected pictures [53,89]. It is interesting to investigate how much space is required for two-dimensional Turing machines to accept T_c. For this problem, we have

Theorem 2.24. (1) n space is necessary and sufficient for TDTM's and TNTM's to accept T_c (see [116]). (2) $T_c \in \mathcal{L}$[AFA] (see [58]). (3) $T_c \in \mathcal{L}$[DMA(1)] (see [3,89]). (4) $T_c^s \notin \mathcal{L}[\text{TATM}^s(L(m))]$ for any $L(m) \ll \log m$, where T_c^s denotes the set of all the square connected pictures (see [64]).

Open problem: $T_c \in \mathcal{L}$[DFA] or $T_c \in \mathcal{L}$[NFA] ?

2.8. Other Topics

In this section, we list up other topics and related references about sequential automata on a two-dimensional tape.

(1) Maze (or labyrinth) search problems: see [1,4,5,7,8,9,10,22,75,104].

(2) Characterizations of one-dimensional languages by two-dimensional automata: see [20,29,32,33].

(3) A relationship between two-dimensional automata and two-dimensional array grammars: see [19,30,73,76,79,84,89,99,115].

(4) Properties of special types of two-dimensional Turing machines (two-dimensional pushdown automata, stack automata, multi-counter automata, multihead automata, and marker automata): see [3,27,46,47,55,56,78,81,89,94,95,113].

(5) Parallel, time, space, and reversal complexities of two-dimensional alternating multihead Turing machines: see [26,50,58,59].

(6) Properties of two-dimensional finite automata over a one-letter alphabet: see [36,40,70].

(7) Properties of two-dimensional automata on a nonrectangular tape: see [77,88,89].

(8) A relationship between two-dimensional alternating finite automata and cellular types of two-dimensional automata: see [62,63,65,66].

The most interesting problem in the future is to investigate time complexity hierarchy of two-dimensional Turing machines.

Two-dimensional (or array) grammars are not discussed here. For this subject, see the excellent book of Rosenfeld [89] and the excellent surveys of Siromoney [97,98].

3. Cellular Types of Two-Dimensional Automata

Many authors investigated language acceptability of one-dimensional cellular automata (for example, see [6,12,14,101,114]). On the other hand, cellular automata on a two-dimensional tape are being investigated not only in the viewpoint of formal language theory but also in the viewpoint of pattern recognition. Cellular automata on a two-dimensional tape can be classified into three types.

The first type, called a two-dimensional cellular automaton (CA for short), is investigated in [2,13,17,29,31,34,35,37,39,53,61-63,65,71,72,87,89,100,112]. CA's make use of two-dimensional cellular arrays. It is shown, for example, that (1) the set T_c of all two-dimensional connected pictures can be accepted by deterministic CA's in linear time [2], (2) the majority problem can be solved by deterministic CA's in linear time, and thus the set of all the two-dimensional tapes over {0,1} with positive Euler number can be accepted by deterministic CA's in linear time [100], (3) the two-dimensional packing problem can be solved by deterministic CA's in linear time [71], (4) NFA's can be simulated by deterministic CA's in linear time [72], and (5) AFA's can be simulated by deterministic CA's in constant state change [62]. (The notion of state change complexity was first introduced in [114]). Many properties of two-dimensional on-line tessellation acceptors (OTA's for short) introduced in [29,35] are investigated in [29,31,34,35,37,39,53,65,112]. The OTA is a restricted type of CA in which cells do not make transitions at every time step; rather, a transition 'wave' passes once diagonally across the array. It is shown, for example, that (1) nondeterministic OTA's are more powerful than NFA's, and deterministic OTA's are incomparable (in accepting power) with NFA's and DFA's [29,35], (2) the set T_c described above cannot be accepted by deterministic OTA's [53], and (3) deterministic OTA's can be used as two-dimensional pattern matching machines [112]. In [17], a generalization of CA's in which each cell is a space-bounded Turing machine rather than a finite automaton, is introduced. Fast algorithms are given for performing various basic image processing tasks by such automata.

The second type of cellular automata on a two-dimensional tape is investigated in [15,30-33,37,38,57,66,78,89,90,92,93,99,107-110].Two typical models of this type are parallel/sequential array automata (PSA's) [90] and one-dimensional bounded cellular acceptors (BCA's) [92,107-110]. The PSA makes use of one-dimensional (e.g., horizontal) cellular array which can move, as a unit, in the vertical direction, and accepts a tape if the leftmost cell (i.e., the cell which reads the first column of the tape) enters an accepting state in some time. The BCA is a restricted type of one-way PSA in which the cellular array moves downwards each time step, and the BCA accepts a tape if the state configuration of the cellular array just after it has completely scanned the tape is an element of the specified regular set (called the accepting configuration set). It is shown, for example, that (1) nondeterministic one-way PSA's are more powerful than deterministic ones, two-way PSA's are more powerful than one-way PSA's, and T_c is accepted by deterministic one-way PSA's [90], (2) deterministic one-way PSA's are incomparable with NFA's and DFA's [15,48], (3) one-way PSA's are more powerful than OTA's [35], (4) nondeterministic BCA's are equivalent to nondeterministic OTA's, and deterministic BCA's are incomparable with deterministic OTA's and DFA's [31,57]. See [30,99] for a relationship between PSA's and two-dimensional grammars, and see [37,38] for closure properties of PSA's. An extension of BCA's in which the accepting configuration set is a context-free language, context-sensitive language, or phrase structure language, is introduced in [107-110].

The third type, called a pyramid cellular acceptor (PCA), is investigated in [16,18,43,54,85,86,89]. The PCA is a pyramid stack of two-dimensional cellular arrays, where the bottom array has size 2^n by 2^n, the next lowest 2^{n-1} by 2^{n-1}, and so forth, the (n+1)st layer consisting of a single cell, called the root. Each cell has nine neighbors -- four son cells in a 2-by-2 block in the level below, four brother cells in the current level, and one father cell in the level above. The transition function of each cell maps 10-tuples of states into states -- or sets of states, in the nondeterministic case. An input tape is stored as initial states of the bottom array; the upper-level cells are initialized to a quiescent state. The root is the accepting cell. A bottom-up pyramid cellular acceptor (UPCA) is a PCA in which the next state of a cell depends only on the current states of that cell and its four sons. It is shown, for example, that (1) both nondeterministic PCA's and nondeterministic UPCA's are equivalent to nondeterministic CA'S [16,85,89], (2) nondeterministic UPCA's are more powerful than deterministic UPCA's [85,89], (3) nondeterministic UPCA's can simulate nondeterministic OTA's, thus NFA's in O(diameter) time [54,86], and (4) O(diameter $\times$ log diameter) time (O((diameter)^2) time) is necessary for deterministic UPCA's to simulate DFA's (NFA's) [54]. See the excellent book [89] of Rosenfeld for image processing task by PCA's and UPCA's.

Open problems:

(1) Can AFA's be simulated by deterministic CA's in linear time ?

(2) Can AFA's be simulated by nondeterministic OTA's ?

(3) Are deterministic CA's equivalent to nondeterministic CA's ?

(4) Is T_c accepted by nondeterministic OTA's or deterministic UPCA's ?

(5) Is T_d accepted by nondeterministic UPCA's in diameter time ?

(6) Can DFA's, NFA's, or AFA's be simulated by deterministic UPCA's ?

4. Conclusions

In this paper, we surveyed several aspects of two-dimensional automata theory. We believe that there are many problems about two-dimensional automata to solve in the future. We hope that this survey will activate the investigation of two-dimensional automata theory.

References

[1] H.Antelmann, L.Budach and H.A.Rollik, On universal traps, EIK 15, 3 (1979),123-131.

[2] T.Beyer, Recognition of topological invariants by iterative arrays, Ph.D.Thesis, MIT, 1970.

[3] M.Blum and C.Hewitt, Automata on a two-dimensional tape, IEEE Symposium on Switching and Automata Theory, 1967, 155-160.

[4] M.Blum and D.Kozen, On the power of the compass, Proc. of the 19th Annual Symp. on Foundations of Computer Science, 1978,

[5] M.Blum and W.J.Sakoda, On the capability of finite automata in 2 and 3 dimensional space, Proc. of the 18th Annual Symp. on Foundations of Computer Science, 1977, 147-161.

[6] W.Bucher and K.Culik II, On real time and linear time cellular automata, Research Report 115, Institute fur Informationsverarbeitung, Technical University of Graz, 1983.

[7] L.Budach, Environments, labyrinths and Automata, Lecture Notes in Computer Science 56, Springer Verlag, 1977.

[8] __, Automata and Labyrinths, Math. Nachr. 86 (1978), 195-282.

[9] L.Budach and C.Meinel, Environments and automata I, EIK 18, 1/2 (1982), 13-40.

[10] __, Environments and automata II, EIK 18, 3 (1982), 115-139.

[11] A.K.Chandra, D.C.Kozen and L.J.Stockmeyer, Alternation, J.Assoc.Comput.Mach. 28, 1 (1981), 114-133.

[12] C.Choffrut and K.Culik II, On real-time cellular automata and trellis automata, Research Report F114, Institute fur Informationsverarbeitung, Technical University of Graz, 1983.

[13] P.Dietz and S.R.Kosaraju, Recognition of topological equivalence of patterns by array automata, JCSS 2 (1980), 111-116.

[14] C.R.Dyer, One-way bounded cellular automata, Information and Control 44 (1980),261-281.

[15] __, Relation of one-way parallel/sequential automata to 2-d finite automata, Information Sciences 23 (1981), 25-30.

[16] C.R.Dyer and A.Rosenfeld, Cellular pyramids for image analysis, University of Maryland, Computer Science Center, TR-544, AFOSR-77-3271, 1977.

[17] __ , Parallel image processing by memory-augmented cellular automata, IEEE Trans. on Pattern Analysis and Machine Intelligence, PAMI-3, 1 (1981), 29-41.

[18] __, Triangle cellular automata, Information and Control 48 (1981), 54-69.

[19] E.M.Ehlers and S.H.Von Solms, A hierarchy of random context grammars and automata, Information Sciences 42 (1987), 1-29.

[20] M.J.Fisher, Two characterizations of the context sensitive languages, IEEE Symp. on Switching and Automata Theory (1969), 149-156.

[21] J.Hartmanis, The structural complexity column, Bulletin of the EATCS, 33 (October 1987), 26-39.

[22] A.Hemmerling, Normed two-plane traps for finite systems of cooperating compass automata, EIK 23, 8/9 (1987),, 453-470.

[23] F.Hoffmann, One pebble does not suffice to search plane labyrinths, Lecture Notes in Computer Science 117 (Fundamentals of Computation Theory), 1981, 433-444.

[24] J.E.Hopcroft and J.D.Ullman, Some results on tape-bounded Turing machines, J.Assoc.Comput.Math. 19, 2 (1972), 283-295.

[25] __ , Introduction to Automata Theory, Languages, and Computation, Addison-Wesley, Reading, Mass. 1979.

[26] J.Hromkovic, K.Inoue and I.Takanami, Lower bounds for language recognition on two-dimensional alternating multihead machines, To appear in JCSS.

[27] O.H.Ibarra and R.T.Melson, Some results concerning automata on two-dimensional tapes, Intern.J.Computer Math. 4-A (1974), 269-279.

[28] N.Immerman, Nondeterministic space is closed under complement, submitted for publication.

[29] K.Inoue, Investigations of two-dimensional on-line tessellation acceptors (in Japanese), Ph.D.Thesis, Nagoya University, 1977.

[30] K.Inoue and A.Nakamura, Some notes on parallel sequential array acceptors (in Japanese), IECE of Japan Trans.(D), March 1975, 167-169.

[31] __ , On the relation between two-dimensional on-line tessellation acceptors and one-dimensional bounded cellular acceptors (in Japanese), IECE of Japan Trans.(D), September 1976, 613-620.

[32] __, Some properties of one-way parallel sequential array acceptors and two-dimensional one-marker automata (in Japanese), IECE of Japan Trans.(D), September 1976, 682-683.

[33] __ , Some properties of parallel sequential array acceptors and two-dimensional two-marker automata (in Japanese), IECE of Japan Trans.(D), September 1976, 680-681.

[34] __, Some properties of two-dimensional on-line tessellation acceptors (in Japanese), IECE of Japan Trans.(D), October 1976, 695-702.

[35] __, Some properties of two-dimensional on-line tessellation acceptors, Information Sciences 13 (1977), 95-121.

[36] __, Some properties of two-dimensional automata with a one-letter alphabet -Recognizability of functions by two-dimensional automata- (in Japanese), IECE of Japan Trans.(D), September 1977, 679-686.

[37] __, Nonclosure properties of two-dimensional on-line tessellation acceptors and one-way parallel sequential array acceptors, IECE of Japan Trans.(E), September 1977, 475-476.

[38] __, Some properties on two-dimensional nondeterministic finite automata and parallel sequential array acceptors (in Japanese), IECE of Japan Trans.(D), November 1977, 990-997.

[39] __, Two-dimensional multipass on-line tessellation acceptors, Information and Control 41, 3 (June 1979), 305-323.

[40] __, Two-dimensional finite automata and unacceptable functions, Intern.J.Computer Math. Section A, 7 (1979), 207-213.

[41] K.Inoue and I.Takanami, A note on closure properties of the classes of sets accepted by tape-bounded two-dimensional Turing machines, Information Sciences 15, 1 (1978), 143-158.

[42] __, Cyclic closure properties of automata on a two-dimensional tape, Information Sciences 15, 1 (1978), 229-242.

[43] __, A note on bottom-up pyramid acceptors, Information Processing Letters 8, 1 (1979), 34-37.

[44] __, Three-way tape-bounded two-dimensional Turing machines, Information Sciences 17, 3 (1979), 195-220.

[45] __, Closure properties of three-way and four-way tape-bounded two-dimensional Turing machines, Information Sciences 18, 3 (1979), 247-265.

[46] __, Three-way two-dimensional multicounter automata, Information Sciences 19, 1 (1979), 1-20.

[47] __, Some properties of three-way two-dimensional multicounter automata over square tapes (in Japanese), IECE of Japan Trans.(D), October 1979, 673-680.

[48] __, A note on deterministic three-way tape-bounded two-dimensional Turing machines, Information Sciences 20, 1 (1980), 41-55.

[49] __, A note on decision problems for three-way two-dimensional finite automata, Information Processing Letters 10, 5 (July 1980), 245-248.

[50] K.Inoue, I.Takanami and J.Hromkovic, A leaf-size hierarchy of two-dimensional alternating Turing machines, Discrete Algorithms and Complexity, Academic Press (1987), 389-404.

[51] K.Inoue, I.Takanami and A.Nakamura, A note on two-dimensional finite automata, Information Processing Letters 7, 1 (1978), 49-52.

[52] __, Nonclosure property of nondeterministic two-dimensional finite automata under cyclic closure, Information Sciences 22, 1 (1980), 45-50.

[53] __, Connected pictures are not recognizable by deterministic two-dimensional on-line tessellation acceptors, Computer Vision, Graphics, and Image Processing 26 (1984), 126-129.

[54] __, A note on time-bounded bottom-up pyramid cellular acceptors, To appear in Information Sciences.

[55] K.Inoue, I.Takanami and H.Taniguchi, Three-way two-dimensional simple multihead finite automata -Hierarchical properties- (in Japanese), IECE of Japan Trans.(D), February 1979, 65-72.

[56] __, Three-way two-dimensional simple multihead finite automata -Closure properties- (in Japanese), IECE of Japan Trans.(D), April 1979, 273-280.

[57] __, The accepting powers of two-dimensional automata over square tapes (in Japanese), IECE of Japan Trans.(D), February 1980, 113-120.

[58] __, Two-dimensional alternating Turing machines, Theoretical Computer Science 27 (1983), 61-83.

[59] A.Ito, k.Inoue, I.Takanami and H.Taniguchi, Two-dimensional alternating Turing machines with only universal states, Information and Control 55, 1-3 (1982), 193-221.

[60] __, A note on space complexity of nondeterministic two-dimensional Turing machines, IECE of Japan Trans.(E), August 1983, 508-509.

[61] __, Hierarchy of the accepting power of cellular space based on the number of state changes (in Japanese), IECE of Japan Trans.(D), September 1985, 1553-1561.

[62] __, Relationships of the accepting powers between cellular space with bounded number of state-changes and other automata (in Japanese), IECE of Japan Trans.(D), September 1985, 1562-1570.

[63] __, State-change bounded rectangular array cellular space acceptors with three-neighbor (in Japanese), IEICE of Japan Trans.(D), December 1987, 2339-2347.

[64] A.Ito, K.Inoue and I.Takanami, A note on three-way two-dimensional alternating Turing machines, Information Sciences 45, 1 (1988), 1-22.

[65] __, Deterministic on-line tessellation acceptors are equivalent to two-way two-dimensional alternating finite automata through 180° rotations, to appear in Theoretical Computer Science.

[66] __, A relationship between one-dimensional bounded cellular acceptors and two-dimensional alternating finite automata, manuscript (1987).

[67] __, The simulation of two-dimensional one-marker automata by three-way two-dimensional Turing machines, to appear in the fifth International Meeting of Young Computer Scientists, November 14-18, 1988, Czechoslovakia.

[68] __, Some closure properties of the class of sets accepted by three-way two-dimensional alternating finite automata, submitted for publication.

[69] K.Iwama, ASPACE(o(loglog n)) is regular, Research Report, KSU/ICS, Institute of Computer Sciences, Kyoto Sangyo University, March 1986.

[70] E.B.Kinber, Three-way automata on rectangular tapes over a one-letter alphabet, Information Sciences 35 (1985), 61-77.

[71] S.R.Kosaraju, On some open problems in the theory of cellular automata, IEEE Trans. on Computers C-23, 6 (1974), 561-565.

[72] __, Fast parallel processing array algorithms for some graph problems, Proc. of the 11th Annual ACM Symp. on Theory of Computing (1979), 231-236.

[73] K.Krithivasan and R.Siromoney, Array automata and operations on array languages, Intern.J.Computer Math. 4-A (1974), 3-30.

[74] R.E.Ladner, R.J.Lipton and L.J.Stockmeyer, Alternating pushdown automata, Proc. of the 19th IEEE Symp. on Foundations of Computer Science (1978), 92-106.

[75] C.Meinel, The importance of plane labyrinths, EIK 18, 7/8 (1982), 419-422.

[76] D.L.Milgram and A.Rosenfeld, Array automata and array grammars, IFIP Congress 71 (1971), Booklet Ta2, 166-173.

[77] D.L.Milgram, A region crossing problem for array-bounded automata, Information and Control 31 (1976), 147-152.

[78] K.Morita, Computational complexity in one- and two-dimensional tape automata, Ph.D. Thesis, Osaka University, 1978.

[79] K.Morita and K.Sugata, Three-way horizontally context-sensitive array grammars (in Japanese), Technical Report No.AL80-66, IECE of Japan (1981).

[80] K.Morita, H.Umeo and K.Sugata, Computational complexity of L(m,n) tape-bounded two-dimensional tape Turing machines (in Japanese), IECE of Japan Trans.(D), November 1977, 982-989.

[81] __, Language recognition abilities of several two-dimensional tape automata and their relation to tape complexities (in Japanese), IECE of Japan Trans.(D), December 1977, 1077-1084.

[82] K.Morita, H.Umeo, H.Ebi and K.Sugata, Lower bounds on tape complexity of two-dimensional tape Turing machines (in Japanese), IECE of Japan Trans.(D), 1978, 381-386.

[83] K.Morita, H.Umeo and K.Sugata, Accepting capability of offside-free two-dimensional marker automata -the simulation of four-way automata by three-way tape-bounded Turing machines-(in Japanese), Technical Report No.AL79-2, IECE of Japan, 1979.

[84] A.Nakamura and K.Aizawa, Acceptors for isometric parallel context-free array languages, Information Processing Letters 13, Nos4-5 (1981), 182-186.

[85] A.Nakamura and C.R.Dyer, Bottom-up cellular pyramids for image analysis, Proc. of the 4th Int.Joint Conf.Pattern Recognition, 1978.

[86] K.Nakazono, K.Morita and K.Sugata, Accepting ability of linear time nondeterministic bottom-up pyramid cellular automata (in japanese), IEICE of Trans.(D), February 1988, 458-461.

[87] J.Pecht, T-recognition of T-languages, a new approach to describe and program the parallel pattern recognition capabilities of d-dimensional tessellation structures, Pattern Recognition 19, 4 (1986), 325-338.

[88] A.Rosenfeld, Some notes on finite-state picture languages, Information and Control 31 (1976), 177-184.

[89] __, Picture Languages (Formal Models for Picture Recognition), Academic Press, New York, 1977.

[90] A.Rosenfeld and D.L.Milgram, Parallel/sequential array automata, Information Processing Letters 2 (1973), 43-46.

[91] W.J.Savitch, Relationships between nondeterministic and deterministic tape complexities, JCSS 4 (1970), 177-192.

[92] S.Seki, Real-time recognition of two-dimensional tapes by cellular automata, Information Sciences 19 (1979), 179-198.

[93] S.M.Selkow, One-pass complexity of digital picture properties, J.Assoc.Comput.Math. 19(2) (1972), 283-295.

[94] A.N.Shah, Pebble automata on arrays, Computer Graphics and Image Processing 3 (1974), 236-246.

[95] __, Pushdown automata on arrays, Information Sciences 25 (1981), 175-193.

[96] M.Sipser, Halting space-bounded computatiopns (Note), Theoretical Computer Science 10 (1980), 335-338.

[97] R.Siromoney, Array languages and Lindenmayer systems -a survey, in 'The Book of L' (eds. G.Rozenberg and A.Salomaa), Springer-Verlag, Berlin, 1985.

[98] __, Advances in array languages, Lecture Notes in Computer Science 291 (Graph-Grammars and Their Application to Computer Science), Ehrig et al. (Eds.), 1987, 549-563.

[99] R.Siromoney and G.Siromoney, Extended controlled table L-arrays, Information and Control 35 (1977), 119-138.

[100] A.R.Smith III, Two-dimensional formal languages and pattern recognition by cellular automata, Proc. of the 12th Switching and Automata Theory (1971), 144-152.

[101] __, Real-time language recognition by one-dimensional cellular automata, JCSS 6 (1972), 233-253.

[102] R.E.Stearns, J.Hartmanis and P.M.Lewis II,, Hierarchies of memory limited computations, IEEE Conf.Rec.on Switching Circuit Theory and Logical Design (1965),, 179-190.

[103] R.Szelepcsenyi, The method of forcing for nondeterministic automata, submitted for publication.

[104] A.Szepietowski, A finite 5-pebble automaton can search every maze, Information Processing Letters 15, 5 (December 1982), 199-204.

[105] __, There are no fully space constructible functions between loglog n and log n, Information Processing Letters 24, 6 (April 1987), 361-362.

[106] __, On three-way two-dimensional Turing machines, manuscript (1987).

[107] H.Taniguchi, K.Inoue, I.Takanami and S.Seki, (k,l)-neighborhood template -type bounded cellular acceptors (in Japanese), IECE of Japan Trans.(D), March 1981, 244-251.

[108] __ , (k,l)-neighborhood template -type bounded cellular acceptors -refinements of hierarchical properties-(in Japanese), IECE of Japan Trans.(D), September 1983, 1062-1069.

[109] __ , Relationship between the accepting powers of (k,l)-neighborhood template -type 1-dimensional bounded cellular acceptors and other types of 2-dimensional automata (in Japanese), IECE of Japan Trans.(D), October 1985, 1711-1718.

[110] __, Closure properties of (k,l)-neighborhood template -type 1-dimensional bounded cellular acceptors (in Japanese), IECE of Japan Trans.(D), March 1986, 279-290.

[111] K.Taniguchi and T.Kasami, Some decision problems for two-dimensional nonwriting automata (in Japanese), IECE of Japan Trans.(C), 1971, 578-585.

[112] M.Toda, K.Inoue and I.Takanami, Two-dimensional pattern matching by two-dimensional on-line tessellation acceptors, Theoretical Computer Science 24 (1983), 179-194.

[113] H.Umeo, K.Morita and K.Sugata, Pattern recognition by automata on a two-dimensional tape, IECE of Japan Trans.(D), November 1976, 817-824.

[114] R.Vollmar, On cellular automata with a finite number of state changes, Comput.Suppl. 3 (1981),181-191.

[115] P.S.P.Wang, Finite-turn repetitive checking automata and sequential/parallel matrix languages, IEEE Trans. on Computers C-30, 5 (May 1981), 366-370.

[116] Y.Yamamoto, K.Morita and K.Sugata, Space complexity for recognizing connectedness in three-dimensional patterns, IECE of Japan Trans.(E), 1981, 778-785.

The Simulation of Two-Dimensional One-Marker Automata by Three-Way Turing Machines

Akira ITO+, Katsushi INOUE++, and Itsuo TAKANAMI++

+*Technical College*, ++*Faculty of Engineering*
Yamaguchi University, Ube, 755 Japan

Abstract We denote a two-dimensional deterministic (nondeterministic) one-marker automaton by "2-DM$_1$" ("2-NM$_1$"), and a three-way two-dimensional deterministic (nondeterministic) Turing machine by "TR2-DTM" ("TR2-NTM"). In this paper, we show that the necessary and sufficient space for TR2-NTM's to simulate 2-DM$_1$'s (2-NM$_1$'s) is $n\log n$ (n^2), and the necessary and sufficient space for TR2-DTM's to simulate 2-DM$_1$'s (2-NM$_1$'s) is $2^{O(n\log n)}$ ($2^{O(n^2)}$), where n is the number of columns of rectangular input tapes.

1. Introduction.

Roughly speaking, a 2-dimensional (multi-)marker automaton is a 2-dimensional finite automaton which can make marks on its input with the restriction that a bounded number of these marks can exist at any given time. This automaton has been widely investigated: For example, 2-markers are strictly more powerful than 1-markers and 1-markers are strictly more powerful than 0-markers, a 1-marker can recognize the connected pictures, nondeterministic 1-markers are strictly more powerful than deterministic ones, and so on [1-3].

In this paper, we characterize 2-dimensional *one-marker* automata in terms of the spaces that *three-way* 2-dimensional Turing machines, which can move left, right, or up, but not down on rectangular input tapes, require and suffice to simulate 1-marker automata. Our research will give a quantitative estimate of the power of 1-marker automata.

We denote a 2-dimensional deterministic (nondeterministic) 1-marker automaton by "2-DM$_1$" ("2-NM$_1$"), and a three-way 2-dimensional deterministic (nondeterministic) Turing machine by "TR2-DTM" ("TR2-NTM"). The results are shown in Table 2, where n is the number of columns of rectangular input tapes. Compare those with the case of 2-dimensional deterministic (nondeterministic) finite automaton which is denoted by "2-DF" ("2-NF") in Table 1.

Table 1. Necessary and sufficient space for Ys to simulate 0-marker Xs [4-6].

X \ Y	TR2-DTM	TR2-NTM
2-DF	$\Theta(n \log n)$	$\Theta(n)$
2-NF	$\Theta(n^2)$	$\Theta(n)$

Table 2. Necessary and sufficient space for Ys to simulate 1-marker Xs.

X \ Y	TR2-DTM	TR2-NTM
2-DM$_1$	$2^{\Theta(n \log n)}$	$\Theta(n \log n)$
2-NM$_1$	$2^{\Theta(n^2)}$	$\Theta(n^2)$

We can know, for example, from the first columns of both tables that the increase of markers from 0 to 1 causes an *exponential increase* of spaces for the simulations.

In this paper, the detailed definitions of two-dimensional marker automata and (space-bounded) three-way two-dimensional Turing machines are omitted. If necessary, refer to [2,6].

2. Preliminaries.

Definition 2.1. Let Σ be a finite set of symbols. A *two-dimensional tape* over Σ is a two-dimensional rectangular array of elements of Σ. The set of all two-dimensional tapes over Σ is denoted by $\Sigma^{(2)}$.

For a tape $x \in \Sigma^{(2)}$, we let $\ell_1(x)$ be the number of rows of x and $\ell_2(x)$ be the number of columns of x. If $1 \le i \le \ell_1(x)$ and $1 \le j \le \ell_2(x)$, we let $x(i,j)$ denote the symbol in x with coordinates (i,j). Furthermore, we define

$$x[(i,j),(i',j')],$$

when $1 \le i \le i' \le \ell_1(x)$ and $1 \le j \le j' \le \ell_2(x)$, as the two-dimensional tape z satisfying the following: (i) $\ell_1(z)=i'-i+1$ and $\ell_2(z)=j'-j+1$, (ii) for each k,r $[1 \le k \le \ell_1(z), 1 \le r \le \ell_2(z)]$, $z(k,r)=x(k+i-1,r+j-1)$.

When a two-dimensional tape x is given to any two-dimensional automaton as an input, x is surrounded by the boundary symbol "#"s.

Definition 2.2. Let x be in $\Sigma^{(2)}$ and $\ell_2(x)=n$. When $\ell_1(x)$ is divided by n, we call

$$x[((j-1)n+1,1),(j\cdot n,n)]$$

an *n-block of x*, for each $j(1 \le j \le \ell_1(x)/n)$.

Definition 2.3. For any two-dimensional automaton M with input alphabet Σ, define $T(M)=\{x \in \Sigma^{(2)} \mid M \text{ accepts } x\}$. Furthermore, define

$\mathcal{L}[2\text{-DM}_1]=\{T \mid T=T(M) \text{ for some 2-DM}_1\ M\}$ and

$\mathcal{L}[2\text{-NM}_1]=\{T \mid T=T(M) \text{ for some 2-NM}_1\ M\}$.

We similarly define $\mathcal{L}$[TR2-DTM(L(m,n))] ($\mathcal{L}$[TR2-NTM(L(m,n))]) as the class of sets accepted by L(m,n) space-bounded TR2-DTMs (TR2-NTMs).

By using an ordinary technique, We can easily show that the following theorem holds.

Theorem 2.1. *For any function $L(n) \ge \log n$, $\mathcal{L}[\text{TR2-NTM}(L(n))] \subseteq \mathcal{L}[\text{TR2-DTM}(2^{O(L(n))})]$.*

3. Sufficient Spaces.

In this section, we investigate the sufficient spaces (i.e., upper bounds) for three-way Turing machines to simulate 1-marker automata. We first show that n log n space is sufficient for TR2-NTM's to simulate 2-DM_1's.

Theorem 3.1. $\mathcal{L}$[2-DM_1] $\subseteq$ $\mathcal{L}$[TR2-NTM(n log n)].

Proof. Suppose that a 2-DM_1 M is given. Let the set of states of M be S. We partition S into two disjoint subsets S^+ and S^- which corresponds to the sets of states when M is holding and not holding the marker in the finite control, respectively. (Rigorously, neither S^+ nor S^- contains the states in which the input head of M positions on the same cell as where the marker is placed.) We assume that the initial state q_0 and the unique accepting state q_a of M are both in S^+. In order to make our proof clear, we also assume that M begins to move with its input head on the rightmost bottom boundary symbol # of an input tape and, when M accepts an input, it enters the accepting state at the rightmost bottom boundary symbol.

Suppose that an input tape x with $\ell_1(x)=m$ and $\ell_2(x)=n$ is given to M. For M and x, we define three types of mappings $f^{\uparrow -}_i: S^- \times \{0,1,\cdots,n+1\} \rightarrow S^- \times \{0,1,\cdots,n+1\} \cup \{\ell\}$, $f^{\uparrow +}_i: S^+ \times \{0,1,\cdots,n+1\} \rightarrow S^+ \times \{0,1,\cdots,n+1\} \cup \{\ell\}$, and $f^{\downarrow -}_i: S^- \times \{0,1,\cdots,n+1\} \rightarrow S^- \times \{0,1,\cdots,n+1\} \cup \{\ell\}$ $(i=0,1,\cdots,m+1)$ as follows.

$f^{\uparrow -}_i(q^-,j)=$
- $(q^{-\prime},j')$: Suppose that we make M start from the configuration $(q^-,(i-1,j))$ with no marker on the input x (i.e., we take away the marker from the input tape by force). After that, if M reaches the i-th row of x in some time, the configuration corresponding to the first arrival is $(q^{-\prime},(i,j'))$;
- ℓ : Starting from the configuration $(q^-,(i-1,j))$ with no marker on the input tape, M never reaches the i-th row of x.

$f^{\uparrow +}_i(q^+,j)=$
- $(q^{+\prime},j')$: Suppose that we make M start from the configuration $(q^+,(i-1,j))$. After that, if M reaches the i-th row of x with its marker held in the finite control in some time (so, when M puts down the marker on the way, it must return to this position again and pick up the marker), the configuration corresponding to the first arrival is $(q^{+\prime},(i,j'))$;
- ℓ : Starting from the configuration $(q^+,(i-1,j))$ with no marker on the tape, M never reaches the i-th row of x with its marker held in the finite control.

$f^{\downarrow -}_i(q^-,j)=$
- $(q^{-\prime},j')$: Suppose that we make M start from the configuration $(q^-,(i+1,j))$ with no marker on the input tape (i.e., we take away the marker from the input tape by force). After that, if M reaches the i-th row of x in some time, the configuration corresponding to the first arrival is $(q^{-\prime},(i,j'))$,
- ℓ : Starting from the configuration $(q^-,(i+1,j))$ with no marker on the tape, M never reaches the i-th row of x.

Below, we show that there exists a TR2-NTM($n\log n$) M' such that T(M')=T(M). Roughly speaking, while scanning from the top row down to the bottom row of the input, M' guesses $f^{\downarrow -}_{i}$, constructs $f^{\uparrow -}_{i+1}$ and $f^{\uparrow +}_{i+1}$, checks $f^{\downarrow -}_{i-1}$, and finally at the bottom row of the input, M' decides by using $f^{\uparrow -}_{m+1}$ and $f^{\uparrow +}_{m+1}$ whether or not M accepts x. (See Figure 1.) In order to record these mappings for each i, O(n) blocks of O($\log n$) size suffice, so in total O($n\log n$) cells of the working tape suffice. More precisely, the working tape must be used as a "multi-track" tape. In the following discussion, we omit the detailed construction of the working tape of M'.

First, set $f^{\uparrow -}_{0}$, $f^{\uparrow +}_{0}$ to the fixed value Ω.
For i=0 to m+1, repeat the following. [$f^{\uparrow -}_{i}$, $f^{\uparrow +}_{i}$ are already computed at the (i-1)st row.]

(0) Go to the i-th row; When i=0, assume the boundary symbols on the first row.

(1) Guess $f^{\downarrow -}_{i}$; if i=m+1, set $f^{\downarrow -}_{m+1}$ to the fixed value Ω.

(2) [compute $f^{\uparrow -}_{i+1}$ from $f^{\uparrow -}_{i}$] When i≠m+1, do the following: Assume that there is no marker on the input tape. For each $(q^-,j) \in S^- \times \{0,1,\cdots,n+1\}$, start to simulate M from the configuration $(q^-,(i,j))$. While M moves only at the i-th row, behave just as M does. On the way of the simulation, if M would go up to the (i-1)st row at the k-th column and would enter the internal state p^-, then search the table $f^{\uparrow -}_{i}$ to know the behavior of M above the i-th row. If the value $f^{\uparrow -}_{i}(p^-,k)$ is "Ω", write "Ω" into the block corresponding to $f^{\uparrow -}_{i+1}(q^-,j)$; If the value $f^{\uparrow -}_{i}(p^-,k)$ is "$(p^{-\prime},k')$", restart the simulation of M from the configuration $(p^{-\prime},(i,k'))$. While continuing to move in this way, if M would go down to the (i+1)st row, then write the pair of the internal state and column number just after that movement into the block corresponding to $f^{\uparrow -}_{i+1}(q^-,j)$ of the working tape. If M never goes down to the (i+1)st row (including the case when M enters a loop), then write "Ω" into the correspondent block.

(3) [compute $f^{\uparrow +}_{i+1}$ from $f^{\uparrow -}_{i}$, $f^{\uparrow +}_{i}$, and $f^{\downarrow -}_{i}$] When i≠m+1, do the following: For each $(q^+,j) \in S^+ \times \{0,1,\cdots,n+1\}$, starting from the configuration $(q^+,(i,j))$, simulate M until M goes down to the (i+1)st row with the marker in the finite control. On the way of the simulation, if M would go up to the (i-1)st row with the marker held, then search the table $f^{\uparrow +}_{i}$ to know the behavior of M above the i-th row. If this value of $f^{\uparrow +}_{i}$ is "Ω", write "Ω" into the block corresponding to $f^{\uparrow +}_{i+1}(q^-,j)$; otherwise, restart the simulation of M from the configuration on the i-th row determined by the table value. If M puts the marker down on the i-th row of the input tape, then record the column number of this position in some track of the working tape and start the simulation of M which has no marker in the finite control. After that, If M would go down to the (i+1)st row or would go up to the (i-1)st row, then search the respective table $f^{\downarrow -}_{i}$ or $f^{\uparrow -}_{i}$ to find the configuration in which M return to the i-th row again. (If M never returns to the i-th row, write "Ω" into the block corresponding to $f^{\uparrow +}_{i+1}(q^+,j)$). From this configuration, restart the simulation of M. After that, if M returns to the position where M put down the marker previously and picks it up, then continue the simulation of M; otherwise write "Ω" into the block corresponding to (q^+,j). At some point of the simulation, If M goes down to the (i+1)st row with the marker held in the finite control, write the pair of the internal state which M would enter just after that time and the row number of this head position into the block corresponding to $f^{\uparrow +}_{i+1}(q^+,j)$. If M never goes down to the (i+1)st row with the

marker held in the finite control, then write "ℓ" into the correspondent block.

(4) [check the validity of $f^{\downarrow -}_{i-1}$ by $f^{\downarrow -}_{i}$] When $i \neq 0$, do the following: In order to check that the table $f^{\downarrow -}_{i-1}$ guessed on the previous row is consistent with the table $f^{\downarrow -}_{i}$ (guessed at the present row), first newly compute a mapping $\underline{f}^{\downarrow -}_{i-1}$, which is uniquely determined from $f^{\downarrow -}_{i}$ and the content of the i-th row of the input. [:Assume that there is no marker on the input tape. For each $(q^-,j) \in S^- \times \{0,1,\cdots,n+1\}$, M' starts to simulate M from the configuration $(q^-,(i,j))$. While M moves only at the i-th row, M' behaves just as M does. On the way of the simulation, if M would go down to the (i+1)st row at the k-th column and would enter the internal state p^-, then M' searches the table $f^{\downarrow -}_{i}$ to know the behavior of M below the i-th row. If the value $f^{\downarrow -}_{i}(p^-,k)$ is "ℓ", M' writes "ℓ" into the block corresponding to $\underline{f}^{\downarrow -}_{i-1}(q^-,j)$; If the value $f^{\downarrow -}_{i}(p^-,k)$ is "$(p^{-\prime},k')$", M' restarts the simulation of M from the configuration $(p^{-\prime},(i,k'))$. While continuing to move in this way, if M would go up to the (i-1)st row, then M' writes the pair of the internal state and column number just after that movement into the block corresponding to $\underline{f}^{\downarrow -}_{i-1}(q^-,j)$ of the working tape. If M never goes up to the (i-1)st row (including the case when M enters a loop), then M' writes "ℓ" into the correspondent block.] After this computation, check that $\underline{f}^{\downarrow -}_{i-1}$ is identical to the mapping $f^{\downarrow -}_{i-1}$ guessed at the previous row. If the equality holds, then continue the process; otherwise, reject and halt.

After the above procedure, on the (m+1)st row, M' begins to simulate M from the initial configuration $(q^+_0,(m+1,n+1))$ to decide whether or not M accepts the input after all. When M goes up to the m-th row with or without the marker, we can know how M returns again to the (m+1)st row, from $f^{\uparrow +}_{m+1}$ or $f^{\uparrow +}_{m+1}$, respectively. If M never returns to the (m+1)st row again, then M' rejects and halts. If M returns to the (m+1)st row, then M' continues the simulation. M' accepts the input x only if M' finds that M enters the accepting configuration $(q^+_a,(m+1,n+1))$. It will be obvious that T(M)=T(M').∎

From Theorem 2.1 and Theorem 3.1, we get the following.

Corollary 3.1. *$\mathcal{L}$[2-DM$_1$] $\subseteq$ $\mathcal{L}$[TR2-DTM($2^{O(n \log n)}$)].*

We next show that n^2 space is sufficient for TR2-NTM's to simulate 2-NM$_1$'s. The basic idea and outline of the proof are the same as those of Theorem 3.1.

Theorem 3.2. *$\mathcal{L}$[2-NM$_1$] $\subseteq$ $\mathcal{L}$[TR2-NTM(n^2)].*

Proof. Suppose that a 2-NM$_1$ M and an input x with $\ell_1(x)$=m and $\ell_2(x)$=n are given. We take the same assumptions and notations for the states of M, initial and accepting configurations of M as in the proof of Theorem 3.1.

From M and x, we define three types of mappings $g^{\uparrow -}_{i}:S^- \times \{0,1,\cdots,n+1\} \rightarrow 2^{S^- \times \{0,1,\cdots,n+1\}}$, $g^{\uparrow +}_{i}:S^+ \times \{0,1,\cdots,n+1\} \rightarrow 2^{S^+ \times \{0,1,\cdots,n+1\}}$, and $g^{\downarrow -}_{i}:S^- \times \{0,1,\cdots,n+1\} \rightarrow$

$2^{S^- \times \{0,1,\ldots,n+1\}}$ (i=0,1,⋯,m+1) as follows.

$g^{\uparrow -}_i(q^-,j) \ni (q^{-\prime},j')$: Suppose that we take away the marker of M from the input tape. Then, there exists a sequence of moves in which M starts from the configuration $(q^-,(i-1,j))$ and reaches the i-th row of x in the configuration $(q^{-\prime},(i,j'))$ for the first time.

$g^{\uparrow +}_i(q^+,j) \ni (q^{+\prime},j')$: There exists a sequence of moves in which M starts from the configuration $(q^+,(i-1,j))$ and reaches the i-th row of x in the configuration $(q^{+\prime},(i,j'))$ for the first time with its marker in the finite control (so, when M puts down the marker on the way, there exists a sequence of moves in which M returns to this position and picks up the marker).

$g^{\downarrow -}_i(q^-,j) \ni (q^{-\prime},j')$: Suppose that we take away the marker from the input tape. Then, there exists a sequence of moves in which M starts from the configuration $(q^-,(i+1,j))$ and M reaches the i-th row of x in the configuration $(q^{-\prime},(i,j'))$ for the first time.

Note that, in order to record these mappings for each i, $O(n^2)$ cells of working tape suffice in total. Roughly speaking, a TR2-NTM M' accepting T(M) acts as follows: While scanning from the top row down to the bottom row of the input, M' guesses $g^{\downarrow -}_i$, constructs $g^{\uparrow -}_{i+1}$ and $g^{\uparrow +}_{i+1}$, checks $g^{\downarrow -}_{i-1}$, and finally at the bottom row of the input, M' decides whether or not M accepts x by using $g^{\uparrow -}_{m+1}$ and $g^{\uparrow +}_{m+1}$.

First, set $g^{\uparrow -}_0=\emptyset$ and $g^{\uparrow +}_0=\emptyset$.
For i=0 to m+1 repeat the following:

(0) Go to the i-th row.

(1) Guess $g^{\downarrow -}_i$; when i=m+1, set $g^{\downarrow -}_{m+1}=\emptyset$.

(2) Compute $g^{\uparrow -}_{i+1}$ from $g^{\uparrow -}_i$ (for $i \neq m+1$). Details are omitted and see (3) below.

(3) [compute $g^{\uparrow +}_{i+1}$ from $g^{\uparrow -}_i, g^{\uparrow +}_i$, and $g^{\downarrow -}_i$ (for $i \neq m+1$)] For each $(q^+,j) \in S^+ \times \{0,1,\ldots,n+1\}$, M' does the following to compute $g^{\uparrow +}_{i+1}(q^+,j)$: M' starts to simulate M from the configuration $(q^+,(i,j))$. Since M is nondeterministic, M' tries to examine the whole possibilities of the moves of M in a systematic way. To this end, M' will construct the list $H^+(q^+,j)$ which is consisting of state and column-position pairs and which implies the set of all the configurations (with the marker in the finite control) on the i-th row which are reachable from $(q^+,(i,j))$ after some steps, with the restriction that M does not move below the i-th row with the marker. Note that the size of the set is O(n). M' constructs the list $H^+(q^+,j)$ as follows. Initially, $H^+(q^+,j)=\{(q^+,j)\}$. M' updates the list by performing all the possible one step simulation of M for each unexamined configuration contained in the list as follows:

(i) While M moves along the i-th row with the marker in the finite control, M simply adds the pair of the state and column-position of such configuration to $H^+(q,j)$.

(ii) If M would go up to the (i-1)st row at some column j_1 with the marker held in the finite control and would enter some state q_1, then search for $g^{\uparrow +}_i(q_1,j_1)$ and add it to $H^+(q^+,j)$.

(iii) If M would put down the marker at the k-th column on the i-th row and would enter the state p^-, then M' must know all the configurations in which M returns to the same position and picks up the marker. To this end, M' calls a subroutine which examines the whole moves of M with no marker after the configuration $(p^-,(i,k))$. In the subroutine, M' constructs another list $H^-(p^-,k)$ of size $O(n)$ which will contain all the possible configurations (without the marker) on the i-th row which are reachable from the configuration $(p^-,(i,k))$ after some steps with the assumption that the marker is placed on the k-th column of the i-th row. Initially, $H^-(p^-,k)=\{(p^-,k)\}$. M' updates $H^-(p^-,k)$ by performing one step simulation of M for each configuration contained in $H^-(p^-,k)$ as follows:

(a) While M move along the i-th row, M' simply adds these configurations to $H^-(p^-,k)$.

(b) If M would go down to the (i+1)st row or would go up to the (i-1)st row, then search the respective table $g^{\downarrow -}{}_i$ or $g^{\uparrow -}{}_i$ to find all the configurations in which M again returns to the i-th row and add those to $H^-(p^-,k)$.

After at most $O(n)$ updates, $H^-(p^-,k)$ does not change any more. The subroutine then terminates. At this time, M' searches the list $H^-(p^-,k)$ for each configuration c in which M returns to the position where M had put down the marker previously (i.e., the k-column of the i-th row), and M' adds to list $H^+(q^+,j)$ all the configurations which are reachable from c by one step simulation of M and which hold the marker in the finite control.

After at most $O(n)$ updates of $H^+(q^+,j)$, M' can construct the desired list $H^+(q^+,j)$. At this time, performing one step simulation of M from each configuration contained in $H^+(q^+,j)$, M' tests if there exist a configuration in which M would go down to the (i+1)st row with the marker held in the finite control, and adds to $g^{\uparrow +}{}_{i+1}(q^+,j)$ the configuration just after that movement. This completes all of the task for (q^+,j).

(4) Check the validity of $g^{\downarrow -}{}_{i-1}$ by $g^{\downarrow -}{}_i$ (for $i \neq 0$). Details are omitted and see (3) above.

After the above procedure, by using the two mappings $g^{\uparrow -}{}_{m+1}$ and $g^{\uparrow +}{}_{m+1}$, M' checks that there exists a sequence of moves of M from the initial configuration $(q^+{}_0,(m+1,n+1))$ to the accepting configuration $(q^+{}_a,(m+1,n+1))$, and decides whether M accepts the input x. If M' find that M accepts x, then M' also accepts x. Otherwise, M' rejects x. It will be obvious that T(M)=T(M').■

From Theorem 2.1 and Theorem 3.2, we get the following.

Corollary 3.2. $\mathcal{L}[2\text{-}NM_1] \subseteq \mathcal{L}[TR2\text{-}DTM(2^{O(n^2)})]$.

4. Necessary spaces.

In this section, we show that the algorithms described in the previous section are optimal in some sense. That is, those spaces are required (i.e., the lower bounds) for three-way Turing machines, when the spaces depend only on one variable n (= the number of columns of the input tapes).

Lemma 4.1. *Let $T_1=\{x\in\{0,1\}^{(2)} \mid \exists n\geq 1[\ \ell_2(x)=n$ & (each row of x contains exactly one "1") & $\exists k\geq 2$[(x has k n-blocks) & (the last n-block is equal to some other n-block)]]\}. Then,*

(1) $T_1 \in \mathcal{L}[2\text{-}DM_1]$, but

(2) $T_1 \notin \mathcal{L}[TR2\text{-}DTM(2^{L(n)})]$ (so, $T_1 \notin \mathcal{L}[TR2\text{-}NTM(L(n))]$) for any function L such that $\lim_{n\to\infty}[L(n)/n\log n]=0$.

Proof. (1): We constructs a 2-DM_1 M accepting T_1 as follows. Given an input x with $\ell_2(x)=x$, M first checks that each row of x contains exactly one "1" by horizontal sweep on each row and that x consists of k n-blocks for some $k\geq 2$ by a zigzag of 45°-direction from top to bottom. Then, M tests whether some n-block is identical to the last n-block (i.e., the k-th n-block) from the first block to the next-to-last block by utilizing its own marker (See Figure 2.): In some n-block and some row of this block, say j-th block and i-th row, M first puts the marker on the position where the input tape symbol is "1", then M starts to zigzag from the rightmost cell of the i-th row of this block until it reaches the bottom boundary. M then goes back to the "1" position on the i-th row of the last block. From this position, M vertically moves up until it encounters the marker put previously by itself or arrives at the top boundary. If M meets the marker again, then the i-th rows of the two blocks are identical and M proceeds to check the (i+1)st rows of the two blocks. If M does not meet the marker again, M can conclude that the j-th n-block and the last n-block are different and must go to the next n-block to test the equality. M accepts x, if M finds that some n-block are identical to the last block (this fact is recognized from the fact that when M reaches the bottom boundary, this is the rightmost position there). It is clear that $T(M)=T_1$.

(2): Suppose to the contrary that there exists a TR2-DTM($2^{L(n)}$) M accepting T_1. Let s and t be the number of states in the finite control and storage tape symbols of M, respectively. We assume without loss of generality that if M accepts an input, then M enters an accepting state at the bottom boundary. For each $n\geq 1$, let

$$V(n)=\{x\in T_1 \mid \exists n\geq 1[\ell_2(x)=n \ \&\ (x \text{ has exactly } (2^{n\log n}+1) \text{ n-blocks})]\}.$$

For each $x\in V(n)$, let

$$B(x)=\{b\in\{0,1\}^{(2)} \mid \exists i(1\leq i\leq 2^{n\log n})[(b \text{ is the i-th n-block of } x)]\},$$

and let $S(n)=\{B(x) \mid x\in V(n)\}$. Note that for each $x\in V(n)$, there is a sequence of configurations of M which leads M to an accepting state. Let conf(x) be the configuration just after M lefts the second-to-last n-block of x.

Proposition 4.1. *For any two tapes $x,y\in V(n)$, if $B(x)\neq B(y)$, then conf(x)$\neq$conf(y).*

Proof. Suppose to the contrary that conf(x)=conf(y) for some x,y in V(n) such that $B(x)\neq B(y)$. Without loss of generality, we assume that there exists an n-block b such that $b\in B(x)$ and $b\notin B(y)$. From this n-block b, we make up a new tape z consisting of ($2^{n\log n}+1$) n-blocks such that the first $2^{n\log n}$ blocks are equal to those of y and the last n-block is b. Clearly, z is not in T_1. On such tape z, M eventually enters an accepting state, because conf(x)=conf(y) and M accepts x, which contradicts the assumption that M does not accept a tape not in T_1.

(End of the proof of Proposition 4.1)

Proof of Lemma 4.1(2) (continued).

There are at most

$$E(n) = (n+2)\cdot s\cdot 2^{L(n)}\cdot t^{2^{L(n)}}$$

different configurations of M when it crosses into the last n-block of tapes in V(n). On the other hand, there exist

$$2^{2^{n\log n}}$$

different elements in S(n). Since $\lim_{n\to\infty}[L(n)/n\log n]=0$, it follows that there exists a integer n such that $|S(n)| > E(n)$ holds. For such n, there exist two tapes x,y in V(n) such that $B(x)\neq B(y)$ and conf(x)=conf(y). This contradicts Proposition 4.1. Therefore, we can conclude that no TR2-DTM($2^{L(n)}$) accepts T_1.■

From Lemma 4.1, we can get the following theorem for 2-DM_1.

Theorem 4.1. *To simulate 2-DM_1's, (1) TR2-NTM's require $\Omega(n\log n)$ space and (2) TR2-DTM's require $2^{\Omega(n\log n)}$ space.*

Lemma 4.2. *Let $T_2=\{x\in\{0,1\}^{(2)} \mid \exists n\geq 1[\ell_2(x)=n\ \&\ \exists k\geq 2[(x \text{ has } k \text{ n-blocks})\ \&\ (\text{the last n-block is equal to some other n-block})]]\}$. Then,*

(1) $T_2\in \mathcal{L}[2\text{-}NM_1]$, but

(2) $T_2\notin \mathcal{L}[TR2\text{-}DTM(2^{L(n)})]$ (so, $T_2\notin \mathcal{L}[TR2\text{-}NTM(L(n))]$) for any function L such that $\lim_{n\to\infty}[L(n)/n^2]=0$.

Proof. It is shown in [3] that Part (1) holds. By using the same technique as in the proof of Lemma 4.1(2), we can show that Part (2) holds.■

From Lemma 4.2, we can get the desired result for 2-NM_1 as follows.

Theorem 4.2. *To simulate 2-NM_1's, (1) TR2-NTM's require $\Omega(n^2)$ space and (2) TR2-DTM's require $2^{\Omega(n^2)}$ space.*

5. Discussion.

In this paper, we have investigated how much space is required and suffices for three-way Turing machines to simulate 2-dimensional 1-marker automata on any vertically long input tapes and given the satisfactory answers to this question.

By a slight improvement of the algorithms in the proofs of Theorem 3.1 and Theorem 3.2 when the number of rows are greater than the number of columns of input tapes and extended argument of the proofs of Lemma 3.4 and Lemma 3.5 in [6], we can get the following results: the necessary and sufficient spaces for TR2-NTMs to simulate 2-DM$_1$'s and 2-NM$_1$'s are

$$n\cdot\min\{\log m, \log n\} \quad \text{and} \quad n\cdot\min\{m, n\} \quad (m\geq 2),$$

respectively, which are the most general expressions as the two-variable space-complexity function L(m,n). The formal proofs will appear in a subsequent paper.

References

[1] M.Blum and C.Hewitt, Automata on a 2-dimensional Tape, *Proceedings of the 8th IEEE symposium of Switching and Automata Theory*, pp.155-160 (1967).

[2] A.Rosenfeld, *Picture Languages -- Formal models for Picture Recognition*, Academic Press (1979).

[3] K.Inoue and A.Nakamura, Some Properties of Two-Dimensional Nondeterministic Finite Automata and Parallel Sequential Array Acceptors, *The Transactions of the Institute of Electronics and Communication Engineers of Japan* Vol.**60-D**, No.11, pp.990-997 (1977).

[4] K.Morita, H.Umeo, and K.Sugata, Accepting Abilities of Offside-free Two-dimensional Marker Automata -- The simulation of Four-way Automata by Three-way Tape-bounded Turing Machines, *The Technical Reports of the Institute of Electronics and Communication Engineers of Japan* Vol.**AL79**,No.19,pp.1-10(1979).

[5] K.Inoue and A.Nakamura, Some Properties of Two-Dimensional On-Line Tessellation Acceptors, *Information Sciences* **13**, pp.95-121 (1977).

[6] K.Inoue and I.Takanami, A Note on Deterministic Three-Way Tape-Bounded Two-Dimensional Turing Machines, *Information Sciences* **20**, pp.41-55 (1980).

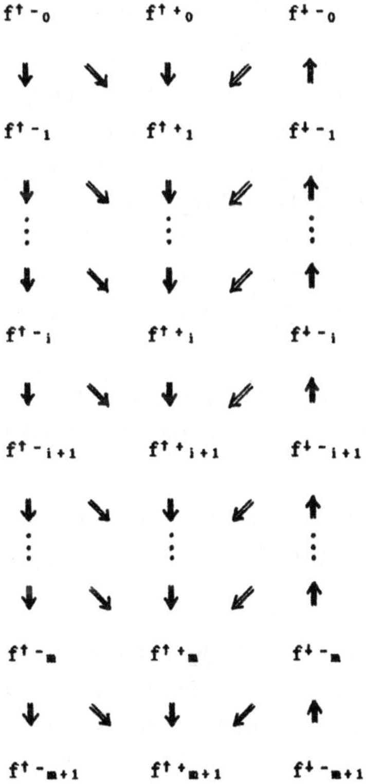

Fig.1. Interdependency of the mappings.

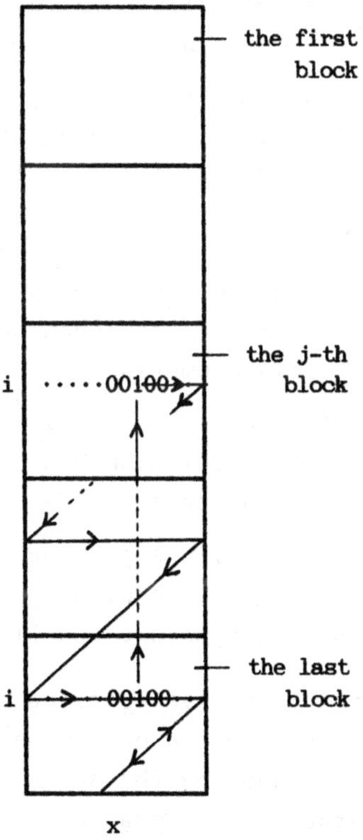

Fig.2. Action of 2-DM$_1$ M on a tape x in T$_1$.

SOME PROPERTIES OF SPACE-BOUNDED SYNCHRONIZED ALTERNATING TURING MACHINES WITH ONLY UNIVERSAL STATES

Anna Slobodová
Department of Theoretical Cybernetics, Comenius University
842 15 Bratislava, Czechoslovakia

1. PRELIMINARIES

During some past years many models of parallel computations have arisen. One of them - alternation, was introduced in |1| as a generalization of nondeterminism. Several types of alternating machines have been introduced and many results about them have been established |4 - 17|. Among the most interesting modifications there are the alternating machines with only universal states. They were investigated by Inoue, Ito, Takanami, Taniguchi, and others |7, 8, 10, 16|. These models are more realistic parallel computation models than ordinary alternating Turing machine because of elimination of nondeterminism.

Another modification of an alternating machine was motivated by the fact that this model does not provide communication among the parallel processes during the computation. Based on the alternation we introduced a more general notion - synchronized alternation, enabling a simple form of communication, via states |17|. The results obtained have witnessed a great power of synchronization. For example, one blind counter suffices to synchronized alternating machine to recognize any recursively enumerable set.

In this paper we are interested in combination of both modifications. We discuss a relationship of synchronization to alternating machines with only universal states.

First of all we give necessary terminology and notations. The most precise definition of general model can be found in |17|. The next section contains our results.

(k - tape) synchronized alternating Turing machine - satm ($satm_k$), is a device which has a read-only input tape with left and right endmarkers, and one (k) semi-infinite read-write storage tape with a left endmarker. Input head and storage tape head can move to the right and also to the left.

The set of states is partitioned into accepting, rejecting, existential and universal states. In addition, some non-final (i.e. existential and universal) states - synchronizing states, have a synchronizing element from a given finite set. Communication is through these elements mediated. When a process enters a sync state, it stops and waits until all parallel processes either enter the states with the same sync element or stop in final states.

A <u>step</u> of satm consists of reading one symbol from each tape, writing one symbol on the storage tape, moving the input and the storage head in specified directions, and entering a new state from a final control, in accordance with the next move relation.

A <u>configuration</u> of satm is given by the input, the input head position, the current state, the contents of the storage tape, and the storage tape head position. The last three components present an <u>internal configuration.</u> The <u>initial configuration</u> of satm M on input x is $I_M(x) = (x,1,q_0, \varepsilon ,1)$, where q_0 is initial state of M and ε is the empty string. A configuration is called existential, universal, accepting, or rejecting, resp., if the state associated with it is existential, universal, accepting, or rejecting, respectively. Similarly we define sync and non-sync configurations.

Given satm M we write $\beta \vdash_M \beta'$ and say β' is a <u>succesor</u> of β if the configuration β' follows from the β in one step of M. $\vdash_M^*$ denotes the reflexive and transitive closure of relation $\vdash_M$.

A <u>computational path</u> of M is a sequence of configurations $\beta_0 \vdash_M \beta_1 \vdash_M \dots \vdash_M \beta_m$, for any $m \geq 0$. If $\beta_0 = I_M(x)$, for some x, we call this sequence the <u>sequential computation</u> of M on x.

Let C be a sequential computation of M and $\beta_1 \vdash_M^* \dots \vdash_M^* \beta_r$ be a subsequence of C that consists of all sync configurations of C. Suppose, for all j, such that $1 \leq j \leq r$, S_j is the sync element of β_j. Then $S_1,\dots,S_r$ is called the <u>sync sequence of C.</u>

A <u>computation</u> of M is a finite nonempty labelled tree V with the following properties:

1. Each node u of V is labelled with a configuration l (u).
2. If u is an internal (non-leaf) node of V and l(u) is existential, then u has exactly one child v such that $l(u) \vdash_M l(v)$.
3. If u is an internal node of V, l(u) is universal and $\{\beta / l(u) \vdash_M \beta\} = \{\beta_1,\dots,\beta_n\}$, then u has exactly n children $v_1,\dots,v_n$ such that $l(v_i) = \beta_i$, for all i; $1 \leq i \leq n$.
4. For any two sync sequences $S^1 = S_1^1,\dots,S_p^1$; $S^2 = S_1^2,\dots,S_r^2$ corresponding

with two paths, beginning in the root of the tree V, $S_i^1=S_i^2$ for all i; $1 \leq i < \min \{p,r\}$ must be true.

An <u>accepting computation</u> of M on x is a computation of M the root of which is labelled with $I_M(x)$, the leaves are labelled with accepting configurations and 4) is true for all i; $1 \leq i \leq \min \{p,r\}$.

The longest sync sequence over all the sequential computations of the accepting computation V is called a <u>sync sequence of V.</u>

We define the <u>language</u> recognized by the satm M as the set $L(M)=\{x|$ there is an accepting computation of M on x $\}$, in natural way. We say that two satm M and N are equivalent if L(M)=L(N).

It is easy to see that satm with empty set of synchronizing elements is an ordinary <u>alternating Turing machine</u> (atm).

(Synchronized) alternating Turing machine which has no existential states is denoted by (s)utm and is called <u>(synchronized) alternating Turing machine with only universal states.</u>

We say satm is a <u>one-way</u> satm (and write 1 satm) if it can move its input head only to the right. Similarly one-way versions of other devices can be defined (and denoted).

Computational complexity of satm is defined as in |17|. It is mentioned as the greatest complexity over all accepting computations of the machine on all inputs with the same length. Suppose M is a satm and V is an accepting computation of M.

For any configuration β let space (β) denote the sum of the length of nonblank storage tapes contents in β. The <u>space</u> of V is

$\mathcal{S}(V) = \max \{ \text{space } (\beta) \mid \beta \text{ occurs in } V \}$.

Let $S_1,\dots,S_m$ be a sync sequence of V and let time (S_i) denote the maximum number of steps of M from the (i-1)-th sync configuration (from the initial configuration if i=1) either to the i-th sync configuration or to an accepting one, if no other sync configuration appears. The maximum is brought over all the computational paths in V. From the above it follows that time (S_i) is generally time between (i-1)-th and i-th synchronization. The <u>time</u> of V is

$$\mathcal{T}(V) = \sum_{i=1}^{m} \text{time } (S_i).$$

The length of the sync sequence of V-syn(V) is called the <u>synchronization</u> of V. We say the function $S_M(n): N \longrightarrow N$ is a <u>space complexity</u> of M if for all positive integers n holds

$S_M(n) = \max \{ \mathcal{S}(W)/W$ is an accepting computation of M on $x \in L(M)$ and $|x|=n$, where $|x|$ denotes the length of x $\}$

The time- and sync complexity of M can be defined in the same way (denoted by $T_M(n)$ and $Syn_M(n)$, resp.).

We say that satm M is f(n)-space bounded and denote satm (f(n)) if $\forall n \in N : S_M(n) \leq f(n)$ holds. A class of languages recognized by some kind of devices is denoted by the same but capital letters as respective device.

2. RESULTS

Alternating Turing machine is able to simulate synchronization because of the same power of synchronized and non-synchronized version of this device |17|. It was shown that any satm M can be simulated by an equivalent atm N such that $T_N(n) \leq 2\ T_M(n)$ and $S_N(n) = Syn_M(n) + S_M(n)$ We do not know whether this simulation the best one is. Since synchronization increases computational power of some simpler kinds of devices - namely alternating finite automata, some increase of space in such simulation is necessary.

The proof of result above has used nondeterminism. Therefore the same technique cannot be applied on utm. The similar assertion concerning relationship between sutm and utm is nevertheless true.

Theorem 1: For any sutm M there is an utm_2 N such that L(M)=L(N). Moreover, for the computational complexity of N holds:

$$T_N(n) \leq 3\ T_M(n)$$

$$S_N(n) = \max \{ Syn_M(n),\ S_M(n) \} .$$

Outline of the proof:
The idea of the proof is the following one:
Recall, that the acceptance of sutm differs from the acceptance of utm solely in one point: for any two synchronizing sequences occured in one computation of sutm must hold -the one is an initial subsequence of the other, or vice versa. The utm simulating the sutm will have one storage tape more than the simulated device to check that condition of acceptance.

Let M be some sutm. An equivalent utm_2 N runs through the simulated computation two times. Its auxiliary storage tape is employed by the sync sequence of M´s computation.

In the first running N writes down the sync elements of the simulated sync configurations on its auxiliary storage tape in order they have come. Hence, at the end of this phase the sync sequence of the corresponding sequential computation of M occurs on this tape. The present phase requires $T_M(n)$ time and $S_M(n) + Syn_M(n)$ space.

During the simulation of an accepting configuration, N returns all its heads at the beginning of the tapes (max $\{Syn_M(n), S_M(n)\}$ is needed for it). Then it runs over the simulated computation once more.

Several simulating computations run parallely now. Each of them has a sync sequence of one sequential computation of M on its storage tape, and vice versa the sync sequence of each sequential computation presents on the auxiliary storage tape in one of these parallel computations. N compares this sequence with the sync sequences of the simulated sequential computations and it checks the condition of the successful synchronization. Any sync sequence have to be an initial subsequense of the sequence stored on the tape, or vice versa. Clearly, this phase of computation uses the same time and space as the first one. □

The next picture can make the above mentioned simulation more clear.

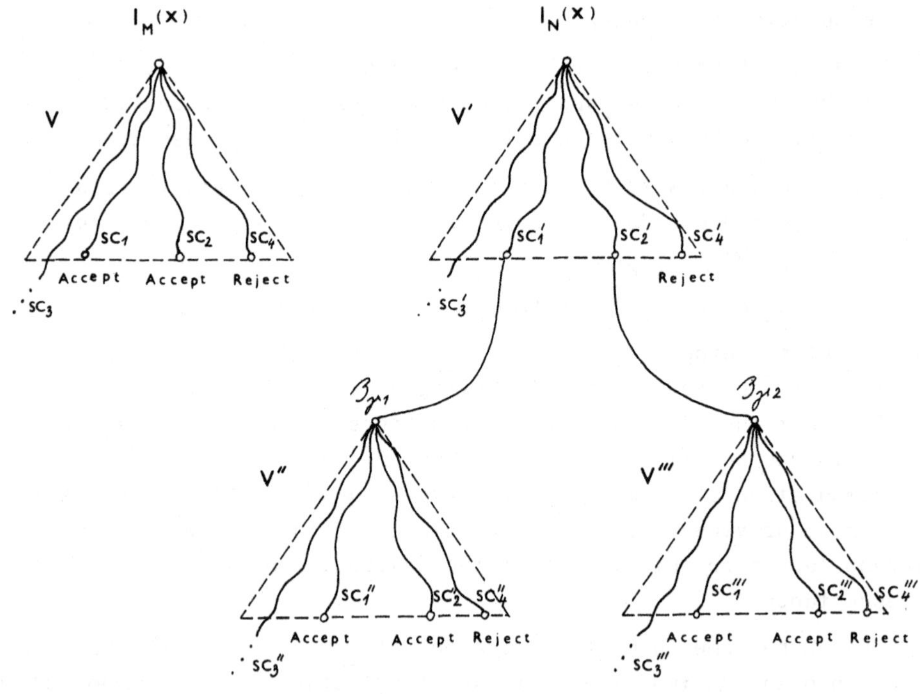

With regard to the preceding assertion synchronization can be compensated by space. This result has motivated us to investigate just the space-bounded devices. We consider the space-bound S(n) such that $\lim_{n \to \infty}(S(n)/n)=0$ ($\liminf_{n\to\infty}(S(n)/n)=0$ suffices in the proofs). It is easily seen that for any function S(n): $S(n) \geq n$, S(n) - space-bounded one-way machines are equivalent to the two-way versions of these devices.

Following results include besides an example of recognition on satm also one lower bound for space. The technique used in the proof has arisen by some modification of a method employed in |10| on (non-synchronized) utm.

<u>Lemma 2</u>: Let $L_1 = \{ w2w' / w, w' \in \{0,1\}^+, w \neq w' \}$.

Then 1. $L_1 \in$ 1 SATM (0)

2. $L_1 \in$ UTM (log n)

3. $L_1 \notin$ 1 SUTM (S(n))

for any $S(n) : N \longrightarrow R$ such that

$$\lim_{n \to \infty} (S(n)/n) = 0$$

Proof:

1. We shall describe the computation of 1 satm M which recognizes L_1 and does not use its storage tape. It can be done deterministically, in one parallel process, whether or not the input string has a form $w2w'$, where $w, w' \in \{0,1\}^+$. Hence we can assume, the input has such a form. We have to check only whether $w \neq w'$.

Suppose $w \neq w'$ and the i-th symbol is the first one in which w and w' differ. Let w(i), and w'(i), respectively, denote this symbol in w, and w', respectively. The next table represents all possible cases.

w(i)	0	1	2	2	0	1
w'(i)	1	0	1	0	$	$

Immediately after the start M nondeterministically decides which case will happen and remembers this decision in a state (say as the ordered pair (u, v)). Afterward the computation branches into two parallel processes. One process enters a synchronizing configuration and the input head remains on the first position. It stores u in the state. The other process situates the input head just behind the symbol 2 and enters a synchronizing configuration. It stores v in the state. After the successful synchronization the both processes run simultaneously. All following configurations are sync configurations.

At first the both processes set sync elements in accordance with the scanned symbol. In certain moment M nondeterministically decides that the symbols scanned in these processes are distinct. In both processes M compares the scanned symbol with the symbol stored in its state. If these symbols agree, M sets a special sync element (say $\bar{S}$). Clearly, the synchronization can be successful only if both decisions were right. Accepting configurations can be reached only after such synchronization.

If w = w´ then such i that w(i) ≠ w´(i) does not exist. Hence the processes cannot set $\bar{S}$ and therefore they cannot accept the input. In opposed to it M rejects the input after that the processes have read w and w´, respectively.

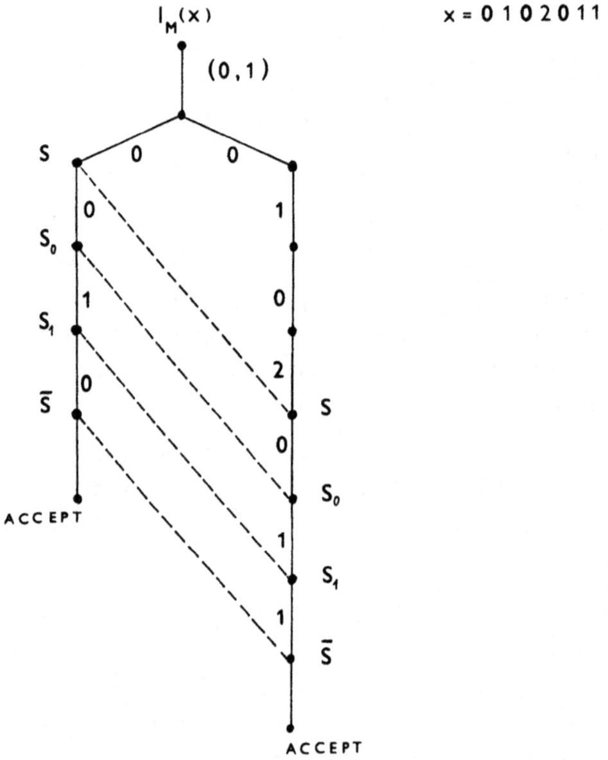

2. The result follows from a stronger result that asserts the following: L_1 is acceptable by deterministic Turing machine in log n space.

First of all the machine (say N) checks whether the input has the form w2w´, where w, w´ ∈ $\{0, 1\}^+$. After that it stores 1 on the storage tape. In every moment this tape contains (in binary form) a position of compared symbols in w and w´.

When N starts the action, its input head is situated on the left end-marker. If the storage tape stores i, then N compares w(i) and w´(i). If w(i) ≠ w´(i) (besides the case w(i)=2 and w´(i)=\$, when N rejects the input) then N accepts the input. If $w(i)=w'(i)$ then N increases the contents of the storage tape by one and repeats its action (like it was described above).

It is easy to see that N recognizes exactly L_1. Moreover it needs to store at most number $\lceil n/2 \rceil$. Hence it requires $\lceil \log n/2 \rceil$ space.

3. Let O be a one-way synchronized alternating Turing machine with only universal states such that $L(O) = L_1$. Suppose O is $S(n)$-space bounded, and $S(n)$ is such a function that $\lim_{n \to \infty}(S(n)/n) = 0$. Let r and s be the members of states and the storage tape alphabet of O, respectively. For each $n \geq 1$ let

$$V(n) = \{ w2w \ / \ w \in \{0,1\}^n \}.$$

For any $x \in V(n)$ we define the following sets of internal configurations:

$S(x) = \{ (q, \alpha, j) \ /$ there is a sequential computation of O on input x such that

$$I_0(x) \vdash_0^+ (x, n+1, q', \alpha', j') \vdash_0 (x, n+2, q, \alpha, j)$$

Clearly, for any $\sigma \in S(x)$ the configuration $(x, n+2, \sigma)$ is the first one in which the input head is placed just behind the symbol 2.

$C(x) = \{ \{\sigma_1, \sigma_2\} \ / \ \sigma_1 \in S(x), \ \sigma_2 \in S(x)$, and one from the following assertions holds:

a) $\sigma_1 = \sigma_2$ and there is a computational path of O which starts in the configuration $(x, n+2, \sigma_1)$ and either terminates in a rejecting configuration or it is infinite.

b) There are two computational paths of O which start in the configurations $(x, n+2, \sigma_1)$ and $(x, n+2, \sigma_2)$, respectively (these configurations may be the same), and they terminate in sync configurations with distinct sync elements.$\}$

Note that each $x \in V(n)$ is not acceptable by O. Hence $C(x) \neq \emptyset$ for any $x \in V(n)$. The next proposition helps us to finish the proof.

<u>Preposition 2.1</u>: For any two different strings x and y in V(n) $C(x) \cap C(y) = \emptyset$.

Proof: (by contradiction)
Let $\{\sigma_1, \sigma_2\} \in C(x) \cap C(y)$, where $x=w2w$, $y=w'2w'$, and $w \neq w'$.

Let $z=w2w'$. Clearly $z \in L_1$.

$\{\sigma_1, \sigma_2\} \in C(x)$ implies $\sigma_1, \sigma_2 \in S(x)$. It is clear that $S(x)=S(z)$ because of the same initial subword w. Hence $\sigma_1, \sigma_2 \in S(z)$. That means, there are two sequential computations (which may be the same in a case $\sigma_1 = \sigma_2$)

$I_0(z) \vdash_0^+ (z, n+2, \sigma_1)$ and $I_0(z) \vdash_0^+ (z, n+2, \sigma_2)$ in which the input head is placed just behind the symbol 2 only in the last configuration.

According to the fact that $\{\sigma_1, \sigma_2\} \in C(y)$ the two following cases appears.

a) $\sigma_1 = \sigma_2$ and there is the computational path of O which starts in the configuration $(z, n+2, \sigma_1)$ and either terminates in a rejecting configuration or it is infinite.

b) There are two distinct computational paths of O. One of them starts in the configuration $(z, n+2, \sigma_1)$ and terminates in a sync configuration associated with some sync element S_1. The other one starts in the configuration $(z, n+2, \sigma_2)$ and terminates in a sync configuration with some sync element S_2 such that $S_1 \neq S_2$. (Notice that in a case $\sigma_1 = \sigma_2$ the configurations $(z, n+2, \sigma_1)$ and $(z,n+2,\sigma_2)$ are the same, which is unimportant.)

In both cases z is not acceptable by O. This contradicts the fact $L_1 = L(O)$.

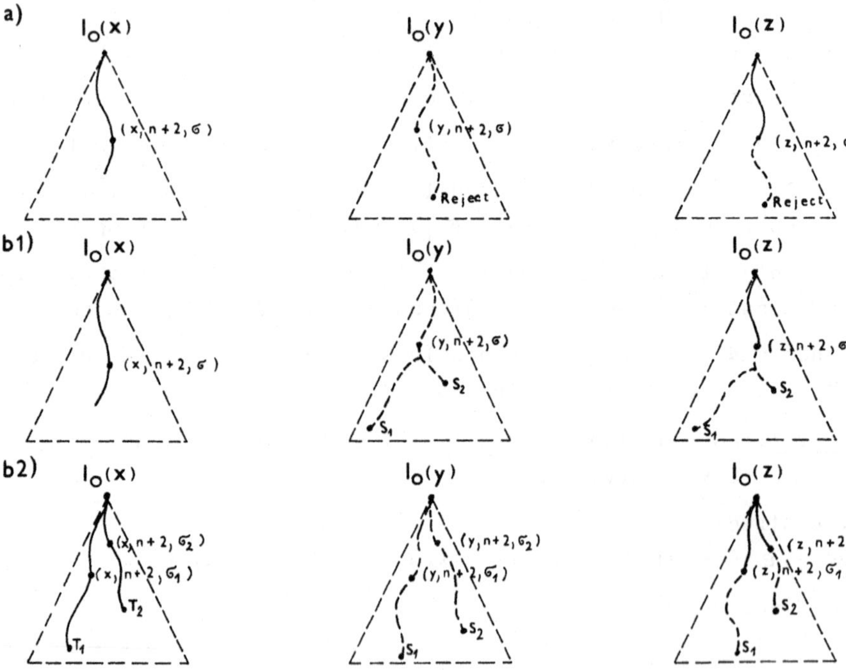

Proof of the Lemma 2 (continued):
Let p(n) denotes the number of pairs of the possible internal configurations of 0 in which the input head is placed just behind the symbol 2.

$$p(n) = \binom{K}{2} + K \text{ , where } K = r.s^{S(2n+1)} . S(2n+1)$$

Hence $p(n) \leq c^{S(2n+1)}$, where c is some appropriate constant.
On the other hand, the number of all elements of V(n) is
$| V(n) | = 2^n$

The fact that $\lim_{n \to \infty} (S(n)/n) = 0$ implies an existence of a positive integer n_0 such that $\forall n \geq n_0 : p(n) < | V(n) |$
Therefore for any large n there must be two different strings x and y in V(n) such that $C(x) \cap C(y) \neq \emptyset$. This contradicts the Proposition 2.1. Consequently there is no 1 sutm (S(n)) which is able to recognize L_1, for any function S(n) such that $\lim_{n \to \infty} (S(n)/n) = 0$.

□

The results of the preceding lemma built up the proof of the next theorem.

Theorem 3: For any function S(n) such that $\lim_{n \to \infty} (S(n)/n) = 0$ the next assertions are true:

1. 1 SUTM (S(n)) $\subsetneq$ 1 SATM (S(n))
2. if also $S(n) \geq \log n$ for any n, then
   1 SUTM (S(n)) $\subsetneq$ SUTM (S(n))

Lemma 4: Let $L_2 = \{ w2w \ / \ w \in \{0,1\}^+ \}$. Then

1. $L_2 \in$ 1 SUTM (0)
2. $\overline{L}_2 \notin$ 1 SUTM (S(n))
   for any function S(n) such that $\lim_{n \to \infty} (S(n)/n) = 0$

Outline of the proof:

1. We can assume inputs have a form w2w′, where w, w′ $\in \{0,1\}^+$, like in the proof of the lemma 2. We have to check only whether or not w = w′.

Computation branches in universal manner into two processes. The first one enters a synchronized configuration in the very first step. The other shifts the input head to right until the first symbol behind the symbol 2 appears. Afterward it reaches a synchronized configuration too. From this time both processes run simultaneously. They set sync elements in accordance with the scanned symbol until symbol 2 (resp.

$) is read in the first (resp. in the second) process.

Hence if there exists such i that w(i) ≠ w′(i), then the (i+1)-th synchronization fails because of the distinct sync elements.

x = 0102010 ∈ L_2 y = 0102011 ∉ L_2

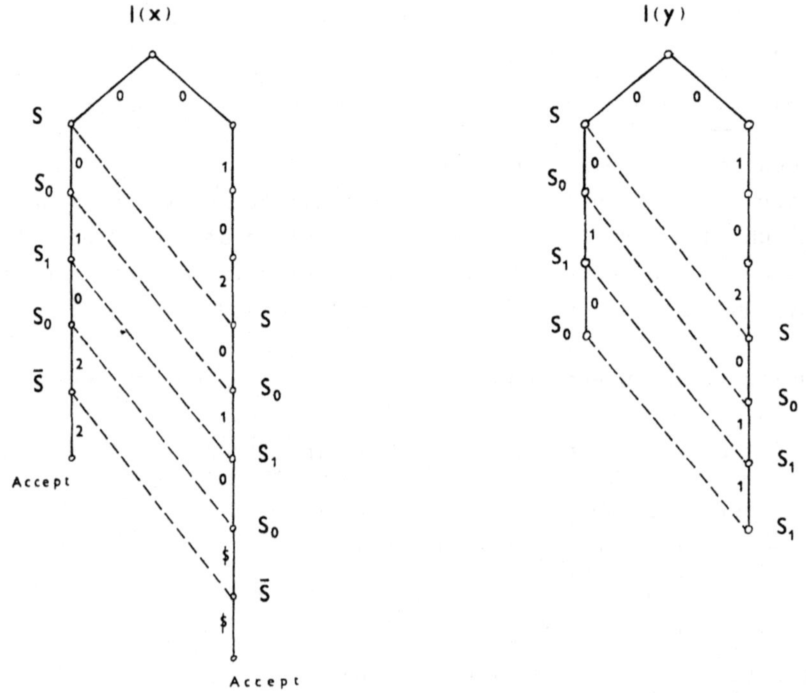

2. This part of the proof can be made by the same technique as the proof of the third assertion of lemma 2. □

<u>Theorem 5</u>: For any function S(n) such that $\lim_{n\to\infty} (S(n)/n) = 0$ the class of languages recognized by S(n)-space-bounded one-way synchronized alternating Turing machines with only universal states is not closed under complementation.

The next table summarizes some preceding results.

classes / S(n)	1 SUTM(S(n)) -1 SATM(S(n))	1 SUTM(S(n)) - SUTM(S(n))	1 ATM (S(n)) -1SATM(S(n))	1 UTM(S(n)) -1SUTM(S(n))
0 log log n	$\subsetneq$	?	$\subsetneq$	$\subsetneq$
log n	$\subsetneq$	?	?	?
n	$\subsetneq$	$\subsetneq$	?	?

References

|1| A.K.Chandra, D.C.Kozen and L.J.Stockmeyer, Alternation J. of ACM 28 (1981) 114-133.

|2| E.M.Gurari and O.H. Ibarra, (Semi-)alternating stack automata, Math. System Theory 15 (1982) 211-224

|3| J.E.Hopcroft and J.D.Ullman, Formal languages and their relation to automata (Addison-Wesley, Reading, MA, 1969).

|4| J.Hromkovič, Alternating multicounter machines with constant number of reversals, Information Processing Letters 21 (1985) 7-9.

|5| J.Hromkovič, On the power of alternation in automata theory, J. of Comp. and Sys. Sci. 31 (1985) 28-39.

|6| J.Hromkovič, Tradeoffs for language recognition on parallel computing models, Proc. 13th ICALP ´86, Lecture Notes in Computer Science 226 (1986) 157-166.

|7| K.Inoue, A.Ito, I.Takanami and H.Taniguchi, A space-hierarchy result on two-dimensional alternating Turing machines with only universal states, Inform. Sciences 35 (1985) 79-90.

|8| K.Inoue, A.Ito, I.Takanami and H.Taniguchi, Two-dimensional alternating Turing machines with only universal states, Inform. and Control 55 (1982) 193-221.

|9| K.Inoue, H.Matsuno, I.Takanami and H.Taniguchi, Alternating simple multihead finite automata, Theoret. Comp. Sci. 36 (1985) 291-308.

|10| K.Inoue, I.Takanami and R.Vollmar, Alternating on-line Turing machines with only universal states and small space bounds, Theoret. Comp. Sci. 41 (1985) 331-339.

|11| K.N.King, Alternating finite automata, Doctoral Dissertation, University of California, Berkeley.

|12| K.N.King, Alternating multihead finite automata, Proc. 8th ICALP ´81, Lecture Notes in Computer Science 115 (1981) 506-520.

|13| R.L.Ladner, R.J.Lipton and L.J.Stockmeyer, Alternating pushdown and stack automata, SIAM J. Comput. 13 (1984) 135-155.

|14| W.J.Paul, E.J.Prauss and R.Reischuk, On alternation, Acta Informatica 14 (1980) 243-255.

|15| W.J.Paul and R.Reischuk, On alternation II., Acta Informatica 14 (1980) 391-403.

|16| S.Sakurayama, H.Matsuno, K.Inoue, I.Takanami, H.Taniguchi, Alternating one-way multihead Turing machines with only universal states, The Transactions of the IECE of Japan, Vol. E 68, No.10 October 1985.

|17| A.Slobodová, On the power of communication in alternating machines, submitted to MFCS ´88.

Chapter 3

Algorithmics

THE VIRTUAL FLOATING GRID FILE
(extended abstract)

Daniele Cortolezzis
Algotech s.r.l., via Biella,10, I-00182 Rome, Italy

ABSTRACT: In this paper, an extension of the grid-file structure is introduced which makes it possible to substantially decrease the number of disk accesses performed during the resolution of range or partial-match queries. An analysis of such decrease is presented for both the general and a particular case.

1. INTRODUCTION

Some specific needs have been introduced by the increased amount of computer application fields. In particular, Cad, Vlsi design and geographical applications have turned the recent past research toward multidimensional data structures that allow to efficiently perform range queries.

An important propriety of these schemes is that they have to preserve the "principle of contiguity": records, whose keys are near in the logical key space, have to be stored in the same or in contiguous physical storage blocks.

Moreover, the increasing interest about interactive application has put in evidence the need to immediately resolve elementary queries, where immediately means, in human physiology, about ten milliseconds, that is the time to perform only a few mass memory accesses.

Thus, the efficiency of methods of data management can be measured by the time used for answering a query. The main part of this measure is the time spent in accessing data on secondary memory. Since present systems use disks, in which the size of transferable data is fixed, the time spent to answer a query may be evaluated in terms of number of disk accesses.

The restrictions presented above, strongly limit the use of tree structures[6][7]: for example, the multidimensional-B-trees [4], introduced as extensions of B-trees, are inefficient for what concerns the execution of queries which involve sets of buckets containing keys adjacent in the logical key space.

In this case, since buckets are stored on tree nodes, in order to retrieve all required information it is necessary to visit the tree structure many times.
Moreover, neighbor keys may not be stored in neighbor subtrees, because the multidimensional-B-tree cannot represent a total order on the logical key space.
The same considerations can be derived for other tree-structures such as k-d trees [8], R-trees [10], quad-trees [11].
As far as trie structures are concerned, it is possible to observe that they fail when partial-match queries are considered [6][7], while inverted files are ineffective when we perform range queries involving wide interval on secondary keys [6][7].
The most efficient structure for this kind of problems is the grid-file [1][2][3][5][6][7][9]: it generalizes the standard single key retrieval hash techniques to multidimensional data, assuring the contiguity of the stored information and answering to exact match queries with, at most, two accesses to mass memory.
But also the grid file presents a weakness when a range query is performed: as it will be shown in the following, the system may transfer a large set of not meaningful data in main memory, inducing a loss in performance proportional to the rate between not meaningful and meaningful information.
In this paper a modified grid file will be presented that reduce the amount of meaningless information retrieved by a range query, in order to limit the number of disk accesses.
Furthermore, we will compare the behaviour of the new structure with the original grid file both in the worst and in the average case.
The paper is organized as follows: first, an overview on grid files is presented, then the new data structure is described and its performance evaluation is given. A brief discussion of results and open problems concludes the paper.

2. GRID-FILE STRUCTURE

In this framework, multidimensional key means that the record key is compounded by more than one field and it may be seen as a point in the multidimensional key space, defined as the Cartesian product of the N domains on which the single key fields can assume value.
Thus grid-file is conceptually based on a partition of the logical key space into subspaces which are associated to buckets, stored in mass memory, where information is placed.

Let $S = X_1 \times X_2 \times \ldots \times X_N$

be the logical key space of the records stored in the file, where $X_1, X_2, \ldots, X_N$ are the domains of the N keys and let

$$P = P_1 \times P_2 \times \ldots \times P_N$$

$$\text{where} \quad P_1 = \{p_{11}, p_{12}, \ldots, p_{1k_1}\}$$
$$P_2 = \{p_{21}, p_{22}, \ldots, p_{2k_2}\}$$
$$\cdot \quad \cdot \quad \cdot \quad \cdot$$
$$P_N = \{p_{N1}, p_{N2}, \ldots, p_{Nk_n}\}$$

be a partition of the logical key space.

In such partition P_J represents the set of values that identify the borders of the intervals in which the j-th dimension is partitioned.

Moreover, let us denote as M the set of references to disk buckets.

Now, the grid-file manager system carries out a function which maps each element of the logical key space to an element of M, or alternatively which joins the single information image on S to the reference to the bucket that stores it.

$F : S \dashrightarrow M \quad ; \quad F : (x_1, x_2, \ldots, x_N) \mid\!\dashrightarrow \mu$

where μ: reference to the bucket containing the record identified by the key values $(x_1, x_2, \ldots, x_N)$.

This function is defined as the composition of two functions, the first with domain S and codomain P, the other with domain P and codomain M.

Moreover, function F_1 is compounded by N functions $F_{11}, F_{12}, \ldots, F_{1N}$ that determine, component by component, the element of the partition to which the information referenced by $(x_1, x_2, \ldots, x_N)$ belongs.

On the other side, function F_2 associates each element of the partition to the reference to the bucket containing its elements.

$$F = F_1 \circ F_2 \quad ; \quad F_1 : S \dashrightarrow P \quad ; \quad F_2 : P \dashrightarrow M$$
$$F_1 (x_1, x_2, \ldots, x_N) = (p_1, p_2, \ldots, p_N) \quad ; \quad F_2 (p_1, p_2, \ldots, p_N) = \mu \ ;$$
$$F_1 (x_1, x_2, \ldots, x_N) = (F_{11}(x_1), F_{12}(x_2), \ldots, F_{1N}(x_N)) = (p_1, p_2, \ldots, p_N)$$

where p_J: compact representation of p_{Ji},

The function F, to which we refer as "find-function", is physically represented by N dynamic arrays (for $F_{11}, F_{12}, \ldots, F_{1N}$)

$$Y_1[1..K_1], \ Y_2[1..K_2], \ \ldots, \ Y_N[1..K_N]$$

in which the generic cell $Y_H[J]$ contains the upper limit of the J-th partition element according to H-th dimension of the space (p_{HJ}), and by one dynamic N-dimensional matrix for F_2

$$G \ [1..K_1, 1..K_2, \ \ldots, 1..K_N]$$

in which every cell contains a reference to mass memory.

Finally, we can observe that the find-function first determines all p_J by a search on arrays Y_j, then, by the look up table G, carries out the reference to the bucket containing the required information (of course if the data is not present then the system carries out the bucket in which the information would be stored).

It is worth noting that there is no bijective correspondence between P's elements and M's elements: the grid-file imposes that all records belonging to the same partition's element have to be stored in the same bucket, but records stored in the same bucket may belong to different partition's element.

This solution is imposed to avoid bucket proliferation in mass memory with a small occupation rate.

Let us now briefly consider how the typical operations are performed on a grid-file.

2.1 INSERTION

If a new record has to be inserted, the find-function determines what is the bucket interested by the insertion.

If the insertion does not cause a bucket overflow, the operation ends normally; on the contrary, if it causes a bucket overflow, we must determine a splitting-value in order to share in two buckets the information contained in the full one.

The choice of the splitting-value differs in dependance of which kind of file management policy is adopted [2][7][9] and depends on whether only one or more references of G point to the full bucket[7][2].

In the first case some of such references will be used to point the new bucket, otherwise, the grid-file management system will provide to spread the arrays properly.

2.2 DELETION

This operation evolves in a dual way with respect to insertion: if two border buckets have less information than the capacity of a single bucket, then the system merges the data contained in the buckets and, eventually, contracts the directory.

2.3 FIND

The method used to find a single information (answer to a exact-match query) is fully explained in the theoretical presentation of grid-file above.

Therefore we will consider only the procedures the system uses to answer to range and partial-match queries.

If we have to retrieve information in order to answer a partial-match query, whose image mapped on the logical key space is the subspace orthogonal to the dimensions relative to the keys specificated in the query, then we must gather all the buckets whose references belong to the cells of G whose indices are $F1V_1(x_{V1}),\ldots,F1V_C(x_{VC})$.

On the other hand, if a range query is to be performed, a N-dimensional hyper-rectangle is specified and all buckets are to be gathered whose image on the logical key space intersected the query's image.

From the definition of the last two kinds of queries it is possible to note that the partial-match query is indeed a particular range-query in which some dimensions are bounded and the others have the same range of the space: in the continuation we will treat them in the same manner.
In such a way a range query involving n records could perform, in the best case, n/b accesses to retrieve information (where b is the bucket size).
This depends on the query structure and on the key distribution in the logical key space.

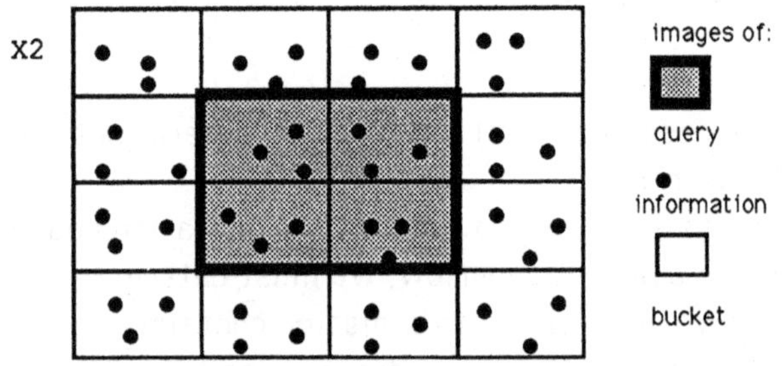

Figure 1:

In figure 1, an example of a query with this good performance is shown: in this case the rectangle query selecting n records requires n/b accesses.
The performance of the data structures for range or partial-match queries on disk depends on the capability to realize and preserve contiguity of adjacent data in the logical key space.
But the grid-file can turn out to be inefficient for particular range queries, since it imposes a fixed partition on the information: in figure 2 we can see an example in which n is the number of accesses to retrieve n records.

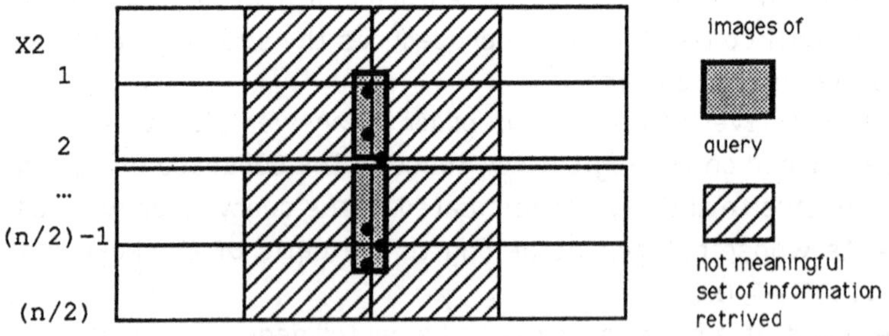

Figure 2

This poor behaviour depends on the fact that the considered query is represented by a rectangle in which the perimeter and the surface involve the same number of buckets and, thus, forces the system to transfer in central memory a large fraction of non meaningful data.

This situation induces a loss in performance proportional to the increase of the rate between non meaningful and meaningful information.

Figure 3 presents this situation: here the non meaningful set has less influence on the performance because the number of accesses tends to n/b anyway.

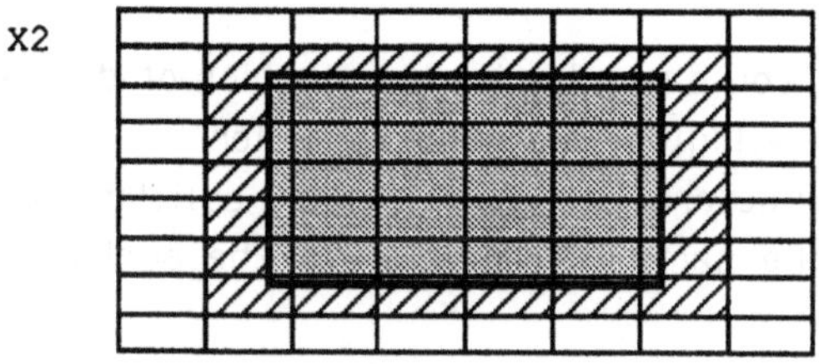

Figure 3:

3. THE VIRTUAL FLOATING GRID-FILE

Since, in order to answer a range-query, the system is often forced to transfer in main memory a set of not meaningful data, our aim is to minimize such redundant set.

Figure 2 presents such a kind of situation, that becomes critical if we work on an interactive application in which queries involve only few buckets that are characterized to have the area of the same size of the perimeter, measured in number of buckets involved.

In order to tackle this problem theoretically we model the shift of a floating grid to frame the query's rectangle into a minimal number of N-dimensional intervals.

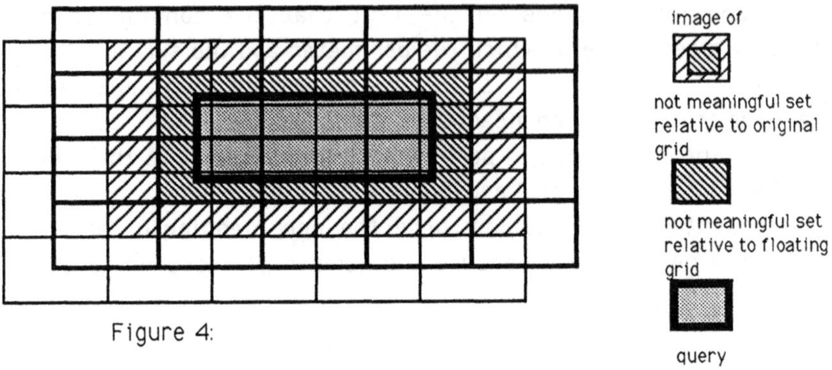

Figure 4:

Physically this operation would require the duplication of data stored in the file and the creation of a new logical key space partition.
It involves that the system determines new different splitting-values, so that no new bucket contains the same information of the buckets of the first partition.
This results in a certain number of file replies (maintained at insertion/deletion time) which approximate the ideal solution considered above.
The implementation of such approach depends on the adopted bucket management policy.
If Nievergelt's approach is considered [7] the determination of splitting-values is performed by choosing the median value between the splitting-values previously determined, independently from the key distribution on the space.
In this case we determine the new grid splitting-values shifting the original grid splitting-values of a fixed quantity δ.
Now, in order to evaluate the number of accesses the method allows to save, we give the following lemma, whose proof is given in [2]:

<u>Lemma 1</u>

Given a function $QM = \sum_{i=1}^{K} q_i \sum_{j=1}^{i} q_j$, such that $0 \leq q \leq 1$ and $\sum_{h=1}^{K} q_h = 1$, the value of QM is maximum iff all q_h elements are equal. In other words

$$QM \text{ is maximum} \iff \forall\, I,J \quad q_I = q_J = 1/K .$$

<u>Theorem 1</u>

If a one-dimensional space with uniform key distribution is considered, the average save it is possible to obtain through the reply and distribution of information in K grids is

$$QM = (K-1)/2K$$

Sketch of proof:

In the first step let us define in mathematical terms the average save; clearly, the query's image onto a one-dimensional space is an interval.

The number of buckets that it is necessary to draw in order to answer to a query, in relation with the R-th grid, is given by the following expression

$$n_R = L + Z_R(p_1, p_2) = [(l/s)+fmin] + 1 + Z_R(p_1, p_2)$$

where l: width of the query (defined by the measure unit of dimension);

s: width of the pages (defined in the same unit; the bucket's images are isomorphic because a uniform key distribution is considered [2].

f_{min}: $\min_{1 \le R \le K} (f_R)$, where f_R: distance between p_1 and the R-th grid splitting-value at the left to p_1;

Z_R: that we will call invasion-function, is defined as follows: $Z_R=0$ if the interval is contained in $[(l/s)+f_{min}]+1$ contiguous elements of R-th partition, while $Z_R=1$ if the query image invades the (L+1)-th element too.

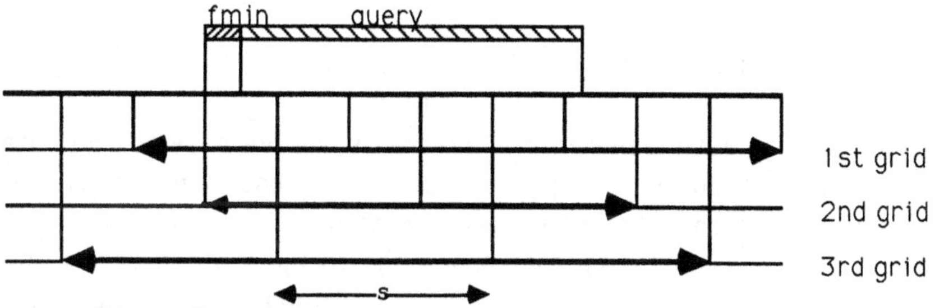

Figure 5

By observing figure 5 it is possible to note that each grid identifies K subsets for each original partition element, whose border is marked by the generic partition splitting-value inside the original partition element.

We will call C_1 the set of intervals included between the splitting-values of original grid (r_1) and the second grid ones (r_2), C_R the one in which the elements are the intervals included between r_R and r_{R+1} ($r_R < p_1 \le r_{R+1}$).

Also we can express the invasion-function in relation with p_1 and p_2:

$$Z_R = \begin{cases} 0 \text{ if } r_R < p_1 \le r_{R+1} \;\&\; r_1 < p_2 \le r_1 + s \\ 0 \text{ if } r_J < p_1 \le r_{J+1} \;\&\; r_1 < p_2 \le r_R \;\&\; J < R \\ 1 \text{ if } r_J < p_1 \le r_{J+1} \;\&\; r_R < p_2 \le r_J \;\&\; J < R \\ 0 \text{ if } r_J < p_1 \le r_{J+1} \;\&\; r_J < p_2 \le r_1 + s \;\&\; J < R \\ 1 \text{ if } r_H < p_1 \le r_{H+1} \;\&\; r_1 < p_2 \le r_H \;\&\; R < H \\ 0 \text{ if } r_H < p_1 \le r_{H+1} \;\&\; r_H < p_2 \le r_R \;\&\; R < H \\ 1 \text{ if } r_H < p_1 \le r_{H+1} \;\&\; r_R < p_2 \le r_1 + s \;\&\; R < H \end{cases}$$

where r_1+s is the right limit of C_K

Formally, we can define the save by the following condition

$\exists R: n_R < n_1$, i.e. $\exists R: Z_R(p_1,p_2) < Z_1(p_1,p_2)$
where the index 1 is used to refer to the original grid.

Using this definition we can introduce the save function (Q_R), that expresses the number of accesses to mass memory we save if we choose the R-th partition rather than the original:

$$Q_R = \begin{cases} 0 & \text{if } n_1 \leq n_R \\ n_1 - n_R & \text{if } n_1 > n_R \end{cases}$$

And we can derive that:

$$Q_R(p_1,p_2) = \begin{cases} 1 & \text{if } r_J < p_1 \leq r_{J+1} \ \& \ r_1 < p_2 \leq r_J \ \& \ J \geq 2 \\ 0 & \text{otherwise} \end{cases}$$

Then the save function results $\quad Q = \max\limits_{1 < R \leq K} Q_R$

Now if we want an estimation of the average save, we have to evaluate the probability that each point belongs to those sets whose combination gives a contribute different from zero to the save-function.

Denoting as q_R the probability that p belongs to C_R, we can derive, by the definition of $Q_R(p_1,p_2)$, that $Q_R=1$ if p_1 belongs to C_R and p_2 belongs to the union of $C_1, \dots, C_{R-1}$. $\left(p_1 \in C_R \ \& \ p_2 \in \bigcup_{i=1}^{R-1} C_i\right)$

Hence, the average save is given by $QM = \sum_{i=1}^{K} q_i \sum_{j=1}^{i} q_j$.

Replacing in the average save expression the results of Lemma 1 we obtain that the average save is given by $QM = (K-1)/2K$. q.e.d.

Theorem 2

If a bidimensional space with uniform keys distribution is considered, the average save it is possible to obtain through the reply and distribution of information in K grids is

$$QM \cong (L1+L2) \left\{\frac{(K^2-K+1)(K-1)^2}{(6K(K-1))(K^2)} + \frac{(15K^2-19K+2)(K-1)^2}{(48K(K-1))(K^2)} + \frac{(2K-1)(K-1)}{6K^3}\right\}$$

$$+ \left|L1-L2\right| \left\{\frac{(K+1)(K-1)}{12K^3} + \frac{(K-2)(K+1)(K-1)^2}{48K^3(K-1)}\right\}$$

with Lj: query's j-th dimension width, defined as the number of partition elements intersecting the query image mapped on the logical key space.

Sketch of proof:

The proof is similar to that of theorem 1.

Lemma 1 gives an indication about the value of the δ quantity: since we have shown that the maximum save is obtained when the intervals, determined through the intersection between the K grids, are equal, then δ will be given by:

$$\delta_q{}^{(j)} = s^{(j)}\ q\ /\ K$$

(with $s^{(j)}$: width of image of original grid buckets along the j-th dimension, expressed in the corrispondent measure unit).

This means that the q-th grid will assume as splitting-values the original grid splitting-values plus $\delta_q{}^{(j)}$.

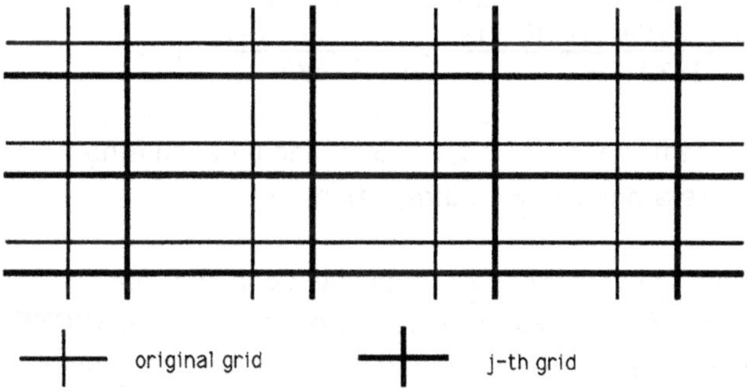

Figure 6

From theorem 2 we obtain, by varying the number of grids and in function of query dimensions L1 and L2:

K=2 --> $QM \cong 0.19\ (L1+L2)$

K=3 --> $QM \cong 0.27\ (L1+L2)$

K=5 --> $QM \cong 0.35\ (L1+L2)$

K=10 --> $QM \cong 0.41\ (L1+L2)$

$$\lim_{k \to \infty} QM \cong 0.48\ (L1+L2)$$

If we want to evaluate the percentual save (QM%), we have to divide QM by the average number of picked buckets, given by (L1*L2).
But in the hypotesis of interactive applications, range queries involve only a few neighbour buckets and (L1+L2) as the same magnitude than (L1*L2).
So the average percent save is around 30% with only three file reproductions, while the asymptotic limit is a little less than 50%.
From this formula we can also see that the behaviour of our structure is better or equal to the original grid-file, but the average save decreases if (L1+L2) << (L1*L2).
In other word, in absence of the hypotesis of interactivity, we expect that the data structures tend to have the same behaviour.
To show this we use the following lemma, whose proof is in [2], and theorem 3.

Lemma 2
The average width of a query edge is given by the evaluation of the average distance between two points that are stochastically arranged on an interval with uniform distribution and, if the length of the interval is equal to N, such average width is given by N/2.

Theorem 3
The expression that determines the medium percent save if we do not make any hypothesis on the dimension of the queries is given by

$$QM\% \cong 4/N \left\{ \frac{(23K^2-27K+10)\,(K-1)^2}{48K^3\,(K-1)} + \frac{(2K-1)\,(K-1)}{6K^3} \right\}$$

Sketch of proof:
It derives from theorem 2 and lemma 2 above, and by assuming $N_1=N_2$, where N_i is the number of splits along the i-th dimension.

From such formula we can derive that, in presence of applications that involve arbitrarily large queries, the medium percent save has order O(QM%)=1/N with respect to the number of splits in a generic dimension of the space.

4. CONCLUSIONS

In order to save disk accesses when range or partial match queries are performed, we have introduced a new structure derived from the grid-file through a finite number of duplications and a different distribution of the information in the buckets.

The results, obtained through the analysis presented in the previous chapters, have shown that the new data structure presents its best behaviour when it is applied to interactive environments, while the average save increases with the number of the grids replied.

On the other side, as we expected, at the increase of the size of the query, the new data structure tends, asymptotically, to behave like the original grid-file, even if its behaviour remains always better or equal than that of the grid-file.

An interesting open problem introduced by the new data structure derives from the fact that replies of information require a great amount of disk space, so that it remains to verify whether it is possible to save mass memory space without losing the obtained benefits.

BIBLIOGRAPHY

[1] G.Ausiello, G.Gambosi, E.Nardelli, M.Talamo:"GEODEQ: UNO STRUMENTO INTERATTIVO PER LA GESTIONE E L'INTERROGAZIONE DI DATI ED IMMAGINI CARTOGRAFICHE INTEGRATI".AICA Conference, Palermo, Italy, 1986.

[2] D.Cortolezzis:"DEFINIZIONE DI STRUTTURE DATI DERIVATE DA GRID-FILE PER GESTIONE EFFICIENTE DI DATI MULTIDIMENSIONALI". Thesis, University of Udine, Italy, 1987.

[3] C.Gaibisso, G.Gambosi, E.Nardelli, G.Soccodato & M.Talamo:"A PROPOSAL FOR THE EFFICIENT REPRESENTATION AND MANAGEMENT OF GEOMETRICS ENTITIES IN A GEOGRAPHIC INFORMATION SYSTEM". Th.Report, University of Rome, Italy, 1987.

[4] H.Gueting, H.P.Kriegel: "MULTIDIMENSIONAL-B-TREE: AN EFFICIENT DYNAMIC FILE STRUCTURE FOR EXACT-MATCH QUERIES". Th.Report, University of Dortmund, RFT, 1985.

[5] K.Hinrichs:"IMPLEMENTATION OF THE GRID-FILE: DESIGN CONCEPTS AND EXPERIENCE". BIT n.25, 1985.

[6] K.Hinrichs, J.Nievergelt:"THE GRID-FILE: A DATA STRUCTURE DESIGNED TO SUPPORT PROXIMITY QUERIES ON SPATIAL OBJECTS". Intern. Workshop on Graph Teoretic Concepts, Linz, Austria,1983.

[7] J.Nievergelt, H.Hinterberger, K.C.Sevcik: "THE GRID-FILE: AN ADAPTABLE SYMMETRIC MULTIKEY FILE STRUCTURE". ACM-TODS, vol.9, n.1, 1984.

[8] M.H.Overmars: "THE DESIGN OF DYNAMIC DATA STRUCTURES". Lecture Notes in Computer Science, vol. VII, Springer Verlag, 1983.

[9] M.Regnier: "ANALYSIS OF GRID-FILE ALGORITHMS". BIT n.25, 1985.

[10] N.Roussopoulos, D.Leifker "DIRECT SPATIAL SEARCH ON PICTORIAL DAATBASE USING PACKED R-TREES". ACM SIGMOD 1985.

[11] H.Samet: "THE QUAD-TREE AND RELATED HIERARCHICAL DATA STRUCTURE". Computer Surveyes, vol.16, n.2, 1984.

[12] H.W.Six, P.Widmayer:"SPATIAL SEARCHING IN GEOMETRIC DATABASES". Th.Report, University of Karlsruhe, RFT, 1987.

A PARTIALLY PERSISTENT DATA STRUCTURE FOR THE SET-UNION PROBLEM WITH BACKTRACKING

Carlo Gaibisso
Istituto di Analisi dei Sistemi ed Informatica del CNR
Viale Manzoni 30, 00185 Rome, Italy

Abstract

An extension of the well known Set-Union problem is considered, where searching in the history of the partition and backtracking over the *Union* operations are possible. A partially persistent data structure is presented which maintains a partitions of an *n-item* set and performs each *Union*, each *Find* and each search in the past in $O(lg\ n)$ time per operation, at the same time allowing to backtrack, over the sequence of *Unions* in costant time. The space complexity of such a structure is $O(n)$.

1. Introduction

The Set-Union problem and its variants has been extensively studied in recent years [1, 2, 3, 5, 6, 7, 8, 9, 10, 11, 12, 13, 14, 15, 16, 17].

The original problem [10] was to maintain a representation of a partition of a set $S\equiv\{1,\ 2,\dots,\ n\}$ under the following two operations:

Union(X,Y,Z): return a new partition of S in which subset X and Y are merged into one subset $Z\equiv X\cup Y$.

Find(x): given an item $x\in S$, return the name of the (unique) subset containing x.

Initially, each element is assumed to be a singleton.

A first naive solution, proposed by Galler and Fischer [8], requires $O(1)$ time per *Union* and $O(n)$ time per *Find* in the worst case.

This bound has been remarkably improved by the use of techniques of balanced linking (link by rank, link by size) [8,15], which made it possible to derive solutions requiring *O(1)* time per *Union* and *O(log n)* time per *Find* in the worst case.

The best solution with this type of approach is due to Blum [2] and requires *O(lg n/lglg n)* single operation worst case time complexity.

After the introduction of the path compression technique [1], the problem has been extensively studied from the point of view of worst case time on sequences of *Union* and *Find* operations [5, 10, 15], i.e. of the amortized complexity of operations [14].

The best solution in this direction has been given in [15]: it requires *O(n)* space and $O(m\ \alpha(m+n,\ n)+n)$ running time, where *m* is the number of *Find* operations performed and $\alpha(\ldots,\ldots)$ is a very slowly increasing function related to the inverse of Ackermann's function. In such a paper it was also proved that such a complexity is also a lower bound for a very general class of algorithms.

As an extension Mannila and Ukkonen [11] proposed a variant of this problem, relevant in the framework of logic programming interpreters design, introducing a new operation defined as follows:

Deunion: undo the last *Union* performed, i.e. return to the state immediately preceding the execution of such *Union*.

In such a paper, an algorithm is presented which is efficient with respect to amortized time complexity.

Successively Westbrook and Tarjan [17] completely characterized such problem giving a *(lg n/glg n)* upper bound of the amortized complexity and proving that such bound is also a lower bound for the class of separable algorithms.

Gambosi, Italiano and Talamo [9] also considered a generalization of such problem to the case where a (real) weight is associated to each *Union* and the *Deunion* operation is substituted by:

Backtrack: returns to the state immediately before the execution of the Union of largest weight thus far performed.

The solution presented in [9] makes it possible to perform *Unions* in *O(lglg n)*, *Finds* in *O(lg n)* and *Backtracks* in *O(1)* time per operation, using a data structure with *O(n)* space complexity.

Gaibisso, Gambosi and Talamo [7] introduced a partially persistent [4] version of the classical Set-Union problem which allows a search in the history of the partition. They introduced a new kind of *Find*, referred to as *PFind*, defined as follows:

PFind(x,k): given an item $x \in S$, return the name of the (unique) subset containing x just after the kth *Union* operation was performed.

Such operation includes the usual *Find* as a particular case.

The partially persistent data structure presented in such a paper maintains a partition of an *n-item* set performing each *Union* in $O(1)$ and each *PFind* in $O(\lg n)$ worst case time, while the space complexity is $O(n)$.

In this paper a further extension of the Set-Union problem is considered where both searching in the history of the partition and backtracking over the sequence of *Union* operations are possible.

Motivations for the study of the *Union-PFind-Backtrack* problem may for example arise from the implementation of search heuristics in the framework of Prolog environment design.

The main results of the paper are concerned with the worst case per operation analysis of the *Union*, *PFind*, and *Backtrack* operations: it is shown how to perform each *Backtrack* in $O(1)$, each *Union* and *PFind* in $O(\lg n)$ worst case times, using a partially persistent data structure which requires $O(n)$ space complexity.

The remainder of this paper is organized as follows. In section 2 a data structure for the *Union-PFind-Backtrack* problem is introduced, in section 3 its worst case time and space complexity are analysed. Section 4 contains concluding remarks.

2. The Data Structure

Recalling the concepts introduced in the last section, the problem considered is that of maintaining a representation of a partition of a set $S \equiv \{1, 2, \ldots, n\}$ under the following three operations:

Union(X,Y,Z): return a new partition of S in which subset X and Y are merged into one subset $Z \equiv X \cup Y$.

PFind(x,k): given an item $x \in S$, return the name of the (unique) subset containing x just after the kth *Union* operation was performed.

Backtrack(k): return to state just after the kth *Union* operation was performed.

In the sequel a *Union* will be referred as *"valid"* if it has not been undone by backtracking and as *"void"* otherwise.

It is not difficult to see that at any time the actual partition is the same that would have been resulted from simply applying the currently valid *Unions* to the initial set of singleton, in exactly the same order in which such *Unions* were performed in the actual sequence: this individuates a virtual sequence, referred to as *VS*, of valid *Unions*. At any time is henceforth possible to univocally denote each valid *Union* by the ordinal number it gets in that virtual sequence.

Furthermore it can be proved that each *Union*, as long as it remains valid, maintains the same ordinal number it was given at the time of its execution.

Since if the parameter k exceeds the number n' of operations currently in *VS*, then it cannot refer to void *Unions* : it follows that *PFind(k)* and *Backtrack(k)*, for $k \geq n'$, reduce respectively to *PFind(n')* and *Backtrack(n')*.

As a consequence, it is worth noting that once a *Backtrack(k)* has been performed the kth *Union* in *VS* can be considered the last *Union* performed.

A data structure able to support the *Union*, *PFind* and *Backtrack* operations is now introduced: as in most of the algorithms which deal with versions of the Set-Union problem, each set of the partition is maintained as a tree whose root contains the name of the set. When a *Union* is performed, exactly one link between two nodes is introduced, which is associated to such an operation: recalling the previously given definitions of valid and void *Union*, also a link is said to be valid or void according to its corresponding *Union* and hence valid links return a connection which has not yet been cancelled by backtracking.

In order to support the *PFind* and *Backtrack* operations such a structure has been modified in the following way:

- if a link has been introduced by the ith *Union* operation performed, such a link is marked with the integer i. The mark associated to a link l will be referred to as *Mark(l)*;
- each node p in the data structure has an associated dictionary *Dictionary(p)*, such that each item in *Dictionary(p)* corresponds to a link l entering p and stores the name and the rank associated to such a node after the *Union* introducing l was performed. Initially, each node p has an associated dictionary with only one item *(0, 0, name_of_p)*;
- each link in the data structure is directly accessible by means of a *(n-1)-item* array *Access*. Two indices i_{valid}, i_{max} allow insertions in the array in such a way that $Access[i], 1 \leq i \leq i_{valid}$, points to the link introduced by the ith valid *Union* in the virtual sequence of *Unions* performed, while $Access[j], i_{valid}+1 \leq j \leq i_{max}$, points to a void links if it exists. In other words i_{valid} and i_{max} point respectively to the last valid and the last void links inserted. It is worth noting that in such a way

the validity of a link l can be tested in costant time by simply comparing $Mark(l)$ with i_{valid}. Initially $i_{valid} = i_{max} = 0$.

In the sequel $Root(X)$ will refer to the root of the tree representing subset X in the data structure.

The different operations can now be implemented as follows:

Union(X,Y,Z): first of all if $i_{valid} < i_{max}$ then at least one void link is present in the data structure. In such a case consider the void link l from node p' to node p pointed to by $Access[i_{valid}+1]$, delete link l from the data structure and the node corresponding to l from $Dictionary(p)$. For what concerns the rank and the name associated to p before l was introduced in the data structure, it is worth noting that they can be retrieved in $Dictionary(p)$ stored in the item corresponding to the live link entering p most recently added, i.e. in the node which stores the maximum mark less than or equal to i_{valid}.

Set, in any case, i_{valid} to $i_{valid}+1$ and i_{max} to the maximum between i_{valid} and i_{max} itself; enter a new link $(Root(X), Root(Y))$ or $(Root(Y), Root(X))$ according to the linking by rank strategy and store a pointer to such a link in $Access[i_{valid}]$.

Finally add a new item (i_{valid}, r, Z) in $Dictionary(Root(Y))$, where r is the new rank of $Root(Y)$ after the *Union* operation was performed.

Figures 2.1.a and 2.1.b show how the data structure evolves when a *Union* operation is performed.

PFind(x,k): starting from node x, which belongs to some tree T, traverse the path from this node to $Root(T)$ until :

1) a node p is reached such that either $p = Root(T)$ or
2) for the (unique) link l outgoing from p the condition $Mark(l)>k$ holds (since the parameter k cannot refer to void *Unions* the above mentioned condition also tests link validity).

Let now $D \equiv \{x \mid x=Mark(l),\ l \text{ enters } p, l \text{ is a valid link}, x \leq k\}$, then return the name stored by the node corresponding to the link L' marked with $max\ D$ in $Dictionary(p)$.

Backtrack(k): set i_{valid} to k.

3. Worst Case Time and Space Complexity Analysis.

As far as the worst case time and space complexity are concerned, the following theorem can be stated:

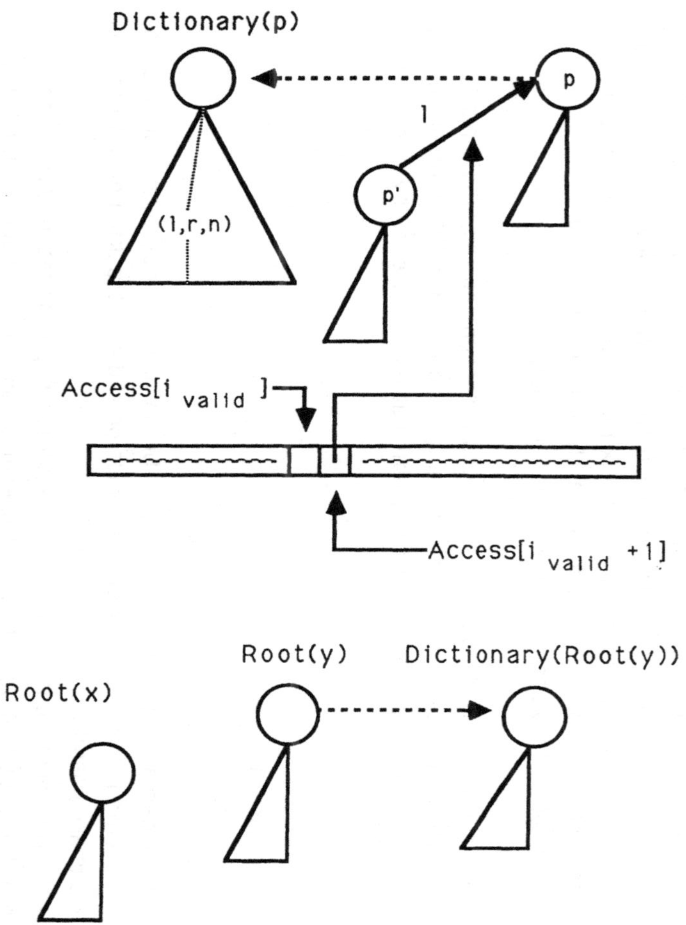

figure 2.1.a

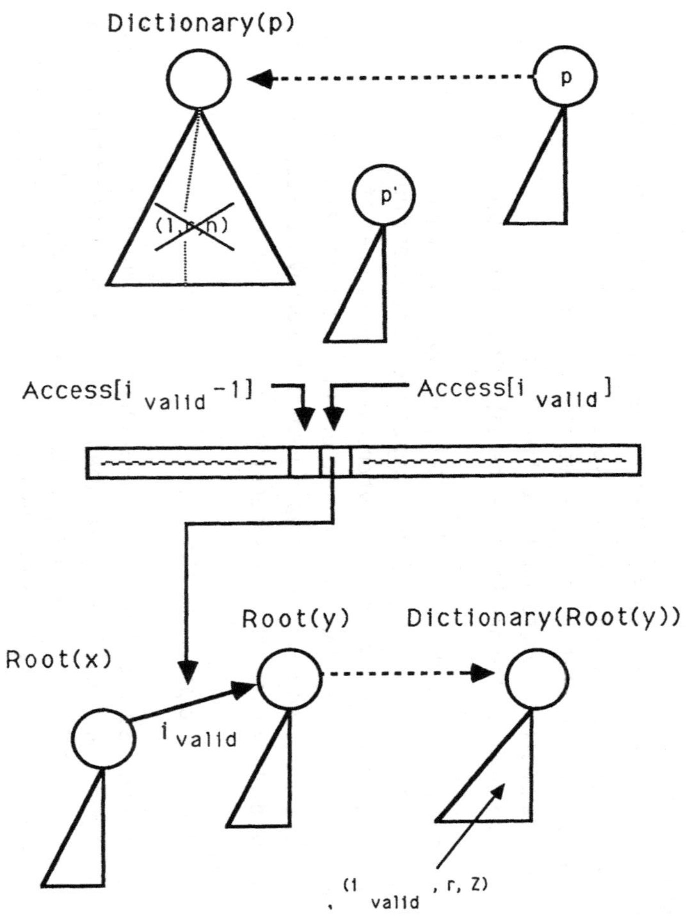

figure 2.1.b

Theorem:

with the previously introduced data structure it is possible to perform:

a) the *Union* operation in $O(lg\ n)$ worst case time;
b) the *PFind* operation in $O(lg\ n)$ worst case time;
c) the *Backtrack* operation in $O(1)$ worst case time;
d) the amount of space to store the data structure is $S(n)=O(n)$.

Let us first note that it is possible to easy implement each dictionary in such a way that inserting an item, deleting an item and searching for an item all require $O(lg\ m)$ worst case time, where m is the number of items in the dictionary. Furthermore, since the number of links, void or valid, in the data structure cannot exceed $n-1$, one for each item in the array *Access*, the sum of items in the dictionaries, and consequently the number of items in a single dictionary, is $O(n)$.

It is now possible to prove the theorem:

a) implementing each *Union* operation requires a costant number of insert, delete, and search operations onto the dictionaries associated to the data structure nodes: each one of such operations requires $O(lg\ n)$ time;
b) each $PFind(x,k)$ implies two searches in the data structure:
the first search, starting from node x to locate a node p such that either p is the root of the tree containing x, or for its outgoing link l the condition $Mark(l)>k$ holds. This search obviously takes $O(lg\ n)$ time.
The other search is performed in *Dictionary(p)* in order to access the name of the subset containing item x just after the kth *Union* operation was performed: also this second search takes $O(lg\ n)$ time.
Hence each *PFind* operation takes $O(lg\ n)$ time;
c) trivial;
d) since the number of nodes in the trees representing the whole partition, the number of items in the dictionaries and the array dimension all are $O(n)$, the space complexity of the whole data structure is obviously $O(n)$.

4. Conclusions

In this paper an extension of the Set-Union problem has been considered, where searching in the history of the partition and backtracking over the *Union* operations are possible.

A partially persistent data structure which supports each *Union* and each search in the past in $O(lg\ n)$ time per operation and allows backtracking in $O(1)$ time, has been proposed. The space required to implement such a structure is $O(n)$.

References

[1] A.V. Aho, J.E. Hopcroft, J.D. Ullman, *"The Design and Analysis of Computer Algorithms"*, Addison-Wesley (1974).

[2] N. Blum, *"On the Single Operation Worst Case Time Complexity of the Disjoint Set-Union Problem"*, Proc. 2nd Symp. on Theretical Aspects of Computer Science (1985).

[3] B. Bollobas, I. Simon, *"On the Expected Behavior of Disjoint Set-Union Algorithms"*, Proc. 17th ACM Symp. on Theory of Computing (1985).

[4] J.R. Driscoll, N. Sarnak, D.D. Sleator, R.E. Tarjan, *"Making Data Structures Persistent"*, Proc. 18th Symp. on Theory of Computing STOC (1986).

[5] M.J. Fischer, *"Efficiency of Equivalence Algorithms"*, in Complexity of Computations, R.E. Miller and J.W. Thatcher, eds., Plenum Press, New York (1972).

[6] H.N. Gabow, R.E. Tarjan, *"A Linear Time Algorithm for a Special Case of Disjoint Set-Union"*, Proc. 15th ACM Symp. on Theory of Computing (1983).

[7] C. Gaibisso, G. Gambosi, M. Talamo, *"A Partially Persistent Data Structure for the Set-Union Problem"*, submitted to RAIRO Theoretical Informatics and Applications (1987).

[8] B.A. Galler, M.J. Fischer, *"An Improved Equivalence Algorithm"*, Comm. ACM 7 (1964).

[9] G. Gambosi, G.F. Italiano. M. Talamo, *"Worst Case Analysis of the Set-Union Problem with Backtracking"*, to appear on "Theoretical Computer Science" (1988).

[10] J.E. Hopcroft, J.D. Ullman, *"Set Merging Algorithms"*, SIAM J. Comput. 2 (1973).

[11] H. Mannila, E. Ukkonen, *"The Set-Union Problem with Backtracking"*, Proc. 13th ICALP (1986).

[12] R.E. Tarjan, *"Efficiency of a Good but not Linear Disjoint Set-Union Algorithm"*, J. ACM 22 (1975).

[13] R.E. Tarjan, *"A Class of Algorithms which Require Linear Time To Maintain Disjoint Sets"*, J. Computer and System Sciences 18 (1979).

[14] R.E Tarjan, *"Amortized Computational Complexity"*, SIAM J. Alg. Discr. Meth. 6 (1985).

[15] R.E. Tarjan, J. van Leeuwen, *"Worst Case Analysis of Set-Union Algorithms"*, J. ACM 31 (1984).

[16] J. van Leeuwen, T. van der Weide, *"Alternative Path Compression Techniques"*, Techn. Rep. RUU-CS-77-3, Rijksuniversiteit Utrecht, The Netherlands.

[17] J. Westbrook, R.E. Tarjan, *"Amortized Analysis of Algorithms for Set-Union with Backtracking"*, Tech. Rep. TR-103-87, Dept. of Computer Sciences, Princeton University (1987).

A NOTE ON THE COMPUTATIONAL COMPLEXITY OF BRACKETING AND RELATED PROBLEMS

MIRKO KŘIVÁNEK
Department of Computer Science
Charles University
Malostranské nám.25,Praha 1, CS-118 00

Abstract. It is shown that the problem of finding the minimum number of bracketing transfers in order to transform one bracketing to another bracketing is an *NP*-complete problem. This problem is related to problems on random walks, planar triangulations of convex polygons and to the problem of comparison of two (labeled) rooted trees. The latter problem is studied with the connection to cluster analysis. Finally, some polynomially solvable classes of bracketing problems are obtained.

I.Introduction and background. Bracketing problems have a long history [1,10]. Though the main emphasis was mainly concentrated on enumerations problems we shall be interested in the computational complexity of evaluation of the distance between two given bracketings. Finally, using the concept of closed random walks we shall stress the connection of bracketing problems to the problem of comparison and evaluation of two labeled rooted trees. This type of problems is often investigated in cluster analysis [7]. Last section is devoted to polynomially solvable classses of bracketing problems which are analyzed by means of planar triangulations of convex polygons.

More precisely, the word w in the alphabet $\Sigma = \{(,)\}$ is said to be a *bracketing* if it is generated by the following production rules :

$$S \longrightarrow SS \mid (S) \mid \Lambda ,$$

where Λ stands for an empty word. The set of all bracketings is often called the Dycklanguage and plays an important part in the theory of formal languages [4]. The abbreviation ℓ^i, $i > 0$, $\ell \in \Sigma$, denotes $\underbrace{\ell\ldots\ell}_{i \text{ times}}$

Let $\mathcal{B}$($\mathcal{B}_n$,resp.) be a set of all bracketings over Σ (... of length n, resp.). Note that n is even. A bracketing $b' \in \mathcal{B}$ is said to be a *sub-bracketing* of b, written $b' \subset b$, if b' is a proper subword of b. The *nesting level* of a sub-bracketing b' of b is the number of different sub-bracketings of b which contain b' as their sub-bracketing. Given two bracketings $b_1, b_2 \in \mathcal{B}_n$ we say that bracketing b_2 arises from bracketing b_1 by one *bracketing transfer* if there is a sub-bracketing b of b_2 such that

$$b_1 = xby \quad \text{and either} \quad b_2 = x_1bx_2y \text{ , where } x_1x_2 = x,$$

or $b_2 = xy_1by_2$, where $y_1y_2 = y$, for $x, x_2, y, y_1 \in \Sigma^+$, $x_1, x_2 \in \Sigma^*$.

By $\beta(b_1,b_2)$ the minimum number of bracketing transfers needed to transform b_1 to b_2 will be denoted, i.e. $\beta(b_1,b_2) = j$ if there is a sequence $s_1, s_2, \ldots , s_{j+1}$ of bracketings from $\mathcal{B}_n$ such that $b_1 \equiv s_1$, $b_2 \equiv s_{j+1}$, $\beta(s_i,s_{i+1}) = 1$ for $i=1,\ldots,j$.

First we have the following straightforward lemma :

LEMMA 1. *The function β is the distance measure on $\mathcal{B}_n$ and $(\mathcal{B}_n,\beta)$ is a metric space.* □

The underlying computational problem **BR** in which lies our main interest is stated as follows :

INSTANCE : Two bracketings $b_1, b_2 \in \mathcal{B}_n$, positive integer k;
QUESTION : Does it hold that $\beta(b_1,b_2) \le k$?

Our *NP*-completeness terminology is that of [3].

II. Complexity results. First we shall prove the following.

THEOREM 1. *The problem* **BR** *is NP-complete.*

Proof. Clearly, the problem **BR** is in the class *NP*. We shall exhibit a polynomial transformation from the problem **BIN PACKING** which is known to be strongly *NP*-complete [3]. **BIN PACKING** has been introduced as follows :

INSTANCE : Positive integers $i_1,\dots,i_s,B,r$ such that $\sum_{j=1}^{s} i_j = rB$;
QUESTION : Is there a partition of $\{i_1,\dots,i_s\}$ into r classes $I_1,\dots,I_r$ such that $\sum_{j\in I_m} i_j = B$, $m = 1,\dots,r$?

Given an instance of **BIN PACKING** the instance of the problem **BR** is constructed in polynomial time by putting

$$b_1 \equiv \underbrace{(^B)^B\dots(^B)^B}_{r\ \text{times}} ,\ b_2 \equiv (^{i_1})^{i_1}(^{i_2})^{i_2}\dots(^{i_s})^{i_s} ,\ k = s - r.$$

Now, the equivalence

$\beta(b_1,b_2) = s - r$ **iff** **BIN PACKING** has "yes"-solution

is easily verified and the theorem is proved.□

Theorem 1 says that it is very unlikely that there exists a polynomial algorithm for the problem **BR**. Therefore we would like to exhibit a polynomial approximation for the problem **BR**. Notice that the proof of Theorem 1 does not exclude the posssible existence of such an algorithm. The so-called "next fit" approximation algorithm has been believed to provide a "good" polynomial approximation for **BR** since **BR** generalizes in some way the **BIN PACKING** problem. Recall that the next fit algorithm was proved to be a "good" approximation both from the worst and average case complexity viewpoint [3,5]. Formally the approximation algorithm $\mathcal{A}$ for **BR** is encoded as follows :

Algorithm $\mathcal{A}$:

(Step 1.) $s_1 := b_1;\ s_2 := b_2;$
(Step 2.) **do** $2n$ **times**
  Scan and compare current letters of s_1 and s_2;
  if they are different **then**
   {*suppose that scanned letter in* s_i *is "(". i.e.* $s_i = x(y$, $x,y \in \Sigma^*$}

(Step 3.) Find in s_2 "next" sub-bracketing b (minimal/maximal with respect to the current nesting level depending on running strategy) such that $s_2 = x)y_1by_2$, $y_1,y_2 \in \Sigma^*$;
$s_2 := xb)y_1y_2$;
endif
endo
endalgorithm.

The correctness and time analysis of the algorithm $\mathcal{A}$ is established in the following theorem :

THEOREM 2. *Algorithm* $\mathcal{A}$ *runs in polynomial time and solves the problem* **BR** *using* $O(n)$ *bracketing transfers.*

Proof. Rough time estimate for Step 3 is $O(n)$. This yields $O(n^2)$ time complexity of the algorithm $\mathcal{A}$. The algorithm $\mathcal{A}$ transforms the bracketing b_1 into the bracketing b_2. This is observed from the fact that that eventually both words s_1,s_2 produced by $\mathcal{A}$ are equal. As possibly both b_1,b_2 and consequently s_1,s_2 are changed the sequences b_1 ---> s_2 and s_2 ---> b_2 provide the sequence of bracketing transfers required for transforming b_1 to b_2. In the worst case the number of bracketing transfers is proportional to the corresponding number of sub-bracketings of b_1 (b_2, resp.) and thus is $O(n)$.□

Reamark. Using so-called balanced search trees [9] as a data structure for the representation of bracketings, Step 3 can be implemented in $O(\log n)$time. Asymptotically $O(n\log n)$ upper bound is the best possible for polynomially solvable instances of **BR** since the well known **SORTING** problem is linearly transformable (assuming an unary representation of input numbers) to the following instance of **BR**:

$$b_1 = ()(())\ldots(^n)^n,\ b_2 = (^{x_1})^{x_1}(^{x_2})^{x_2}\ldots(^{x_n})^{x_n},$$

$$\text{where } \{x_1,\ldots,x_n\} = \{1,\ldots n\}$$

constitute an instance of **SORTING**. Recall that **SORTING** is solvable in $\Theta(n\log n)$time [9].□

Let us deal with the question how good the approximation produced by $\mathcal{A}$ is. Regretablly, no constant bounded worst case error ratio is guaranteed.

THEOREM 3. *Algorithm* $\mathcal{A}$ *has a* $\Theta(n)$ *worst case error ratio.*

Proof. Let $b_1 = xy$, $b_2 = yx$, $x = ()$, $y = ()(\underbrace{()\ldots()}_{O(n)\text{ times}})$. In this case $\beta(b_1,b_2) = 1$. However algorithm $\mathcal{A}$ constructs a sequence of $O(n)$ bracketing transfers regardless of the nesting level of the "next" sub-bracketing in Step 3.□

The failure of the algorithm $\mathcal{A}$ is due to the fact that $\mathcal{A}$ does not search for identical sub-bracketings in b_1 and b_2. Therefore its behavior could be slightly improved by preprocessing, i.e. by decomposing b_1 and b_2 into their corresponding sub-bracketings, say , maximal up to inclusion. This approach supposes setting up a data structure where nesting level and sub-bracketing can be directly accessed. This way we avoid pathological behavior of $\mathcal{A}$ on the current nesting level but complexity problems remain unchanged when dealing with identical sub-bracketings on different nesting levels.

Let us conclude this section by a remark that some preliminary calculations indicate that algorithm $\mathcal{A}$ also has the average case error ratio of order $\Theta(n)$. The details will appear in a full paper.

III. Random walks and rooted trees. The aim of this section is to discuss a 1-1 correspondence between bracketings, random walks and rooted trees. It will enable us to extend the results of the previous section to trees embedded to the plane. Our exposition is based on [6].

Random walk of length n is $(n+1)$-tuple $\Phi = (\phi(0),\phi(1),\ldots,\phi(n))$ where ϕ is a mapping to non-negative integers such that

$$\phi(0) = \phi(n) = 0,\ \Phi(i) \in \{\phi(i-1)-1,\phi(i-1)+1\},\ i = 1,\ldots,n.$$

LEMMA 2. *There is a one-to-one correspondence between $\mathcal{B}_n$ and the set of all random walks of length n.*

Proof. Let $b \in \mathcal{B}_n$. Define a random walk Φ of length n as follows

$$\phi(i) = \begin{cases} 0, & \text{if } i \in \{0,n\} \\ \phi(i-1)+1, & \text{if the } i\text{-th letter of } b \text{ is "("} \\ \phi(i-1)-1, & \text{if the } i\text{-th letter of } b \text{ is ")".} \end{cases}$$

The correspondence is visualized on Figure 1.□

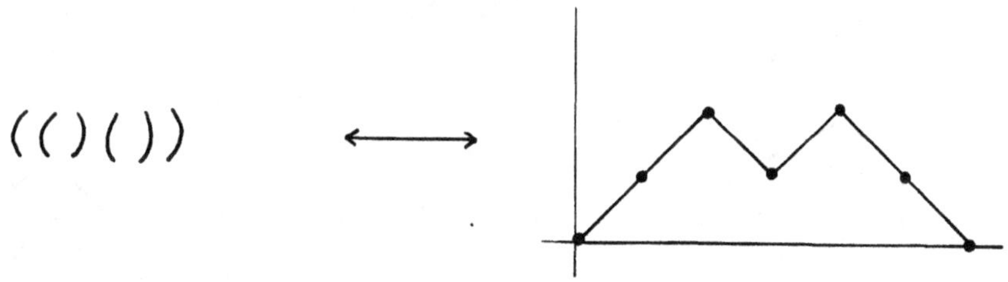

Figure 1.

Let T be a rooted tree on n vertices embedded into the plane. Let us consider a topological ordering $\omega_T = v_0v_1\ldots v_{2n-2}$ of its vertices which is recursively defined as follows :

(1) If $T = \{v_0\}$ then $\omega_T = v_0$,

(2) If T has a root v_0 with the subtrees $T_1,T_2,\ldots,T_k$ then $\omega_T = v_0\omega_{T_1}v_0\omega_{T_2}v_0\ldots\omega_{T_k}v_0$.

The set of all trees on n vertices with the root v_0 embedded into the plane will be denoted by $\mathcal{T}_n$. Let $T_1, T_2 \in \mathcal{T}_n$. T_1 is said to be obtained from T_2 by one *edge rotation* if

$$T_1 \approx T_2 - uv + uw, \text{ where } uv \in E(T_2) \ \& \ uw \notin E(T_2),$$

where symbol $\approx$ expresses that both trees have the same topology of plane embedding, i.e. they are topologically isomorphic. The *edge rotation distance* $\rho(T_1,T_2)$ between T_1 and T_2 is defined as the minimum number of edge rotations needed to be performed on T_1 in order to obtain a tree which is topologically isomorphic to T_2. Notice that the root v_0 is supposed to be fixed. Here the edge rotation distance is a special case of edge rotation distance defined between isomorphic classes of graphs (or trees). Recently in [8] the underlyingdecision problem for latter problems was shown to be *NP*-complete. Our aim is to extend this result for the computation of edge rotation distance ρ between topologically isomorphic classes of trees. Note that topologically isomorphic trees correspond to derivation trees for different bracketings from $\mathcal{B}_n$. This connection clarifies the following observation :

LEMMA 3. *The pair $(\mathcal{T}_n,\rho)$ forms a metric space.*□

LEMMA 4. *There is a one-to-one correspondence between $\mathcal{T}_n$ and random walks of length* $2n-2$.

Proof. Let $T \in \mathcal{T}_n$. Let $d(v_i,v_0)$ be the distance of the i-th vertex v_i of ω from v_0. The corresponding random walk Φ is defined as follows

$$\phi(i) = \begin{cases} 0, & \text{if } i \in \{0,2n-2\} \\ d(v_i,v_0), & \text{otherwise.} \end{cases}$$

The correspondence is depicted on Figure 2.□

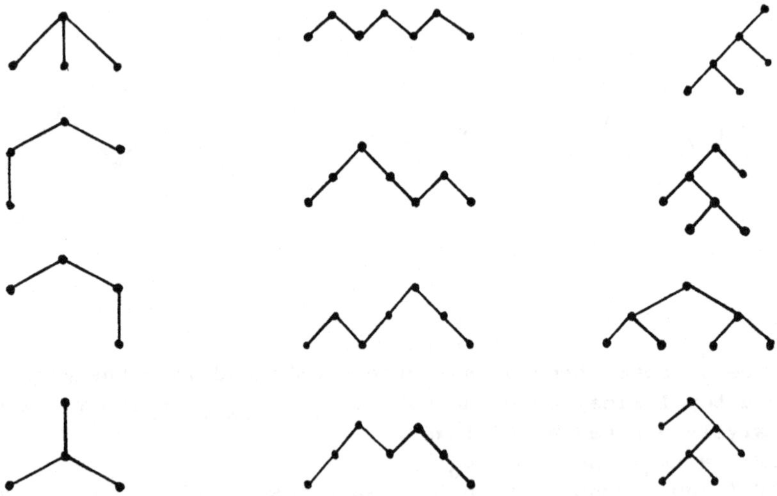

Figure 2.

Now we are ready to prove the following :

THEOREM 4. *Given* $T_1,T_2 \in \mathcal{T}_n$, *the underlying decision problem of computing* $\rho(T_1,T_2)$ *is NP-complete.*

Proof. Choose $b_1,b_2 \in \mathcal{B}_n$ and by virtue of Lemma 4 consider two corresponding trees $T_1,T_2 \in \mathcal{T}_n$. By the aid of Lemma 2 and Lemma 4 we have $\beta(b_1,b_2) = \rho(T_1,T_2)$. It implies that graphs $\mathcal{G}_1=(\mathcal{B}_n,\mathcal{E}_1)$ and $\mathcal{G}_2=(\mathcal{T}_n,\mathcal{E}_2)$, where $\{b_1,b_2\} \in \mathcal{E}_1$ iff $\beta(b_1,b_2) = 1$ and $\{T_1,T_2\} \in \mathcal{E}_2$ iff $\rho(T_1,T_2). = 1$, are isomorphic. The use of Theorem 1 completes the proof.□

Trees from $\mathcal{T}_n$ are very often constructed by hierarchical clustering procedures. The study of the consensus between these trees is one of the most important problems encountered in cluster analysis [7]. However, special attention is mostly paid to binary trees [2]. The concept of random walks can be used for proving similar results for binary trees, too.

Let $T \in \mathcal{T}_{2n-1}$ be a binary rooted tree on n leaves, i.e. having all internal vertices of degree 3 except of the root v_0 which is of degree 2. A given binary rooted tree T induces a topological ordering $\omega_T = v_0v_1...v_{2n-2}$ which is defined recursively as follows :

(1) If $T = \{v_0\}$ then $\omega_T = v_0$,

(2) If T has a root v_0 with the subtrees T_1,T_2 then $\omega_T = \omega_{T_1}\omega_{T_2}v_0$.

The set of all binary trees on n leaves and with the root v_0 embedded into the plane will be denoted by $\mathcal{D}_n$. Given $T_1,T_2 \in \mathcal{D}_n$ we say that T_2 is obtained by one *(binary) subtree rotation* if

$$T_2 \approx T_1 - \{\{u_1,v_2\},\{u_1,w\}\} + \{\{u_2,v\},\{u_2,w\}\}$$

where

$$\{u_1,v\},\{u_1,w\} \in E(T_1) \text{ and } \{u_2,v\},\{u_2,w\} \notin E(T_1).$$

Notice that u_2 is a leaf. The *(binary) subtree rotation distance* δ is defined as the minimum number of subtree rotations required to obtain a tree T_2 from T_1. Similarly as in the general case the following propositions hold

LEMMA 5. *The pair* $(\mathcal{D}_n,\delta)$ *forms a metric space.*□

LEMMA 6. *There is a one-to-one correspondence between binary rooted trees on* n *leaves and random walks of length* $2n-2$.

Proof. Let $T \in \mathcal{D}_n$, $\omega_T = v_0...v_{2n-2}$. The corresponding random walk Φ is defined as follows (c.f.Figure 2):

$$\phi(i) = \begin{cases} 0, & \text{if } i \in \{0,2n-2\} \\ \phi(i-1)+1, & \text{if } v_i \text{ is a leaf in } T \\ \phi(i-1)-1, & \text{if } v_i \text{ is an internal vertex in } T. \end{cases}$$ □

Combining Lemma 2, Lemma 6 and Theorem 1 we get

THEOREM 5. *Given $T_1,T_2 \in \mathcal{D}_n$, the underlying decision problem of computing $\delta(T_1,T_2)$ is NP-complete.*□

IV. Labeled rooted trees. In this section a polynomially solvable classes of bracketing problems will be explored by means of labeled rooted trees and planar triangulations of convex polygons. Let $T \in \mathcal{T}_n$ and let ω_T be its topological ordering. Let us define on the set of vertices of T a labeling ξ, $\xi:\{v_0,\ldots,v_n\} \longrightarrow \{0,\ldots,n\}$ as follows

$$\xi(x) = \begin{cases} 0, & \text{if } x \equiv v_0 \\ i, & \text{if vertex x occurs as the } i\text{-th new vertex in } \omega_T . \end{cases}$$

Let us suppose that we are given a fixed labeling ξ on $\{v_0,\ldots,v_n\}$ Let $\mathcal{T}_n^{\xi}$ denote the set of all labeled trees on n vertices with the root v_0 and with same labeling ξ. Now we can define a subtree rotation distance ρ^{ξ} formally as in the previous case with the only exception that now the labeling ξ must be preserved. Note that now we deal with the very special case of previous general problem since the changes in the structure of trees caused by subtree rotations locally depend on labels of vertices. This observation justifies the following theorem :

THEOREM 6. *Given $T_1,T_2 \in \mathcal{T}_n^{\xi}$, the problem of the computation of ρ^{ξ} is polynomially solvable.*

Proof. Let us consider the following algorithm :

(Step 1.) **do** traverse the tree T_1 using so-called breath-first search
(Step 2.) **if** childrens of current vertex of T_1 and T_2 are diffferent **then** update locally T_1 by T_2
endo

The loop involved in Step 1 requires $O(n)$ time , Step 2 can be implemented in $O(\log n)$time using search trees as data structures for the fast search and update in T_1 and T_2.□

The another type of bracketing problems can be described by means of planar triangulations of convex polygons,cf.[1,11]. In this case we deal with so-called labeled bracketings. Each labeled n-bracketing is obtained by putting brackets in the product $x_1. \ldots .x_n$ of labels in such a way that it corresponds to multiplications— each time of exactly two labels. By a *planar triangulation* of a convex n-gon we mean a set of diagonals that partition its interior into triangles.

LEMMA 7. *There is a one-to-one correspondence between labeled n-bracketings and planar triangulations of convex $(n+1)$-gon.*

Proof. Figure 3 clearly explains the correspondence.□

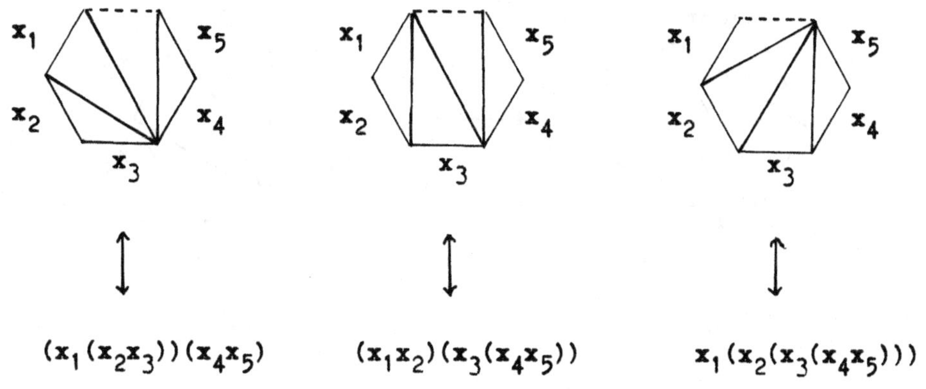

Figure 3.

Now, we shall define the distance measure between two labeled n-bracketings with the aid of triangulations. Two triangulations T_1, T_2 have distance 1, written $\tau(T_1, T_2) = 1$, if one triangulation from the other one can be obtained by one *diagonal flip*, i.e. by converting a diagonal to oposite diagonal of the quadrilateral which is determined by two triangles sharing the first diagonal in common, see Figure 4.

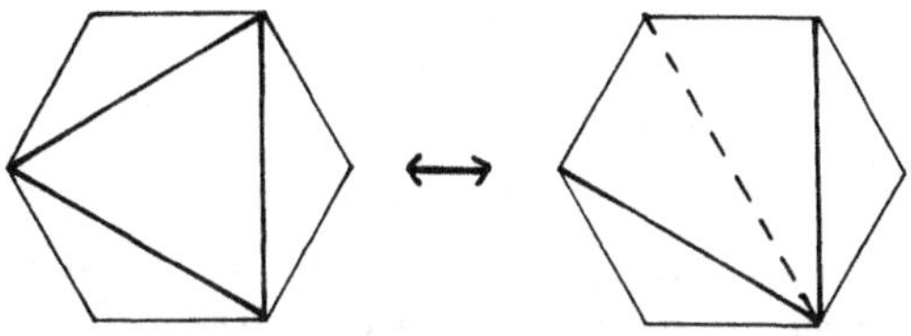

Figure 4.

We would like to emphasise the other interesting connection of diagonal flips on triangulations and rotations in trees. Clearly, any labeled n-bracketing can be represented by a rooted binary tree with labeled vertices, cf. Figure 5. Using triangulation representation diagonal flips are exactly *rotations* inbinary search trees which are thoroughly studied in the theory of data structures, cf. [9].

Note that both diagonal flips and rotation preserves the fixed labeling from left to right in planar embedding. Let us define the distance measure τ between planar triangulations under the fixed labeling $x_1 \dots x_n$ as the minimum number of diagonal flips required to convert one triangulation to another. It will enable us to develop a polynomial algorithm for the computation of τ.

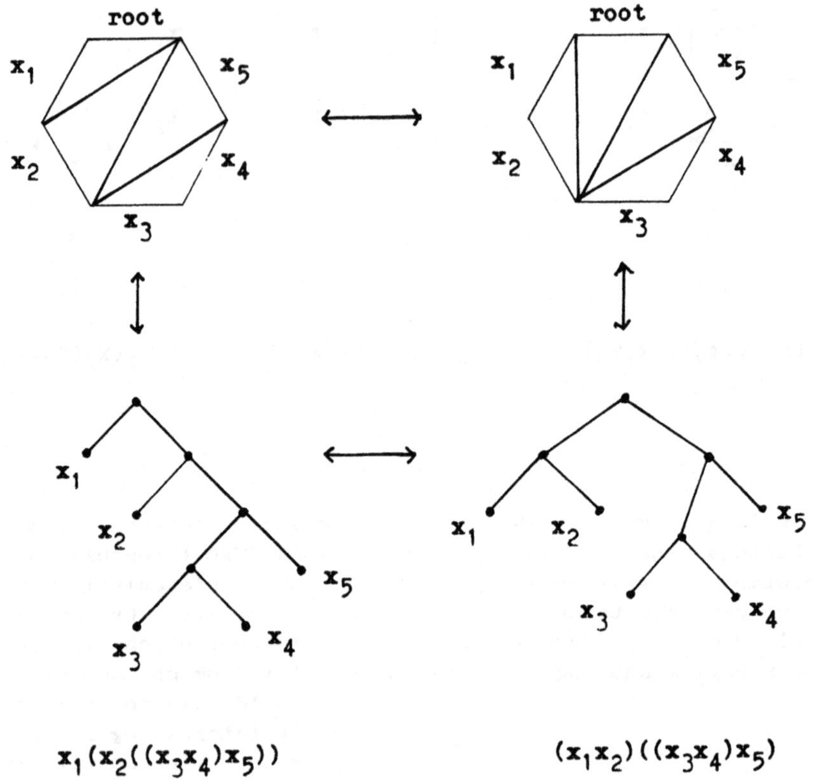

Figure 5.

THEOREM 7. *Given two planar triangulations T_1, T_2 of a convex $(n+1)$-gon the distance $\tau(T_1, T_2)$ is computable in polynomial time.*

Proof. Let us consider the following algorithm which constructs a shortest sequence of triangulations between T_1, T_2:

(Step 1.) **for** each diagonal d of T_2 **do**
Determine $i(d) \equiv \#$ of intersections of d with diagonals in T_1; Set up a data structure $\wp$ that mainatain this information;
endfor

(Step 2.) **while** $T_1 \neq T_2$ **do**
Find a diagonal d in T_2 with minimum positive $i(d)$;
In T_1 perform diagonal flips of diagonals that intersect d creating a "new" T_1 that has one more diagonal in common with T_2 than the "old" T_1 had;
Update $\wp$
endwhile

Now, we are to verify the correctness and estimate the time efficiency of our algorithm. Clearly, the main loop of Step 1 is repeated $O(n)$ times. Using balanced hierarchical representation of convex polygons (in fact (2,4)-trees of [9]) for $\mathcal{P}$ we observe that Step 1 consumes $O(n\log n)$ time. The loop in Step 2 is executed $O(n)$ times since the maximum distance of two triangulations is $\leq 2n-10$, see [11]. The operations on $\mathcal{P}$ take $O(\log n)$ time. Hence the overall upper time bound is $O(n\log n)$. On the other hand **SET EQUALNESS** problem which cannot be solved in $o(n\log n)$ time [9] constitute a special case of an input instance of our algorithm (in case where $T_1 \equiv T_2$). Hence our algorithm is assymptotically optimal. The correctness of the algorithm follows from the fact that there exists a shortest sequence of triangulations converting T_1 to T_2 which never flips the common diagonals and which continues by a diagonal flip that creates one more diagonal in common of T_2 and "new" T_1 .□

REFERENCES

[1] L.COMTET: Advanced combinatorics. D Reidel, Boston 1974.

[2] K.CULIK II,D.WOOD :A note on some tree similarity measures, Information Processing Letters, 15(1982),39-42.

[3] M.R.GAREY,D.S.JOHNSON : Computers and Intractability. W.H.Freeman, San Francisco,1979.

[4] M.A.HARRISON: Introduction to formal language theory. Addison-Wesley,1978.

[5] M.HOFRI: Probabilistic analysis of algorithms. Springer,1987.

[6] R.KEMP: Fundamentals of the average case analysis of particular algorithms.Willey-Teubner, Stuttgart, 1984.

[7] M.KRIVANEK: The computational complexity of the consensus between hierarchical trees. Proc IMYCS'84, Smolenice, 119-125.

[8] M.KRIVANEK: A note on the computational complexity of computing the edge rotation distance between graphs. Cas.pest.mat. 113(1988),52-55.

[9] K.MEHLHORN: Data structures and algorithms, Vol.1 and 3, Springer,1984.

[10] SCHRODER: Vier ccombinatorische Probleme,Z.fur M.Phys.,15(1870), 361-376.

[11] D.D.SLEATOR,R.E.TARJAN,W.P.THURSTON: Rotation distance, triangulations, and hyperbolic geometry. Proc ACM STOC(1986),122-135.

POSTORDER HIERARCHY FOR PATH COMPRESSIONS AND SET UNION

Martin Loebl and Jaroslav Nešetřil
Department of Applied Mathematics (KAM), Charles University
Prague

In this note we introduce several variants of the notion of the postorder and we relate it to the Systems of Compressions of paths in a tree and to the Set Union problem. Although most of these definitions appeared earlier we feel a necessity to unify and to compare these various approaches in order to clarify a confusion which appeared already in the existing literature (compare /1/, /2/, /4/). This paper is a pendant to our papers /2/ and /3/.

§ 1 Basic definitions

Let $T = (V,E)$ be an arbitrary rooted tree. We use selfexplanatory notions father, ancestor, son and descendant of a vertex according to the common usage (see e.g. /1/, /5/). A vertex is called a leaf if it has no sons. Let x be a vertex of T. Then T_x is a subtree of T formed by all descendants of x; x is considered as the root of T_x.

The following is the central notion of this paper (see /1/,/5/ for the historical remarks):

1.1. Definition

Let T be a tree. Let $x_1, x_2, \ldots, x_k$ be a path of T such that x_i is a haf of T. The <u>path compression</u> (PC for short) $C = (x_1, x_2, \ldots x_k)$ is an operation that modifies T as follows:

(i) the edges (x_i, x_{i+1}), $i = 1, \ldots, k-1$, are deleted,

(ii) we make each vertex x_i, $i = 1, 2, \ldots, k-1$, a son of x_k,

(iii) we delete all new sons of x_k with degree 1 which may occur (particularly x_1 is deleted).

The vertex x_k is called the <u>root</u> of C. We also say that C <u>starts</u> from x_1. The <u>length</u> of the compressions c is equal to $k - 1$. It is denoted by $|C|$.

1.2. Definition

A sequence $S = (C_1, \ldots, C_m)$ of PC's on a tree T is called <u>Path Compression System</u> (PCS) if

(i) Each C_i is a PC on the tree T_i obtained from T after the path

compressions $C_1, \ldots, C_{i-1}$ have been executed (with $T_1 \equiv T$ for $i=1$).
(ii) From each end-vertex of T starts exactly one PC belonging to S.

The length of S, $|S|$, is defined as $\sum |C_i|$. To simplify the notation we denote by i the end-vertex of T where the path compression C_i starts. If (ii) is replaced by the condition that from each end-vertex of T goes at most one PC then S is called an Incomplete Path Compression System. Now we give two easy propositions about the structure of PCS´s.

1.3 Proposition

Let $S = (C_1, C_2)$ be an incomplete PCS on a tree T and $V(C_1) \cap V(C_2) = \emptyset$. Then $S' = (C_2, C_2)$ is also an incomplete PCS on T and the trees obtained from T after S or S´ have been executed are equal.

□

1.4. Proposition

Let $S = (C_1, C_2, \ldots, C_m)$ and $S' = (D_1, D_2, \ldots, D_n)$ be two incomplete PCS´s on a tree T and let the following conditions are satisfied:

(i) $\{C_1, C_2, \ldots, C_m\} \subseteq \{D_1, \ldots, D_n\}$; explicitely, for a choice of indexes $i_1 < i_2 < \ldots < i_k$ the set $\{D_1, D_2, \ldots, D_n\}$ is the disjoint union of $\{C_1, C_2, \ldots, C_m\}$ and $\{D_{i_1}, D_{i_2}, \ldots, D_{i_k}\}$;

(ii) If $D_i = C_{i'}$, $D_j = C_{j'}$ and the indexes satisfy $i > y$ and $i' < j'$ then $D_i \cap D_j = \emptyset$,

(iii) If $D_i = C_{i'}$, $D_j = D_{i_{j'}}$, and $i > j$ then $D_i \cap D_j = \emptyset$.

Then $S'' = (C_i, C_2, \ldots, C_m, D_{i_1}, D_{i_2}, \ldots, D_{i_k})$ is an incomplete PCS on T and the trees obtained from T after S´ or S´´ have been executed are equal.

Proof

We proceed by induction on n. If n = 1 then 1.4. is clearly true.
Let $n \geq 2$. If $C_1 = D_1$ then we use induction assumption for $(C_2, \ldots C_m)$ and $(D_2, \ldots, D_n)$.
Thus let $C_1 = D_\ell$ It follows from (ii) and (iii) that $D_\ell \cap D_i = \emptyset$ for $i = 1, \ldots, \ell - 1$. Using $(\ell - 1)$ times Proposition 3 we get two trees obtained from T after the execution of the systems S´ and $(D_\ell, D_1, D_2, \ldots, D_{\ell-1}, D_{\ell+1}, \ldots, D_n)$ are equal. We apply the induction assumption. □

1.5. Definition

A Set Union System (SUS) on a tree T is a sequence of the form $(x_1, C_1, \ldots, C_{n_1}, x_2, C_{n_1+1}, \ldots, C_{n_2}, x_3, \ldots, x_m, C_{n_{m-1}+1},$

$\ldots, C_{n_m}$),

where $x_1, x_2, \ldots, x_m$ are vertices of T such that if $i < j$ then x_j is not a descendant of x_i, $(C_1, \ldots, C_{n_1}, C_{n_1+1}, \ldots, C_{n_m})$ is a PCS on T, and for each $i \in \{n_j + 1, \ldots, n_{j+1}\}$, the compression C_i roots in x_{j+1}.

Remark: Note that possibly $n_i = 0$ for some i. A connection between PCS and SUS is simply described using "raising roots condition" in /4/.

1.6. Definition

A Postorder on a tree T is a linear order of the nodes of T induced by a linear order of the sons of each vertex.

Remark:

A given tree T may have many postorders. Note that a given postorder can be visualized by a planar embedding and the left-right rule.

This completes the list of the basic definitions. The idea of the postorder may be combined with Path Compressions Systems and with Set Union Systems in various ways. We list three possibilities which refine each other and thus may be regarded as a hierarchy.

1.7. Definition

A Set Union System $(x_1, C_1, \ldots, C_{n_1}, x_2, C_{n_1+1}, \ldots, C_{n_2}, x_3, \ldots, C_{n_m})$ on a tree T is called Fixed Postorder Set Union System (FPSUS) if $(1, 2, \ldots, n_1, n_1 + 1, \ldots, n_2, \ldots, n_m)$ is a linear order of the end-vertices of T induced by some (fixed) postorder of T.

1.8. Definition

A Set Union System $S = (x_1, C_1, \ldots, C_{n_1}, x_2, C_{n_1+1}, \ldots, C_{n_2}, x_3, \ldots, C_{n_m})$ on a tree T is called On Line Postorder Set Union System (OLPSUS) if, for each vertex x_i, $i = 1, 2, \ldots, m$, the following condition is satisfied:

Let $(C_{i_1}, C_{i_2}, \ldots, C_{i_{p(i)}})$ be all the path compressions from S satisfying

(i) $i_j \in T_{x_i}$, for each $j = 1, \ldots, p(i)$,

(ii) $i_j > n_{i-1}$, for each $j = 1, \ldots, p(i)$,

(iii) $i_j < i_{j'}$ whenever $1 \leq j < j' \leq p(i)$.

Then $(i_1, \ldots, i_{p(i)})$ is a linear order (of some end - vertices of T_{x_i}) induced by a (fixed and independent on i) postorder of T.

1.9. Definition

A path compression system $S = (C_1, \ldots, C_m)$ on a tree T is called Strong Postorder Path Compression System (SPPCS) if

(i) $(1, 2, \ldots, m)$ is a linear order of the end-vertices of T induced by a fixed postorder of T,

(ii) Let the root of a compression C_i, $i \leq m$, be a vertex x of T. Then all the compressions C_j such that $j < i$ and $j \in T_x$ have the root in a descendant of x.

1.10. Definition

A path compression system $S = (C_1, \ldots, C_m)$ on a tree T is called Postorder Path Comprelssion System (PPCS) if $(1, 2, \ldots, m)$ is a linear order of end-vertices of T induced by a fixed postorder of T.

§ 2 Results

The hierarchy of the above defined systems FPSUS, OLPSUS, WPPCS and PPCS is established in the following propositions.

2.1. Proposition

Each FPSUS is OLPSUS.

Proof. If follows directly by comparing the definitions 1.5 and 1.6. □

2.2. Proposition

Each SPPCS is PPCS.

Proof. It follows directly from the definitions 1.9. and 1.10. □

2.3. Proposition

Let $S = (x_1, C_1, \ldots, C_{n_1}, x_2, C_{n_1+1}, \ldots, x_3, \ldots, C_{n_m})$ be an OLPSUS on a tree T. Let $(\pi(1), \pi(2), \ldots, \pi(n_m))$ be the linear order of the end-vertices of T induced by the postorder of T which correspond to the OLPSUS S (see Definition 1.8). Then $(C_{\pi(1)}, C_{\pi(2)}, \ldots, C_{\pi(n_m)})$ is a SPPCS on T.

Proof

We denote by T_i' the tree obtained from T after executing $C_1, C_2, \ldots, C_{i-1}$.

Let us consider the following situation: - $i \in \{1, \ldots, n_m\}$

- the root of a compression $C_{\pi(i)}$ is a vertex $\overline{x}$ of T.

- $\pi(j)$ is an end-vertex of $T_{\overline{x}}$.

For such pair i, j we show the following three statements:

(1) If $\pi(j) < \pi(i)$ then $C_{\pi(j)}$ roots in a descendant of $\overline{x}$.

(2) If $j < i$ then $\pi(j) < \pi(i)$,

(3) If $\pi(j) < \pi(i)$ and $j > i$ then $C_{\pi(i)} \cap C_{\pi(j)} = \emptyset$.

ad(1): It follows from the definition of SUS.

ad(2): For a contradiction let $\pi(j) > \pi(i)$. By (1) the compressions C_ℓ, $\ell \in T_{\overline{x}}$ and $\ell < \pi(i)$, root above $\overline{x}$. Hence $\pi(j)$ is an end-vertex of $[T'_{\pi(i)}]_{\overline{x}}$. But $j < i$ which contradicts the definition of OLPSUS, as $C_{\pi(j)}$ should be executed in $T'_{\pi(i)}$ instead of $C_{\pi(i)}$.

ad(3): For a contradiction let there be a vertex in common. Let x' be the root of $C_{\pi(j)}$.

As $C_{\pi(i)} \cap C_{\pi(j)} \neq \emptyset$ we have that $\pi(i) \in [T'_{\pi(j)}]_{x'}$.

However this contradicts (as above) the definition of OLPSUS, as $C_{\pi(i)}$ should be executed in $T'_{\pi(j)}$ instead of $C_{\pi(j)}$.

This finishes the proof of (1), (2) and (3) .

Continuing in the main line of the proof we show first that $(C_{\pi(1)}, C_{\pi(2)}, \ldots, C_{\pi(n_m)})$ is a PCS on T. For a contradiction suppose that i_0 is minimal such that $C_{\pi(i_0)}$ is not a PC in the tree T_{i_0} obtained from T after executing compressions $C_{\pi(1)}, C_{\pi(2)}, \ldots, C_{\pi(i_0-1)}$.

Let x' be the root of $C_{\pi(i_0)}$.

Let $(\pi(j_0), \pi(j_0+1), \ldots, \pi(i_0-1))$ be the postorder inherited from T of the end-vertices of $T_{x'}$ preceeding $\pi(i_0)$ (it has this interval form by the definitionn of the postorder).

We have by (1) and by the minimality of i_0 that the system $S_1 = (C_{\pi(j_0)}, C_{\pi(j_0+1)}, \ldots, C_{\pi(i_0-1)})$ is an incomplete PCS on $T_{x'}$. Let $S_2 = (C_i;\ i < \pi(i_0)$ and i is an end-vertex of $T_{x'})$.

By (1) S_2 is also an incomplete PCS on $T_{x'}$.

Further if $j_0 \leq j \leq i_0 - 1$ then the compression $C_{\pi(j)}$ belongs to S_2 by (2). Hence the set $\{C_i;\ i < \pi(i_0)$ and i is an end - vertex of $T_{x'}\}$ coincides with the set $\{C_{\pi(j_0)}, \ldots, C_{\pi(i_0-1)}\} \cup \{C_{\pi(i)};\ \pi(i)$ is an end-vertex of $T_{x'}$, $i > i_0$ and $\pi(i) < \pi(i_0)\}$.

Moreover by (3) we have that both S_2 and S_1 satisfy the conditions of Proposition 1.4. (for S and S′).

Finally we proceed as follows:

Let $T^1_{x'}$ be the tree obtained from $T_{x'}$ after executing S_1. Let $T^2_{x'}$ be the tree obtained from $T_{x'}$ after executing S_2. As $T^2_{x'} = [T'_{\pi(i)}]_{x'}$ we have that $C_{\pi(i_0)}$ is a PC in $T^2_{x'}$, i.e. $C_{\pi(i_0)}$ is a path in $T^2_{x'}$ from $\pi(i_0)$ to x'.

Observe that if we apply the above statement (3) for a pair $i > i_0$ then we get the following:

If $i_0 < i$, $\pi(i) < \pi(i_0)$ and $\pi(i)$ is a leaf of $T_{x'}$ then

$C_{\pi(i)} \cap C_{\pi(i_0)} = \emptyset$. Combining this with Proposition 1.4. we get that the path in $T^1_{x'}$, from $\pi(i_0)$ to x' is equal to the path in $T^2_{x'}$ from $\pi(i_0)$ to x' (which equals $C_{\pi(i_0)}$).
Hence $C_{\pi(i_0)}$ is a PC in $T^1_{x'} = [T_{i_0}]_{x'}$ which contradicts the choice of $\pi(i_0)$.
Hence we proved that $(C_{\pi(1)}, \ldots, C_{\pi(n_m)})$ is a PCS on T.
Property (ii) of the definition of SPPCS follows from (1). □

The fact that there are several postorder systems caused some confusions. Now we list the results.

2.4. Hart and Sharir conjectured in /1/ that there is a linear upper bound for maximal length of PPCS´s. As far we know this is stil an open problem.

2.5. In Theorem 1 /2/ we announced "postorder set union systems have linear length". Moreover we assumed originally that this solves the above conjecture of Hart and Sharir. Using the terminology developed here we may reformulate Theorem 1 of /2/ as follows: There is a linear upper bound for the maximal length of OLPSUS´s. This is proved in /3/ where we derive a linear upper bound for more general WPPCS ´s.

2.6. J.Lucas /4/ obtained independently a linear upper bound for the maximum length of FPSUS´s (solved already by a more general Theorem 1 /2/).

2.7. We mention, finally, that in /2/ we introduced more complex systems called Local Postorder Set Union Systems and we proved that the existence of linear upper bound for the maximal length of these systems cannot be proved or disproved in Finite Set Theory.

Reference.

/1/ S.Hart, M.Sharir: Non-linearity of Davenport-Schinzel sequences and of generalized path compression schemes, Combinatorica 6, 2(1986), 151-177; see also proc. 24th FOCS Symposium (1985), 313-319
/2/ M.Loebl, J.Nešetřil: Linearity and Unprovability of the set union problem strategies, STOC (1988), 360-366
/3/ M.Loebl, J.Nešetřil: (to appear)
/4/ J.M.Lucas: Postorder disjoint set union is linear, Rutgers Technical Report (September 1988)
/5/ R.E.Tarjan: Application of Path Compression on Balanced Trees, J.ACM 26 (1979), 690-715.

The Convex Hull Problem on Grids
Computational and Combinatorial Aspects

Kristel Unger
Karl-Weierstraß-Institut für Mathematik
Mohrenstr. 39, Berlin, DDR-1086

1. Introduction

For some years research in the field of computational geometry has became more intensive. First of all, this is caused by increased applications. We refer to computer graphics, CAD/CAM at all, digital image processing and layout verification as fields of application. A great manifold of articles, but also of monographs, e.g. /PS/, are proofs of this intensive interest. In /PS/ one finds an extensive list of references.

One of the most investigated problems is the problem of the planar convex hull. The special interest to this problem is caused by its simplicity which allows to investigate exemplary certain aspects. On the other hand, this interest is also caused by different applications.

Usually, the problem is given as following.

Problem R:

Given a set P of n points from $\mathbb{R}^2$, the two-dimensional Euclidean space, find its convex hull as enumeration of the engaged points in clockwise order.

Theorem 1:

Problem R can be solved by $\Theta(n \log n)$ comparisons and $\Theta(n)$ multiplications in the worst case. Algorithms solving problem R with this effort are time optimal in the model of binary decision trees, quadratic resp. linear decision trees and in the model of algebraic computation trees, too. □

These are well known results which can be found in /PS/. Now, it is a general trend of research in computational geometry to specialize already well known problems by reasonable restrictions. Chiefly, these restrictions are motivated by application. E.g. problem R was investigated under the conditon that the point set P forms a simple polygon /PS/. This condition is reasonable from the angle of application in layout verification. Generally, the investigation of such restricted problems consists of three parts:

- Is the restricted problem relevant to applications?
- What is the complexity of algorithms solving the general problem under the restriction? Are there better algorithms?
- Are lower bounds known for the general problem valid under the restriction?

We'll investigate these three aspects in the case of an restricted problem defined in section 2. Finally, we refer to two further restrictions of problem R (Section 8). Our main interest is directed to lower bounds of all three problems in different models of computation.

2. A special convex hull problem

Problem $Z(m_1,m_2)$:

Given a set P of n points from $G = [0,m_1) \times [0,m_2) \cap \mathbb{Z}^2$, in which m_1, m_2 are positive integers depending on n, find the convex hull of P as enumeration of the engaged points in clockwise order. $m_1m_2 \geq n$.

We call the set $\{i\} \times ([0,m_2)\cap\mathbb{Z})$ with $i \in [0,m_1)\cap\mathbb{Z}$ column i and analogously the set $([0,m_1)\cap\mathbb{Z}) \times \{j\}$ with $j \in [0,m_2)\cap\mathbb{Z}$ row j. The condition $m_1m_2 \geq n$ ensures that all n points can be placed in the grid G.

This problem means all cases of application in which the input data are significantly discrete, i.e. the input data are integer multiples of a constant like e.g. the layout constant or the scanning constant of a camera. The field of view has finite dimensions. According with this, fields of application are the layout verification and the processing of digital images. Compare this approach with those of Karlsson and Overmars /KO/, /O/ which refer to the same field of application. The problem of the convex hull as defined in problem $Z(m_1,m_2)$ seems to be especially important in the area of digital image processing. Observe that the concept of orthogonal convex hulls /KO/ is more interesting in the field of layout verification. We are on the opinion, that both concepts are interesting in its own rights. At least, they differ much from each other.

Now, we will give an upper bound, i.e. we will investigate algorithms solving problem $Z(m_1,m_2)$. We derive such algorithms from algorithms, solving the general problem, by a very simple fact. Observe that we can reduce P to $P' := P_m \cup P_M$ with $p = (x,y) \in P_m$ iff $p \in P$ and for all $(x,y') \in P$ $y \leq y'$ and analogously $p = (x,y) \in P_M$ iff $p \in P$ and for all $(x,y') \in P$ $y \geq y'$. P' consists of the upper and lower points of any column. Other points than those of P' cannot take part in the convex hull. (The convex hull is marked by "-", the points of P' are marked by "x" in the following illustration.)

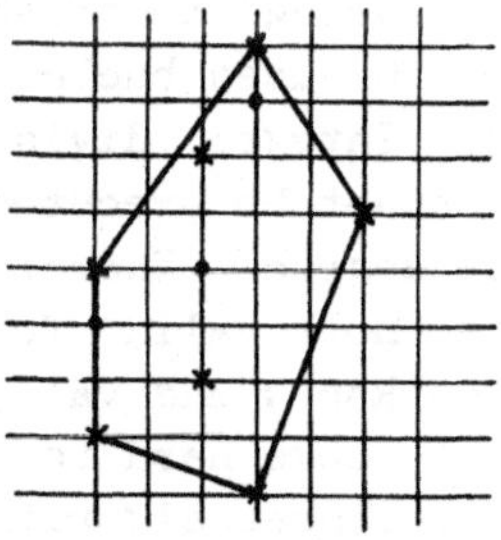

The costs of this approach consist of the costs reducing P to P' and constructing the convex hull of P'. Of course, we will use a time

optimal algorithm for this later step. Determining P' costs $O(n\log n_1)$ comparisons where $n_1 = \min(n, 2m_1)$. n_1 is an upper bound for the size of P'. From theorem 1 we can conclude that constructing the convex hull of P' costs $O(n_1 \log n_1)$ comparisons and $O(n_1)$ multiplications. One multiplication on the grid $G = [0,m_1)x[0,m_2) \cap \mathbb{Z}^2$ can be done by $O(\log(m_1 \cdot m_2))$ comparisons. Therefore, our approach, to which we will refer as algorithm HULL, needs $O(n\log n_1 + n_1 \log(m_1 m_2))$ comparisons to solve $Z(m_1,m_2)$.

We note that HULL solves also the general problem R. But in the worst case, all x-coordinates of the input P are different from each other, and no reduction can be done. Nevertheless, HULL is time-optimal for problem R too, because reduction costs $\Theta(n\log n)$ in the worst case.

For simplicity, we suppose in the following

$$m_1 \leq m_2 \qquad (1)$$

$$m_2 = O(n^{\alpha}) \text{ with } \alpha > 0 \qquad (2)$$

$$m_1 \leq n \qquad (3)$$

Condition (1) is rather of technical importance, i.e. it simplifies the following explanations. With condition (2) and (3) we try to choose such a domain of the parameters $m_1(n)$ and $m_2(n)$ which is of interest, i.e. in which problem $Z(m_1,m_2)$ differs essentially from problem R. Intuitively, we mean by this "well filled" grids. Furthermore, condition (1), (2), (3) make the two components $O(n\log n_1)$ and $O(n_1 \log(m_1 m_2))$ in the costs of algorithm HULL comparable.

<u>Theorem 2:</u>

Under the condition (1), (2), (3) the algorithm HULL solves problem $Z(m_1,m_2)$ with $\Theta(n\log m_1)$ coordinate comparisons in the worst case. □

<u>3. Lower bounds are related to computational models</u>

In the following, we search for lower bounds of $Z(m_1,m_2)$. For this end, we have to define the model of computation, in which we investigate $Z(m_1,m_2)$. That this is necessary, will become clear, if we compare the upper bound provided by HULL with those of Karlsson and Overmars /KO/, /O/ gained for similar problems. The later two approaches provide algorithms which are of linear time and storage requirements under conditons (1),(2) and (3). /KO/ uses a result of Kirkpatrick and Reisch /KR/ concerning the sorting of integers on random access machines (RAM), namely using the capability of integer division resp. shift operations. /O/ uses bucket sort, i.e. the capability of indirect addressing. Integer division and indirect addressing are operations which cannot be executed by a constant number of decisions with finite out degree. Therefore, lower bounds based on decision tree models are not valid for RAM-algorithms. Furthermore, lower bounds valid on RAM's and valid for inputs from restricted ranges are unknown and it seems hard to obtain such lower bounds, /DO'D/. But obviously, any linear algorithm (linear in time and storage) on RAM's can be treated as optimal, at most in a weak sense. Thus, our main argument against the application of RAM's remains that $Z(m_1,m_2)$ can be solved in the frame of models with much more simpler basic operations, i.e. with coordinate comparisons only.

4. Lower bounds for $Z(m_1,m_2)$ in the model of binary decision trees

In this model we suppose only that any inner node possesses two edges. At any inner node a binary decision has to be made. The leaves contain the answers. Therefore, a tree correctly answering a question possesses at least so many leaves as there are different answers. The number of leaves is bounded by 2^h in which h is the hight of the tree. This well known argument provides us with the so-called information theoretic lower bound $h \geq \log m$ in which m denotes the number of distinct answers.

Here, we have to estimate the number m of distinct convex hulls. Two convex hulls are distinct iff they consist of different points or they consist of the same points, but the points are enumerated in different cyclic orders. h_{max} denotes the number of vertices in a convex hull for $Z(m_1,m_2)$ with maximally many vertices. Then,

$$m = \sum_{i=2}^{h_{max}} \binom{n}{i} (i-1)! \qquad (n \geq 2)$$

Obviously, $h_{max} \leq \min(n,2m_1,2m_2) = \min(n,2m_1)$ by condition (1). But, h_{max} does not reach this upper bound in any case. This depends on the relation of m_1 and m_2. Lemma A gives insight into this question, but it cannot give a complete answer.

<u>Lemma A:</u>

a) A convex hull with exactly $2m_1$ elements exists only for

$$m_2 \geq 2 + \left(\left\lfloor\frac{m_1+1}{2}\right\rfloor - 2\right)\left(\left\lfloor\frac{m_1+1}{2}\right\rfloor - 1\right) = \frac{m_1^2}{2} + O(m_1) \text{ and } 2m_1 \leq n.$$

b) There exists a convex hull with $\Theta(m_1)$ many points for $m_1^2 = O(m_2)$.

c) There exists a convex hull with $\Theta(\sqrt{m_2})$ many points for $\sqrt{m_2} = O(m_1)$. □

If we replace the condition $m_1 m_2 \geq n$ from the problem definition of $Z(m_1,m_2)$ by

$$\exists\, \varepsilon > 0\ \exists\, n_0\ \forall\, n \geq n_0 \quad m_1 m_2 (1-\varepsilon) \geq n \qquad (4)$$

then we can show the following theorem by means of lemma A. (Condition (4) means that the number of empty places in the grid G is at least proportional to n.)

<u>Theorem 2a:</u>

The algorithm HULL is time optimal for $Z(m_1,m_2)$ in the model of binary decision trees under condition (1)-(4) and (a) or (1)-(4) and (b).

(a) $m_1 = \Theta(n)$ and $m_1^2 = O(m_2)$

(b) $\sqrt{m_2} = \Theta(n)$ and $\sqrt{m_2} = O(m_1)$.

HULL is not time optimal in the same model under condition (1)-(4) and (c) $m_1 = o(n)$. □

By this theorem one can see that there exists a gap between the upper bound $O(m_1 \log n)$ of the information theoretic lower bound and the worst case behaviour of HULL, e.g. in the case $m_1 = o(n)$. This gap can only be closed when using more special computational models.

5. $Z(m_1,m_2)$ in other known computational models

Models of this kind are the model of quadratic resp. linear decision trees or more generally the model of k-th order decision trees resp. the model of algebraic computation trees /PS/. One sees at once that HULL solves $Z(m_1,m_2)$ in any of these models. Recall the well known result from the literature that problem R, i.e. the general problem is not solvable in the model of linear decision trees. Lower bounds are generally obtained in the models mentioned above by determining the number of different connection components of the input space. The curves bounding the components are quadratic, linear or more generally polynomial resp. algebraic depending on the chosen model. However, the decisive fact is the continuity of the input space. At most, the input space is $\mathbb{R}^n$. Compare e.g. with /PS/. /U2/ gives a method to prove lower bounds in the model of k-th order decision trees which bases rather on the density of the input space than on its continuity. As already mentioned, this model can be characterized by the fact that at any inner node polynomials of the input of maximal degree k are compared with zero, /YS/. The discrete nature of $Z(m_1,m_2)$ makes all these approaches apparently difficult or even impossible. That's why we looked for a model of computation which reflects the discrete nature of $Z(m_1,m_2)$ in a more adequate way. The finiteness of grid G suggests to choose coordinate comparisons as basic unit of the complexity measure.

6. A special model - the model of $CC(m_1,m_2)$-trees

For our interest is directed towards geometric problems on planar point sets we presume the input to be in form of n coordinate pairs $r_1 =(x_1,y_1),\dots,r_n=(x_n,y_n)$.

Definition:

A coordinate comparison tree, shortly <u>CC-tree</u> is a binary decision tree parameterized by n in which the comparison at node ν is of form

1) $x_{i_\nu} \geq x_{j_\nu}$, shortly x-comparison
2) $y_{i_\nu} \geq y_{j_\nu}$, shortly y-comparison
3) $x_{i_\nu} \geq c_\nu$ resp. $x_{i_\nu} \leq c_\nu$, shortly xc-comparison or
4) $y_{i_\nu} \geq d_\nu$ resp. $y_{i_\nu} \leq d_\nu$, shortly yd-comparison or
5) $x_{i_\nu} \geq y_{j_\nu}$ resp. $x_{i_\nu} \leq y_{j_\nu}$, shortly xy-comparison

with $i_\nu, j_\nu \in \{1,\dots,n\}$ and c_ν, $d_\nu \in$ R.

A <u>$CC(m_1,m_2)$-tree</u> with $m_1(n), m_2(n)$ functions over $\mathbb{Z}^+$ and with values from $\mathbb{Z}^+$ is a CC-tree parameterized by m_1 and m_2 in which it holds for c_ν from 3) and d_ν from 4) of the previous definition $c_\nu \in [0,m_1) \cap \mathbb{Z}$ and $d_\nu \in [0,m_2) \cap \mathbb{Z}$.

Observations:

1a) The model of CC-trees is at least such powerful as the model of $CC(m_1,m_2)$-trees for arbitrary m_1,m_2.

1b) Any CC-tree applicated to point sets from $[0,m_1) \times [0,m_2) \cap \mathbb{Z}^2$ can be replaced in a canonical way by a $CC(m_1,m_2)$-tree possessing the same structure as the original CC-tree.

2) The model of linear decision trees (shortly L-trees) is at least such powerful as the model of CC-trees.

3) The algorithm HULL solves $Z(m_1,m_2)$ by $CC(m_1,m_2)$-trees.

Theorem 3:

a) The model of L-trees is more powerful than the model of CC-trees, i.e. there exist problems which can be solved by L-trees but which cannot be solved by CC-trees, actually the problem "$y \geq rx$?" - Decide for an arbitrarily given point (x,y) and arbitrary, but fixed parameter $r \in R$, if $y \geq rx$, $r > 1$.

b) The model of L-trees is exactly such powerful as the model of $CC(m_1,m_2)$-trees if inputs are restricted to G. Any problem can be solved in both models or in none of them.

c) The model of L-trees is more efficient on G than the model of $CC(m_1,m_2)$-trees. Actually, "$y \geq rx$?" for $r > 2$ can be solved by one comparison in the model of L-trees. Any arbitrary $CC(m_1,m_2)$-trêe has at least hight

$$\left\lceil \log\left(\min\left(m_1-1\ ,\ \left\lfloor\frac{m_2-1}{r}\right\rfloor\right)\right)\right\rceil -1\ .\square$$

After we have classified the CC-model into the hierarchy of the well known computational models we return to $Z(m_1,m_2)$.

7. Lower bounds for $Z(m_1,m_2)$ in the model of $CC(m_1,_2)$-trees

The following theorem contains the main result of this paper.

Theorem 4:

The asymptotic lower bound $\Omega(n\log m_1)$ for problem $Z(m_1,m_2)$ holds in the model of $CC(m_1,m_2)$-trees under the following conditions:

$\lim_{n\to\infty} m_1(n) = \infty$ (5)

$\exists\ \varepsilon > 0\ \exists\ \varepsilon_2 > 0\quad n(1+\varepsilon) < m_2(1-\varepsilon_2)$, if n large enough (6)

$m_1(n) = o(n)$. (7)

Condition (5) is a rather technical condition. It seems to be not too strong. Condition (6) and (7) are crucial for the proof. They can be summarized to the following: One coordinate (here the x-coordinate) is really smaller than n. The other coordinate (here the y-coordinate) grows faster as n. Observe that condition (7) is stronger than condition (3).

Sketch of Proof:

At first, we define special point configurations being inputs of $Z(m_1,m_2)$ which are called admissible, in the following way. m+2 points form the convex hull, in which $m := \min(m_1, \sqrt{2\varepsilon_2 m_2})$. These points are marked by "x". The remaining points are equally distributed in the first m columns directly above the convex curve formed by $r_1,\ldots,r_m$. They are marked by blocks (▮). As an important observation we mention the fact that these blocks don't overlap each other.

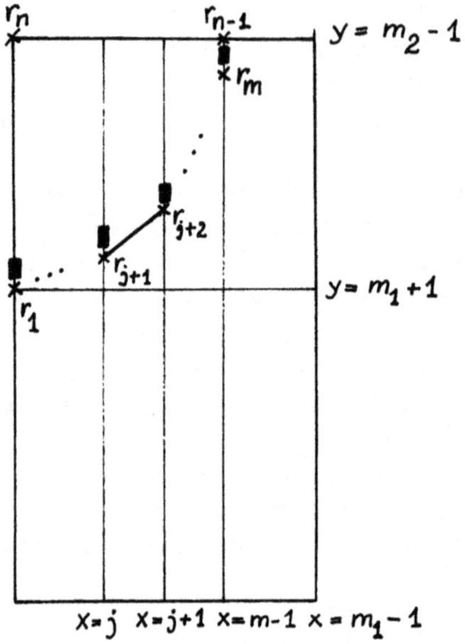

At first, we have to show that admissible configurations are input of $Z(m_1,m_2)$. This can be done by means of condition (5)-(7). Admissible point configurations are called partially monotonous or shortly <u>pma-configurations</u> if the indices of the points in each block ordered by increasing y-values form a monotonously increasing sequence.
Now, one can show the following lemma.

<u>Lemma B:</u>

Distinct pma-configurations lead to distinct leaves in any $CC(m_1,m_2)$-tree correctly solving $Z(m_1,m_2)$. □

This is the main point of the proof. The remaining part of the proof is canonical.

<u>Lemma C:</u>

There are at least $(m!)^{\lfloor \frac{n}{m} \rfloor -1}$ distinct pma-configurations. □

<u>Lemma D:</u>

$$\log\left((m!)^{\lfloor \frac{n}{m} \rfloor -1}\right) = \Theta(n\log m_1).\ □$$

By these lemmas, the assertion of theorem 4 follows. □

From theorem 4 and theorem 2 follows at once

<u>Theorem 2b:</u>

Algorithm HULL solves problem $Z(m_1,m_2)$ time optimally in the model of $CC(m_1,m_2)$-trees under condition (5),(6),(7), and (2). □

8. Two related problems - R-n_1 and ZM(m_1,m_2)

Problem R-n_1:
is the same as problem R, but furthermore we know

$\#\pi(P) := \#\{ x \mid \exists p = (x,y) \in P \} \leq n_1(n) \leq n$.

Obviously, $Z(m_1,m_2)$ is a special problem R-n_1 with $n_1 = \min(n,2m_1)$. But, $Z(m_1,m_2)$ is much more simpler than problem R-n_1. This is demonstrated by the following results on R-n_1.

Theorem 5:
HULL solves problem R-n_1 with $\Theta(n\log n_1)$ coordinate comparisons and $\Theta(n_1)$ multiplications in the worst case. □

Multiplications cannot be executed by a finite number of coordinate comparisons or more generally of comparisons of linear function on the input. It holds

Theorem 6:
Problem R-n_1 is not solvable in the model of linear decision trees. □

The proof can be found in /U1/.

Theorem 5a:
It holds the lower bound $\Omega(n_1\log n)$ for R-n_1 in the model of binary decision trees. □

Theorem 5b:
It holds the lower bound $\Omega(n\log n_1)$ for R-n_1 in the model of k-th order decision trees. □

The proof can be found in /U2/. This theorem asserts that the gap between upper and lower bound for R-n_1 can be closed in the model of k-th order decision trees, which is more general than the model of CC-trees. In /U1/ we investigate also

Problem ZM(m_1,m_2):
which is the same as $Z(m_1,m_2)$, but there can be points with equal coordinates but different indices in the input. The convex hull consists of the engaged points including their multiplicities, i.e. a sequence of sets of indices. A condition similar to $n \leq m_1 \cdot m_2$ is not necessary due to the allowed multiplicity.

Theorem 7:
HULL solves ZM(m_1,m_2) with $\Theta(n\log m_1)$ coordinate comparisons under condition (1),(2),(3) in the worst case. □

Theorem 7a:
It holds the lower bound $\Omega(n\log m_1)$ for ZM(m_1,m_2) in the model of binary decision trees, i.e. HULL is time optimal in this model under conditon (1),(2),(3). □

The proof can be found in /U1/.

9. Final remarks

We showed that restrictions of the well known convex hull problem which were motivated by application can be solved time optimally in special, but adequate models. The main result in this paper is the lower bound of $Z(m_1,m_2)$ in the model of CC(m_1,m_2)-trees, defined here, under conditions intended to describe well filled images.

During looking for the information theoretic lower bound of $Z(m_1,m_2)$ we investigated also the combinatoric problem standing in the background of this question - What is the maximal number of vertices of a convex hull formed by finitely many points with vertices only in $G = [0,m_1)x[0,m_2)\cap\mathbb{Z}^2$.

Problem:

Determine the maximal length, i.e. the number of vertices lying on a concave, strictly monotonic increasing function where its curve consists of finite lines between points of the grid $G = [0,k_1)x[0,k_2)\cap\mathbb{Z}^2$ with $k_1,k_2 \in \mathbb{Z}^+$ starting in (0,0) and ending in (k_1-1,k_2-1).

$l(k_1,k_2)$ denotes this length. Some partial results on $l(k_1,k_2)$ and a related problem can be found in [13]. There can be also found a PASCAL-program computing $l(k_1,k_2)$.

References

/DO'D/ Dittert,E.; M.J.O'Donnell: Lower bounds for sorting with realistic instruction sets. IEEE Trans.Comp. 34(1985), 311-317.

/KO/ Karlsson,R.G.; M.H.Overmars: Scanline Algorithms on a Grid. Dep. of Comp. Science and Inf. Science, University of Linköping, Linköping 1986, Research Report LITH-IDA-86-30.

/KR/ Kirkpatrick,D., Reisch,S.: Upper Bounds for Sorting Integers on Random Access Machines, Theoretical Computer Science 28(1984), 263-276.

/O/ Overmars,M.H.: Computational geometry on a grid an overview. Dep.of Comp. Sc., University of Utrecht, Utrecht 1987, Technical Report RUU-CS-87-4.

/PS/ Preparata,F.P., M.I.Shamos: Computational Geometry, Springer 1985, New York.

/SY/ Steele,J.M.; A.C.Yao: Lower bounds for algebraic decision trees. J. of Algorithms 3(1982), 1-8.

/U1/ Unger,K.: The convex hull problem on special planar point sets. K.-Weierstraß-Institut Berlin, Berlin 1988, Report R-MATH-05/88.

/U2/ Unger,K.:Another method for proving lower bounds in the model of k-th order decision trees, (in preparation).

The Riches of Rectangles

Derick Wood

Data Structuring Group
Department of Computer Science
University of Waterloo
WATERLOO, Ontario N2L 3G1
CANADA

Abstract

In this paper we consider some of the rectangle problems that have been studied in the literature of computational geometry. Our aim is to demonstrate that although rectangles are, perhaps, the simplest of geometrical figures, they occur naturally in many situations and, thus they are a rich source for intriguing and challenging problems.

1 Introduction

A title such as "The Riches as Rectangles" suggests that there may be sequels such as "The Treasures of Triangles", "The Quandries of Quadrilaterals", and "The Horrors of Octagons" to name but a few. I believe this to be the case for some of these topics, since like rectangles some of them occur profusely in the real world. But, if this is the case, why have I chosen rectangles first?

I have two responses to this question. First, I have studied many rectangle problems over the last ten years and, therefore, claim some expertise with them. And, second, a rectangle is the simplest polygon apart from the square, which is a special case of a rectangle. Why is this so? Because rectangles have four sides, but these sides have only two orientations, and their angles are all right angles. (A triangle has fewer sides, but it has more orientations and more angles.)

We consider some problems for rectangles that have been studied in computational geometry and some that have not. Our hope is that the reader will obtain a little of the flavor of the types of questions, the types of results, and the types of approaches that are to be found in this rapidly growing area. In other words, we use rectangles to provide the reader with the flavor of computational geometry. [1]

2 What Are Rectangles

We assume that rectangles are given by quadruples of the form $(x_{left}, x_{right}, y_{bottom}, y_{top})$ that determine their corner points. Hence, we assume they have sides parallel to the two axes in two-dimensional space. For the purposes of this paper we assume that all coordinate values are integral. A rectangle with sides parallel to the axes is termed *isothetic* or *orthogonal*. Many problems involve isothetic sets of rectangles.

[1] The term computational geometry has been in use in the areas of computer graphics and solid modeling for many years with a more restrictive meaning. We are interested in computational aspects of combinatorial geometry problems here.

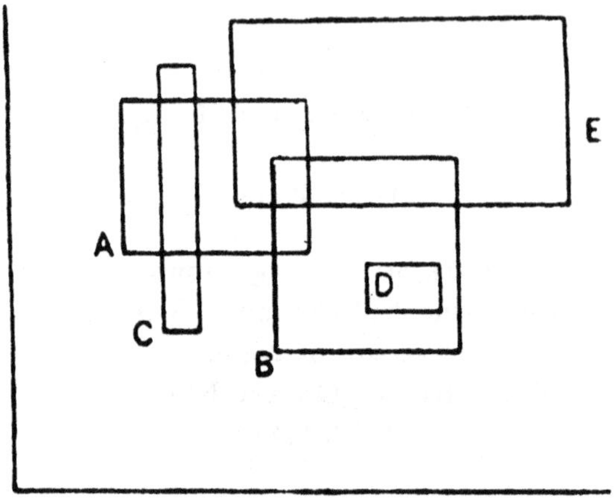

Figure 1: Some orthogonal rectangles.

Given two rectangles $R^i = (x_l^i, x_r^i, y_b^i, y_t^i)$, $i = 1, 2$, we say that R^1 is a *zoom* or *homothet* of R^2 if $(x_r^1 - x_l^1)(y_t^2 - y_b^2) = (x_r^2 - x_l^2)(y_t^1 - y_b^1)$, that is, one is a magnification of the other. It is clear that every square is a zoom of every other square, but this is not true for rectangles. Therefore, for rectangles we may wish to restrict our attention to those rectangles in a homothetic class generated by some given rectangle. The most restricted class of rectangles we might consider are those consisting of a single rectangle or a single *tile*. In this case, we consider only *translates* of such a set.

Throughout this paper, as is usual, we use the term to mean either the closed set of points it defines or its boundary alone; the meaning will always be clear from the context.

3 The Combinatorial-Computational Relationship

We begin by exploring the differences between the combinatorial approach and the computational approach to geometric problems. Essentially, combinatorics characterizes when a property occurs, whereas computation computes when a property occurs, almost occurs, or doesn't occur.

As our first example, consider the following theorem. (Note that we assume all rectangles are isothetic throughout the remainder of this paper.)

Theorem 3.1 *Given n rectangles in the plane, they share a common point (or have a nonempty intersection) if and only if every pair share a common point (or intersect).*

Computationally, we might turn this into:

Problem 3.1 *Given n rectangles in the plane, do they share a common point? How fast can this be determined?*

If the rectangles have an empty intersection as the ones in Figure 1 do it is unclear how to proceed combinatorially, but computationally we can easily weaken the question.

Problem 3.2 *Given n rectangles in the plane, what is the maximum number of them that share a common point?*

This value is called the *thickness* of the rectangles; in Figure 1 the thickness is three. If we can solve the thickness problem efficiently, it should be clear that we can solve the common point problem as efficiently. This follows by observing that the n rectangles share a common point if and only if their thickness is n.

A different approach is found by considering the common point (when it exists) rather than the rectangles that share it. Given n rectangles and a point p, all rectangles containing p are said to be *stabbed* by p. This gives rise to:

Problem 3.3 *Given n rectangles in the plane and a point p, which rectangles does p stab?*

This is an example of a *searching* problem. Also, this particular problem is a fundamental one, so we return to it in Section 4.

In order to consider a second weakened version of Problem 3.1, we first introduce an intermediate problem.

Problem 3.4 *Given n rectangles in the plane and a set P of points, is every rectangle stabbed by at least one point in P? (We say that P* stabs *the rectangles if this is the case.)*

Now we turn to the second weakened version of Problem 3.1.

Problem 3.5 *Given n rectangles in the plane, determine a smallest set P of points that stabs the rectangles.*

To see that this is a weakened version of Problem 3.1 observe that the n rectangles share a common point or are pairwise disjoint if and only if the smallest set P of points that stabs them has size 1 or n, respectively. We say that $\#P$ is the *stabbing number* of the given rectangles. The rectangles in Figure 1 have stabbing number three. The problem can also be viewed as a thumbtack problem. Given n notices, what is the fewest thumbtacks needed to attach them to a noticeboard with a particular overlap pattern. Of course, in practice, the notices might rotate and we would like to prevent this. We can prevent rotation of notices by using at least two thumbtacks for each notice. This gives rise to:

Problem 3.6 *Given n rectangles in the plane, determine a smallest set P of points such that each rectangle is stabbed by at least two disjoint points from P. (We say each rectangle is* 2-stabbed *and P 2-stabs the rectangles.*

The rectangles in Figure 1 have a 2-stabbing number of six.

We can weaken our concerns even further by looking at groups of fixed size that share a common point. Perhaps, the most obvious group size is two, in which case we have:

Problem 3.7 The Rectangle Intersection Problem
Given n rectangles in the plane, determine all intersecting pairs.

This problem was my initiation into the field of computational geometry. Together with Jon Bentley (but more of Jon than of me) we proved in [2]:

Theorem 3.2 *The R.I.P. for n rectangles can be solved in $O(a + n \log n)$ time and $O(n \log n)$ space, where a is the number of answers or intersecting pairs.*

If $k = O(n^2)$, this algorithm outperforms the naive algorithm that examines the $\binom{n}{2}$ pairs. Our algorithm was subsequently improved by Edelsbrunner and McCreight independently. They both showed that $O(n)$ space to be sufficient (see [5,6,12]), but McCreight's solution did not have a provable worst case time bound of $O(a + n \log n)$. Later, McCreight gave a second alternative approach that also met these optimal time and space bounds; see [13].

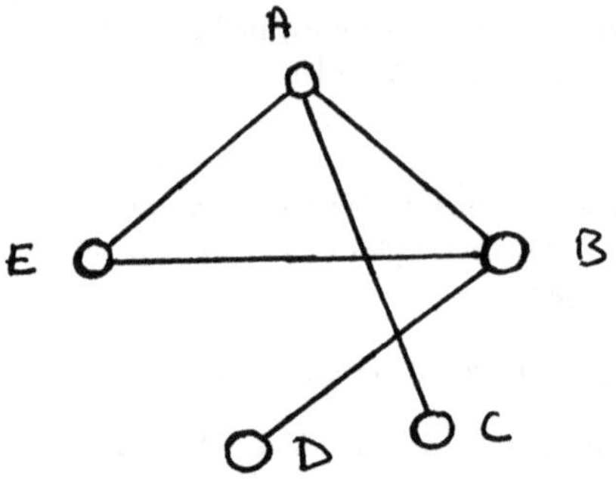

Figure 2: A rectangle intersection graph.

The interesting point about these algorithms is that they introduced novel data structures to the computer science community — the *segment tree*, the *range tree*, the *interval tree*, and the *priority search tree* — that have become basic data structures in many other computational geometry algorithms.

The original motivation for the R.I.P. was from the area of VLSI design checking. in this setting, components, wires, and input-output pads could, at that time, be viewed as rectangles. Hence, between different layers of the chip some intersections were essential, while others were design faults. Finding all pairwise intersections so that these could be examined in more detail was one of the design checking steps.

Corresponding to the n rectangles in the plane we have their *rectangle intersection graph* in which rectangles are nodes and two nodes are incident to the same edge if the associated rectangles intersect. In Figure 2 we display the rectangle intersection graph of the rectangles in Figure 1. The R.I.P. is equivalent to determining the rectangle intersection graph of the given rectangles. This simple notion leads to a nontrivial combinatorial problem:

Problem 3.8 *Characterize the rectangle intersection graphs.*

The one-dimensional version of this problem, for line segments, has been well studied. In this case we obtain *interval graphs* which have many different characterizations; see [17].

The graph-theoretic view of rectangles leads naturally to:

Problem 3.9 *Given n rectangles in the plane, determine their connected components (in the rectangle intersection graph sense).*

This is yet another important problem in VLSI design. It can be solved using the standard algorithms of graph theory. This leads to solutions that require $O(a+n)$ time, where a is the number of pairwise intersections. When $a = \omega(n \log n)$, this solution technique can be improved substantially. The basic idea is to avoid the explicit construction of the intersection graph. Edelsbrunner et al. [8] proved:

Theorem 3.3 *Given n rectangles in the plane, their connected components can be computed in $O(n \log n)$ time and $O(n)$ space.*

4 Stabbing Search

Recall that in this problem we are given n rectangles and a query point. We wish to determine all rectangles that the query point stabs.

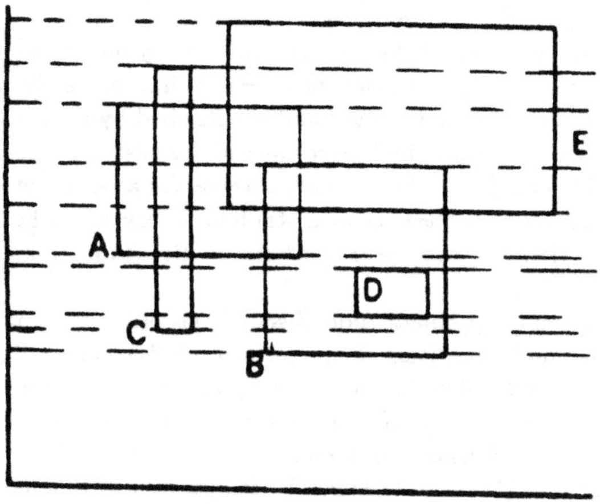

Figure 3: The slabs induced by some rectangles.

Clearly, if this is all we are given we cannot do better than exhaustive search — test each rectangle to see if it is stabbed by the query point. However, usually we expect many query points, not just one. In this case, we can do better by *preconditioning* or *preprocessing* the rectangles in some way. For example, extend all horizontal edges of the rectangles to partition the plane into at most $2n+1$ horizontal slabs; see Figure 3. Each horizontal slab is immediately partitioned into at most $2n+1$ cells by the rectangle's vertical edges and each rectangle has been partitioned into a number of cells that only intersect at their boundaries. Therefore, we associate with each cell, in each horizontal slab, the "names" of the rectangles that they belong to.

Given a query point $p = (x, y)$, we can perform binary search with y to determine the slab in which it lies. (Assuming that we keep the y-coordinates of the slabs in sorted order in an array.) Similarly, once we know the slab that contains y, we can perform a binary search with x within the slab to determine the cell that contains p.

This slab technique provides $O(a + \log n)$ query time, where a is the number of answers. Unfortunately, it requires $O(n^3)$ space in the worst case and, therefore, $O(n^3)$ time to preprocess the rectangles. The reader is invited to provide n rectangles that achieve this bound.

Can we do better? Fortunately, yes we can. Observe that an orthogonal rectangle can be defined as the cross-product of the two intervals given by its x- and y-projections. Moreover, a point $p = (x, y)$ is in a rectangle R if and only if x is in its x-projection and y is in its y-projection. This suggests an approach, similar to the slab technique, except that we first perform a binary search on the y-projections of the rectangles. Second, we perform a binary search on the x-projections of only those rectangles that were not excluded in the first search. The resulting rectangles must be stabbed by p and none of the excluded rectangles are. Using tree data structures first proposed by Edelsbrunner, Six, and Wood [5,6,20] the rectangles can be preprocessed in $O(n \log^2 n)$ time to give a structure that requires $O(n \log n)$ space. Furthermore, a stabbing query can be solved in $O(a + \log^2 n)$ time. This structure is, essentially, a search tree for y-intervals and each node is a second-level search tree for x-intervals.

It is possible to do even better than this by once more changing our view of the problem. Consider the simpler stabbing problem in which we are only given y-intervals on the y-axis, rather than rectangles placed arbitrarily. Then, this problem can be solved with $O(n \log n)$ preprocessing time and $O(n)$ space using the structure of either Edelsbrunner [4] or McCreight [13]. In both cases, the query time is $O(a + \log n)$; the best we can hope for in the worst case with a comparison-based model of computation.

But now consider a modification of this problem in which y-intervals are inserted and deleted over time and we want to ask ***historical stabbing queries***. That is, we give a y-value and a time t and we want all y-intervals that exist at time t and are stabbed by y. A little thought shows that the two-dimensional space-time chart for the y-intervals consists of a set of rectangles. In this framework a rectangle denotes the existence of a y-interval for a period of time and the historical stabbing query is nothing more nor less than a stabbing query with the point (t, y). Based on this idea, Sarnak and Tarjan [18] used ***persistent search structures*** to solve the stabbing query problem efficiently.

Yet one more approach to the problem under discussion is based on another simple observation. The boundaries of the rectangles partition the plane into subdivisions. In this setting the stabbing query becomes: In which subdivision does the given point lie? This is a basic problem that has been studied intensely since the dawn of computational geometry and is usually known as the point location (in a planar subdivision) problem.

The interested reader should consult the texts by Preparata and Shamos [15] and Edelsbrunner [7] and the paper of Sarnak and Tarjan [18] and the references therein.

All of the above mentioned material is concerned with worst case and amortized case behavior. Thus, it leaves open the question of whether there are solutions that do well on average and are easy to implement in practical situations. We conclude this section by examining three variants of the general stabbing problem.

The first variant occurs when multiple windows are allowed in a work station environment.

Problem 4.1 The Window Selection Problem
Given n rectangles (or windows) and a point p, determine the closest rectangle that p stabs.

Think of the rectangles as carpets on the floor and the query point as someone standing on them, then the answer to the query will be the carpet that the person is touching (We assume point feet.) Or, alternately, the windows are hanging in three-space rather than in the plane and the answer to the query is the closest window to the observer that is stabbed by the point. Based on this interpretation we can use our first approach where we also keep a sorted list of rectangles associated with each cell. The second approach can also be modified to take into account the third coordinate, but this means that the preprocessing time becomes $O(n \log^3 n)$ and the query time becomes $O(a + \log^3 n)$ in the worst case. Whether the other approaches can be modified to give efficient solutions is not so clear. Also, in practice the windows are changing dynamically — shrinking, expanding, translating, being removed, and being added. We are currently reconsidering this problem, since we know of no method that is good under all circumstances.

The second variant is also motivated by a work station environment, namely, the problem of menu selection.

Problem 4.2 The Menu Selection Problem
Given n disjoint rectangles in the plane and a query point p, determine whether p stabs a rectangle and if so, which one.

The motivation for this problem is obvious; all PC's use menu selection, to some extent, as a system language; perhaps the MacIntosh is the most thorough example. Menus are rectangles and a stabbing query is a cursor.

Since the x- and y-projections of the rectangles result in $O(n)$ intervals, the first and second approaches are no better than before, except that the number of answers does not appear in the time bounds. But we, typically, cannot afford the space overhead. Field [9] gave a solution using hashing that has $O(1)$ expected query time and requires $O(n)$ space.

The third variant is found in one approach to querying in a geographic database.

Problem 4.3 *Given n rectangles in the plane and a query rectangle, determine all rectangles the query rectangle stabs.*

This problem was motivated by range queries in a geographic database for Baden-Württemberg in West Germany. Bounding rectangles were used to surround the municipalities of this province, yielding 1211 rectangles and in a second more detailed situation 48,500 rectangles were obtained. In both cases, the query of most interest was the range query or rectangle query.

This problem is easily solved using the techniques of [4,5], but it requires $O(a + \log^3 n)$ time and $O(n \log n)$ space. In a practical environment this is unacceptable.

Recently, Six and Widmayer [19] introduced a method based on the grid file of [14] which is very promising for large databases of rectangles. However, one hopes that some further improvement is possible.

The stabbing query continues to fascinate algorithmicists, since it is an easy problem to grasp, yet good efficient solutions seem to be difficult to find.

5 An Update

Since this paper was written in January, 1988, there have been some new developments that are worthy of mention. First, Kratochvíl has proved that deciding whether a graph is a rectangle intersection graph is NP-complete[Private communication, 1989]. This results follows by arguments similar to those in [10,11].

Second, performing hidden surface elimination for orthogonal rectangles hanging in 3-space — the window rendering problem — has received considerable attention in the last twelve months. Specifically, Bern [3] obtained an $O(n \log n \log\log n + k \log n)$ time algorithm and Preparata, Vitter, and Yvinec [16] independently found an $O(n \log^2 n + k \log n)$ time algorithm. These output-sensitive algorithms have been followed more recently by an $O(n^{1.5} + k)$ time algorithm due to Atallah and Goodrich [1].

These results have demonstrated that we have only touched the surface of rectangle problems and solutions; there are many more that are waiting to be explored or whose present solutions are waiting to be improved.

Acknowledgement

This work was supported under a Natural Sciences and Engineering Research Council of Canada Grant No. A-5692 and under a grant from the Information Technology Research Centre.

References

[1] M.J. Atallah and M.T. Goodrich. Output-sensitive hidden surface elimination for rectangles. Technical Report 88-13, The John Hopkin's University, Department of Computer Science, Baltimore, 1988.

[2] J.L. Bentley and D. Wood. An optimal worst case algorithm for reporting intersections of rectangles. *IEEE Transactions on Computers*, EC-29:571–576, 1980.

[3] M. Bern. Hidden surface removal for rectangles. In *Proceedings of the 4th ACM Symposium on Computational Geometry*, pages 183–192, 1988.

[4] H. Edelsbrunner. Dynamic rectangle intersection searching. Technical Report F 47, Institut für Informationsverarbeitung, Technische Universität Graz, 1980.

[5] H. Edelsbrunner. New approach to rectangle intersections: Part I. *International Journal of Computer Mathematics*, 13:209–219, 1983.

[6] H. Edelsbrunner. New approach to rectangle intersections: Part II. *International Journal of Computer Mathematics*, 13:221–229, 1983.

[7] H. Edelsbrunner. *Algorithms in Combinatorial Geometry.* Springer-Verlag, New York, 1987.

[8] H. Edelsbrunner, J. van Leeuwen, Th. Ottmann, and D. Wood. Computing the connected components of simple rectilinear geometrical objects in d-space. *RAIRO Informatique théorique*, 18:171–183, 1984.

[9] D.E. Field. Fast hit detection for disjoint rectangles. Technical Report 85-53, Department of Computer Science, University of Waterloo, 1985.

[10] J. Kratochvíl. String graphs I: The number of critical nonstring graphs is infinite. Technical Report 88-83, Charles University, Department of Mathematics and Physics, Prague, Czechoslovakia, 1988.

[11] J. Kratochvíl. String graphs II: Recognizing string graphs is NP-hard. Technical Report 88-86, Charles University, Department of Mathematics and Physics, Prague, Czechoslovakia, 1988.

[12] E.M. McCreight. Efficient algorithms for enumerating intersecting intervals and rectangles. Technical Report CSL-80-9, Xerox Palo Alto Research Center, 1980.

[13] E.M. McCreight. Priority search trees. *SIAM Journal on Computing*, 14:257–276, 1985.

[14] J. Nievergelt, H. Hinterberger, and K.C. Sevcik. The grid file: An adaptable, symmetric multikey file structure. *ACM Transactions on Database Systems*, 9:38–71, 1984.

[15] F.P. Preparata and M.I. Shamos. *Computational Geometry.* Springer-Verlag, New York, 1985.

[16] F.P. Preparata, J.S. Vitter, and M. Yvinec. Computation of the axial view of a set of isothetic parallelopipeds. Technical Report 88-1, Labatoire d'Informatique de l'Ecole Normale Supérieure, Paris, France, 1988.

[17] F.S. Roberts. *Graph Theory and Its Applications to Problems of Society.* Society for Industrial and Applied Mathematics, Philadelphia, Pennsylvania, 197?

[18] N. Sarnak and R.E. Tarjan. Planar point location using persistent search trees. *Communications of the ACM*, 29:669–679, 1986.

[19] H.-W. Six and P. Widmayer. Spatial searching in geometric databases. Technical Report 176, Institut für Angewandte Informatik, Universität Karlsruhe, 1987.

[20] H.-W. Six and D. Wood. Counting and reporting intersections of d-ranges. *IEEE Transactions on Computers*, C-31:181–187, 1982.

Chapter 4

Artificial Intelligence

The limitations of partial evaluation

Frank van Harmelen
Department of Artificial Intelligence
University of Edinburgh
Edinburgh EH1 1HN
Scotland
frankh%uk.ac.ed.aiva@nss.cs.ucl.ac.uk

1 Introduction

There is widespread agreement in the literature on expert system about the desirability of the separate and explicit representation of control knowledge in reasoning architectures. Such separate and explicit representation of control knowledge, preferably in a declarative format, has the following advantages:

- Ease of development and debugging because of increased modularity.
- Multiple usage of same domain knowledge for different tasks (e.g. problem solving, teaching, etc), by combination with different control knowledge.
- Improved possibilities for explanation of the behaviour of the system, because both control knowledge and domain knowledge can be part of the explanation.
- Fully declarative nature of the domain knowledge, since all procedural aspects can be moved into the control knowledge.

On the basis of these arguments, many workers in AI have implemented architectures to support the explicit and separate representation of control knowledge. One family of architectures that has been particularly successful in this respect are the so called *meta-level architectures*. These systems provide two levels, the *object-level*, used for representing domain knowledge, and the *meta-level*, used for representing control knowledge. In particular, when logic is used as the knowledge representation formalism, a meta-level architecture will provide both an object-level and a meta-level *theory*, with the object-level theory refering to domain knowledge, and with the meta-level theory refering to formulae of the object-level theory, and how to use them. An *interpreter* for both levels will be provided to make *logical inferences* with the expressions from the meta- and object-level theories.

Although a large number of logic-based meta-level systems have been successfully reported in the literature, a serious deficiency that prohibits their use as a practical tool in many situations is the overhead which is incurred by the extra layer of interpretation by the meta-level. The advantage of an explicit meta-level theory is of course (among others) that it is possible to write specialised control regimes for particular applications, which can significantly cut down the search space, and consequently significantly reduce the number of logical inferences needed to compute the desired object-level result. However, this advantage comes at the price of an increased cost per logical inference made at the object-level. After all, a system with a hardwired control strategy can be optimised for that particular strategy, and current object-level logic programming systems routinely achieve speeds of 100K logical inferences per second, whereas meta-level systems that have their control regime explicitly specified in the meta-level theory will have to perform expensive meta-level inference in order to execute the object-level strategy. Thus, the trade-off is between cutting down the number of logical inferences made at the object-level versus an increase in cost per logical inference due to the extra time spent interpreting the meta-level theory.

It is of course impossible to say anything in general about the reduction in the number of object-level logical inferences, since this depends entirely on the effectiveness of the control strategy as formalised at the meta-level, but simple quantitative models (see for instance [Rose83]) show that in realistic situations there will be a diminishing return on the effectiveness of meta-level effort, and that as a result, there will be a point where the meta-level effort (ie. the increase in cost per logical inference) outweighs the savings made at the object-level (ie. the reduction in number of logical inferences). Where this break-even point lies depends of course entirely on the characteristics of a particular system, but experiments described in [O'Ke88], [Lowe88] and [Owen88a] indicate that the increase in costs for a single object-level inference is often a factor in the range 10-100. This factor was found to be stable across a number of different applications, implemented in different systems.

Although many of the papers in the literature dealing with the use of meta-level interpreters for control issues acknowledge the inefficiency that is inherent in the multiple layers of interpretation, very few of them offer any solutions to this problem. An important section of the limited work on reducing meta-level overhead in recent years has been based on the idea of specialising the general purpose formulation of the meta-level control regime with respect to the particular object-level theory that is being used in the system. Most of the work on this idea is based on the use of *partial evaluation* as an optimisation technique.

Work reported in for example [Venk84], [Take86], [Take85], [Safr86], [Levi88] and [Gall86], is all based on this technique. In this paper we will first describe this technique, and its application to meta-level interpreters in logic-based systems. In the second part of this paper we will explore some of the limitations of this technique in the context of meta-level interpreters for logic-based expert systems, which remain largely undiscussed in the literature.

2 A description of partial evaluation

The main goal of partial evaluation is to perform as much of the computation in a program as possible without depending on any of the input values of the program. The theoretical foundation for partial evaluation is Kleene's S-M-N theorem from recursive function theory [Klee52]. This theorem says that given any computable function f of n variables ($f = f(x_1,\ldots,x_n)$), and k ($k \leq n$) values $a_1,\ldots,a_k$ for $x_1,\ldots,x_k$, we can effectively compute a new function f' such that

$$f'(x_{k+1},\ldots,x_n) = f(a_1,\ldots,a_k,x_{k+1},\ldots,x_n)$$

The new function f' is a specialisation of f, and is easier to compute than f for those specific input values. A partial evaluation algorithm can be regarded as the implementation of this theorem, and is, in fact, slightly more general in the context of logic programming: it allows not only that a number of input variables are instantiated to constants, but also that these variables can be partially instantiated to terms that contain nested variables. Furthermore, a partial evaluation algorithm allows k in the above theorem (the number of instantiated input variables), to be 0, that is, no input to f is specified at all. Even in this case a partial evaluation algorithm is often able to produce a definition of f' which is equivalent to f but more efficient, since all the computations performed by f that are independent of the values of the input variables can be precomputed in f'. Thus, a partial evaluation algorithm takes as its input a function (program) definition, together with a partial specification of the input of the program, and produces a new version of the program that is specialised for the particular input values. The new version of the program may then be less general but more efficient than the original version.

A partial evaluation algorithm works by symbolically evaluating the input program while trying to (i) propagate constant values through the program code, (ii) unfold procedure calls, and (iii) branching out conditional parts of the code. If the language used to express the input program is logic, then the symbolic evaluation of the program becomes the construction of the proof tree corresponding to the execution of the program.

A special case of partial evaluation is when none of the values for the input variables $x_1, \ldots, x_k$ are given (in other words, $k = 0$). In this case, the partial evaluation algorithm cannot do as much optimisation of the input program, and as a result the new program will not be as efficient. However, the new program is no longer only a specialisation of the original program, but indeed equivalent to it. Thus, in this way partial evaluation can be used as a way of reformulating the input program in an equivalent but more efficient way.

As a simple example of partial evaluation, consider the following function in Lisp:

```
(defun assoc (key alist)
       (cond ((null alist) nil)
             ((eq key (caar alist)) (car alist))
             (t (assoc key (cdr alist)))))
```

This function accesses the standard Lisp assoc-list data-structure. If we specify a partial input, such as

```
alist = '((key1 . val1)(key2 . val2))
```

then we can partially evaluate `assoc`, using the following call to the partial evaluator:[1]

```
(peval '(assoc key '((key1 . val1)(key2 . val2))))
```

to return the derived program `assoc'`:

```
(defun assoc' (key)
       (cond ((eq key 'key1) '(key1 . val1))
             (t (cond ((eq key 'key2) '(key2 . val2))
                      (t nil)))))
```

One problem with partial evaluation in general is that the partial evaluator has to handle uninstantiated variables. This is because the input of the source program is only partially specified and some of the variables in the source program will not have a value at partial evaluation time. In most programming languages it is hard to deal with uninstantiated variables, and the partial evaluator has to be very careful about what it evaluates, and what not.

This is exactly the reason why logic programming is especially suited for partial evaluation. Unification is a fundamental computational operation in logic programming, and handling uninstantiated variables in unification is no problem at all. In fact, uninstantiated variables arising

[1]This call to the partial evaluator only specifies half of its input: the partially specified input to the source program. The other half of the input to the partial evaluator (the actual definition of the source program) is assumed to be globally available in the execution environment of this call. This argument could be made explicit in the obvious way.

```
theory(t1,
      [o1(a) & h1(X) => c1(X, a),
       o2(a) & h2(X) => c1(X, a),
       o3(X, Y) => h2(Y),
       o3(b, c),
       o2(a)
      ]).
```

Figure 1: An object-level theory in Prolog

from partially specified input[2] can be treated like any other term. For instance, in the example above, care had to be taken not to further evaluate the eq's and cond's, since the variable key was uninstantiated at partial evaluation time. However, in Prolog, the program assoc:

```
assoc(_, [], []).
assoc(Key, [[Key, Value]|_], Value).
assoc(Key, [_|Alist], Value) :-
        assoc(Key, Alist, Value).
```

plus a call to the partial evaluator:

```
:- peval(assoc(Key, [[key1, val1], [key2, val2]], Val)).
```

partially evaluates into:

```
assoc'(key1, [[key1, val1], [key2, val2]], val1).
assoc'(key2, [[key1, val1], [key2, val2]], val2).
assoc'(_, [[key1, val1], [key2, val2]], []).
```

without having to worry about evaluation at all, since even with an uninstantiated variable Key, the procedure evaluates to the equivalent specialised code, which now contains no further calls to be executed at run time.

This technique of specialising a program with respect to its (partial) input to derive a more efficient version, can also be applied in the special case when the source program is itself the definition of an interpreter (i.e. a meta-level program). This will then produce a version of the meta-level interpreter which is specialised for the particular object-level theory program that was given as input specification.

Example in Prolog: Consider an object-level theory, called t1, as in figure 1 and a meta-level interpreter that specifies how to use these clauses, as in figure 2.

This meta-level interpreter assumes that the predicate object_level_interpreter generates all possible formulas derivable from the input formula using the available object-level inference rules. A full instantiation of the input to the meta-level interpreter consists of the object-level theory, plus the top goal that should be proved. So, if the above meta-level program is partially evaluated with the arguments:

[2]In the context of logic programming G' is a partial specification of G if G' is subsumed by G. We also say that G' is an *instantiation* of G (notation: $G' \leq_{inst} G$): there exists a substitution θ for variables in G such that θ applied to G gives G': $G' = \theta G$. G' is a *strict instantiation* of G (notation: $G' <_{inst} G$) if there is a non-empty substitution θ for variables in G such that $G' = \theta G$.

```
[1] proof(Goal, Theory) :-
        lookup(Goal, Theory).
[2] proof(Goal, Theory) :-
        object_level_inference(Goal, Theory, New_Goals),
        proof(New_Goals, Theory).

[3] proof([],_).
[4] proof([Goal|Goals], Theory) :-
        proof(Goal, Theory),
        proof(Goals, Theory).
```

Figure 2: A meta-level interpreter in Prolog

```
[1]  proof(o1(a) & h1(X) => c1(X,a), t1).
[2]  proof(o2(a) & h2(X) => c1(X,a), t1).
[3]  proof(o3(X,Y) => h2(Y), t1).
[4]  proof(o3(b,c), t1).
[5]  proof(o2(a), t1).
[6]  proof(h2(c), t1).
[7]  proof(c1(c,a), t1).
[8]  proof(X & Y, t1) :-
         proof(X, t1),
         proof(Y, t1).
[9]  proof([X|Y], t1) :-
         proof(X, t1),
         proof(Y, t1).
[10] proof([], t1).
```

Figure 3: The programs after partial evaluation

```
Goal = c1(X, a)
Theory = t1
```

with the following call to the partial evaluator:

```
:- peval(proof(c1(X, a), t1)).
```

then, assuming that the inference rules Modus Ponens and And Introduction are in the object-level inference rules, the derived version of the meta-level program becomes:

```
proof(c1(c, a), t1).
```

However, we do not want to specify the top goal of the query, since we cannot predict which goal we will want to prove. So, we underspecify the input to the source program (the meta-level interpreter): we leave the query uninstantiated, and only specify the object-level theory that we want to use. In the example above we would call the partial evaluator with

```
:- peval(proof(Goal, t1)).
```

giving us the remarkably transformed source program as shown in figure 3. This program contains the direct results for all the successful proofs that could be performed by the meta-level interpreter, namely:

- clauses [1]-[5] contain all the results derived via clause [1] of the meta-level interpreter (using `lookup`),
- clauses [6]-[7] contain all the results derivable via application of Modus Ponens (via clause [2] of the meta-level interpreter),
- clause [8] contains a precomputed scheme for applying And Introduction (based on clauses [2]-[4] of the meta-interpreter),
- clauses [9] and [10] repeat the code from the meta-interpreter for iterating over conjunctive goals. This code will never be used by the partially evaluated version, since the iteration over conjunctive goals has already been precomputed in clause [8]. The fact that this superfluous code still appears in the partially evaluated version is due to the difference in status of clauses [1]-[2] and [3]-[4] of the meta-level interpreter: clauses [1]-[2] are meant to be called by the user of the meta-level interpreter, whereas clauses [3]-[4] are only meant to be called by the code itself. If this information had been conveyed to the partial evaluator (for instance by introducing a new predicate name, clauses [9]-[10] would not have occurred in the partially evaluated code.

The partially evaluated code from figure 3 is of course much more efficient than the original code from figures 1 and 2: Any of the facts mentioned in clauses [1]-[5] of figure 3 can now be proved in 1 logical inference[3] instead of taking anywhere between 4 and 8 logical inferences (depending on their place in the object-level theory). Similarly, the facts from clauses [6]-[7] can now be proved in 1 logical inference, instead of 18 and 41 logical inferences respectively. The speedup for conjunctive goals is 3 logical inferences per conjunction. These speedups may be quite small as absolute figures, but taken as a proportion of the small amount of inference done by this toy example it amounts to about an order of magnitude speedup.

3 Problems of partial evaluation

Although the above example indicates the power of partial evaluation, there are some serious problems associated with partial evaluation as a tool for reducing meta-level overhead. Experiments with partial evaluation of small Prolog programs that were executed by a simple meta-level interpreter indicated two main problems. The first of these is related to the definition of the object-level program (which is one of the arguments of the meta-level procedure that is instantiated at partial evaluation time), and the second problem is to do with the amount of information that is available to the partial evaluator.

3.1 Changing object-level programs at run time

In partial evaluation, programs are specialised with respect to their (partial) input. This gives a derived program that is specialised with respect to its input, and obviously this specialised program cannot be used to do computations on different inputs.

[3]One logical inference corresponds roughly to one procedure call.

```
proof(X,t1) :-
        lookup(X,t1).
proof(X,t1) :-
        proof([Y=>X,Y],t1).
proof(X&Y,t1) :-
        proof([X,Y],t1).
proof([X|Y],t1) :-
        proof(X,t1),
        proof(Y,t1).
proof([],t1).
```

Figure 4: The programs after restricted partial evaluation

In our specific case, the only part of the input to the source program (the meta-level interpreter) that is specified is the object-level theory. However, this object-level theory is likely to change while the meta-level interpreter is running. We are likely to want to add to the object-level theory during the proof of a particular query, thereby invalidating the optimised version of the meta-level program.

Furukawa and Takeuchi [Take86] describe a solution for the special case when the object-level theory grows monotonically. This involves constructing a version of a partial evaluator which is specialised for the meta-level interpreter plus the current version of the object-level theory, by applying the partial evaluator to itself with the meta-level interpreter and object-level theory as input. When a clause is added to the object-level theory, the specialised version of the partial evaluator can be used to construct both a partially evaluated version of the meta-level interpreter for the increased object-level theory, as well as a new version of the specialised partial evaluator, which is in turn to be used when the next clause is added to the object-level theory. Since this process can be performed incrementally, the overhead of repeated partial evaluation is greatly reduced. However, although this incremental approach might be useful during the development stages of a system, it is doubtful whether the price of repeatedly constructing a new specialised version of both meta-level interpreter and partial evaluator at run time does not cost more than it gains, especially when the object-level theory changes frequently. In the context of the problem of changing object-level theories, Sterling and Beer [Ster86] talk about "open programs", which are programs whose definition is not complete, for instance because input data for the expert system needs to be provided at run time. They do not provide a solution for this problem, since they

> "assume that a goal which fails during partial evaluation time will also fail at run time, that is, we assume that a system to be partially evaluated is closed."

Another solution to the problem of run time changes to the object-level theory would be not to include the object-level theory in the specialisation process. This would leave us with only the object-level rules of inference as input for specialisation of the meta-level interpreter. In terms of the example meta-level interpreter from figure 2 this would mean that we do not supply the object-level theory from figure 1 but that we do supply the definition of the predicate `object_level_interpreter`. This restricted version of the partial evaluation process would not generate a very efficient program like the one in figure 3 but the code in figure 4. Although this code is not as optimal as the code in figure 3 (since a lot of computation is still to be done at run time), it is still more efficient than the original version from figure 2. The new program will not be invalidated by run time changes, since the object-level theory was not used in the specialisation process (the predicate `lookup` will still be executed at run time, and was not precomputed by the partial evaluator, as it was in figure 3. The rules of inference (which were used in the specialisation process) are not very likely to be the subject of run time changes.

3.2 Lack of static information

An important distinction can be made between so called *static* and *dynamic* information. Static information is information which is part of, or can be derived from, the program code, whereas dynamic information is dependent on the run time environment of the program. For the purposes of partial evaluation we include the values of input variables supplied at partial evaluation time in our definition of static information. For example, in the following or statement

```
(or (eq x 'a)(eql y 2))
```

under the partial input specification

```
y = 3
```

both arguments to the call to `eql` are statically available (and therefore so is the result of the call to `eql`), whereas only one argument to the call to `eq` is statically available, since the value of x can only be dynamically determined.

[Beet87] distinguishes three different types of information that can influence the search strategy:

1. Information that is independent of the current problem and the current state of the problem solving process.

2. Information that is dependent on the current problem, but independent of the current state of the problem solving process.

3. Information that is dependent on both the current problem and the current state of the problem solving process.

Since both the second and the third type of control information will only be dynamically available, search strategies that use such information can not be optimised (or only to a limited extent) by using partial evaluation. Only search strategies that are independent of both the input problem and the current state of the problem solving process can make full use of partial evaluation. However, such search strategies are very weak and general, and do not typically play a very important role in expert systems applications. It is notable that all the examples given in the literature on partial evaluation show programs that employ only the first type of information.

In order to analyse the problem of dynamic information in more detail, we can distinguish three techniques that are used by a partial evaluator to produce more efficient code:

1. branching out conditional parts of the code,

2. propagating data structures,

3. opening up intermediate procedure calls (unfolding).

We will argue that each of these techniques is crucially dependent on a large proportion of the information being statically available. If most of the information is only dynamically available, partial evaluation will generate quite poor results.

The first technique deals with *conditional branches in the code.* If the condition for such a branch cannot be evaluated at partial evaluation time, because its value is dependent on dynamic information, the partial evaluator either has to stop its evaluations at this point, or it has to generate code for both branches of the conditional, and leave it to the run time evaluation to determine which of these branches should be taken. Neither of these strategies is very successful: if a partial evaluator has to stop optimising the source code at the first dynamically determined conditional it encounters in the code, the resulting code may be not very different at all from the original code, and hence will not be any more efficient. The other strategy (generating code for all possible branches) is also usually not very attractive, given the high branching rates of most programs. This will result in very bulky output code (possibly exponential in the size of the original code), most of which will not be executed at run time. In the context of Prolog, this will mean a large number of clauses that will have to be tried at run time, even though most of them will fail in most cases.

The second technique (*propagating data structures*) tries to pass on data structures through the code in the program. This passing of data structures can be done both *forward* (for input values), and *backward* (for output values)[4]. Obviously, the forward passing of data structures only works for those parts of the data that have been provided statically as partial input. The backward passing of data structures is typically dependent on the values of the input, and is therefore also blocked if most information is only available dynamically. A special problem occurs with the so called built-in predicates that are provided by the Prolog interpreter. These predicates often depend on the full instantiation of a number of their arguments (e.g. `is`), and can therefore not be executed by the partial evaluator if the argument-values are not available. Other built-in predicates cause side effects that must occur at run time (e.g. `write`), and such predicates must also be suspended by the partial evaluator.

The third technique (*unfolding*) tries to insert code for procedure calls as 'in line code', rather than explicitly calling the procedures at run time. This technique runs into trouble as soon as the source program contains recursive calls. Although a particular recursive program may in practice always terminate at run-time, this is not necessarily the case at partial-evaluation time, due to the lack of static information. In the case of a logic program this means that the proof tree may contain infinite paths for some uninstantiated goals, and the partial evaluation would be non terminating. Since these infinite computations only arise from the lack of information at partial-evaluation time, and do not occur at run time, we will use the phrase *pseudo-infinite* computation. Two different types of pseudo-infinite computation can be distinguished. The first type, *pseudo-infinitely deep* computation, is caused by programs whose recursive clauses always apply (at partial evaluation time), but whose base clauses never apply, due to the lack of static information. This gives rise to a proof tree with infinitely long branches. The second type, *pseudo-infinitely wide* computation, is caused by programs whose recursive clauses always apply, but whose base clauses also apply sometimes. This gives rise to a proof tree with infinitely many finite branches. A mixture of both types of pseudo-infinite computation is of course also possible. Pseudo-infinitely deep computation corresponds to a program that needs an infinite amount of time to compute its first output, and pseudo-infinitely wide computation corresponds to a program that computes an infinite number of outputs (on backtracking, in the case of Prolog).

---

[4]It is exactly this passing of data structures which makes logic programs so suited for partial evaluation, since both the forward and the backward passing is done automatically by the unification mechanism that is provided by the standard interpreter for the language.

A good example of both problems is the predicate num-elem given below, which selects numeric elements from a list:

```
num-elem(X, [X|_]) :- number(X).
num-elem(X, [_|L]) :- num-elem(X,L).
```

If this predicate is partially evaluated with no input specified, then the base case will never apply, and an infinitely deep computation will result. If this predicate is partially evaluated with the first argument bound to a specific number, but the second argument still unbound, then the base case will always apply, but so will the recursive clause, resulting in an infinitely wide computation. (Notice that when this predicate is partially evaluated with the second argument bound, then none of these problems occur).

In certain cases, the occurrence of breadth-infinity does not need to lead to problems during partial evaluation, in particular if it is known at partial evaluation time how many outputs are required of the source program. If it is known that at most n different outputs are needed from the source program, then the partial evaluator can unfold the proof tree of the source program until the base clauses have applied n times. A realistic example of this is where a predicate P is immediately followed by a cut in a Prolog program:

$$\mathtt{Q_1,\ldots,Q_i,P,!,Q_{i+1},\ldots,Q_k}$$

or more generally

$$\mathtt{Q_1,\ldots,Q_i,P,Q_{i+1},\ldots,Q_j,!,Q_{j+1},\ldots,Q_k}$$

where all the conjuncts $\mathtt{Q_{i+1},\ldots,Q_j}$ are known to be deterministic (that is: given an input they compute exactly one output). In such a case $n = 1$, i.e. only 1 output will ever be required from P. This sort of analysis does of course presuppose that the partial evaluation algorithm has knowledge about properties of cut and of determinateness of predicates in the source program.

In the more general case, where such information about n is not known, or for pseudo-infinitely deep programs, it is necessary for a partial evaluation program to select a finite subtree from the infinite proof tree, in order to guarantee termination of the partial evaluation algorithm. Let π be a source program, θ an input substitution to π, $P(\pi,\theta)$ a partial evaluation procedure, and let $\pi(\theta)\downarrow$ mean that π terminates on input θ, then we would at least require P to terminate whenever π would terminate on θ (or on some instantiation of θ). Formally:

$$\forall\pi\forall\theta : (\exists\theta' \leq_{inst} \theta : \pi(\theta')\downarrow) \rightarrow P(\pi,\theta)\downarrow .$$

This can of course always be achieved by trivial means, such as not unfolding recursive predicates at all, or only unfolding them once (as in [Venk84]), or in general only unfolding them to a fixed maximum depth. However, a more sophisticated solution would be to incorporate a stop criterion in the partial evaluation procedure that will tell us whether a branch of the proof tree for $\pi(\theta)$ is infinite. Thus, we need a stop criterion S such that:

$$\forall\pi\forall\theta : (\forall\theta' \leq_{inst} \theta : \pi(\theta')\uparrow) \leftrightarrow S(\pi,\theta). \tag{1}$$

As soon as S becomes true on a branch for $\pi(\theta)$, the partial evaluation procedure should stop. The problem with such a criterion S is that it amounts to solving the halting problem for Prolog, and that therefore it is undecidable. The halting problem for a given language L is to find a predicate H_L that will decided whether an arbitrary program P written in L will halt on an arbitrary input I or not:[5]

$$\forall P\forall I : P(I)\uparrow \leftrightarrow H_L(P,I) \tag{2}$$

[5]The reader should be aware of a possible confusion: the stop criterion S from 1 is true not when $\pi(\theta)$ will stop, but when $\pi(\theta)$ will *not* stop, indicating that the partial evaluator *should be stopped.* In analogy, 2 has been formulated using $P(I)\uparrow$ instead of the usual $P(I)\downarrow$.

One of the fundamental theorems of the theory of computation states that this problem is undecidable for any sufficiently powerful language L. Prolog is certainly sufficiently powerful, since it is Turing complete [Tarn77]. Since having S from 1 would also give us H_{Prolog} from (2), S must also be undecidable. This means that the best we can hope for regarding a stop criterion for partial evaluation is one that is either too strong or too weak. A stop criterion which is too strong will satisfy the $\rightarrow$ direction of 1, but there will be some π_0 and θ_0 such that

$$S(\pi_0, \theta_0) \wedge \exists \theta' \leq_{inst} \theta_0 : \pi(\theta') \downarrow,$$

in other words, S will tell us that π_0 will not terminate on θ_0 (or any instantiation of it), while in fact it would. This would result in stopping the unfolding of the partial evaluation algorithm prematurely, thereby producing suboptimal results. Conversely, a stop criterion which is too weak will satisfy the $\leftarrow$ direction of 1, but there will be some π_0 and θ_0 such that

$$\neg S(\pi_0, \theta_0) \wedge \forall \theta' \leq_{inst} \theta_0 : \pi(\theta') \uparrow,$$

in other words, S will tell us that π_0 will terminate on θ_0 (or some instantiation of it), while in fact it would not. This would result in a non-terminating partial evaluation.

In the practical use of a stop criterion, a partial evaluator would keep a stack of goals that are unfolded during the expansion of the input program. If we call the original goal $G = G_0$, and we describe the stack of unfolded goals by $G_i(0 > i > j)$, then a number of useful termination criteria are:

1. unification: $\exists i < j, \exists \theta : \theta G_j = \theta G_i$. We write $G_j =_{unif} G_i$.
2. instantiation: $\exists i < j, \exists \theta : G_j = \theta G_i$, i.e. $G_j \leq_{inst} G_i$.
3. strict instantiation: $\exists i < j, \exists \theta (non\text{-}empty) : G_j = \theta G_i$, i.e $G_j <_{inst} G_i$.
4. alphabetic variancy: $G_j \leq_{inst} G_i$ and $G_i \leq_{inst} G_j$, i.e. $G_j =_{inst} G_i$ (G_i and G_j are identical up to renaming of variables).

It is not necessary to consider another variation, namely ($G_j >_{inst} G_i$) where G_i is a strict instantiation of G_j, since any chain of ever more general subgoals (a chain $G_0, \ldots, G_n$ where $G_i <_{inst} G_j$ if $i < j$) will always have a most general goal as its limit, and therefore such a computation must always terminate. However, we can have two different variations of (1), namely unification without occurs-check (1a) and unification with occurs-check (1b). These stop criteria relate to each other as follows:

$$(3 \vee 4) \leftrightarrow 2$$
$$2 \rightarrow 1b \rightarrow 1a$$

Simple examples can show that none of these criteria performs satisfactorily. In particular, none of these criteria deals satisfactorily with pseudo-infinitely wide computations. Consider for example a predicate like:

```
p1(X,Y).
p1(X,Y) :- p1(s(X),Y)
```

which generates on backtracking all terms $s^n(0)$ after the call

```
:- p1(0,Y).
```

None of the above stop criteria is able to prevent a partial evaluator from looping while trying to partially evaluate p1 with the first argument instantiated. The point here is not that we would expect a great optimisation from the partial evaluation (it is not clear what such optimisation could possibly be), but rather that the presence of a predicate like p1 in any code makes the partial evaluation non-terminating. An example that illustrates the difference between some of the termination criteria is partially evaluating the above predicate p1 with no input specified. In this case stop criterion 3 is too weak, and lets the partial evaluator loop infinitely, while criteria 4 (and by implication 2, 1a and 1b) properly halt the partial evaluator and reproduce the original code. However, the roles of 3 and 4 swap over on the predicate:

```
p2(0).
p2(s(X)) :- p2(X).
```

which will succeed on any input of the form $s^n(0)$. Partially evaluating p2 with no input specified will be properly stopped by 3 (and by implication also by 2, 1a and 1b), but not by 4 which will loop forever.

For a more realistic example, we can turn to the example that was used in the previous section to describe the use of partial evaluation for meta-level interpreters, shown in figures 1, 2 and 3. The partially evaluated code in figure 3 was computed from the code in figures 1 and 2 using stop criterion 3 (strict instantiation). Had we used the stronger stop criterion 2 (non-strict instantiation), the partial evaluator would have produced the same code in as figure 3 but with clauses [6]-[7] replaced by the following clause:

```
[6a] proof(X, t1) :-
          proof([Y => X, Y], t1).
```

This new clause represents a precomputed version of Modus Ponens, but the partial evaluator has stopped short of actually applying this rule, as in in figure 3, due to the stronger stop criterion. As a result, this new code is not as efficient as the code from figure 3. An advantage of the stronger stop criterion is that it takes significantly less time to execute the partial evaluator (the difference between the execution times of the partial evaluator with stop criteria 2 and 3 is more than a factor 100).

A different situation occurred while computing the code for figure 4. Fewer bindings for variables were known for that partial evaluation, since the object-level theory was not included in the input specification. As a result, the stronger stop criterion 2 had to be used to produce the result in figure 4. Any weaker stop criterion would result in either a non-terminating partial evaluation, or in code with many spurious branches.

3.3 Summary of problems

Summarising, we can say that although in principle a powerful technique, partial evaluation is rather restricted in its use for optimising meta-level interpreters for two reasons.

- Firstly, if the object-level theory is going to be changed at run time, at least part of the object-level theory cannot be included as input to the partial evaluation algorithm, thereby negatively affecting the optimisations achieved by partial evaluation.
- Secondly, if most of the information in a program is only dynamically available (i.e. at run time), partial evaluation suffers from the following disadvantages:
  - If the source code contains conditional expressions, then a partial evaluator will either have to stop the optimisation process at that point, or produce very bulky code.

- Data structures cannot be propagated throughout the code.
- If the source code contains recursive procedures, then, unless specific termination criteria are programmed for particular predicates, a partial evaluator will either produce suboptimal code, or termination of the partial evaluator is no longer guaranteed.

It has to be stressed that although the above discussion quotes examples in Prolog, the problems are not due to this choice, and are fundamental to the concept of partial evaluation.

4 Heuristic guidance to partial evaluation

Although the problems discussed above seriously limit the applicability of partial evaluation as a tool for reducing meta-level overhead, a number of heuristics solution can be found to alleviate the problems to a certain extent. The heuristics discussed below are all based on the idea that we will try to build a specific partial evaluator for a particular application, rather than a general, application independent one. More precisely, we can maintain the general framework for a partial evaluator as discussed above, but identify specific places in the algorithm where a user can tune the algorithm to suit a particular application. In particular, we will point out a number of places in the partial evaluation algorithm where we can insert specific knowledge about the behaviour of components of the program to be evaluated. In our case these components will be meta-level predicates, ie. predicates occurring in the meta-level interpreter.

An obvious candidate for removing over-generality is the stop criterion used to determine when to stop unfolding recursive predicates. This criterion can never be correct in the general case (since such a criterion would solve the halting problem for Prolog programs, and hence for Turing machines). As a result, any general criterion is either going to be too weak (i.e. not halting on some infinite recursion), or too strong (i.e. halting too early on some finite recursion). However, if we know the intended meaning of particular parts of a program we can construct specialised termination criteria that are just right for these particular procedures. As example, consider the definition of `member/2`:

```
member(X, [X|_]).
member(X, [_|T]) :- member(X,T).
```

We know that this predicate is guaranteed to terminate as long as the length of the second argument is decreasing. A good specialised stop criterion for this predicate would therefore be:

$$\exists i,j : i > j,\ member_i(X, L_i) \& member_j(X, L_j) \wedge \parallel L_i \parallel \geq \parallel L_j \parallel,$$

where $member_i$ represents the i-th call to `member`. This stop criterion would successfully unfold all calls to `member/2` where the second argument is instantiated, but will not loop on those calls where the second argument is uninstantiated (due to a lack of static information). This corresponds to the notion that `member/2` will be used to test membership of a given list, and not to generate all possible lists containing a certain element. This criterion will even work for partially instantiated second arguments. A call to `member/2` like

```
:- member(X, [1,2|L]).
```

will properly partially evaluate to:

```
member(1, [1,2|L]).
member(2, [1,2|L]).
member(X, [1,2,X|_]).
member(X, [1,2,_|T]) :- member(X, T).
```

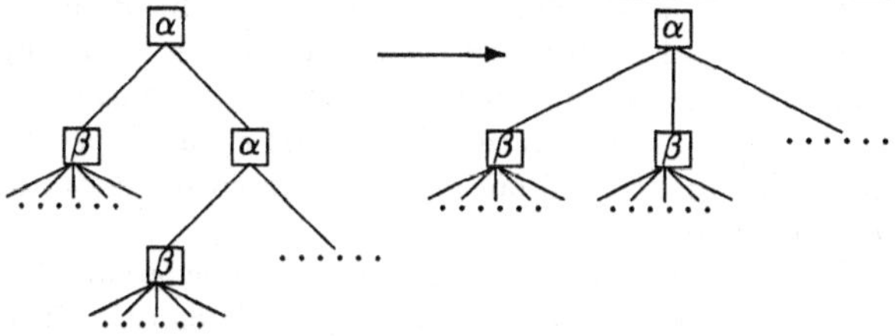

Figure 5: Heuristically limited partial evaluation

The partial evaluation has generated all possible results based on the available static information, while stopping short of looping on the uninstantiated part of the input.

The above halting criterion is based on the intended meaning and use of the predicate member/2, and cannot be generally used, since it would again be either too strong or too weak for certain predicates. Consider for instance the predicate nlist/2 which generates a list of length n:

```
nlist(0, []).
nlist(s(X), [_|T]) :- nlist(X, T).
```

(We use terms $s^n(0)$ for representing the number n to avoid problems with the built in arithmetical predicates. More about this below). This predicate should not be stopped when its second argument is increasing in length, as with member/2, but rather when its first argument is increasing in depth. Such metrics should be devised where possible for predicates used in a meta-level interpreter, and the stop criterion should be specialised for these cases.

A second heuristic that we can inject in the partial evaluation algorithm is a special treatment for certain predicates which are known to be easy to compute at run time, but possibly hard or impossible to compute with only static information. This idea is based on the notion of an *operational predicate* as introduced in the explanation-based generalisation algorithm [Mitc86] which turns out to be closely related to the partial evaluation algorithm [Harm88]. The partial evaluation algorithm should stop when encountering such an operational predicate (which is declared as such beforehand), no matter what amount of precomputation could potentially be done using the definition of such a predicate. For instance, it is possible that the definition of such a predicate has a very high branching rate, leading to an explosion of the size of the code generated by partial evaluation, while only one of the many branches would be chosen and computed at low cost at run time, pruning all the other branches. In such a case it is better not to generate the highly branched search space explicitly at partial evaluation time, but to leave it for run time computation.

An example of this specialised treatment of the partial evaluation algorithm for certain predicates is the standard logic programming technique where a predicate, when applied to a list, unpacks the list into its elements, and then takes a specific action for each of the elements in the list. If these specific actions have a very high branching rate, a good strategy for the partial evaluator is to precompute the process of unfolding the list into its elements (a deterministic operation), but to stop short of partially evaluating the actions taken for the individual elements. These actions will have to be performed at run time, when extra available dynamic information will possibly cut down the branching rate. Graphically, this optimisation process can be depicted as in figure 5. Figure 5a shows the search tree of original code before partial evaluation, with the α nodes doing the unfolding of the list, and the β nodes doing the highly non-deterministic actions for the individual nodes. If we designate β to be an operational predicate, the limited partial evaluation described above will produce code that has a search space as in figure 5b showing that the limited partial evaluation still optimises the search space, but does not get bogged down in the explosive parts of it.

Another heuristic to optimise partial evaluation is *mixed computation*. This involves declaring certain meta-level predicates to be executable at partial evaluation time. If the partial evaluator comes across such a predicate during unfolding, it does not unfold that predicate using its ordinary unfolding strategy, but rather it calls the hardwired interpreter that would normally execute the meta-level code (i.e. in our examples the Prolog interpreter) to execute the particular predicate. The resulting variable bindings are then taken into account during the rest of the unfolding process, but the predicate itself can be removed from the code.

A final heuristic to be embodied in the partial evaluator concerns the evaluable predicates, as typically built into a Prolog system. These predicates can be divided into three types, and for each of the types a different partial evaluation strategy should be used.

- The first type of evaluable predicates are those that perform *side-effects* (e.g. input-output). These predicates can never be performed at partial evaluation time, and must always be postponed until run time.

- The second type of predicates are those that can be partially evaluated if certain conditions hold. These conditions are specific for each particular predicate. For instance, the predicate `var/1` (which tests if its argument is a variable), can be partially evaluated (to `false`, pruning branches from the code) if its argument is not a variable. The reason for this is of course that if the argument is not a variable at partial evaluation time, it will never become a variable at run time, since variables only get more instantiated, not less. On the other hand, if the predicate `var/1` succeeds at partial evaluation time, it must remain in the code, since its argument might or might not have become instantiated at run time. Another example is the predicate `==/2` (testing if its arguments are the same Prolog object). This predicate can be evaluated (to `true`, that is: removed), if it succeeds at partial evaluation time. The argument here is that if it succeeds at partial evaluation time, it will also succeed at run time (since objects that are the same can never become different again), but when the arguments are different at partial evaluation time the predicate should remain in the code, since the objects might or might not have become the same at run time[6]. A third example of this category is the predicate `functor/3` (which computes functor and arity of a Prolog term). This predicate can be partially evaluated if either the first or both the second and third arguments are (at least partially) instantiated. Further criteria could be provided for a number of other built in Prolog predicates.

- The final class of evaluable predicates are those which can be either fully evaluated (if they are fully instantiated at partial evaluation time), or translated into a number of simplified constraints. A good example of this class of predicates are the arithmetic predicates. Obviously, a goal like `X is 5+4` can be fully computed at partial evaluation time, as well as goals like `9 is X+4` and `X>10, X<5` (although a somewhat more sophisticated algorithm is required). In general a goal like `X is Y` ⟨op⟩ `Z`, where ⟨op⟩ is any of the functions `+`, `-` and `*` can be fully computed at partial evaluation time if at least 2 out of the 3 arguments are

[6]This criterion for `==/2` is quite different from that used in the partial evaluator described in [Prie87], where it is incorrectly treated the same as `=/2` (unification), which can always be performed at partial evaluation time, unlike `==/2`.

instantiated. Some types of calls cannot be fully computed at partial evaluation time, but can be transformed into simplified conditions, for instance `X<10, X<11` can be reduced to `X <10`, and the integer division `4 is X/3` can be transformed into `X>11, X<15`. The partial evaluator incorporated in the PROLEARN system [Prie87] implements these heuristics.

4.1 Summary of heuristics

The partial evaluator can be tailored to specific applications by

- incorporating specialised stop criteria for certain recursive predicates.
- using knowledge about operational predicates to stop the partial evaluation process
- using knowledge about the branching factor of certain predicates to stop the partial evaluation process
- allowing execution during partial evaluation, the so called mixed computation
- using specialised knowledge to deal with evaluable predicates, dividing them in three ways:
  - predicates that can never be partially evaluated (predicates with side effects).
  - predicates that can only be evaluated if certain conditions hold
  - predicates that can be transformed into simpler constraints.

5 Related work in the literature

Much related work has been done in the last few years on partial evaluation and its application to meta-programming (e.g. [Bjor87] and [Lloy88]). Some of these papers analyse and discuss the limitations of partial evaluation in a similar way as we have done in this paper, and we will discuss two of these papers in particular.

A well known problem with the use of negation in logic programming is that it is only sound when applied to fully instantiated goals. If applied to partially uninstantiated subgoals, the negation is said to "flounder" [Lloy84], and produces unsound results. This problem is particularly urgent during partial evaluation. A partial evaluation algorithm cannot unfold a negated subgoal if it is not fully instantiated. However, due to the lack of dynamic information at partial evaluation time, many negated subgoals will not be fully instantiated, thus hampering the performance of partial evaluation. As a result, the partial evaluation algorithm given in [Lloy87] is restricted to either evaluate negated subgoals completely (if they are fully instantiated), or not at all otherwise. To solve this problem, [Chan88] gives two techniques for dealing with negated subgoals. This solution is based on two separate techniques for eliminating negation from a program, or at least splitting up into smaller pieces, so that the partial evaluation algorithm can optimise larger parts of the source program.

A second paper that explores the limitations of partial evaluation is [Owen88b]. Owen applied partial evaluation to a number of meta-interpreters that were developed for a particular application, and compared the results of this with hand-coded optimisations of the same set of interpreters. This careful analysis revealed many problems with the practical use of partial evaluation, some of which have also been discussed in this paper:

- Partial evaluation should not always suspend built-in meta-logical predicates (see section 4).

- Partial evaluation causes significant fruitless branches in the object-level program (see section 3.2).
- Partial evaluation systems always suspend the execution of Prolog's cut, even when this is not necessary.

In order to deal with these problems, Owen proposes a number of enhancements to the partial evaluation algorithm. The most significant of these is what he calls a *folding transformation*, which folds a sequence of conjuncts into a new, uniquely named procedure. This is the opposite of the unfolding operation described in section 2. The main goal of this extra operation is to control the branching rate of the code produced by partial evaluation. However, the introduction of this new operation makes a partial evaluation algorithm non-deterministic (the algorithm will have to choose between different possible operations at each step), whereas this was not the case before. This introduces a search component in the partial evaluation procedure that was not present without the folding operation. Further extensions that Owen proposes to the partial evaluation algorithm are the merging of clauses with identical heads, or with heads that only differ in positions which contain local variables, and rules that allow the treatment of cuts in certain under certain conditions at partial evaluation time. Unfortunately, even with these an many other special purpose extensions to his partial evaluation algorithm, Owen found the results of partial evaluation on his meta-level interpreters suboptimal, and it would require open ended theorem proving and consistency checking to achieve the same results as his hand-code optimisations.

References

[Beet87] M. Beetz. *Specifying Meta-Level Architectures for Rule-Based Systems.* Technical Report SEKI No. SR-87-06 (Diploma Thesis), Universität Kaiserslautern, Fachbereich Informatik, Kaiserlautern, 1987.

[Bjor87] D. Bjorner, A.P. Ershov, and N.D. Jones, editors. *Workshop on Partial Evaluation and Mixed Computation*, Avernaes, Denmark, October 1987.

[Chan88] D. Chan and M. Wallace. A treatment of negation during partial evaluation. In J. Lloyd, editor, *Proceedings of the Meta'88 Workshop on meta-programming in logic programming*, pages 227–240, Bristol, June 1988.

[Gall86] J. Gallagher. Transforming logic programs by specialising interpreters. In *Proceedings of the Seventh European Conference on Artificial Intelligence, ECAI '86*, pages 109–122, Brighton, July 1986.

[Harm88] F. van Harmelen and A. Bundy. Explanation-based generalisation = partial evaluation. *Artificial Intelligence Journal*, 30(3):401–412, October 1988.

[Klee52] S. Kleene. *Introduction to Metamathematics.* Van Nostrand, New York, 1952.

[Levi88] G. Levi. Object level reflection of inference rules by partial evaluation. In P. Maes and D. Nardi, editors, *Meta-level architectures and reflection*, North Holland Publishers, 1988.

[Lloy84] J. Lloyd. *Foundations of Logic Programming. Symbolic Computation Series*, Springer Verlag, 1984.

[Lloy87] J.W. Lloyd and J.C. Shepherdson. *Partial evaluation in logic programming.* Technical Report CS-87-09, Department of Computer Science, University of Bristol, 1987.

[Lloy88] J. Lloyd, editor. *Proceedings of the Meta'88 Workshop on meta-programming in logic programming*, Bristol, June 1988.

[Lowe88] H. Lowe. *Empirical Evaluation of Meta-Level Interpreters.* Master's thesis, Department of Artificial Intelligence, University of Edinburgh, 1988.

[Mitc86] T.M. Mitchell, R.M. Keller, and S.T. Kedar-Cabelli. Explanation-based generalization: a unifying view. *Machine Learning*, 1(1):47–80, 1986.

[O'Ke88] R. O'Keefe. Practical prolog for real programmers. August 1988. Tutorial No. 8 of the Fifth Internation Conference and Symposium on Logic Programming, Seattle.

[Owen88a] S. Owen. *The development of explicit interpreters and transformers to control control reasoning about protein topology.* Technical Memo HPL-ISC-TM-88-015, Hewlett-Packard Laboratories Bristol Research Centre, 1988.

[Owen88b] S. Owen. Issues in the partial evaluation of meta-interpreters. In J. Lloyd, editor, *Proceedings of the Meta'88 Workshop on meta-programming in logic programming*, pages 241–254, Bristol, June 1988.

[Prie87] A.E. Priedites and J. Mostow. PROLEARN: towards a Prolog interpreter that learns. In *Proceedings of AAAI-87*, American Association for Artificial Intelligence, Seattle, Washington, July 1987.

[Rose83] J.S. Rosenschein and V. Singh. *The Utility of Meta-level Effort.* Technical Report No. HPP-83-20, Stanford Heuristic Programming Project, March 1983.

[Safr86] S. Safra and E. Shapiro. *Meta Interpreters for Real.* Technical Report No. CS86-11, Department of Computer Science, The Weizmann Institute of Science, May 1986.

[Ster86] L. Sterling and R.D. Beer. Incremental flavor-mixing of meta-interpreters for expert system construction. In *Proceedings of the 3rd Symposium on Logic Programming*, pages 20–27, Salt Lake City, Utah, September 1986.

[Take85] T. Takewaki, A. Takeuchi, S. Kunifuji, and K. Furukawa. *Application of Partial Evaluation to the Algebraic Manipulation System and its Evaluation.* Technical Report TR-148, Tokyo, ICOT Research Centre, December 1985.

[Take86] A. Takeuchi and K. Furukawa. Partial evaluation of Prolog programs and its application to meta programming. In *Proceedings of IFIPS '86*, Dublin, 1986.

[Tarn77] S.Å. Tarnlund. Horn clause computability. *BIT*, 17:215–226, 1977.

[Venk84] R. Venken. A Prolog meta-interpreter for partial evaluation and its application to source to source transformation and query-optimisation. In *Proceedings of the Sixth European Conference on Artificial Intelligence, ECAI '84*, pages 91–100, Pisa, September 1984.

ALGORITHMIC LEARNING FROM INCOMPLETE INFORMATION: PRINCIPLES AND PROBLEMS

Klaus P. Jantke
Leipzig University of Technology
Dept. of Mathematics & Informatics
P.O.Box 66
Leipzig
DDR - 7030

This papers is intended to provide a painless introduction into inductive inference, which is a mathematically well-based theory of algorithmic learning from possibly incomplete information. The paper is more a tutorial than a technical one, and it should provide the students of the author´s lecture at **IMYCS´88** with some basic concepts and helpful examples. Additionally, the author wants to offer some basic motivations of algorithmic learning from incomplete information as well as some fundamental theses about the interconnections of artificial intteligence and mathematical research work. The paper is not a survey of inductive inference research. Therefore, the author avoids to refer to the huge number of topical publications. A bibliography on inductive inference would contain some hundred titles. The reader is directed to /01/ and /04/ for surveys as well as for a considerable number of references.

1. Inductive Inference and Artificial Intelligence

It is quite obvious that learnability is a fundamental characteristics of natural intelligence. Consequently, learning belongs to the central issues of artificial intelligence, never mind how to characterize artificial intelligence in detail. But surprisingly, the results of applying machine learning in the development of artificial intelligence systems turns out to be very poor compared to other areas of artificial intelligence. The key reason may be that learning is a phenomenon much more difficult than expected in the early days of artificial intelligence. This implies that successful applications of machine learning results require a much more comprehensive and deeper fundamental research work. For the author, this is the underlying motivation for doing mathematically well-based investigations which are ultimately aimed at the development of learnable systems.

Inductive inference is a mathematical theory of algorithmic learning from incomplete information. Inductive inference research work is primarly characterized by stressing the problem of processing information which may be incomplete with respect to the goal under consideration.

In human communication, it is widely accepted that in many cases providing incomplete information about some object to be communicated is sufficient for understanding. If one tries to explain to someone else a certain algorithm, for example, this is usually done by explaining some key ideas, some crucial cases, and by giving some typical examples in the form of sample computations, e.g. Human experience proves that this suffices usually. Moreover, there are a lot of interesting cases where human beings when faced to the problem of understanding some completely described phenomenon, give up some information for reducing the complexity of the given description. From the remaining incomplete description, they are able to understand the phenomenon to be learned. A typical case is the complete description of some algebraically described abstract data type. Such a description consists of a couple of sorts, a couple of operators together with their corresponding arity, and a finite number of axioms describing the behaviour of these operators (under some assumed semantics). For understanding the meaning of some operator, one usually considers the defining axioms by substituting simple constant terms for the occurring variables. By investigating the resulting basic cases one usually gets the intended meaning. This works in general, although, a finite number of instances of some set of axioms rarely reflects all the information contained in the full theory. Naturally, this important human ability to learn from incomplete information is based on a large amount of implicitly given basic knowledge.

The goal of inductive inference research work is to understand, model and analyse this human ability described above for enabling computers to learn from incomplete information. There have been found lots of reasonable formalizations, a large number of principle algorithms and theorems about possibilities and boundaries, and a huge amount of illustrative examples. A considerable part is reported in /01/.

However, the number of successful applications is still disappointing. In the author´s opinion, there are two main reasons for the unsatisfying situation. (1) Inductive inference algorithms are usually of a high complexity. The theory of inductive inference contains a large number of results in this regard. Therefore, many algorithms developed are not really feasible. For exploiting these algorithms it is necessary to embed these algorithms into some non-mathematical framework, e.g. using heuristics for switching between different approaches to be applied. (2) The mathematical approaches to inductive learning are usually not explicitly concerned with the huge amount of basic knowledge accessible to humans when learning from incomplete information. So they are missing an important source which has to be used under real circumstances. Therefore, making inductive inference explicitly knowledge based is an important research topic. To sum up, bringing mathematical ideas and results of algorithmic learning from incomplete information to real applications in AI systems requires mathematical research work as well as integration of mathematical research and artificial intelligence approaches.

2. Principles of Inductive Inference

Before presenting some formalism, the key features of inductive inference shall be illuminated by means of an example. It is assumed that every reader knows about the puzzle of the "*Towers of Hanoi*". This puzzle is briefly explained in the sequel. The places where towers may occur are named by **X**, **Y**, and **Z**. Towers are represented by lists or queues of their elements. Every tower consists of a finite number of objects of a different size. There is an integrity constraint that large objects has to be queued before smaller ones. The initial situation of the *Towers of Hanoi* puzzle is that there is a tower T of some height at place **X**, whereas the other places **Y** and **Z** are empty. Admissible steps are to pop an object from some place and to push it to another place, if the integrity constraint is not violated. The final goal is to clear place **X** and to erect the original tower T at place **Z**. Place **Y** must be finally clear, too. The puzzle is stepwise solved for the trivial case of a tower of height 2 in Figure 1.

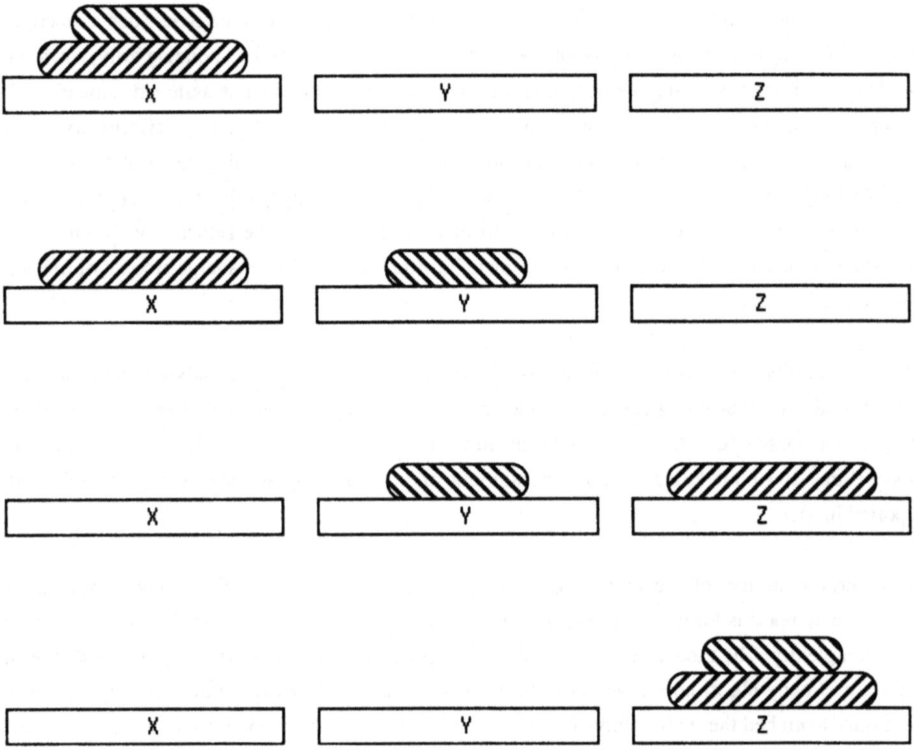

Figure 1

The single steps may be presented in a textual form by

Y := push(**Y** , top(**X**)) ;
X := pop(**X**) ;
Z := push(**Z** , top(**X**)) ;
X := pop(**X**) ;
Z := push(**Z** , top(**Y**)) ;
Y := pop(**Y**) .

The whole procedure above is called ToH(2 , **X** , **Y** , **Z**) . Obviously, everyone who knows about this puzzle is easily able to perform it for towers of height 2 or 3, e.g.

Let us assume, that for the height 3 the sample solution ToH(3 , **X** , **Y** , **Z**) is given, too.

ToH(3 , **X** , **Y** , **Z**) =
Z := push(**Z** , top(**X**)) ;
X := pop(**X**) ;
Y := push(**Y** , top(**X**)) ;
X := pop(**X**) ;
Y := push(**Y** , top(**Z**)) ;
Z := pop(**Z**) .
Z := push(**Z** , top(**X**)) ;
X := pop(**X**) ;
X := push(**X** , top(**Y**)) ;
Y := pop(**Y**) ;
Z := push(**Z** , top(**Y**)) ;
Y := pop(**Y**) ;
Z := push(**Z** , top(**X**)) ;
X := pop(**X**) .

An inductive inference algorithm for processing sample computations as above could proceed as follows. Given two or more examples it attempts to express the largest example in terms of the smaller. In the case above, the sequence describing ToH(2 , **X** , **Y** , **Z**) does not occur as a subsequence of ToH(3 , **X** , **Y** , **Z**). So, the simplest way of expressing ToH(3 , **X** , **Y** , **Z**) in terms of the smaller sample ToH(2 , **X** , **Y** , **Z**) does not work. Next the inductive inference algorithm checks whether some renamed version of ToH(2 , **X** , **Y** , **Z**) occurs in ToH(3 , **X** , **Y** , **Z**). This is the case in exactly two positions. The reader may easily recognize that the first 6 lines as well as the last 6 lines of ToH(3 , **X** , **Y** , **Z**) are renamed versions of ToH(2 , **X** , **Y** , **Z**). This yields

ToH(3 , **X** , **Y** , **Z**) = ToH(2 , **X** , **Z** , **Y**) ;
Z := push(**Z** , top(**X**)) ;
X := pop(**X**) ;
ToH(2 , **Y** , **X** , **Z**).

The following inference step consists in a generalisation intended to make the recurrence relation found above applicable to much more (in fact, infinitely many) cases. Generalisation means in many cases the replacement of constant terms by new variables. In the case of the *Towers of Hanoi* puzzle this yields

ToH(n+1 , **X** , **Y** , **Z**) = ToH(n , **X** , **Z** , **Y**) ;
Z := push(**Z** , top(**X**)) ;
X := pop(**X**) ;
ToH(n , **Y** , **X** , **Z**).

Indeed, this equality inductively synthesised from the two examples above together with the equality defining ToH(2 , **X** , **Y** , **Z**)

ToH(2 , **X** , **Y** , **Z**) =
Y := push(**Y** , top(**X**)) ;
X := pop(**X**) ;
Z := push(**Z** , top(**X**)) ;
X := pop(**X**) ;
Z := push(**Z** , top(**Y**)) ;
Y := pop(**Y**) .

gives a correct inductive definition of all solutions for towers of a height greater than or equal to 2 . Note that, in fact, we have used some basic knowledge about arithmetic for interpreting 3 as 2+1 . If this knowledge is not available, the generalisation step above is not possible.

So, our example illustrates two quite opposite aspects of inductive learning. On the one hand, it illustrates that already a considerably small number of sample computations may be sufficient for automatically synthesizing algorithms. On the other hand, this assumes some basic knowledge which may be easily forgotten, although it is crucial for a correct automatic solution. Whereas the first aspect is encouraging for everyone who tries to invoke mathematically based approaches to algorithmic learning for progress in the development of AI systems, the second aspect recalls that a considerable progress requires the ability to incorporate a large amount of suitable and well-specified knowledge.

The example above was intended to explain the principles of inductive inference which are formally summarized in the sequel and illustrated by figure 2.

Every particular inductive inference problem is characterized by the following 7 parameters. Different instantiations of these parameters yield different concepts. The parameters are:

- **(P1)** The class of objects under consideration to be learned (or synthesized, equivalently).
- **(P2)** The way of presenting (possibly incomplete) information about some object to be synthesized.
- **(P3)** The semantics of information sequences describing which object is presented by a possibly infinite sequence of information.
- **(P4)** The family of algorithms or devices taken into account for doing the inductive inference.
- **(P5)** The space of possible hypotheses which may be produced during some learning process.
- **(P6)** The concept of convergency which specifies under which circumstances a generated sequence of hypotheses approximates some final hypothesis.
- **(P7)** The semantics on the space of hypotheses explaining the meaning of intermediate and final hypotheses generated resp. approximated during some learning process.

In the example discussed above, the parameter **(P1)** is implicitly given as some class of primitive recursive functions. **(P2)** allows sample computations using certain standard functions (like pop, push, and top) and assumes some syntactical rules like separating statements by ";" and closing a sample by "." . **(P3)** relates sample computations to programs in the usual way. This requires that a sequence of samples according to **(P2)** contains only computation traces which may be generated from a unique program. **(P4)** is an implicitly given class of algorithms described by natural language sentences (as above) which consist of two basic procedures: a) expressing later sample computations in terms of one or more preceeding samples, b) generalizing the resulting recurrence relation(s) by insertion of variables. **(P5)** is given as the language of recursive definitions using the assumed standard functions and following the same syntactical rules as **(P2)** does. As concept of convergency **(P6)** we prefer the so-called discrete limit, i.e. a sequence of hypotheses is said to be convergent, if and only if after a finite number of mind changes there is a unique hypothesis being the final one which will never changed again. **(P7)** This hypothesis describes the function computable by recursively processing the definitions given.

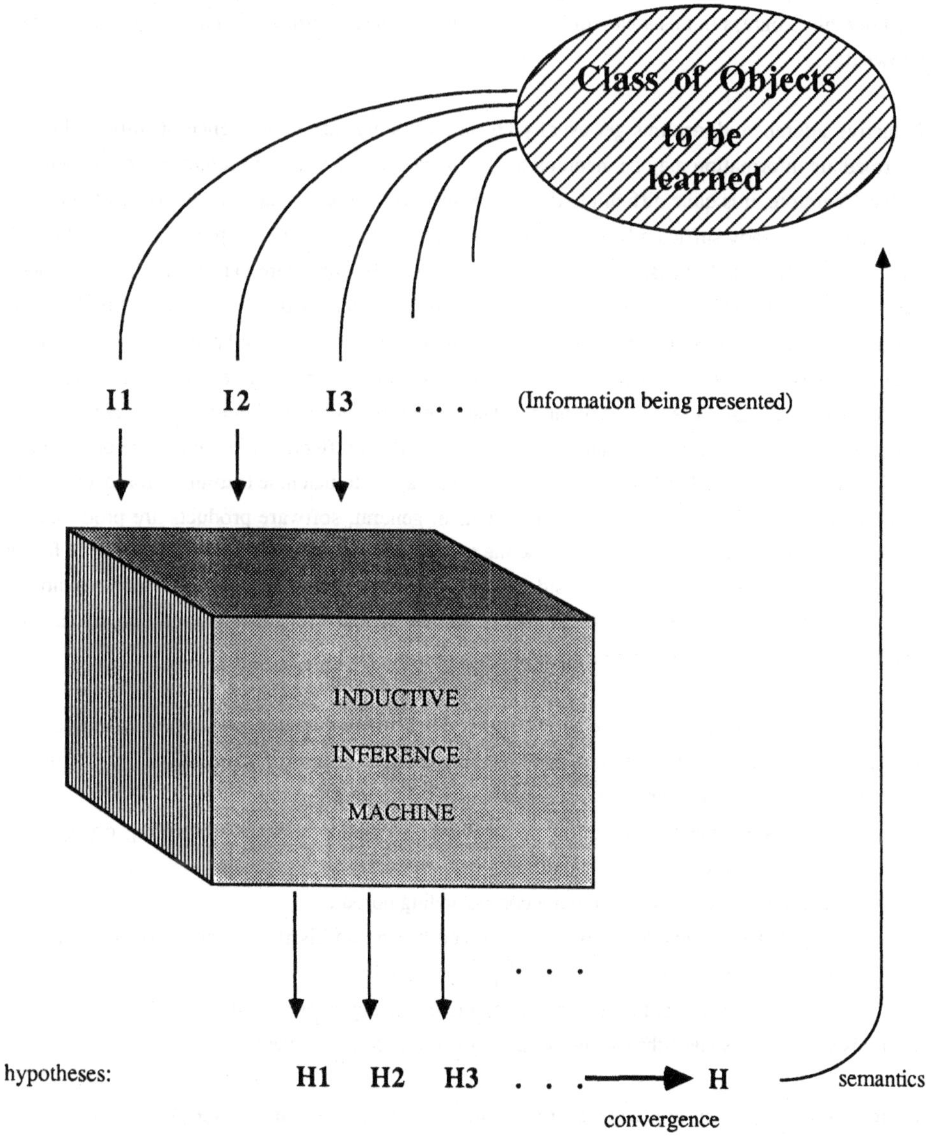

Figure 2

Obviously, the explanation in the paragraph before is rather imprecise. This exhibits that every particular inductive inference approach is based on a considerably large number of complex implicit assumptions. For example, it includes two formal languages (namely **(P2)** and **(P5)**) as well as the corresponding semantics. Additionally, it is fundamental to fix the class of considered inductive inference algorithms **(P4)**, as it is the most important task of inductive inference research to develop feasible inductive inference algorithms which may lead to really learning components of certain AI systems. This, naturally, requires an agreement about the type of algorithms to be constructed, e.g. Prolog programs, finite deterministic automata, LISP programs of a polynomial time complexity, and so on. With respect to our ultimate goal of inventing learnable AI systems, this proves that a considerable progress in this area requires a considerably large number of underlying formalisms and knowledge.

Inductive inference algorithms get usually fed in a possibly infinite sequence of information. Each intermediate information may be incomplete with respect to the object presented by the sequence as a whole. Therefore, it is quite difficult to determine, whether or not a certain amount of (still incomplete) knowledge is already sufficiently comprehensive for identifying the object presented in the limit. The choice of the discrete limit (see **(P6)** above) guarantees only that there exists some finite number of steps such that after reaching this point the object has been identified. This is a typical problem of all approaches to learning from possibly incomplete information. Only under very particular circumstances, there is some way to check hypotheses being generated, whether they are already final or not. This may seem to be an important disadvantage of the inductive inference approach as a whole. But this is not true. The problem under consideration is just reflecting a basic feature of learning, in general, which is ignored or hidden in several AI approaches to machine learning. Moreover, it is quite similar to the practice of software development. In general, software products are produced in an iterative way, where after some initial phase the product is used and assumed to be correct. In fact, it is rarely correct. Instead, it may be considered as some intermediate hypothesis which has not been proved to be the final one. If mistakes are found, the hypothesis will be slightly changed. This is regularly done repeatedly, forming a potentially infinite process.

The characteristics described above is reflected by the inductive inference notion of "*identification in the limit*". If for some instantiation of the 7 parameters above, and for some class of problems of the type under consideration, there exists some inductive inference algorithm,

- which stepwise accepts all admissible information sequences describing objects of the underlying class,
- which generates for every input a corresponding output,
- such that for every given object presented by any admissible sequence of information the sequence of hypotheses become stable past some point,
- where the final hypothesis correctly describes the object presented,

then it is said that this algorithm identifies all objects of this class in the limit.

In the author's opinion, approaches to algorithmic or machine learning should be classified with respect to the question, whether or not they consider learning from possibly incomplete information. If incompleteness of information provided is generally possible, one has to consider sequences of information. This results in sequences of hypotheses generated. And this leads directly to the concept of identification in the limit. Learning from complete information is closer to transformation techniques or compilation than to learning.

3. Inductive Inference of Formal Languages

The seminal paper /02/ of inductive inference is faced to problems of learning formal languages belonging to some class of the *Chomsky* hierarchy from incomplete information. This information about some given language L may consist of a sequence of all words of L (called text) or of a sequence containing both words from L and counterexamples, which are indicated by + and - , respectively (called informant).

Under this approach, the 7 parameters above can be easily specified. We are considering one instantiation: **(P1)** There has been chosen some class of languages, e.g. the class of finite languages over any finte alphabet. **(P2)** A language L is given by any sequence which contains exactly all words of L. **(P3)** The semantics of a sequence is just the set of all its members. **(P4)** As algorithms we take into account effective procedures for processing finite lists of words. We assume that it is possible, in principle, that those procedures may be implemented in LISP. **(P5)** Outputs of an inductive inference algorithm are finite lists of words. **(P6)** The limit of a given sequence of lists is defined to be the union of all its members, i.e. the list containing exactly all words occurring somewhere in the sequence. **(P7)** The meaning of such a list is obvious. It simply describes the finite language of all the elements listed. For this approach, there is an almost trivial result:

Theorem 1
For every fixed finite alphabet, there is an inductive inference algorithm for synthesizing every finite language in the limit.

Let us consider a second instantiation of the 7 parameters: **(P1)** The class of objects to be synthesized is the class of all regular languages. **(P5)** Hypotheses are regular grammars. (Note that we could choose finite deterministic or non-deterministic automata or regular terms, equivalently.) **(P6)** A sequence of hypotheses is concergent, if it becomes stable past some point. **(P7)** The meaning of a regular grammar is the language generated, as usual. All other parameters remain unchanged. For a subproblem of the inference problem presented, /02/ contains the following negative answer:

Theorem 2
For every finite alphabet, and for every class C of languages which contains all finite languages over this alphabet and, additionally, at least one infinite language, there is no computable inductive inference algorithm for identifying every language of C in the limit.

The *proof* is a typical one for inductive inference investigations. One assumes any such class C and any computable inductive inference algorithm identifying every language from C in the limit. If the infinite language of C is presented by some sequence of information, there must be some point n such that the algorithm is never changing its mind again, independently of the information presented afterwards. Let us assume that up to this point, there have been presented certain finite sets $I_1, \dots, I_n$ containing exactly the words $w_1, \dots, w_m$. How does the inductive inference algorithm behave, if from now on only the word w_m is presented infinitely many times? It can never change its mind again! In case of a mind change, it had not identified the infinite language at this point. By repeatedly applying this argument, the inductive inference algorithm would never identify the infinite language of C. Thus, it converges to some hypothesis describing this infinite language, when getting fed in the infinite sequence $I_1, \dots, I_n, \{ w_m \}, \{ w_m \}, \{ w_m \}, \dots$ This already contradicts the assumption, as the information sequence under consideration is an admissible description of the finite language $L_0 = \{ w_1, \dots, w_m \}$, too. The Hypothesis found in the limit describes the infinite language of C, hence L_0 is not identified, when $I_1, \dots, I_n, \{ w_m \}, \{ w_m \}, \dots$ is presented.■

4. Inductive Program Synthesis in a Recursion-Theoretic Setting

This chapter is intended to provide information illuminating that there is a paramount number of cases in which inductive inference works successfully. Additionally, it is aimed at exhibiting the importance of seemingly natural properties in algorithmic learning. These properties are frequently assumed in AI approaches to machine learning. A formally exact treatment exhibits that these properties are crucial conditions which usually heavily influence the solvability resp. unsolvability of learning problems. The results presented as well as a large number of additional similar results may be found in /03/.

Before going into technical details, we are sketching two important features of the chosen approach helpful for relating the purely theoretical results to intended applications. 1) In the recursion-theoretic setting, programming languages are represented by *Gödel numberings*. Every real program may be translated, at least in principle, into each Gödel numbering. Therefore, every result about the non-existence of an inductive inference algorithm implies the unsolvability of the corresponding problems in practice. In particular, if propositions are stating the unsolvability of inductive inference problems under certain seemingly natural properties, this proves that these properties under consideration are serious obstacles for constructing real learning programs resp. machines. 2) The information presented to some inductive inference algorithm is chosen *as weak as possible*. In particular, when allowing incomplete logical or abstract data type specifications as a basis for program synthesis, the investigated weak information occurs as a special case. Therefore, if propositions are stating the solvability of inductive inference problems from this weakest form of information, this implies the solvability of the corresponding versions of inductive program synthesis from more realistic information in practice.

The following concepts require some basic notions and notations which are briefly listed. N denotes the set of all natural numbers. By P and R we denote the class of unary partial recursive resp. total recursive functions. In the sequel, we assume any Gödel numbering φ. Note that all the results are independent of the particular choice of φ. If a Gödel numbering φ is assumed, programs are represented by natural numbers which may be understood as effective encodings of the corresponding program texts. For each number $a \in \mathcal{N}$, where a is understood as the encoding of a particular program P, φ_a denotes the unary partial recursive function computed by P. For avoiding the problem how to present the fact that some program to be synthesized must be undefined for some input, we take into account only total recursive functions as objects to be learned. Functions $f \in \mathcal{R}$ will be presented by input/output examples, i.e. by enumerations of the graph. This is really the weakest form of information about some function to be learned. Input/output examples are presented with respect to some enumeration of the input set $\mathcal{N}$. $\mathcal{F}$ denotes the set of all complete sequences of natural numbers taken as ordering of the graphs of functions to be presented. For guaranteeing the uniqueness of a function presented, we assume that orderings X are repetition-free. For $X \in \mathcal{F}$, $f_X[n]$ denotes an encoding of the initial segment of length n+1 of f with respect to the underlying sequence X, i.e. it encodes the list $(x_0,f(x_0)),\dots,(x_n,f(x_n))$, where $X = x_0, x_1, \dots$. If f is represented with respect to the standard enumeration $0, 1, 2, \dots$, the corresponding initial segment of some function f is written as $f[n]$.

Let us briefly relate the present approach to the general concept and the 7 parameters introduced above. **(P1)** The class of objects to be learned or synthesized is some class **U** of unary total recursive functions. **(P2)** Each particular function is presented by an enumeration of its graph with respect to some sequence $X \in \mathcal{F}$. An intermediate (incomplete) information is given as an initial segment of this enumeration, i.e. $f_X[n]$. **(P3)** For a given sequence $(x_0,f(x_0)), (x_1,f(x_1)), (x_2,f(x_2)), \dots$, the defined function f is uniquely defined, as the input sequence $x_0, x_1, x_2, \dots$ is complete and repetition-free, by assumption. **(P4)** We don´t want to restrict the class of possible inductive inference algorithms. The only requirement is that they should be computable, i.e. programmable in principle. Therefore, we take as inductive inference algorithm any function from $\mathcal{P}$. **(P5)** Hypotheses are natural numbers interpreted as Gödel numbers with respect to some underlying Gödel numbering φ. **(P6)** As concept of convergency we choose the discrete limit, as before. **(P7)** If a hypothesis a is generated, it means the function φ_a. In particular, if a sequence of hypotheses converges to some a, φ_a is the function learned or synthesized. The following definitions are reflecting this approach and some reasonable refinements. We are introducing so-called *identification types*, i.e. families of classes of total recursive functions identifiable in a uniform way. These identification types are dentoed by **LIM**, **CONS**, and so on.

Definition 1

A class $\mathbf{U} \subseteq \mathcal{R}$ is idenfiable in the limit by some inductive inference algorithm $S \in \mathcal{P}$

iff $\forall f \in U$ (1) $\forall n \in \mathcal{N}$ $S(f[n])$ is defined,

(2) the sequence of hypotheses converges to some number a,

(3) $\varphi_a = f$.

This is abbreviated by $U \in$ **LIM**(S) resp. $U \in$ **LIM**, if some S exists.

The following definition allows arbitrary arrangements of input/output examples. All similar versions of identification types are indicated by the upper index "arb", i.e. when defining below the identification types **CONS**, **FIN**, and so on, their "arb"-variants have to be defined as in the following case for **LIM**.

Definition 2

A class $\mathbf{U} \subseteq \boldsymbol{R}$ is idenfiable in the limit by some inductive inference algorithm $S \in \boldsymbol{P}$ for arbitrary information sequences

iff $\forall X \in \boldsymbol{F}$ $\forall f \in U$ (1) $\forall n \in \boldsymbol{N}$ $S(f_X[n])$ is defined,

(2) the sequence of hypotheses converges to some number a,

(3) $\varphi_a = f$.

This is abbreviated by $U \in$ **LIM**$^{\mathbf{arb}}$ (S) resp. $U \in$ **LIM**$^{\mathbf{arb}}$, if some S exists.

Some first folklore results of inductive inference are:

Theorem 3

(1) **LIM** = **LIM**$^{\mathbf{arb}}$

(2) $\boldsymbol{R} \notin$ **LIM**

The most frequently used seemingly natural property of machine learning algorithms is called *consistency*. A learning algorithm is said to be consistent, if every hypothesis generated is compatible with the information processed. Naturally, this concept heavily depends on a reasonable concept of compatibility. One usually requires that a consistent hypothesis allows to reconstruct the information where it comes from. In the present recursion-theoretic framework, there is a quite natural way to formalize consistency.

Definition 3

A class $\mathbf{U} \subseteq \boldsymbol{R}$ is idenfiable in the limit by some consistent inductive inference algorithm $S \in \boldsymbol{P}$

iff $\forall f \in U$ (1) $\forall n \in \boldsymbol{N}$ $S(f[n])$ is defined,

(2) $\forall n \in \boldsymbol{N}$ $\varphi_{S(f[n])}(m) = f(m)$ (for all $m = 0,\dots,n$),

(3) the sequence of hypotheses converges to some number a

(4) $\varphi_a = f$.

This is abbreviated by $U \in$ **CONS** (S) resp. $U \in$ **CONS**, if some S exists.

A class $\mathbf{U} \subseteq \boldsymbol{R}$ is idenfiable in the limit by some consistent inductive inference algorithm $S \in \boldsymbol{P}$ for arbitrary information sequences

iff $\forall X \in \boldsymbol{F}$ $\forall f \in U$ (1) $\forall n \in \boldsymbol{N}$ $S(f_X[n])$ is defined,

(2) $\forall n \in \boldsymbol{N}$ $\varphi_h(x_m) = f(x_m)$ (for all $m = 0,\dots,n$, where h abbreviates the intermediate hypothesis $S(f_X[n])$),

(3) the sequence of hypotheses converges to some number a,

(4) $\varphi_a = f$.

This is abbreviated by $U \in$ **CONS**$^{\mathbf{arb}}$ (S) resp. $U \in$ **CONS**$^{\mathbf{arb}}$, if some S exists.

It is a basic insight to detect the following fact:

Theorem 4

CONS $\subset$ **LIM**

In other words, there are solvable inductive inference problems which become unsolvable under the additional requirement of consistency. Recall that this is of a particular importance, as almost all current methods of machine learning are assumed to be consistent.

Inductive inference algorithms above are arbitrary partial recursive functions. For applications, it seems to be more secure, if an inference algorithm is always defined. In the present recursion-theoretic setting, this means to consider total recursive functions as inductive inference algorithms. The corresponding identification types, where in the definition as above $S \in \boldsymbol{P}$ is replaced by $S \in \boldsymbol{R}$, are indicated by a prefix "***R***-". So we get ***R*-LIM** , ***R*-CONS** , and ***R*-CONS**^{arb} .The following theorem summarizes the knowledge about the introduced identification types.

Theorem 5

(1) **LIM** = ***R*-LIM** = **LIM**^{arb} = ***R*-LIM**^{arb}

(2) ***R*-CONS** $\subset$ **CONS** , **CONS**^{arb} $\subset$ **CONS**

(3) ***R*-CONS** and **CONS**^{arb} are incomparable.

(4) ***R*-CONS**^{arb} $\subset$ ***R*-CONS** , ***R*-CONS**^{arb} $\subset$ **CONS**^{arb}

The theorems 4 and 5 together illuminate the importance of seemingly natural properties in algorithmic learning from incomplete information, in particular in inductive program synthesis.

At the end of chapter 2 we were discussing the difficulty to decide, whether or not some hypothesis generated is already correct. The following definition reflects this approach within the considered framework.

Definition 4

A class $U \subseteq \boldsymbol{R}$ is finitely identifiable in the limit by some inductive inference algorithm $S \in \boldsymbol{P}$

<u>iff</u> $\exists d \in \boldsymbol{P}$ $\forall f \in U$

(1) $\forall n \in N$ $S(f[n])$ is defined,

(2) the sequence of hypotheses converges to some number a,

(3) $\varphi_a = f$,

(4) $\forall n \in N$ $d(f[n]) = 0$, if $S(f[n])$ will be changed later,

(5) $\forall n \in N$ $d(f[n]) = 1$, if $S(f[n])$ will never be changed again .

This is abbreviated by $U \in$ **FIN**(S) resp. $U \in$ **FIN**, if some S exists. **FIN**^{arb} is defined similarly.

If some function class belongs to **FIN** resp. **FIN**^{arb} , the function d allows to decide whether any constructed hypothesis is already the final one. The following theorem shows that one can rarely expect such a decidability property.

Theorem 6

(1) **FIN** = **FIN**^{arb}

(2) **FIN** $\subset$ **CONS** $\subset$ **LIM**

(3) **FIN** is incomparable to all other identification types investigated.

The results presented here are intended to illustrate that there is a large number of different inductive inference problems solvable under several requirements. Only a small number of function classes belonging to one of the discussed identification types is effectively enumerable. The majority is much more complex in structure. Because of $\boldsymbol{R} \notin \mathbf{LIM}$ (see theorem 3), there is no universal program synthesis methodology. For the infinite number of solvable problems in **LIM**, there exists an inifinte family of inductive inference algorithms.

It is an exciting and currently almost unsolved problem to bring inductive inference algorithms known in the recursion-theoretic setting to applications in inductive program synthesis or in other areas of machine learning.

5. Inductive Generalisation of Sequences of Rewrite Rules

In this chapter we are going to investigate inductive inference problems in a very restricted area. This enables to present quite easy inductive inference algorithms and to prove their correctness under certain circumstances. We are considering term rewriting systems which offer an operational framework for handling equational knowledge. It is not intended to give a complete introduction into the area of term rewriting systems. There is also no space for comprehensive motivations. Some remarks will do.

In a considerably large area, knowledge may be expressed by finite sets of equations. Abstract data type specifications are a typical example. From a logical point of view, equations are understood as symmetric objects without any particular orientation. But for processing equational knowledge, an orientation of the given equations may be helpful. Let us consider, as an example, the following set $\mathbf{E_1}$ of term equations over some implicitly given signature:

(A1) $x + 0 = x$

(A2) $0 + x = x$

(A3) $x + S(y) = S(x + y)$

(A4) $S(x) + y = S(x + y)$

(A5) $(x + y) + z = x + (y + z)$

There has been presented some elementary knowledge about arithmetics, where 0 is assumed to be some constant name, x,y,z are variables, and S and + are operators with an obvious arity. This equational knowledge implies the validity of formulae like

$$S(0) + S(S(u)) = S(S(S(u))) + 0 \quad ,$$

where u is assumed to be a variable.The reader may consider this statement as a trivial one. However, it remains to explain how a computer could check the validity of formulae, in general. In the case under consideration, it is almost trivial to consider $\mathbf{E_1}$ as a rewrite rule system **R** (This system will be used later, when investigating particular examples of sequences of rewrite rules.):

(R1)	$x + 0 \rightarrow x$
(R2)	$0 + x \rightarrow x$
(R3)	$x + S(y) \rightarrow S(x + y)$
(R4)	$S(x) + y \rightarrow S(x + y)$
(R5)	$(x + y) + z \rightarrow x + (y + z)$

Some term t is rewritable by means of some rewrite rule system, if there exists some subterm which turns out to be the instance of some left hande side of a rule in the given rewrite rule system. The result of rewriting is constructed in replacing this subterm by the corresponding right hand side. Such a derivation step on the basis of some rewrite rule system **R** is denoted by $\longrightarrow_{\mathbf{R}}$ .In the example above, it holds

$$S(0) + S(S(u)) \longrightarrow_{\mathbf{R}} S(0 + S(S(u))) \qquad \text{(by (R4))}$$
$$S(0 + S(S(u))) \longrightarrow_{\mathbf{R}} S(S(S(u))) \qquad \text{(by (R2))}$$

This demonstrates that $S(0) + S(S(u))$ rewrites by finitely many steps to $S(S(S(u)))$ .The formal notion is $S(0) + S(S(u)) \xrightarrow{*}_{\mathbf{R}} S(S(S(u)))$. More formally, $\xrightarrow{*}_{\mathbf{R}}$ is the reflexive, transitive closure of $\longrightarrow_{\mathbf{R}}$. Similar to the two steps above, one gets $S(S(S(u))) + 0 \xrightarrow{*}_{\mathbf{R}} S(S(S(u)))$. Thus, the validity of $S(0) + S(S(u)) = S(S(S(u))) + 0$ has been verified by reducing both sides into the same normal form. The proof is correct, as the reflexive, symmetric and transitive closure of $\longrightarrow_{\mathbf{R}}$ denoted by $\xleftrightarrow{*}_{\mathbf{R}}$ turns out to be identical with the equality relation defined by $\mathbf{E_1}$. In some cases, this may be much more difficult.

Consider $\mathbf{E_2}$ to be the system of associativity and idempotence for some binary operator + :

(A)	$(x + y) + z = x + (y + z)$
(I)	$x + x = x$

One can easily check that an orientation of these two equations does not yield an appropriate rewrite rule system, as obviously valid equations do not become provable as in the example before. The situation is much more unpleasant: There is no finite rewrite rule system **R** such that $\xleftrightarrow{*}_{\mathbf{R}}$ equals the equivalence relation induced by $\mathbf{E_2}$.

In the area of term rewriting systems, there are some techniques for searching for finite rewrite rule systems as above. (Note that the desired rewrite rule system should satisfy two conditions: 1) It should allow only finite chains of derivations. 2) Every term should have a unique irreducible form. Systems meeting both conditions are called *canonical.*) But these techniques are sometimes generating infinite sequences of rewrite rules.

Inductive inference algorithms may help to replace infinite sequences of rewrite rules by a finite system defining the same equivalence relation. Thus, algorithmic learning techniques allow to solve problems which remained unsolvable by the classical term rewriting techniques. Before a more formal treatment, there will be investigated an example. Consider the following infinite sequence $\mathbf{R}'$ of rewrite rules:

(R11) $f(S(0),g(z)) \longrightarrow h(S(S(0)))$
(R12) $f(S(S(0)),g(z)) \longrightarrow h(S(S(S(0))))$
(R13) $f(S(S(S(0))),g(z)) \longrightarrow h(S(S(S(S(0)))))$
and so on

The regularity of the given sequence is obvious and may be expressed by a single rule

(G1) $f(S(x),g(z)) \longrightarrow h(S(S(x)))$

said to be a generalisation of the infinite sequence (R11) , (R12) , (R13) , ... But there do exist several other generalisations like

(G1′) $f(x,g(z)) \longrightarrow h(S(x))$
(G1″) $f(S(x),y) \longrightarrow h(S(S(x)))$

In dependence on the underlying signature, the generalisations (G1′) and (G1″) may be to general. For example, (G1′) has the instance $f(0,g(z)) \longrightarrow h(S(0))$ which does not occur in the given sequence. For exactly expressing the knowledge given by some infinite sequence of rewrite rules, one has to construct generalisations which fit the given sequence as close as possible. This is reflected by the following definitions. (Implicitly, we assume any many-sorted finite signature.)

Definition 5
Assume a term t and a set of terms T.
t generalises T ($t \sqsupseteq_1 T$)
iff For every term $t' \in T$ there exists some substitution σ such that $t\sigma = t'$.

Definition 6
Assume a term t and a set of terms T. For every term t′, $\mathcal{L}(t')$ denotes the set of all ground instances of t′. $\mathcal{L}(T) = \bigcup_{t' \in T} \mathcal{L}(t')$.
$t \sqsupseteq_2 T$ **iff** $\mathcal{L}(t) \supseteq \mathcal{L}(T)$

Whereas the definition of $\sqsupseteq_1$ is technically much easier, the concept $\sqsupseteq_2$ may be more intuitive. In particular, definition 6 suggests a concept of exactness.

Definition 7
A term t is called an exact generalisation of a set T of terms
iff (1) $t \sqsupseteq_2 T$
(2) $\mathcal{L}(t) = \mathcal{L}(T)$.

By the way, condition (2) implies condition (1), which may be dropped, therefore.

If in the example above, the signature and the arity of the unary operator S are such that 0 and S are generating the argument sort of S, than (G1) is an exact generalisation of the infinite sequence of rules (R11) , (R12) , ... Note that the presented rewrite rules are understood as terms with $\longrightarrow$ being the outermost operator.

We are investigating a more interesting example. **R″** is the following infinite sequence of rewrite rules

(R21) f(z,g(S(0))) $\longrightarrow$ h(0,S(z))
(R22) f(z,g(S(S(0)))) $\longrightarrow$ h(S(0),S(S(z)))
(R23) f(z,g(S(S(S(0))))) $\longrightarrow$ h(S(S(0)),S(S(S(z))))
and so on

There is no way to generalise the set **R″** in an exact manner. Let us assume additionally, that there is a system **R** consisting of the rules (R1) , ... , (R5) above describing some available knowledge about arithmetics. This allows a weaker form of generalisation:

(G2) f(z,g(S(x))) $\longrightarrow$ h(x,S(z+x))

We are investigating a particular ground instance of this new rule. Suppose that x is substituted by the term S(S(0)) and z by 0. The ground instance is

f(0,g(S(S(S(0))))) $\longrightarrow$ h(S(S(0)),S(0+S(S(0))))

This ground rule is no instance of any rule from **R″** . But its reduced form, derived by means of **R**,

f(0,g(S(S(S(0))))) $\longrightarrow$ h(S(S(0)),S(S(S(0))))

turns out to be a ground instance of (R23). Therefore, (G2) may be considered as a generalisation of **R″** with respect to the basic knowledge **R** .This concept is now introduced more formally.

Definition 8

(1) Assume a term t and a set of terms T. For every term t′, $\mathcal{L}$(t′) denotes the set of all ground instances of t′. $\mathcal{L}(T) = \bigcup_{t' \in T} \mathcal{L}(t')$. Suppose **R** to be some canonical rewrite rule system. For any set M of terms, $\downarrow_{\mathbf{R}}M$ denotes the set of all irreducible forms (w.r.t. **R**) of terms from M.

$t \sqsupseteq_3 T$ <u>**iff**</u> $\downarrow_{\mathbf{R}}\mathcal{L}(t) \supseteq \downarrow_{\mathbf{R}}\mathcal{L}(T)$.

(2) t is said to be an exact normal generalisation of T

<u>**iff**</u> $\downarrow_{\mathbf{R}}\mathcal{L}(t) = \downarrow_{\mathbf{R}}\mathcal{L}(T)$.

If there is some sort, say **nat**, such that **R** contains exactly all knowledge about this sort, and if the operators f,g,h are mapping into some other sorts, the sort **nat** is generated by the constant 0 and the unary operator S. Under these assumptions, (G2) is an exact normal generalisation of the infinite set **R″** .

Note that the different concepts of generalisation introduced above are logically different. But, fortunately, under quite weak assumptions, $\sqsupseteq_1$ and $\sqsupseteq_2$ become equivalent.

Theorem 7

Assume any finite, heterogeneous and finitary signature such that 1) every sort contains at least one constant and 2) in every sort there are at least two different ground terms,

then $\sqsupseteq_1$ and $\sqsupseteq_2$ are equivalent.

This result suggests, whenever possible, to search for a generalisation with respect to $\sqsupseteq_1$ first, and to try a proof of exactness with respect to $\sqsupseteq_2$ afterwards. It is considerably easy to define an inductive inference algorithm constructing for any finite set of terms T_n a generalisation with respect to $\sqsupseteq_1$ which fits as close as possible. This is generally possible, as the set of all generalisations (w.r.t. $\sqsupseteq_1$) forms a complete lattice.

This is a brief description of the ***rule generalisation algorithm*** : Roughly spoken, given any finite set $\{ t_1, \dots, t_m \}$ of terms, the inductive inference algorithm searches for all positions, where some terms are distinguished by different occurring subterms. These subterms are chosen as small as possible. Subterms in the same position are replaced by a unique variable. If there are distinguished positions, such that in every t_i the corresponding subterms are identical, these subterms are replaced by the same variable. As a result, there is constructed a generalisation of $\{ t_1, \dots, t_m \}$ w.r.t. $\sqsupseteq_1$. This generalisation is a rewrite rule of the form $l \longrightarrow r$. If all variables of r occur in l, this rule is called *acceptable*, otherwise not. This algorithm, when getting as input a finite set of rules, always generates some output. In the worst case, the output is a rule of the form $x \longrightarrow y$, where both x and y are variables. Such an output is not acceptable. This may be understood as a failure message.

Theorem 8

For finite sets of rewrite rules, it is decidable whether or not there exists an acceptable generalisation w.r.t. $\sqsupseteq_1$.

Theorem 9

For every finite set of rewrite rules, the rule generalisation algorithm either constructs an acceptable generalisation w.r.t. $\sqsupseteq_1$ or terminates with a failure message.

This suggests to invoke the rule generalisation algorithm as an inductive inference method.

Theorem 10

Assume any infinite sequence $t_1, t_2, \dots$ of rewrite rules.

(1) If there exists an acceptable generalisation t of $\{ t_1, t_2, \dots \}$ w.r.t. $\sqsupseteq_1$, then the rule generalisation algorithm getting $\{ t_1, t_2 \}, \{ t_1, t_2, t_3 \}, \dots$ as input information identifies t in the limit.

(2) If there does not exist an acceptable generalisation of $\{ t_1, t_2, \dots \}$ w.r.t. $\sqsupseteq_1$, then the rule generalisation algorithm getting $\{ t_1, t_2 \}, \{ t_1, t_2, t_3 \}, \dots$ as input information generates a failure message past some point n.

Note that a generalisation is only necessary, if at least two different terms are given. We are now prepared to study a more complex and interesting example. Throughout the rest of the paper, **R** denotes the following rewrite rule system:

(A1) $x + 0 \longrightarrow x$
(A2) $0 + x \longrightarrow x$
(A3) $x + S(y) \longrightarrow S(x + y)$
(A4) $S(x) + y \longrightarrow S(x + y)$
(A5) $(x + y) + z \longrightarrow x + (y + z)$
(B1) $f(g(f(x))) \longrightarrow h(S(0),x)$
(B2) $f(g(h(y,x))) \longrightarrow f(h(S(y),x))$
(B3) $f(h(z,h(y,x)) \longrightarrow h(z + y,x)$

For simplicity, the sort of which 0 is a constant is called **nat** . S is a unary and + is a binary operator over **nat** . The other operators are assumed to map into some other sort. The given rewrite rule system is terminating. In particular, the subsystem consisting of (A1) , ... , (A5) is canonical. When applying a *critical pair / completion procedure* to **R**, i.e. a certain procedure which checks **R** for confluence (uniqueness of irreducible forms), this procedure constructs additional rules for completing the non-confluent system. Unfortunately, it does not succeed, i.e. there will be generated an infinite sequence of rules to be added for completion. This sequence is

(C1) $f(h(S(0),g(f(x)))) \longrightarrow f(h(S(S(0)),x))$
(C2) $f(h(S(0),g(h(y,x)))) \longrightarrow f(h(S(S(y)),x))$
(C3) $f(h(S(S(0)),g(f(x)))) \longrightarrow f(h(S(S(S(0))),x))$
(C4) $f(h(S(S(0)),g(h(y,x)))) \longrightarrow f(h(S(S(S(y))),x))$
(C5) $f(h(S(S(S(0))),g(f(x)))) \longrightarrow f(h(S(S(S(S(0)))),x))$
(C6) $f(h(S(S(S(0))),g(h(y,x)))) \longrightarrow f(h(S(S(S(S(y)))),x))$
(C7) $f(h(S(S(S(S(0)))),g(f(x)))) \longrightarrow f(h(S(S(S(S(S(0))))),x))$
and so on

An exact or normal exact generalisation seems to be impossible. Therefore, we separate the given sequence into two subsequences for generalisation.

(C1) $f(h(S(0),g(f(x)))) \longrightarrow f(h(S(S(0)),x))$
(C3) $f(h(S(S(0)),g(f(x)))) \longrightarrow f(h(S(S(S(0))),x))$
(C5) $f(h(S(S(S(0))),g(f(x)))) \longrightarrow f(h(S(S(S(S(0)))),x))$
(C7) $f(h(S(S(S(S(0)))),g(f(x)))) \longrightarrow f(h(S(S(S(S(S(0))))),x))$
and so on

(C2) $f(h(S(0),g(h(y,x)))) \longrightarrow f(h(S(S(y)),x))$
(C4) $f(h(S(S(0)),g(h(y,x)))) \longrightarrow f(h(S(S(S(y))),x))$
(C6) $f(h(S(S(S(0))),g(h(y,x)))) \longrightarrow f(h(S(S(S(S(y)))),x))$
and so on

It is currently open, whether or not such a classification of subsequences suitable for generalisation may be done automatically for all sequences as above (or, at least, for a considerably large number of cases) which have been generated by a critical pair/completion procedure. The original rules of **R** may give some hint how to divide a sequence into subsequences. In the case under consideration, all new rules from the first sequence have been generated by means of (B1), whereas all rules of the second sequence stem from (B2).

We are now applying the rule generalisation algorithm to the first sequence. Applied to the first sample of this sequence, i.e. to { (C1) , (C3) } , it yields the following rule (where **y** is a new variable):

$$(G^*) \quad f(h(S(\mathbf{y}),g(f(x)))) \longrightarrow f(h(S(S(\mathbf{y})),x))$$

Note that over the underlying signature, this rule can not be an exact generalisation, as there do exist terms of the sort **nat** containing the operator + . These terms may be substituted for **y** , but the do not occur as subterms in { (C1) , (C3) , (C5) , ... } .

Proposition 1: (G*) is already a normal exact generalisation of { (C1) , (C3) , (C5) , ... } . The rule generalisation algorithm will never change this hypothesis, when getting further samples.

Applied to { (C2) , (C4) } , there will be generated a failure message. The reason is that on the right hand side of both rules there are occurring the subterms y resp. S(y) in corresponding positions. But S(y) does not occur in the left hand side of (C4). Therefore, there is no way to construct an acceptable generalisation, although a generalisation w.r.t. $\sqsupseteq_1$ exists.

Proposition 2: The rule generalisation algorithm, when applied to the samples from the second sequence above, recognizes already for the input { (C2) , (C4) } that there does not exist an acceptable generalisation.

When searching for a generalisation w.r.t. $\sqsupseteq_1$, one finds

$$(G^{**})\ f(h(S(\mathbf{z}),g(h(y,x)))) \longrightarrow f(h(S(S(\mathbf{z}+y)),x)) \ .$$

This turns out to be a normal exact generalisation of the whole sequence { (C2) , (C4) , (C6) , ... } . In general, it may be quite complex or even impossible to prove a generalisation exact resp. normal exact.

Proposition 3: From the rewrite rule system **R** and the underlying structural knowledge, it is provable 1) that (G*) is a normal exact generalisation of { (C1) , (C3) , (C5) , ... } and 2) that (G**) is a normal exact generalisation of { (C2) , (C4) , ... }.

For *proving* proposition 3, one first proves that the sort **nat** is generated by 0 and S. This may be done using the fact that (A1) , ... , (A5) is canonical. Second, one uses the knowledge about the construction of both sequences. Every rule (C2n+1), where n = 1,2,3,... , is generated from (B1) and

(C2n-1). This yields that the resulting subterm at the position where **y** will be introduced is just $S^n(0)$. And this implies that the sequence of subterms replaced by **y** is exactly the sequence of all normal forms of the sort **nat**. Thus, substituting any term t of the sort **nat** for **y** in (G*) yields a term, where the particular subterm of sort **nat** may be rewritten into some $S^n(0)$, i.e. it becomes a version occuring in the sequence { (C1) , (C3) , (C5) , ... } .This completes the proof idea for the first subsequence. The second part of the proof may be performed completely similar, as each (C2n) is constructed from (B2) and (C2n-3), where n = 2,3,4,... . ■

The propositions above characterizing the behaviour of the rule generalisation algorithm in a particular case are listed for illustrating a general approach to divergence problems of critical pair/completion procedures. Roughly spoken, we propose to invoke inductive inference methods. More precisely, one should first try a generalisation w.r.t. $\geqq_1$. It is decidable, whether such a generalisation exists or not. In case it does not exist, one tries to find a generalisation w.r.t. $\geqq_3$. This is only possible by an enumeration method which, perhaps, does not terminate. If a generalisation has been found, one may try to prove exactness. For a generalisation w.r.t. $\geqq_3$, it is only possible to prove normal exactness, whereas a generalisation w.r.t. $\geqq_1$ may be exact or normal exact.

Acknowledgement

A considerable number of results presented (chapter 5 and 4) stem from common work with **Muffy Thomas** (Glasgow) resp. **Hans-Rainer Beick** (Berlin). Cooperating with both is always fruitful and a great pleasure. Other results are taken from the huge source of inductive inference research (cf. /01/ and /04/, e.g.). Discussions with **Steffen Lange** (Berlin) are of a growing importance for my own research in inductive inference at all. Finally, this paper has been finished during my visit to **Jürgen Avenhaus** (Kaiserslautern). I gratefully acknowledge the excellent working conditions at the Fachbereich Informatik of the Kaiserslautern University provided by Jürgen Avenhaus and his colleagues.

References

/01/ **Dana Angluin** and **Carl Smith**, A survey of inductive inference: theory and methods, Computing Surveys 15 (1983), 237-269

/02/ **E. Mark Gold**, Language identification in the limit, Information and Control 14 (1967), 447-474

/03/ **Klaus P. Jantke** and **Hans-Rainer Beick**, Combining postulates of naturalness in inductive inference, EIK 17 (1981) 8/9, 465-484

/04/ **Reinhard Klette** and **Rolf Wiehagen**, Research in the theory of inductive inference by GDR mathematicians - a survey, Inf. Sciences 22 (1980), 149-169

Chapter 5

Cryptography

A CRYPTOSYSTEM BASED ON PROPOSITIONAL LOGIC

Jarkko Kari
Mathematics Department
University of Turku
SF-20500 Turku, Finland

Abstract

A new public key cryptosystem based on propositional calculus is presented. The system is proved optimal in the sense that any cryptanalytic method against it can be used to break other cryptosystems as well. Such a cryptanalytic method could also be used to solve in polynomial time the membership problem of any language in $\mathcal{NP}\cap Co\mathcal{NP}$. Only worst case complexities are considered.

1. Introduction

Diffie and Hellman introduced the idea of public key cryptography in [1]. Since then several new cryptosystems have been proposed. At the same time difficulties in proving the security of systems have become obvious. Many systems are claimed to be safe just because their breaking *seems* to require resolving some intractable problem. For other systems some particular cryptanalytic methods may have been showed intractable. But no system is known to be secure against all possible attacks.

This paper investigates public key cryptosystems that encrypt the message in a bitwise manner using probabilistic encryption algorithms. A new system of that kind, that is based essentially on simple propositional calculus is studied. Readers not familiar with the standard terminology of cryptography are adviced to consult e.g. [3].

The notion of *probabilistic encryption* was first introduced by Goldwasser and Micali in [2]. To encrypt a message we use a fair coin. The cryptotext depends not only on the plaintext but also on the results of consecutive coin tosses. So there are many possible cryptotexts for each plaintext. The encryption is done *bit-by-bit* so that each bit of the plaintext is encrypted separately and independently of the other bits. When describing a cryptosystem it is enough to explain how a single bit is encrypted.

More formally, throughout this work a *cryptosystem* is supposed to consist of the following items:

- a *key space* $\mathcal{K} \subseteq \mathcal{K}_e \times \mathcal{K}_d$. The keys are pairs (e,d) where e is the public encryption key from $\mathcal{K}_e$ and d is the corresponding secret decryption key from $\mathcal{K}_d$. Both keys are represented by words over some alphabet. With the size of a key (e,d) is meant the sum of the lengths of e and d as words.

  In the new cryptosystem presented later the set $\mathcal{K}_e$ will contain pairs of propositional statements, and $\mathcal{K}_d$ will be the set of truth value assignments for variables. A pair (e,d) is a legal key, that is, belongs to $\mathcal{K}$ if e and d satisfy special conditions explained later in chapter 2.

- a *cryptotext space* $\mathcal{C}$. These are the items that the bits are encrypted into. In our cryptosystem $\mathcal{C}$ will be the set of propositional statements.

- *encryption algorithms* $\mathcal{E}_0$ and $\mathcal{E}_1$. Given an encryption key $e \in \mathcal{K}_e$ and a sequence $x \in \{0,1\}^*$ representing the coin tosses, the algorithms compute a cryptotext $c \in \mathcal{C}$. The cryptotext corresponding to bit i (= 0 or 1) and key (e,d) is any $\mathcal{E}_i(e,x)$ where x is a binary word. Because we want the encryption to be fast the algorithms $\mathcal{E}_0$ and $\mathcal{E}_1$ should work in polynomial time with respect to the size of e. Then the number of bits in the sequence x that the algorithm $\mathcal{E}_i$ has time to use is also bound by a polynomial of the size of e.

- a *decryption algorithm* $\mathcal{D}$ that computes a function from $\mathcal{K}_d \times \mathcal{C}$ to $\{0,1\}$. $\mathcal{D}$ finds the encrypted bit from the cryptotext. For each key $(e,d) \in \mathcal{K}$, bit i and sequence x of coin tosses we have

$$\mathcal{D}(d, \mathcal{E}_i(e,x)) = i.$$

The algorithm $\mathcal{D}$ should work in polynomial time with respect to the size of the decryption key d.

Consider for example the well known quadratic residue system of Goldwasser and Micali [2]. In their system the private key d consists of two prime numbers p and q, and the corresponding public key is their product $N = p \cdot q$. In this case the encryption algorithms $\mathcal{E}_0$, $\mathcal{E}_1$ and the decryption algorithm $\mathcal{D}$ work in polynomial time with respect to logN, the size of the keys.

2. Description of the cryptosystem

In this chapter a public key cryptosystem based on propositional logic is developed. In effect the system works as follows: The public encryption key includes two statements p_0 and p_1 of proposition calculus. The secret decryption key is some truth value assignment for the variables of p_0 and p_1. The assignment makes p_0 false and p_1 true. The encryption of bit i is done by shuffling the statement p_i into an equivalent but different looking statement p_i' which is the cryptotext. Decryption is done simply by computing the value of p_i' under the secret truth value assignment. If you get false then the encrypted bit must have been 0, if you get true then the bit was 1.

Let us now look at the details. In the following $\mathcal{P}_X$ will denote the set of *propositional statements* over the finite variable set X. So $\mathcal{P}_X$ is the smallest set such that

(i) True, False $\in \mathcal{P}_X$,
(ii) $X \subseteq \mathcal{P}_X$ and
(iii) if $p, q \in \mathcal{P}_X$ then $(\neg p)$, $(p \vee q)$, $(p \wedge q) \in \mathcal{P}_X$.

Unnecessary parentheses will be omitted using the normal precedeces of connectives.

A mapping

$$\alpha : X \longrightarrow \{\text{True,False}\}$$

is called a *truth value assignment* of the variable set X. The mapping α is in the traditional way extended into a mapping

$$\hat{\alpha} : \mathcal{P}_X \longrightarrow \{\text{True,False}\}$$

that gives truth values for all proposition statements over X.

Definition. Let X and Y be finite, disjoint variable sets, α a truth value assignment of X and p_0 and p_1 two statements from $\mathcal{P}_{X \cup Y}$. Suppose that the truth value of p_0 is false and the truth value of p_1 is true (or vice versa) under every truth value assignment of $X \cup Y$ that gives the variables of X the same values as α. So, if the variables of X are given truth values according to α, then the truth values of variables of Y have no effect on the values that p_0 and p_1 get. Then p_0 and p_1 form a public encryption key of the cryptosystem, while α constitutes the corresponding secret decryption key.

Example. Let $X=\{x_1,x_2\}$ and $Y=\{y_1,y_2\}$. These variable sets are of course far too small for any practical purposes. In practice there should be several hundreds of variables in the sets. Let α be defined by

$$\begin{aligned} \alpha : x_1 &\longrightarrow \text{False} \\ x_2 &\longrightarrow \text{True} \end{aligned}$$

and let

$$\begin{aligned} p_0 &= \neg y_1 \wedge y_2 \wedge x_2 \wedge (y_1 \vee x_1 \vee (\neg y_2 \wedge x_2)) \qquad \text{and} \\ p_1 &= (y_2 \vee x_2) \wedge (y_1 \vee x_1 \vee (\neg y_1 \wedge x_2)) \end{aligned}$$

be the two public propositional statements. In order to verify that these α, p_0 and p_1 indeed constitute legal keys of the cryptosystem we compute the truth values of p_0 and p_1 under the truth value assignment α:

$$\begin{aligned} \hat{\alpha}(p_0) &\equiv \neg y_1 \wedge y_2 \wedge (y_1 \vee \neg y_2) \equiv \text{False} \\ \hat{\alpha}(p_1) &\equiv \text{True} \wedge (y_1 \vee \neg y_1) \equiv \text{True} \end{aligned}$$

If the variables of X get there truth values from α then the truth value of p_0 is false and the truth value of p_1 is true, no matter what truth values the variables of Y are given.

Let us now look at how the keys α, p_0 and p_1 are used to encrypt a message. The encryption is done bit-by-bit, so that it is enough to describe how a single bit is encrypted. Suppose you want to encrypt bit i (0 or 1). First select an arbitrary truth value assignment β for the variables of Y and substitute the truth values to Y-variables of p_i. After that you have a propositional statement whose variables belong to X. The final cryptotext is obtained by shuffling this statement using the rules below. The rules are given in the form $p \longrightarrow q$ which tells that any occurence of p may be replaced by q. in the rules p,q and r mean arbitrary statements.

$\neg\text{True} \longrightarrow \text{False}$	$\neg\text{False} \longrightarrow \text{True}$
$(\text{True} \vee p) \longrightarrow \text{True}$	$(\text{False} \wedge p) \longrightarrow \text{False}$
$(\text{True} \wedge p) \longrightarrow p$	$(\text{False} \vee p) \longrightarrow p$
$(p \vee q) \longrightarrow (q \vee p)$	$(p \wedge q) \longrightarrow (q \wedge p)$
$(p \vee (q \vee r)) \longrightarrow ((p \vee q) \vee r)$	$(p \wedge (q \wedge r)) \longrightarrow ((p \wedge q) \wedge r)$
$(p \vee p) \longrightarrow p$	$(p \wedge p) \longrightarrow p$
$(p \vee \neg p) \longrightarrow \text{True}$	$(p \wedge \neg p) \longrightarrow \text{False}$

The statement of $\mathcal{P}_X$ that is obtained after the shuffling is a possible cryptotext for bit i. A sequence of bits is encrypted into a sequence of propositional statements, separated by some special marker. We want that the time needed to encrypt a bit is polynomial with respect to the size of the encryption key. So we fix some polynomial upper bound on the number of applications of the shuffling rules.

Obviously the rules above keep the proposition statement equivalent. They do not change its truth value. Consequently the decryption can be done by computing the truth value of the cryptotext under the secret asignment α. If it is false then the encrypted bit was 0, otherwise it was 1.

Example. Consider the encryption and decryption keys defined in the previous example. Suppose you want to encrypt bit 0. First you select the arbitrary truth value assignment β for the variables of Y, for example

$$\beta : y_1 \longrightarrow \text{False}$$
$$y_2 \longrightarrow \text{True}.$$

Then you substitute these truth values to p_0 obtaining

$$\neg\text{False} \wedge \text{True} \wedge x_2 \wedge (\text{False} \vee x_1 \vee (\neg\text{True} \wedge x_2)).$$

Using the shuffling rules this can be reduced to $x_2 \wedge x_1$. So this is one possible cryptotext for bit 0.

A possible cryptotext for bit 1 is for example x_2. It can be obtained with the assignment

$$\beta : y_1 \longrightarrow \text{True}$$
$$y_2 \longrightarrow \text{False}.$$

If one substitutes these values to p_1 one gets first

$$(\text{False} \vee x_2) \wedge (\text{True} \vee x_1 \vee (\neg\text{True} \wedge x_2))$$

and this can be further reduced into x_2 using the shuffling rules.

The decryption is easily done with the secret α. It makes $x_2 \wedge x_1$ false and x_2 true.

The important question about how the keys p_0, p_1 and α are constructed is not considered here. Let us just mention one possible approach. First the variable sets X and Y are fixed and an arbitrary truth value assignment $\alpha : X \longrightarrow \{\text{True,False}\}$ is selected. Then statements p_0' and p_1' over the variable set Y are formed such that p_0' is a contradiction and p_1' is a tautology. This may be done with the help of backward resolution for instance. One should make sure that p_0' and p_1' include many occurrences of symbols True and False. Now every True in p_0' and p_1' is replaced with some variable $x \in X$ such that $\alpha(x)=\text{True}$. Similarly occurences of False are replaced with some other variables of X. The resulting statements over $X \cup Y$ are the public p_0 and p_1.

3. Security of the cryptosystem

When we prove facts about the safety of our cryptosystem we make use of an *oracle* that is able to break the cryptosystem. When given the public keys p_0 and p_1 and a possible cryptotext p the oracle tells the bit that p is obtained from. With illegal instances the oracle may work arbitrarily. In the following we prove that this kind of oracle is powerful, that is, we can solve difficult problems using it.

Theorem. Let L_0 and L_1 are languages in $\mathcal{NP}$. There is a deterministic polynomial time algorithm using oracle that, when given a word w in $L_0 \Delta L_1$ ($= (L_0 - L_1) \cup (L_1 - L_0)$), decides whether $w \in L_0$ or $w \in L_1$.

Proof. Because the satisfiability problem of propositional logic is $\mathcal{NP}$-complete, statements q_0^X and q_1^X of $\mathcal{P}_X$ such that, for i=0 and i=1

$$q_i^X \text{ is satisfiable} \iff w \in L_i,$$

can be constructed in polynomial time. Since w is in $L_0 \Delta L_1$ there exists a truth value assignment $\alpha : X \longrightarrow \{\text{True,False}\}$ that makes either q_0^X or q_1^X true, while the other is a contradiction.

Let Y be another variable set with the same cardinality as X. Let q_0^Y and q_1^Y be copies of q_0^X and q_1^X where only the variables have been replaced by new ones.

Statements $(q_0^X \wedge \neg q_1^Y)$ and $(q_1^X \wedge \neg q_0^Y)$ constitute possible encryption keys p_0 and p_1 of the cryptosystem with α as the secret decryption key. Namely, suppose without loss of generality that q_0^X is a contradiction and $\hat{\alpha}(q_1^X)$=True. Then regardless what values the variables of Y are given the truth value of the statement $(q_0^X \wedge \neg q_1^Y)$ is false and the truth value of $(q_1^X \wedge \neg q_0^Y)$ is true if the variables of X get their truth values from α.

The trivial statement False is a possible cryptotext. Assume again that q_0^X is a contradiction while α makes q_1^X true. Then there is a truth value assignment $\beta : Y \longrightarrow \{\text{True,False}\}$ that makes q_1^Y true. The arbitrary truth value assignment used in the encryption may accidently be chosen to be this β. Using the shuffling rules $\hat{\beta}(q_0^X \wedge \neg q_1^Y)$ can be reduced to False:

$$\hat{\beta}(q_0^X \wedge \neg q_1^Y) \rightarrow^* q_0^X \wedge \neg \text{True} \rightarrow q_0^X \wedge \text{False} \rightarrow \text{False}.$$

If one consults the oracle with public keys $(q_0^X \wedge \neg q_1^Y)$ and $(q_1^X \wedge \neg q_0^Y)$, and with cryptotext False then the oracle tells the key that False can be obtained from and thus settles the question whether $w \in L_0$ or $w \in L_1$. ∎

In the following two interesting corollaries of the theorem are presented. The first corollary states that the cryptanalysis of our cryptosystem is $\mathcal{NP} \cap Co\mathcal{NP}$-hard.

Corollary 1. Let L be a language in $\mathcal{NP} \cap Co\mathcal{NP}$. There exists a deterministic polynomial time algorithm using oracle that determines whether a given word w is in L or not.

Proof. Choose L and its complement as L_0 and L_1 and apply the theorem. ∎

The second corollary states that the cryptanalysis of any other cryptosystem can be reduced to the cryptanalysis of our system. Before presenting it, however, it is necessary to look at the cryptanalysis problem of cryptosystems in general. Suppose the eavesdropper knows only the public encryption key e and the cryptotext c. He/she wants to find out the bit that c is obtained from. The pair (e,c) constitutes a legal instance for cryptanalysisproblem. The following lemma is an immediate consequence of our notion of cryptosystem presented in chapter 1.

Lemma. For every cryptosystem (in the sense of chapter 1) there are languages L_0 and L_1 in $\mathcal{NP}$ such that for each encryption key e, bit i and cryptotext c

$$\text{c is obtained from bit i using the encryption key e} \implies (e,c) \in L_i - L_{1-i}.$$

Proof. Define L_i to be the set of instances (e,c) recognized by the following nondeterministic algorithm: First the algorithm guesses a sequence x of coin tosses. Then it computes $E_i(e,x)$. The pair (e,c) is accepted if and only if $E_i(e,x) = c$. Obviously this algorithm works in polynomial time with respect to the size of e (since E_i does), and the languages L_0 and L_1 recognized have the required property. ∎

Apply now the theorem to the languages L_0 and L_1 of the lemma. The theorem says that for every cryptosystem there is a deterministic polynomial time algorithm using oracle that, when it is given an encryption key e and a cryptotext c that is created using e, decides whether c is obtained from bit 0 or from bit 1. We have thus proved

Corollary 2. The cryptanalysis of any other cryptosystem can be reduced to the cryptanalysis of our system. ∎

4. Conclusions

A new cryptosystem based on propositional calculus was presented and studied. It was proved safe in the sense that the cryptanalysisproblem encountered by an eavesdropper is $\mathcal{NP}\cap\mathrm{Co}\mathcal{NP}$-hard. Moreover the system was showed optimal in the sense that any cryptanalytic method against it can be used to break other cryptosystems as well.

Unfortunately these facts do not seem to prove that the cryptosystem is unquestionable safe. Consider for instance the following degenarate system:

The public key e consists of two statements p_0 and p_1 in proposition calculus. They have been constructed so that one of them is a contradiction while the other is satisfiable. The secret key d is the index k where p_k is the satisfiable statement.

The encryption of a bit i is done as follows. First select an arbitrary truth value assignment for the variables existing in p_i and compute the truth value of p_i under this assignment. If the result is True then the cryptotext is a special marker #, otherwise it is the bit i itself.

The decryption algorithm simply changes # to k and leaves 0 and 1 unaltered.

This is indeed a cryptosystem in the sense of chapter 1. It is easy to prove for this cryptosystem a theorem similar to the one presented in chapter 3. Yet no one can seriously claim that this system is safe. If there are many truth value assignments that make p_k true then the cryptanalyst can simply generate assignments until either p_0 or p_1 comes true and so decide the meaning of #. On the other hand, if p_k is rarely true then the symbol # is not likely to occur as the cryptotext.

Unfortunately the theorem of chapter 3 does not say anything more about our cryptosystem than it says about this degenerate system. The problem is apparent: The complexity theory as used here deals with worst case complexities only — it says nothing about the complexity on the average. In a more accurate measure of safety the probabilities of different cryptotext should be taken into account.

An interesting feature of the theorem is that it concerns all possible cryptanalytic attacs against our cryptosystem. Nothing was said about how the oracle is implemented. For other cryptosystems it is usual that only some particular cryptanalytic methods have been proved intractable.

References

[1] W. Diffie and M. Hellman, New directions in cryptography, IEEE Transactions on Information Theory IT-22 (1976), 644-654.

[2] S. Goldwasser and S. Micali, Probabilistic encryption & how to play mental poker keeping secret all partial information, in: Proceedings of the 14th ACM Symposium on the Theory of Computing (1982), 365-377.

[3] A. Salomaa, Computation and Automata (Cambridge University Press, 1985).

TUTORIAL: CRYPTOGRAPHY AND DATA SECURITY

Arto Salomaa
Mathematical Department
University of Turku, Finland

1. Cryptosystems and cryptanalysis

The art and science of cryptography consists of two worlds. There is the world of legal communications: parties such as legal users of a data bank exchanging messages. This world can be viewed as open and sunlit. There is also the dark world of the enemy who illegally tries to intercept the messages and do all kinds of vicious things. For people in the legal world, it is desirable that the enemy understands very little of the messages. The enemy, on the other hand, would like to have easily understandable messages.

Cryptography is continuing struggle between the two worlds. A success by the enemy leads to a need to strengthen the methods in the sunlit world. This means a new challenge for the enemy. And so the struggle goes on. Eternal mathematical results are likely to be impractical.

How to present the two worlds? There is no difficulty as regards things past. One just describes a method in the sunlit world and then goes on telling how the enemy made a successful attack. The situation is different if one wants to say something about present things. Whenever one describes a successful enemy attack, one has to admit that the corresponding methods in the legal world were not safe after all. No exposition can claim success in both worlds.

What one can do is to give details for the legal world and then outline some possible enemy attacks, at the same time telling why the attacks are not likely to succeed. This of course has no implications concerning the eventual success of some other, maybe very ingenious enemy attacks. Anyway, this approach will be followed in the sequel. Although mathematical certainty cannot be reached, the likelihood of the safety of the methods is often very high.

The following observation should be made of the two worlds. Although we called them "legal" and "dark", it is not always the case that the former is inhabited by "good guys" and the latter is Mordor where Sauron lives. The roles can be interchanged in practical situations. For instance, the interception of messages may be attempted by our country in a war, whereas messages are interchanged by our enemy. Of course, we have justice on our side! Or the legal users of a data bank may be criminals, and the police tries to find out their activities. In fact, the terminology we will introduce below is going to be impartial in the sense that no value judgments will be attached to the two opposing parties.

We are now ready to introduce the very fundamental notions of cryptography. It is to be emphasized that the terminology is by no means uniform and fixed in different expositions on secret writing. When introducing the terminology, we often mention also some other terms used for the same notion by some other authors.

Our over-all term for secret writing is cryptography. It includes the activities in both worlds. Some authors use the term cryptology for this over-all purpose and reserve the term "cryptography" for the activities of the legal world.

The basic set-up is depicted in the following figure. A message is being sent through an insecure channel, where it may be intercepted by an eavesdropper.

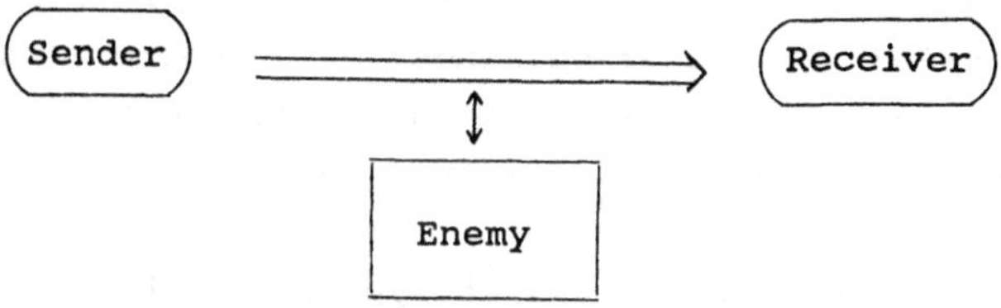

The picture is the same, no matter whether we speak of a horseback courier or electronic mail. We cannot secure the channel and, therefore, interception is possible. The foremost goal of the enemy is to violate the secrecy of the communication and benefit from the secret information. More sophisticated goals might be the following ones. The enemy might want to alter the message, thus confounding the receiver with a corrupted message. In this fashion the enemy also deceives the receiver about the identity of the sender.

For instance, the sender might have sent the message "I will give no support to the Greens." If the enemy alters this into "I will give $ 10.000 to the Greens," the receiver has no idea from whom this essentially different message came.

The enemy might also deceive the sender about the identity of the receiver, for instance, by grabbing the whole message and failing to forward it.

In all of these cases it is of great advantage to the original sender and receiver if the enemy does not understand the message after intercepting it. For this purpose, some method of encryption will be used.

The message in its original form will be referred to as the plaintext. Thus, the sender encrypts the plaintext. The result will be referred to as the cryptotext. The cryptotext is then sent via the insecure channel. Finally, the receiver decrypts the cryptotext, after which he/she has the original plaintext.

Thus, sender's translation activity is:

Encrypt plaintext to cryptotext.

Receiver's translation activity is the reverse one:

Decrypt cryptotext to plaintext.

We may use also the shorter symbolic expressions

$$E(pt) = ct \quad \text{and} \quad D(ct) = pt.$$

In the literature the terms "cleartext" and "ciphertext" or briefly "cipher" are often used instead of "plaintext" and "cryptotext". The verbs for translation are in this case "encipher" and "decipher". The word "code" and the corresponding verbs "encode" and "decode" have also been used, although not any more recently. The reason is that the word "code" is loaded with other meanings: error-correcting codes, automata-theoretic codes, etc. The word "code" will be used in some special contexts below, not however in the general sense of the word "cryptotext".

We now analyze the encryption and decryption further. Both translations happen within the framework of a cryptosystem. A cryptosystem consists of the following items.

(i) A plaintext space PT, that is, the collection of all possible plaintexts pt.

(ii) A key space K. Each key k in K determines an encryption method E_k and a decryption method D_k. If E_k is applied to a plaintext pt, and D_k to the result, then pt is obtained.

(iii) A cryptotext space CT, that is, the collection of all possible cryptotexts ct. Elements of CT result from the elements of PT by applying the encryption methods E_k, where k ranges over K.

We need some very basic language-theoretic notions. We begin with a finite nonempty set Σ, called an alphabet. The elements of Σ are referred to as letters. Finite strings of elements of Σ are referred to as words. The same letter may occur several times in a word. Also the string consisting of zero letters is counted as a word, the empty word λ. The length of a word w is the number of letters in w, where each letter is counted as many times as it occurs. The set of all words over Σ is denoted by Σ^*. Subsets of Σ^* are referred to as (formal) languages over Σ.

For instance, if Σ is the English alphabet {A, B, C, ..., Z} then ABBA, HORSE and KOKOOKOKOONKOKOKOKKO are words over Σ. (Whether a word has a meaning is irrelevant. In fact, the third word has a meaning in Finnish.) We may also add to Σ the lower case letters, all punctuation marks and the empty space needed in an ordinary text. Then the collected works of Shakespeare, written one after the other, constitute a word over this extended alphabet.

We now return to the notion of a cryptosystem, analyzing the different items further. The plaintext space PT is usually either the set Σ^*, for some alphabet Σ, or else consists of all meaningful expressions of a natural language. We want to emphasize already now that these two possibilities are essentially different from many points of view. If the plaintext space is Σ^* then every letter in the message is significant: there is no leeway in the process of decryption. On the other hand, every natural language is highly redundant in the sense that a message is usually understood correctly even if many individual characters have been distorted. This is a definite advantage for the eavesdropper: he/she might understand the message correctly although the analysis is wrong in several spots! Let us illustrate this further.

Example. Assume first that the English language constitutes the plaintext space. Consider the plaintext message WEMEETTOMORROW. (We have disregarded the spaces between individual words. This will be often done in the sequel.) This is encrypted as UBQBBNNFIVPNFOOB. (We do not tell how the encryption is done - the method is a bit surprising.) If the eavesdropper's analysis of the cryptotext gives the result WIMIIDTUMAROV, he/she is quite well off: the result should be understandable correctly.

Assume, secondly, that the plaintext space is Σ^* for the binary alphabet $\Sigma = \{0,1\}$. Assume further that the sender and the receiver have made the following previous agreement concerning the messages. The messages are of length 12 and give information about a fleet consisting of 12 vessels. More specifically, a message sent in the morning indicates which vessels participate in the mission of that particular day. For instance, according to the message 010011000001 the only vessels participating are the second, fifth, sixth and twelfth one. The messages are sent in an encrypted form. Now the analysis of our eavesdropper must produce the original plaintext quite accurately. Even if one bit is wrong, a grave error may occur in the resulting action.

Often when the plaintext is English it is first encoded into the binary alphabet, for instance, by replacing each letter with the binary number indicating the position of the letter in the English alphabet. Since $2^4 < 26 < 2^5$, words of length five are needed for this purpose:

A = 00001, B = 00010, C = 00011, ..., N = 01110, ..., Z = 11010.

We will use the terms encoding and decoding for translations of the message without any purpose of concealment. An encoding might be needed, for instance, in the transmission of the message. Thus, the message is first encoded and then encrypted. Of course, the redundancy of a natural language is not at all affected by an encoding.

After this discussion about the plaintext space, we give some comments on the key space. The cardinality of the key space should not be very small: the illegal party should not have the possibility of testing all keys. In most cases the key space is (denumerably) infinite.

We have said only that each key k determines an encryption method E_k and a decryption method D_k and, further, that E_k and D_k cancel each other. We do not want to give a more specific mathematical characterization of E_k and D_k. In fact, we do not even want to require that E_k is a function.

There is not much to say about the third item, the cryptotext space. It is determined by the first two items: all possible encryptions of all possible plaintexts.

What makes a cryptosystem good? Sir Francis Bacon proposed the following three requirements, given now in our terminology.

(i) Given E_k and pt, the computation of E_k(pt) is easy. Given D_k and ct, the computation of D_k(ct) is easy.

(ii) Without knowing D_k, it is impossible to find pt from ct.

(iii) The cryptotext should be without suspicion: innocent looking.

One can still agree with Sir Francis, with the following reservations in mind. Requirement (iii) is not any more considered to be important.

Requirement (i) says that for legal users the cryptosystem should not be too complicated. "Easy" refers here to complexity theory. It is assumed that the users have available a reasonable amount of computing power. In (ii) "impossible" is replaced by "computationally intractable". The eavesdropper is also assumed to have computing power.

Before the advent of computers, everything in the application of a cryptosystem had to be done by hand. For instance, an army general responsible for cryptography used children in the first grade to test a new cryptosystem. If it was too complicated for the children, it was not accepted for army usage!

Let us begin here with a very old and not at all good cryptosystem: CAESAR. Many variants of it have been in use at different times.

It is not important how we fix the plaintext space. CAESAR is based on <u>substitutions</u>: each letter is substituted by another letter. The latter is obtained from the former by advancing k steps in the alphabet. At the end of the alphabet one goes cyclically to the beginning.

Thus, for k = 3, substitutions are as follows.

Old:	A	B	C	D	E	F	G	H	I	J	K	L	M	N	O	P	Q	R	S	T	U	V	W	X	Y	Z
New:	D	E	F	G	H	I	J	K	L	M	N	O	P	Q	R	S	T	U	V	W	X	Y	Z	A	B	C

In this case, the plaintext TRY AGAIN is encrypted as WUB DJDLQ.

Thus, the key space of the CAESAR system consists of the 26 numbers 0, 1, 2, ..., 25. The encryption method E_k determined by the key k is: advance k steps in the alphabet. The corresponding decryption method D_k is: go back k steps in the alphabet. Some further illustrations:

$$E_{25}(\text{IBM}) = \text{HAL} \quad , \quad E_6(\text{MUPID}) = \text{SAVOJ} \quad ,$$
$$E_3(\text{HELP}) = \text{KHOS} \quad , \quad E_1(\text{HOME}) = \text{IPNF} \quad ,$$
$$D_6(\text{SAVOJ}) = E_{20}(\text{SAVOJ}) = \text{MUPID} \ .$$

Some general properties of the E's and D's can be stated here. One of them is <u>commutativity</u>: whenever some E's and D's are applied one after the other, the order of application does not matter. For instance,

$$E_3D_7E_6D_{11} = E_3E_6D_7D_{11} = D_9 = E_{17} \ .$$

Commutativity will be a crucial property. Also the following relations hold for any k satisfying $1 \leq k \leq 25$:

$$D_k = E_{26-k} \quad , \quad D_kE_k = E_0 = D_0 \ .$$

The latter expresses the fact that the effects of E_k and D_k cancel each other as they should.

The decryption key D_k can be immediately computed from the encryption key E_k. For any cryptosystem, D_k is determined (in a mathematical sense) by E_k. However, the computation of D_k from E_k may be intractable.

In every classical cryptosystem also D_k is given away if E_k is publicized. Anybody who knows E_k is able to compute also D_k. Of course, the computation is not so immediate as in case of CAESAR but is can always be done within a reasonable time. Hence, E_k cannot be publicized.

A property characteristic for public-key-cryptosystems is that E_k can be made public without compromising the secrecy. The keys are so skillfully constructed that the computation of D_k from E_k is intractable, and so is the computation of pt given E_k and $E_k(pt)$.

After discussing the basics of cryptosystems, let us now go to the other world. From now on we refer to the eavesdropper as the cryptanalyst. Thus, the difference between cryptanalysis and decryption is that the cryptanalyst has to manage without the decryption key D_k. The purpose is the same in both cases: to find the plaintext pt.

The illustration is as follows.

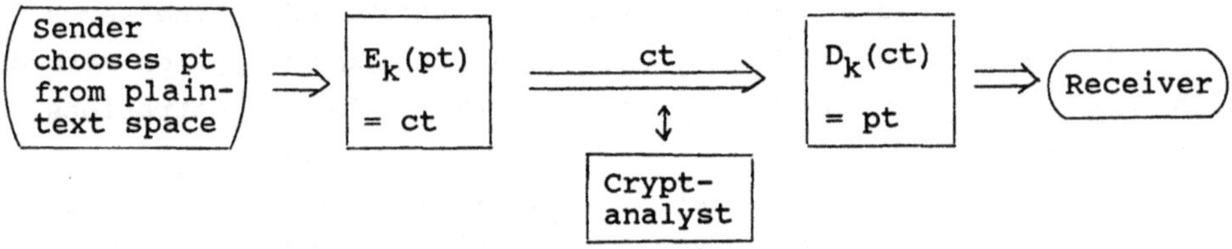

The sender (resp. receiver) knows in advance E_k (resp. D_k). For instance, the two parties might have agreed upon the matters in a previous meeting. The details of this agreement depend on the cryptosystem used. The procedure is essentially different for classical and public-key cryptosystems.

Observe that we have, for any key k and plaintext pt,

$$D_k(E_k(pt)) = D_k(ct) = pt \ .$$

We now make some over-all remarks about cryptanalysis. We begin by emphasizing the following principle.

Golden rule for designers of cryptosystems: Never underestimate the cryptanalyst.

The golden rule should be applied to all activities of the cryptanalyst: spying information in advance, inventing methods of attack, computing effectively, etc. As regards the advance information, we apply the following convention in the sequel: the cryptanalyst knows the cryptosystem used. This is reasonable also bacause of the following reason. Even if the cryptanalyst has to try out a few cryptosystems, the complexity of the procedure is essentially the same as when working with one system.

Although the cryptanalyst knows the cryptosystem, he/she does not know the key. However, if the number of all possible keys is small, like in the CAESAR system, then all keys can be tried out. (Recall that the cryptanalyst has excellent computing facilities!) This means that a cryptosystem with a small number of keys is useless in practice. However, such systems are sometimes still useful for illustrating specific points, as is the case in this exposition.

The essential condition for a cryptosystem to be good is that it is intractable to recover the plaintext pt from the cryptotext ct without knowing the decryption method D_k. We now discuss in more detail the possible initial setups for the cryptanalyst. We mention below four basic setups. Some symmetric modifications of them are also possible, as well as some combinations of the basic setups. They will not be discussed below. Recall, however, that in each setup the cryptanalyst is assumed to know the cryptosystem used.

<u>Setup (i): Cryptotext only.</u> Here the cryptanalysis has to be based on only one sample of cryptotext. For the cryptanalyst it is always better that the sample is longer. In simple systems, such as CAESAR, even short samples will suffice because usually only one key will produce meaningful plaintext. In more complicated systems long samples of cryptotext are necessary. Efficient cryptanalytic methods can be based on statistical information concerning the plaintext language, for instance, information about the frequency of individual letters in English.

<u>Setup (ii): Known plaintext.</u> Here the cryptanalyst knows in advance some pairs (pt, E_k(pt)). The knowledge of such pairs may essentially aid the analysis of the given cryptotext ct. A very simple example is again CAESAR: any pair of any length gives away the key.

<u>Setup (iii): Chosen plaintext.</u> The cryptanalyst knows also now in advance some pairs (pt, E_k(pt)). However, pt has now been chosen by the cryptanalyst. In situations where the cryptanalyst has definite conjectures about the key, it is clear that this setup is essentially better than (ii). On the other hand, this setup (iii) is likely to be realistic at least in such cases where the cryptanalyst has the possibility of masquerading himself or herself as an authorized user of the information system in question.

Before discussing setup (iv), we give an example of a cryptosystem where the initial setup (iii) often gives much better possibilities for the cryptanalyst than the initial setup (ii).

<u>Example.</u> The cryptosystem is based on linear algebra and has been quite important historically. It is originally due to Hill.

The plaintext and cryptotext spaces are both equal to Σ^*, where Σ is the English alphabet. We number the letters in the alphabetic order: A gets the number 0, B the number 1 and Z the number 25.

All arithmetic operations are carried out modulo the total number of letters: 26. This means that 26 is identified with 0, 27 with 1, 28 with 2, and so forth.

We choose an integer $d \geq 2$. It indicates the dimension of the matrices involved. In the encryption procedure, d-tuples of letters of the plaintext are encrypted together. In what follows d will be 2.

Let now M be a d-dimensional square matrix. The entries of M are integers between 0 and 25. Furthermore, M is assumed to be invertible in our arithmetic, that is, M^{-1} exists. For instance,

$$M = \begin{pmatrix} 3 & 3 \\ 2 & 5 \end{pmatrix} \quad \text{and} \quad M^{-1} = \begin{pmatrix} 15 & 17 \\ 20 & 9 \end{pmatrix}.$$

recall that arithmetic is carried out modulo 26. This implies that we have, for instance,

$$2 \cdot 17 + 5 \cdot 9 = 79 = 1 + 3 \cdot 26 = 1 ,$$

as we should, the number being on the main diagonal of the identity matrix.

The encryption is carried out by the equation

$$MP = C ,$$

where P and C are d-dimensional column vectors. More specifically, each d-tuple of plaintext letters defines the vector P where the components are the numerical encodings of the letters. Finally, C is again interpreted as a d-tuple of cryptotext letters.

For instance, the plaintext HELP defines the two vectors

$$P_1 = \begin{pmatrix} H \\ E \end{pmatrix} = \begin{pmatrix} 7 \\ 4 \end{pmatrix} \quad \text{and} \quad P_2 = \begin{pmatrix} L \\ P \end{pmatrix} = \begin{pmatrix} 11 \\ 15 \end{pmatrix} .$$

From the equations

$$MP_1 = \begin{pmatrix} 7 \\ 8 \end{pmatrix} = C_1 \quad \text{and} \quad MP_2 = \begin{pmatrix} 0 \\ 19 \end{pmatrix} = C_2$$

we obtain the cryptotext HIAT.

Consider now the world of our cryptanalyst. Assume the cryptanalyst has guessed that $d = 2$. He has to find the matrix M or, better still, the inverse M^{-1}. For this purpose he chooses the plaintext HELP and learns that the corresponding cryptotext is HIAT. This choice of the plaintext was good because of the following reasons.

The cryptanalyst knows that

$$M \begin{pmatrix} 7 \\ 4 \end{pmatrix} = \begin{pmatrix} 7 \\ 8 \end{pmatrix} \quad \text{and} \quad M \begin{pmatrix} 11 \\ 15 \end{pmatrix} = \begin{pmatrix} 0 \\ 19 \end{pmatrix} .$$

This can be written in the form

$$M = \begin{pmatrix} 7 & 0 \\ 8 & 19 \end{pmatrix} \begin{pmatrix} 7 & 11 \\ 4 & 15 \end{pmatrix}^{-1} = \begin{pmatrix} 7 & 0 \\ 8 & 19 \end{pmatrix} \begin{pmatrix} 19 & 19 \\ 14 & 21 \end{pmatrix} = \begin{pmatrix} 3 & 3 \\ 2 & 5 \end{pmatrix} .$$

The inverse M^{-1} is immediately calculable from M. Anything can be decrypted using M^{-1}.

The point in these calculations is that the inverse $\begin{pmatrix} 7 & 11 \\ 4 & 15 \end{pmatrix}^{-1}$ exists. On the other hand, our cryptanalyst chose the plaintext HELP giving rise to the matrix $\begin{pmatrix} 7 & 11 \\ 4 & 15 \end{pmatrix}$. Thus, he has to make the choice in such a way that the resulting matrix is invertible.

Assume now that the cryptanalyst is working under different preconditions: the initial setup is "known plaintext." More specifically, the cryptanalyst knows CKVOZI is the cryptotext corresponding to the plaintext SAHARA. Although we have here a longer sample of text than before, the information obtained is still much less.

Indeed, the plaintext-cryptotext equations are now

$$M\begin{pmatrix} 18 \\ 0 \end{pmatrix} = \begin{pmatrix} 2 \\ 10 \end{pmatrix}, \ M\begin{pmatrix} 7 \\ 0 \end{pmatrix} = \begin{pmatrix} 21 \\ 14 \end{pmatrix} \text{ and } M\begin{pmatrix} 17 \\ 0 \end{pmatrix} = \begin{pmatrix} 25 \\ 8 \end{pmatrix} .$$

No invertible square matrix can be formed of the three column vectors appearing as coefficients of M.

The cryptanalyst finds out that any invertible square matrix

$$M' = \begin{pmatrix} 3 & x \\ 2 & y \end{pmatrix}$$

can be the basis of the cryptosystem because it encrypts SAHARA as CKVOZI. Thus, the cryptanalyst might settle for the matrix

$$M' = \begin{pmatrix} 3 & 1 \\ 2 & 1 \end{pmatrix}$$

whose inverse is

$$(M')^{-1} = \begin{pmatrix} 1 & 25 \\ 24 & 3 \end{pmatrix} .$$

The cryptanalyst is ready for a cryptotext. He/she receives the text NAFG. The cryptanalyst now computes

$$\begin{pmatrix} 1 & 25 \\ 24 & 3 \end{pmatrix} \begin{pmatrix} 13 \\ 0 \end{pmatrix} = \begin{pmatrix} 13 \\ 0 \end{pmatrix} \text{ and } \begin{pmatrix} 1 & 25 \\ 24 & 3 \end{pmatrix} \begin{pmatrix} 5 \\ 6 \end{pmatrix} = \begin{pmatrix} 25 \\ 8 \end{pmatrix} .$$

The two column vectors give rise to the plaintext NAZI. However, the legal user knows the original M and its inverse and computes

$$\begin{pmatrix} 15 & 17 \\ 20 & 9 \end{pmatrix}\begin{pmatrix} 13 \\ 0 \end{pmatrix} = \begin{pmatrix} 13 \\ 0 \end{pmatrix} \text{ and } \begin{pmatrix} 15 & 17 \\ 20 & 9 \end{pmatrix}\begin{pmatrix} 5 \\ 6 \end{pmatrix} = \begin{pmatrix} 21 \\ 24 \end{pmatrix},$$

getting the plaintext NAVY.

Our cryptanalyst made a rude error which may lead to an entirely false action!

2. Classical cryptosystems: a survey

There are many classifications of cryptosystems, one of which will now be mentioned. If the use of substitutes remains unaltered throughhout the text, the cryptosystem is called monoalphabetic. This term reflects the idea that there is only one sequence of substitute letters: every plaintext letter is represented everywhere by the same substitute. If the plaintext is some natural language, cryptanalysis can always be based on the statistical distribution of letters. Examples are given in our article in EATCS Bulletin 26 (1985) 101-120.

Monoalphabetic substitution systems are to be contrasted with polyalphabetic ones: the use of substitutes varies in different parts of the plaintext. The wellknown PLAYFAIR system is discussed in detail in our column in EATCS Bulletin 33 (1987) 42-53. PLAYFAIR cryptanalysis is based on the distribution of pairs of letters.

To conclude this section, we still mention some cryptosystems of an entirely different nature. The system CODE BOOK is often referred to as the aristocrat of all cryptosystems. There is some truth in this statement since many aspects, such as making the cryptotext innocent-looking, can be taken into account in the CODE BOOK.

Both legal parties have a dictionary translating plaintext words (at least the most necessary ones) into sequences of numbers, some nonsense words, or preferably, into some other meaningful words. Thus, a part of the dictionary might look like:

Original	Translation
ATTACK	FISHING
⋮	⋮
IN	BETWEEN
⋮	⋮
MORNING	WORK HOUR
⋮	⋮
THE	THE

Then the plaintext ATTACK IN THE MORNING will become the cryptotext FISHING BETWEEN THE WORK HOURS. Suitable endings have to be added to the cryptotext to make it syntactically correct.

What about the cryptanalysis of CODE BOOK? If nothing is known about the dictionary, then the initial setup "cryptotext only" is impossible. On the other hand, the initial setups "known plaintext" and "chosen plaintext" necessarily disclose some details of the dictionary. It depends on the details how much this is going to help.

Are there cryptosystems which guarantee perfect secrecy? Briefly stated, perfect secrecy means that the cryptotext does not give away any information whatsoever to the cryptanalyst. The cryptanalyst may or may not intercept the cryptotext: he/she has exactly the same knowledge in both cases. The cryptotext gives away no information about the plaintext.

An example of a cryptosystem with perfect secrecy is ONE-TIME PAD. The plaintext is a sequence of bits with bounded length, say a sequence of at most 20 bits. The key is a sequence of 20 bits. It is used both for encryption and decryption and communicated to the receiver via some secure channel. Take the key 11010100001100010010.

A plaintext, say 010001101011, is encrypted using bitwise addition with the bits of the key, starting from the beginning of the key. Thus, the cryptotext is 100100101000. This gives no information to the cryptanalyst because he/she has no way of knowing whether a bit in the cryptotext comes directly from the plaintext or has been changed by the key. Here it is essential that the key is used only once, as also the name of the cryptosystem indicates. A previous plaintext together with the corresponding cryptotext give away the key, or at least a prefix of the key. Also a set of previous cryptotexts, with plaintexts remaining unknown, give away some information. Of course, legal decryption is obvious: use bitwise addition of the plaintext and the beginning of the key.

The obvious disadvantage of ONE-TIME PAD is the difficult key management. The key, at least as long as the plaintext, has to be communicated separately via some secure channel. Nothing has been accomplished: the difficulties in secret communication have only been transferred to a different level! Of course, the system is still useful for really important one-time messages.

In some variants of ONE-TIME PAD the key management is easier but the secrecy is not quite 100 %.

DES (Data Encryption Standard) is not dealt with in this article. It is possibly the most widely used cryptosystem of all time. It is presented in detail in our article in EATCS Bulletin 26 (1985) 101-120.

3. Cryptographic machines

The cryptosystems considered so far can be made more complicated and, at the same time, more secure by the use of cryptographic machines. Such machines make the encryption and (legal) decryption processes much faster, and also provide an enormous number of possible keys to choose from.

The history of cryptographic machines extends already over hundreds of years. While the early mechanical devices took several seconds for the encryption of a character, the modern electronic machines encrypt millions of characters in a second.

As an illustration of mechanical machines, we discuss the machine C-36 of the famous manufacturer of cryptographic machines Boris Hagelin. It is also known as the M-209 Converter and was used by the U.S. Army still in the early 50s.

Verbal descriptions of a mechanical device are extremely hard to follow when no specimen of the device is available. Since it is rather unlikely that the reader has C-36 at hand (indeed, you are lucky if you get one for $ 20.000!), we describe its operation in abstract terms. The machine is depicted in our column in EATCS Bulletin 36 (1988) 85-95. Its basic components are six disks, usually called rotors, and a cylinder called the lug cage.

Consider a 6 × 27 matrix M with entries from {0,1}. It is also assumed that every one of the 27 columns of M has at most two 1's. Such matrices are called lug matrices. The Matrix

$$M = \begin{pmatrix} 0&0&0&1&0&0&0&0&1&0&1&0&0&0&1&1&1&0&0&0&0&0&0&0&0&0&1 \\ 1&0&0&0&1&0&0&0&1&0&0&1&1&0&0&0&1&0&0&1&0&0&1&0&1&0&0 \\ 0&0&0&0&0&0&0&0&0&0&0&0&0&0&0&0&0&0&0&0&0&0&0&0&0&0&0 \\ 0&0&1&1&0&0&0&1&0&1&0&0&0&0&1&0&0&1&0&0&0&1&1&1&1&1&1 \\ 0&0&1&0&1&0&0&0&0&0&0&1&0&0&0&1&0&0&1&0&0&0&0&0&0&0&0 \\ 0&0&0&0&0&0&0&1&0&0&1&0&0&1&0&0&0&0&0&1&0&0&0&1&0&0&0 \end{pmatrix}$$

is an example of a lug matrix.

Obviously, if v is a 6-dimensional row vector with entries from {0,1}, then vM is a 27-dimensional row vector with entries from {0,1,2}. For instance, if v = (1,0,1,1,0,0) then

$$vM = (0,0,1,2,0,0,0,1,1,1,1,0,0,0,2,1,1,1,0,0,0,1,1,1,1,1,2).$$

(Here we use the above M.) The number of positive entries in vM is called the hit number of v with respect to M. In our example the hit number is 16. In general, the hit number can be any integer between 0 and 27.

A <u>step figure</u> is constructed as follows. Pile 6 sequences of numbers from {0,1}. The sequences, from top to bottom, should have lengths 17, 19, 21, 23, 25, 26 and start from the same point. For instance,

```
0 1 1 0 0 0 1 0 0 0 0 0 0 1 1 0
0 1 1 1 1 1 0 0 0 0 0 0 0 0 0 0 0 0 0
0 0 1 0 0 0 0 0 1 0 0 0 0 0 0 0 0 0 0 0 0
0 0 0 0 0 0 0 0 0 0 0 1 0 0 1 0 0 0 1 0 0 0 1
1 0 1 0 0 0 0 0 0 0 0 0 0 0 0 0 0 0 0 0 0 0 0 0 0
1 1 0 0 0 0 0 0 0 0 0 0 0 0 1 0 0 0 1 0 0 0 0 0 0 1
```

is a step figure. Contrary to lug matrices, there are no restrictions concerning the position of 1's in step figures.

A step figure <u>generates</u> an infinite sequence of 6-dimensional (row) vectors as follows. The first 17 vectors are read directly from the columns. Thus,

(0,0,0,0,1,1) and (1,1,0,0,0,1)

are the first two vectors generated by the step figure above. Whenever some row ends, it is restarted from the beginning. Thus, the vectors from 17th to 47th are:

(0,0,0,0,0,0) , (0,0,0,0,0,0) , (1,0,0,1,0,1) , (1,0,0,0,0,0),
(0,1,0,0,0,0) , (0,1,0,0,0,0) , (0,1,0,1,0,0) , (1,1,1,0,0,0),
(0,1,0,0,0,0) , (0,0,0,0,1,1) , (0,0,0,0,0,1) , (0,0,0,0,1,1),
(0,0,0,0,0,0) , (0,0,1,0,0,0) , (0,0,0,0,0,0) , (1,0,0,0,0,0),
(1,0,0,0,0,0) , (0,0,0,0,0,0) , (0,0,0,1,0,0) , (1,0,0,0,0,0),
(1,0,0,0,0,0) , (0,0,0,1,0,0) , (0,0,0,0,0,0) , (0,1,0,0,0,0),
(1,1,0,0,0,1) , (0,1,0,1,0,0) , (0,1,0,0,0,0) , (0,1,0,0,0,0),
(0,0,1,0,0,1) , (0,0,0,1,0,0) , (0,0,0,0,0,0) .

Having defined the lug matrix and the step figure, we are now in the position to tell how the cryptotext is obtained. We use the following numerical encoding of the letters: A gets the number 0, B gets the number 1 and so forth. Z gets the number 25. Arithmetic is carried out modulo 26.

Assume that α is the ith letter in the plaintext and that h is the hit number of the ith vector generated by the step figure, with respect to the lug matrix. Then α is translated into the letter

$$\gamma = h - \alpha - 1$$

in the cryptotext.

For instance, consider the plaintext

GOVERNMENTOFTHEPEOPLEBYTHEPEOPLEANDFORTHEPEOPLE ,

as well as the lug matrix and the step figure given above. The numerical encoding of the plaintext is as follows. We use commas only for clarity.

6, 14, 21, 4, 17, 13, 12, 4, 13, 19, 14, 5, 19, 7, 4, 15,
4, 14, 15, 11, 4, 1, 24, 19, 7, 4, 15, 4, 14, 15, 11, 4,
0, 13, 3, 5, 14, 17, 19, 7, 4, 15, 4, 14, 15, 11, 4,

The length of the plaintext is 47. As we often do, we have disregarded the spaces between two words. When using cryptographic machines, the spaces are sometimes filled with the letter Z.

Thus, we have to compute the hit numbers of the first 47 vectors generated by the step figure. This is straightforward because the first 17 vectors can be seen directly from the step figure and the other vectors we already computed above. The hit numbers are:

10, 17, 16, 9, 9, 9, 7, 0, 0, 0, 0, 12, 0, 0, 18, 7, 0, 0,
18, 7, 9, 9, 19, 14, 9, 10, 5, 10, 0, 0, 0, 7, 7, 0, 12,
7, 7, 12, 0, 9, 17, 19, 9, 9, 5, 12, 0 .

By the formula $\gamma = h - \alpha - 1$, we now compute the numerical encodings of the cryptotext letters:

3, 2, 20, 4, 17, 21, 20, 21, 12, 6, 11, 6, 6, 18, 13, 17,
21, 11, 2, 21, 4, 7, 20, 20, 1, 5, 15, 5, 11, 10, 14, 3,
6, 12, 8, 1, 18, 20, 6, 1, 12, 3, 4, 20, 15, 0, 21 .

Hence, we obtain the following cryptotext:

D C U E R V U V M G L G G S N R V L C V
E H U U B F P F L K O D G M I B S U G B
M D E U P A V .

The three occurrences of PEOPLE in the plaintext have been encrypted as RVLCVE, PFLKOD and DEUPAV, whereas the three occurrences of THE have been encrypted as GSN, UBF and GBM.

Several additional remarks concerning the machine C-36 are in order. The rotors and the lug cage correspond to the step figure and the lug matrix, respectively. Any prechosen step figure is obtained by activating suitable pins in the rotors. Similarly, any prechosen lug matrix is obtained positioning the lugs suitably.

The lug matrix and the step figure constitute the key for the C-36 encryption. The machine itself can be viewed as a physical realization of the cryptosystem described above: it operates according to a prechosen key after suitable pins have been activated and lugs positioned suitably.

The equation $\gamma = h - \alpha - 1$ can be written also in the form $\alpha = h - \gamma - 1$. This means that the same key can be used both for encryption and decryption. This is the reason why the basic equation is of Beaufort type rather than of Vigenère - Caesar type.

A combinatorially minded reader might want to compute the number of all possible keys in the C-36 encryption. The additional requirement for the lug matrix should be kept in mind. As will be seen below, all possible keys are not good from the point of view of secrecy.

It is obvious that the step figure generates vectors in a periodic fashion. Hence, the C-36 encryption can be viewed as the usage of the Beaufort square with a keyword. But how long is the keyword? Usually it is much longer than any conceivable plaintext. Hence, no periodicity due to the keyword can appear in the cryptotext.

Indeed, the lengths of the rows in the step figure are all pairwise relatively prime. This implies that only after

$$17 \cdot 19 \cdot 21 \cdot 23 \cdot 25 \cdot 26 = 101.405.850$$

steps we can be sure that we are back in the initial position again, that is, the step figure restarts the generation of the same sequence. In the general case the period is no shorter than this number which, in fact, exceeds the number of characters in a fairly big encyclopedia. However, in special cases the period can be much shorter. For instance, if the step figure contains no 0's then (1,1,1,1,1,1) is the only generated vector and, hence, the period equals 1. The period will be short if there are very few 1's in the lug matrix, or if there are very few 0's or very few 1's in the step figure. Thus, such choices of the key should be avoided.

There is no compelling mathematical reason for the step figure to consist of 6 rows. This number is just a compromise between security and technical feasibility. Of course, in general the period increases together with the number of rows. The number of rows should obviously be the same in the step figure and in the lug matrix. It is also a great advantage that the lengths of the rows in the step figure are pairwise relatively prime: this guarantees the maximal period. Everything else is arbitrary: the lengths of the rows both in the step figure and in the lug matrix, as well as the additional requirement made for the lug matrix. Physically this requirement corresponds to the number of lugs on a bar in the lug cage.

Some famous cryptographic machines, such as the German ENIGMA, American SIGABA and the Japanese RED and PURPLE from World War II, are electro-mechanical. The basic building block, a wired codewheel also called a rotor, is an insulating disk on which electrical contacts are placed on the circumference, as well as on each side. The latter contacts make the concatenation of rotors possible. As with C-36, the resulting substitution can be varied from letter to letter.

4. The idea of public keys

Think about any of the cryptosystems presented above, or any other similar system. There will be no difficulties in the decryption process for a cryptanalyst who has learned the encryption method. The encryption and decryption keys coincide even in such a sophisticated system as DES. So you give away your secrets if you work with one of the systems mentioned and publicize your encryption method.

This is not necessarily the case. There are systems in which you can safely publicize your encryption method. This means that also the cryptanalyst will know it. However, he/she is still unable to decrypt your cryptotext. This is what public-key cryptography is all about: the encryption method can be made public.

The idea was presented by Diffie and Hellman. Although revolutionary, the idea is still very simple.

In mathematics, as well as in real life, there are some one-way streets. It is easy to go along the street from A to B, whereas it is practically impossible to go from B to A. Encryption is viewed as the direction from A to B. Although you are able to go in this direction, this does not enable you to go in the opposite direction: to decrypt.

Take the telephone directory of a big city. It is easy to find the number of any specific person. On the other hand, it is hard - one might say hopeless! - to find the person who has a certain specified number. The directory consists of several thick volumes. In principle, you have to go through all of them carefully.

This gives an idea for a public-key cryptosystem. The encryption is letter by letter. For each letter of the plaintext, a name beginning with that letter is chosen at random from the directory. The corresponding telephone number constitutes the encryption of that particular occurrence of the letter in question. Thus, the system is polyalphabetic: two different occurrences of the same letter are very unlikely to be encrypted in the same way.

Observe that the encryption method is nondeterministic. Enormously many cryptotexts result from one and the same plaintext. On the other hand, each cryptotext gives rise to only one plaintext.

A legal receiver of the plaintext message should have a directory listed according to the increasing order of the numbers. Such a directory makes the decryption process easy. According to the customary terminology, the reverse directory constitutes the secret <u>trapdoor</u> known only to the legal users of the system.

Without knowledge of the trapdoor, i.e., without possessing a copy of the reverse directory, the cryptanalyst will have a hard time. This in spite of the fact that the encryption method has been publicized, and so the cryptanalyst knows, in principle, how he/she should interpret the number sequence intercepted.

The system based on telephone directories is intended to be only an initial illustration, rather than a cryptosystem for serious use. After all, the "reverse" directories are not so hard to come by.

The idea of public-key cryptography is closely related with the idea of <u>one-way functions</u>. Given an argument value x, it is easy to compute the function value f(x), whereas it is intractable to compute x from f(x). Here "intractable" is understood in the sense of complexity theory. The situation can be depicted as follows:

$$x \underset{\text{intractable}}{\overset{\text{easy}}{\rightleftarrows}} f(x)$$

General principles for the construction of public-key cryptosystems are explained in our article in EATCS Bulletin 26 (1985) 101-120.

We now list some very fundamental number-theoretic problems that have so far defied all attempts to classify their complexities. Indeed, none of the subsequent problems is known either to possess a deterministic polynomial time algorithm, or to be complete for any natural complexity class. The problems have turned out to be very useful for many aspects of public-key cryptography. Some mutual reductions among the problems are also known: which of them are "easier" and which are "harder".

FACTOR(n). Find the factorization of n.

PRIMALITY(n). Decide whether or not n is prime.

FIND-PRIME(>n). Find a prime number >n.

SQUAREFREENESS(n). Decide whether or not a square of a prime divides n.

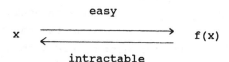

QUAD-RESIDUE(a,n). Decide whether or not $x^2 \equiv a \pmod{n}$ holds for some x.

SQUAREROOT(a,n). Find, if possible, an x such that $x^2 \equiv a \pmod{n}$.

DISCRETE-LOG(a,b,n). Find, if possible, an x such that $a^x \equiv b \pmod{n}$.

A number-theory minded reader might want to think of some natural reductions among the problems mentioned. For instance, if we are able to factor n, we are also able to tell whether or not n is prime. In fact, the primality problem is essentially simpler than factorization because there are many easily computable criteria to the following effect: if n is prime then a certain condition A (for instance, a congruence) is satisfied. Hence, if A is not satisfied then we are able to conclude that n is composite, without being able to factorize n.

From the theoretical point of view it would be desirable to be able to formally establish some lower bounds for the amount of work the cryptanalyst has to do in order to break a public-key cryptosystem. Unfortunately, no such theoretical lower bounds are known for the most widely used public-key cryptosystems. For instance, FACTOR(n) might be in low polynomial time, which would mean that RSA and related systems would collapse. On the other hand, it is not likely that FACTOR(n) is in low polynomial time. After all, people have investigated FACTOR(n) (more or less intensely) already for more than two thousand years.

The advantages of public-key cryptography are tremendous, provided the idea can be realized without any too harmful side-effects. The most far-reaching innovation due to public keys concerns <u>key management</u>: how to handle and send keys.

Consider any classical (that is, symmetric) cryptosystem. The encryption key gives away the decryption key and, hence, the former cannot be publicized. This means that the two legal parties (sender and receiver) have to agree <u>in advance</u> upon the encryption method. This can happen either in a meeting between the two parties, or else by sending the encryption key via some absolutely secure channel.

If a public-key cryptosystem is used, the two parties do not have to meet - they do not even have to know each other or be in any kind of previous communication! This is a huge advantage, for instance, in the case of a big data bank, where there are numerous users and some user wants to communicate only with a specific another user. Then he/she can do so just by applying the information in the data bank itself.

One can compare classical and public-ley cryptosystems also as regards the <u>length</u> of a key. Since every key has to be described somehow, the description being a sequence of letters of some alphabet (that is, a word), it is natural to talk about the length of a key. There is a remarkable difference between classical and public-key cryptosystems.

Consider first a classical cryptosystem. If the key is longer than the plaintext, nothing has really been achieved. Since the key has to be transmitted securely, one could transmit the plaintext instead of the key via this secure channel. Of course, in some situations the key is transmitted earlier to wait for the crucial moment.

Consider next a public-key cryptosystem. The length of the encryption key is largely irrelevant. The key is publicized anyway. This means that also the length of the decryption key is largely irrelevant: the receiver only has to store it in a secure place.

The easiness of key management can justly be regarded as the chief advantage of public-key cryptography. Let us now consider some other advantages.

One of a computer system's central strongholds is the <u>password</u> file. The following might be an entry in such a file.

login: JOHNSON   password: KILLER

If the password file is exposed - accidentally or otherwise - to an inspection by an intruder, then the intruder will have free access, for instance, to Mr. Johnson's electronic mail. We assume here that the mail is not encrypted and, thus, security is provided only by the passwords.

Suppose now that <u>one-way</u> functions f are used in connection with the password file. The entry mentioned above is now as follows.

login: JOHNSON   password: KILLER   function: f_J

Here f_J is a description of a one-way function. The idea is that KILLER is Mr. Johnson's "public" password, whereas only Mr. Johnson knows his "secret" password PURR such that

$$f_J(\text{PURR}) = \text{KILLER}.$$

In fact, he "publicized" the password KILLER after computing f_J(PURR).

Mr. Johnson types in the secret password PURR, after which the computer checks whether or not f_J applied to PURR gives the correct result KILLER. The computer does not store PURR in any way. The password file may now be inspected by an intruder without loss of security because the function f_J cannot be inverted.

5. RSA

The most widely studied public key cryptosystem was originally introduced by Rivest, Shamir, and Adleman and is usually referred to as RSA. It is based on the fact that it is almost impossible to recover two large primes p and q from their product n = pq - at least according to the presently known factorization algorithms. On the other hand, large random primes can be generated quickly.

The public key encryption is based on n, whereas decryption requires that we know p and q. We now present the details.

Let p and q be two large random primes (typically, having at least 100 digits in their decimal representation). Let

$$n = pq \quad \text{and} \quad \varphi(n) = (p - 1)(q - 1) .$$

(In fact, φ is the well-known Euler function.) Choose a number $e > 1$ relatively prime to $\varphi(n)$ and a number d satisfying the congruence

$$ed \equiv 1 \pmod{\varphi(n)} .$$

(Since e and $\varphi(n)$ are relatively prime, the congruence has a solution. It can be found rapidly by Euclid's algorithm.)

The numbers n and e, referred to as the <u>moludus</u> and the <u>encryption exponent</u>, respectively, constitute the public encryption key. Basically, the cryptotext c will be the least positive remainder of w^e (mod n), where w is the plaintext.

More specifically, we first express the plaintext as a word over the alphabet {0,1,2,...,9}. The word is divided into blocks of suitable size. The blocks are encrypted separately by applying the pair (n,e) in the way described earlier. A suitable size of the blocks is the unique integer i satisfying the inequalities $10^{i-1} < n < 10^i$.

We now show that decryption is easy if you are in the possession of the secret trapdoor information - that is, the number d, referred to as the <u>decryption exponent</u>. At this point, the knowledge of d is already intimately connected with the knowledge of p and q. The next result shows that d is, indeed, a proper decryption exponent.

Let c be the cryptotext corresponding to a plaintext w obtained in the RSA way described above, and let d satisfy the above congruence. Then $c^d \equiv w \pmod{n}$.

Proof. There exists an integer j such that $ed = j\varphi(n) + 1$. According to Euler's well-known theorem,

$$w^{\varphi(n)} \equiv 1 \pmod{n} ,$$

assuming that neither p nor q divides w. Hence, under this same assumption,

$$w^{j\varphi(n)+1} \equiv w \pmod{n} .$$

On the other hand, it is easy to see that this also holds true in the case where at least one of p and q divides w.

Consequently, we obtain

$$c^d \equiv (w^e)^d \equiv w^{j\varphi(n)+1} \equiv w \pmod{n} .$$

Indeed, no cryptanalytic attack against the RSA cryptosystem has so far been successful. Factoring a number seems to be much harder than determining whether the number is prime or composite.

Even if one admits that factoring is intractable, it would still be conceivable that $\varphi(n)$ (and, hence, d) could be determined by some "direct" approach. However, if this were the case, we would then immediately obtain the following fast-factoring algorithm.

Assume, thus, that we have been able to compute $\varphi(n)$. Then $p + q$ is immediately obtainable from $\varphi(n) = n - (p + q) + 1$ and the public information n. On the other hand, $p - q$ is the square root of $(p + q)^2 - 4n$ and, thus, also immediately obtainable. Finally, q can be immediately computed from $p + q$ and $p - q$.

However, we want to emphasize that there is no mathematical proof showing that

(1) Factorization is not, say, in linear time, or

(2) Factorization is needed for breaking RSA.

A very interesting result is that in RSA certain parts are as hard as the whole. For instance, if there is an $\varepsilon > 0$ such that you can always guess the least significant bit of the plaintext with probability $\geq 1/2 + \varepsilon$, then you can break the whole RSA. More specifically, there is a stochastic polynomial-time algorithm for the breaking of RSA.

We now give an example of RSA that involves larger primes than normally given in a written exposition. For a computer, the primes are still much too small but the reader will have difficulties in cracking the system with a programmable pocket calculator. Kimmo Kari did the numerical calculations.

We first give the two primes, their product, Euler function and the two exponents.

$$p = 3336670033$$
$$q = 9876543211$$
$$h = 32954765761773295963$$
$$\varphi(n) = 32954765748560082720$$
$$e = 1031$$
$$d = 31963885304131991$$

Here is the actual example.

Plaintext	Numerical encoding	Cryptotext
S A U N A S T O V	19 01 21 14 01 00 19 20 15 22	77 68 59 05 32 12 45 52 88 2
E S A R E E I T	05 19 00 01 18 05 00 05 09 20	65 88 88 60 45 38 59 07 62 7
H E R P R E H E A	08 05 18 00 16 18 05 08 05 01	32 30 30 08 02 45 53 15 02 1
T E D O R C O N	20 05 04 00 15 18 00 03 15 14	21 31 77 47 34 19 91 66 56 23
T I N U O U S L Y	20 09 14 21 15 21 19 12 25 00	26 79 96 17 49 12 44 73 93 50
H E A T E D P R E	08 05 01 20 05 04 00 16 18 05	18 60 12 14 55 08 02 97 74 69
H E A T E D M E A	08 05 01 20 05 04 00 13 05 01	19 30 82 41 72 78 36 62 37 92
N S T H A T T H	14 19 00 20 08 01 20 00 20 08	35 47 75 55 08 13 82 04 12
E S T O V E I S	05 00 19 20 15 22 05 00 09 19	80 96 51 86 11 93 31 35 21 6
N O T H E A T E	00 14 15 20 00 08 05 01 20 05	25 46 95 14 53 92 13 01 51 16
D D U R I N G T	04 00 04 21 18 09 14 07 00 20	11 50 97 64 43 79 13 53 82 16
H E A C T U A L	08 05 00 01 03 20 21 01 12 00	96 92 29 81 62 23 05 20 47 5
B A T H I N G A	02 01 20 08 09 14 07 00 01 00	11 99 79 09 82 55 26 46 28 0
S M O K E S A U N	19 13 15 11 05 00 19 01 21 14	22 99 97 58 47 09 33 93 11 63
A I S A S P E	01 00 09 19 00 01 00 19 16 05	15 47 01 66 62 00 54 88 57 52
C I A L T Y P E	03 09 01 12 00 20 25 16 05 00	22 65 30 11 10 28 72 92 14 02
O F P R E H E A T	15 06 00 16 18 05 08 05 01 20	47 67 27 30 05 30 01 66 95 8
E D S A U N A T	05 04 00 19 01 21 14 01 00 20	28 37 02 12 22 45 44 72 69 48
H E R E I S N O	08 05 18 05 00 09 19 00 14 15	78 35 61 58 44 89 02 37 47 7
C H I M N E Y B	00 03 08 09 13 14 05 25 00 02	19 24 51 71 60 60 29 84 87 09
U T S M O K E G	21 20 00 19 13 15 11 05 00 07	86 93 19 88 53 33 12 57 13 8
O E S O U T T H	15 05 19 00 15 21 20 00 20 08	13 19 81 25 97 20 43 78 79 88
R O U G H H O L E	18 15 21 07 08 00 08 15 12 05	99 62 60 55 25 34 65 19 66 3
S I N T H E W	19 00 09 14 00 20 08 05 00 23	29 63 96 70 80 42 70 59 54 77
A L L S A N D R	01 12 12 19 00 01 14 04 00 18	20 74 91 50 78 95 85 53 07 11
O O F	15 15 06 00 00 00 00 00 00 00	38 93 59 39 67 42 08 73 67 8

6. Protocols

In general, a cryptographic protocol involves a sequence of message exchanges. The number of communicating parties may be also greater than two. A specific, usually public-key, cryptosystem is used. The security of a protocol usually means protection against a passive or an active eavesdropper but often also protection against cheating by some of the parties. In the latter case a protocol may provide for arbitration procedures if the parties happen to disagree about their adherence to the protocol. Protocols are no more secure than the cryptosystem applied. It is difficult to prove that a specific cryptosystem possesses certain security properties. It is also difficult to prove that if the underlying cryptosystem satisfies certain security conditions then the protocol possesses certain security properties. We mention some examples.

Suppose elections are held over a computer network. A protocol should make it impossible for non-registered voters to vote although they might be legal users of the network. Furthermore, ballots should be kept secret and the publicized outcome of the elections should be fair.

Also some new types of secret votings can be carried out using appropriate protocols. Such protocols seem to open new vistas for confidential communication.

Some members of a council might have the right of veto. When an appropriate protocol is followed, nobody knows whether a negative decision is based on the majority, or somebody using the veto-right, or on both!

Let us consider a specific example. The parties A, B, C_1, ..., C_n want to make a yes or no decision. All parties can vote yes or no. Moreover, A and B have two additional votes, super-yes and super-no. Such a voting may be visualized as arising in the United Nations, with A and B being the two superpowers. If no supervotes are cast, the majority decides. If at least one supervote is cast, then the ordinary votes have no significance. The decision is yes in case of a draw. After the voting all parties know the decision but nobody knows why the decision was made. Was it due to a supervote, majority, or to both? Of course, it is possible to construct a voting machine to satisfy the requirements. But nobody would trust such a machine: it could be tampered to leak information and/or announce a false outcome for the voting.

We now mention three problems that require cryptographic protocols for their solution. The protocols devised for these problems are often used as a part of a protocol for a more complicated problem.

A and B want to flip a coin by telephone without any impartial judge. As always, both parties should at some later stage be able to check that the other party did not cheat. This may happen after the result of the coin flipping has been used for some other purpose.

An oblivious transfer allows A to transfer a secret to B with probability 1/2. After the completion of the protocol, B knows whether or not the secret was transferred successfully, but A does not know.

Two or more parties want to share a part of their secrets but do not want to give away their secrets entirely. For instance, two people want to find out who is older without learning anything else about each other's age. After going through the protocol both know who is older but neither one knows how much older. Our book "Computation and Automata", Cambridge University Press, 1985, contains detailed expositions of some further protocols.

Zero-knowledge proofs constitute an interesting recent aspect. You convince your partner that you can prove something without revealing a single bit of the proof!

Zero-knowledge proof of identity means the following. Suppose you have to tell your ID-number to a security guard. You can just say it. But then somebody might hear it and, later on, masquerade as you. However, you can also convince the guard that you know the number without revealing a single bit of it! (Some interesting conflicts with the U. S. Department of Defense, as well as the protocol in detail, are explained in: S. Landau, Notices of the American Math. Soc. 35 (1988) 5-12.)

Some useful books

D.E. Denning. Cryptography and Data Security. Reading, Mass.: Addison-Wesley (1982).

Concentrates on various aspects of data security.

H.F. Gaines. Cryptanalysis. New York: Dover Publications (1939).

A classic on cryptanalysis.

D. Kahn. The Codebreakers: The Story of Secret Writing. New York: Macmillan (1967).

The Bible of classical cryptography.

Lecture Notes in Computer Science

Vol. 270: E. Börger (Ed.), Computation Theory and Logic. IX, 442 pages. 1987.

Vol. 271: D. Snyers, A. Thayse, From Logic Design to Logic Programming. IV, 125 pages. 1987.

Vol. 272: P. Treleaven, M. Vanneschi (Eds.), Future Parallel Computers. Proceedings, 1986. V, 492 pages. 1987.

Vol. 273: J.S. Royer, A Connotational Theory of Program Structure. V, 186 pages. 1987.

Vol. 274: G. Kahn (Ed.), Functional Programming Languages and Computer Architecture. Proceedings. VI, 470 pages. 1987.

Vol. 275: A.N. Habermann, U. Montanari (Eds.), System Development and Ada. Proceedings, 1986. V, 305 pages. 1987.

Vol. 276: J. Bézivin, J.-M. Hullot, P. Cointe, H. Lieberman (Eds.), ECOOP '87. European Conference on Object-Oriented Programming. Proceedings. VI, 273 pages. 1987.

Vol. 277: B. Benninghofen, S. Kemmerich, M.M. Richter, Systems of Reductions. X, 265 pages. 1987.

Vol. 278: L. Budach, R.G. Bukharajev, O.B. Lupanov (Eds.), Fundamentals of Computation Theory. Proceedings, 1987. XIV, 505 pages. 1987.

Vol. 279: J.H. Fasel, R.M. Keller (Eds.), Graph Reduction. Proceedings, 1986. XVI, 450 pages. 1987.

Vol. 280: M. Venturini Zilli (Ed.), Mathematical Models for the Semantics of Parallelism. Proceedings, 1986. V, 231 pages. 1987.

Vol. 281: A. Kelemenová, J. Kelemen (Eds.), Trends, Techniques, and Problems in Theoretical Computer Science. Proceedings, 1986. VI, 213 pages. 1987.

Vol. 282: P. Gorny, M.J. Tauber (Eds.), Visualization in Programming. Proceedings, 1986. VII, 210 pages. 1987.

Vol. 283: D.H. Pitt, A. Poigné, D.E. Rydeheard (Eds.), Category Theory and Computer Science. Proceedings, 1987. V, 300 pages. 1987.

Vol. 284: A. Kündig, R.E. Bührer, J. Dähler (Eds.), Embedded Systems. Proceedings, 1986. V, 207 pages. 1987.

Vol. 285: C. Delgado Kloos, Semantics of Digital Circuits. IX, 124 pages. 1987.

Vol. 286: B. Bouchon, R.R. Yager (Eds.), Uncertainty in Knowledge-Based Systems. Proceedings, 1986. VII, 405 pages. 1987.

Vol. 287: K.V. Nori (Ed.), Foundations of Software Technology and Theoretical Computer Science. Proceedings, 1987. IX, 540 pages. 1987.

Vol. 288: A. Blikle, MetaSoft Primer. XIII, 140 pages. 1987.

Vol. 289: H.K. Nichols, D. Simpson (Eds.), ESEC '87. 1st European Software Engineering Conference. Proceedings, 1987. XII, 404 pages. 1987.

Vol. 290: T.X. Bui, Co-oP A Group Decision Support System for Cooperative Multiple Criteria Group Decision Making. XIII, 250 pages. 1987.

Vol. 291: H. Ehrig, M. Nagl, G. Rozenberg, A. Rosenfeld (Eds.), Graph-Grammars and Their Application to Computer Science. VIII, 609 pages. 1987.

Vol. 292: The Munich Project CIP. Volume II: The Program Transformation System CIP-S. By the CIP System Group. VIII, 522 pages. 1987.

Vol. 293: C. Pomerance (Ed.), Advances in Cryptology — CRYPTO '87. Proceedings. X, 463 pages. 1988.

Vol. 294: R. Cori, M. Wirsing (Eds.), STACS 88. Proceedings, 1988. X, 404 pages. 1988.

Vol. 295: R. Dierstein, D. Müller-Wichards, H.-M. Wacker (Eds.), Parallel Computing in Science and Engineering. Proceedings, 1987. V, 185 pages. 1988.

Vol. 296: R. Janßen (Ed.), Trends in Computer Algebra. Proceedings, 1987. V, 197 pages. 1988.

Vol. 297: E.N. Houstis, T.S. Papatheodorou, C.D. Polychronopoulos (Eds.), Supercomputing. Proceedings, 1987. X, 1093 pages. 1988.

Vol. 298: M. Main, A. Melton, M. Mislove, D. Schmidt (Eds.), Mathematical Foundations of Programming Language Semantics. Proceedings, 1987. VIII, 637 pages. 1988.

Vol. 299: M. Dauchet, M. Nivat (Eds.), CAAP '88. Proceedings, 1988. VI, 304 pages. 1988.

Vol. 300: H. Ganzinger (Ed.), ESOP '88. Proceedings, 1988. VI, 381 pages. 1988.

Vol. 301: J. Kittler (Ed.), Pattern Recognition. Proceedings, 1988. VII, 668 pages. 1988.

Vol. 302: D.M. Yellin, Attribute Grammar Inversion and Source-to-source Translation. VIII, 176 pages. 1988.

Vol. 303: J.W. Schmidt, S. Ceri, M. Missikoff (Eds.), Advances in Database Technology – EDBT '88. X, 620 pages. 1988.

Vol. 304: W.L. Price, D. Chaum (Eds.), Advances in Cryptology – EUROCRYPT '87. Proceedings, 1987. VII, 314 pages. 1988.

Vol. 305: J. Biskup, J. Demetrovics, J. Paredaens, B. Thalheim (Eds.), MFDBS 87. Proceedings, 1987. V, 247 pages. 1988.

Vol. 306: M. Boscarol, L. Carlucci Aiello, G. Levi (Eds.), Foundations of Logic and Functional Programming. Proceedings, 1986. V, 218 pages. 1988.

Vol. 307: Th. Beth, M. Clausen (Eds.), Applicable Algebra, Error-Correcting Codes, Combinatorics and Computer Algebra. Proceedings, 1986. VI, 215 pages. 1988.

Vol. 308: S. Kaplan, J.-P. Jouannaud (Eds.), Conditional Term Rewriting Systems. Proceedings, 1987. VI, 278 pages. 1988.

Vol. 309: J. Nehmer (Ed.), Experiences with Distributed Systems. Proceedings, 1987. VI, 292 pages. 1988.

Vol. 310: E. Lusk, R. Overbeek (Eds.), 9th International Conference on Automated Deduction. Proceedings, 1988. X, 775 pages. 1988.

Vol. 311: G. Cohen, P. Godlewski (Eds.), Coding Theory and Applications 1986. Proceedings, 1986. XIV, 196 pages. 1988.

Vol. 312: J. van Leeuwen (Ed.), Distributed Algorithms 1987. Proceedings, 1987. VII, 430 pages. 1988.

Vol. 313: B. Bouchon, L. Saitta, R.R. Yager (Eds.), Uncertainty and Intelligent Systems. IPMU '88. Proceedings, 1988. VIII, 408 pages. 1988.

Vol. 314: H. Göttler, H.J. Schneider (Eds.), Graph-Theoretic Concepts in Computer Science. Proceedings, 1987. VI, 254 pages. 1988.

Vol. 315: K. Furukawa, H. Tanaka, T. Fujisaki (Eds.), Logic Programming '87. Proceedings, 1987. VI, 327 pages. 1988.

Vol. 316: C. Choffrut (Ed.), Automata Networks. Proceedings, 1986. VII, 125 pages. 1988.

Vol. 317: T. Lepistö, A. Salomaa (Eds.), Automata, Languages and Programming. Proceedings, 1988. XI, 741 pages. 1988.

Vol. 318: R. Karlsson, A. Lingas (Eds.), SWAT 88. Proceedings, 1988. VI, 262 pages. 1988.

Vol. 319: J.H. Reif (Ed.), VLSI Algorithms and Architectures – AWOC 88. Proceedings, 1988. X, 476 pages. 1988.

Vol. 320: A. Blaser (Ed.), Natural Language at the Computer. Proceedings, 1988. III, 176 pages. 1988.

Vol. 321: J. Zwiers, Compositionality, Concurrency and Partial Correctness. VI, 272 pages. 1989.

Vol. 322: S. Gjessing, K. Nygaard (Eds.), ECOOP '88. European Conference on Object-Oriented Programming. Proceedings, 1988. VI, 410 pages. 1988.

Vol. 323: P. Deransart, M. Jourdan, B. Lorho, Attribute Grammars. IX, 232 pages. 1988.

Vol. 324: M.P. Chytil, L. Janiga, V. Koubek (Eds.), Mathematical Foundations of Computer Science 1988. Proceedings. IX, 562 pages. 1988.

Vol. 325: G. Brassard, Modern Cryptology. VI, 107 pages. 1988.

Vol. 326: M. Gyssens, J. Paredaens, D. Van Gucht (Eds.), ICDT '88. 2nd International Conference on Database Theory. Proceedings, 1988. VI, 409 pages. 1988.

Vol. 327: G.A. Ford (Ed.), Software Engineering Education. Proceedings, 1988. V, 207 pages. 1988.

Vol. 328: R. Bloomfield, L. Marshall, R. Jones (Eds.), VDM '88. VDM – The Way Ahead. Proceedings, 1988. IX, 499 pages. 1988.

Vol. 329: E. Börger, H. Kleine Büning, M.M. Richter (Eds.), CSL '87. 1st Workshop on Computer Science Logic. Proceedings, 1987. VI, 346 pages. 1988.

Vol. 330: C.G. Günther (Ed.), Advances in Cryptology – EUROCRYPT '88. Proceedings, 1988. XI, 473 pages. 1988.

Vol. 331: M. Joseph (Ed.), Formal Techniques in Real-Time and Fault-Tolerant Systems. Proceedings, 1988. VI, 229 pages. 1988.

Vol. 332: D. Sannella, A. Tarlecki (Eds.), Recent Trends in Data Type Specification. V, 259 pages. 1988.

Vol. 333: H. Noltemeier (Ed.), Computational Geometry and its Applications. Proceedings, 1988. VI, 252 pages. 1988.

Vol. 334: K.R. Dittrich (Ed.), Advances in Object-Oriented Database Systems. Proceedings, 1988. VII, 373 pages. 1988.

Vol. 335: F.A. Vogt (Ed.), CONCURRENCY 88. Proceedings, 1988. VI, 401 pages. 1988.

Vol. 336: B.R. Donald, Error Detection and Recovery in Robotics. XXIV, 314 pages. 1989.

Vol. 337: O. Günther, Efficient Structures for Geometric Data Management. XI, 135 pages. 1988.

Vol. 338: K.V. Nori, S. Kumar (Eds.), Foundations of Software Technology and Theoretical Computer Science. Proceedings, 1988. IX, 520 pages. 1988.

Vol. 339: M. Rafanelli, J.C. Klensin, P. Svensson (Eds.), Statistical and Scientific Database Management. Proceedings, 1988. IX, 454 pages. 1989.

Vol. 340: G. Rozenberg (Ed.), Advances in Petri Nets 1988. VI, 439 pages. 1988.

Vol. 341: S. Bittanti (Ed.), Software Reliability Modelling and Identification. VII, 209 pages. 1988.

Vol. 342: G. Wolf, T. Legendi, U. Schendel (Eds.), Parcella '88. Proceedings, 1988. 380 pages. 1989.

Vol. 343: J. Grabowski, P. Lescanne, W. Wechler (Eds.), Algebraic and Logic Programming. Proceedings, 1988. 278 pages. 1988.

Vol. 344: J. van Leeuwen, Graph-Theoretic Concepts in Computer Science. Proceedings, 1988. VII, 459 pages. 1989.

Vol. 345: R.T. Nossum (Ed.), Advanced Topics in Artificial Intelligence. VII, 233 pages. 1988 (Subseries LNAI).

Vol. 346: M. Reinfrank, J. de Kleer, M.L. Ginsberg, E. Sandewall (Eds.), Non-Monotonic Reasoning. Proceedings, 1988. XIV, 237 pages. 1989 (Subseries LNAI).

Vol. 347: K. Morik (Ed.), Knowledge Representation and Organization in Machine Learning. XV, 319 pages. 1989 (Subseries LNAI).

Vol. 348: P. Deransart, B. Lorho, J. Maluszyński (Eds.), Programming Languages Implementation and Logic Programming. Proceedings, 1988. VI, 299 pages. 1989.

Vol. 349: B. Monien, R. Cori (Eds.), STACS 89. Proceedings, 1989. VIII, 544 pages. 1989.

Vol. 350: A. Törn, A. Žilinskas, Global Optimization. X, 255 pages. 1989.

Vol. 351: J. Díaz, F. Orejas (Eds.), TAPSOFT '89. Volume 1. Proceedings, 1989. X, 383 pages. 1989.

Vol. 352: J. Díaz, F. Orejas (Eds.), TAPSOFT '89. Volume 2. Proceedings, 1989. X, 389 pages. 1989.

Vol. 354: J.W. de Bakker, W.-P. de Roever, G. Rozenberg (Eds.), Linear Time, Branching Time and Partial Order in Logics and Models for Concurrency. VIII, 713 pages. 1989.

Vol. 355: N. Dershowitz (Ed.), Rewriting Techniques and Applications. Proceedings, 1989. VII, 579 pages. 1989.

Vol. 356: L. Huguet, A. Poli (Eds.), Applied Algebra, Algebraic Algorithms and Error-Correcting Codes. Proceedings, 1987. VI, 417 pages. 1989.

Vol. 357: T. Mora (Ed.), Applied Algebra, Algebraic Algorithms and Error-Correcting Codes. Proceedings, 1988. IX, 481 pages. 1989.

Vol. 358: P. Gianni (Ed.), Symbolic and Algebraic Computation. Proceedings, 1988. XI, 545 pages. 1989.

Vol. 359: D. Gawlick, M. Haynie, A. Reuter (Eds.), High Performance Transaction Systems. Proceedings, 1987. XII, 329 pages. 1989.

Vol. 360: H. Maurer (Ed.), Computer Assisted Learning – ICCAL '89. Proceedings, 1989. VII, 642 pages. 1989.

Vol. 361: S. Abiteboul, P.C. Fischer, H.-J. Schek (Eds.), Nested Relations and Complex Objects in Databases. VI, 323 pages. 1989.

Vol. 362: B. Lisper, Synthesizing Synchronous Systems by Static Scheduling in Space-Time. VI, 263 pages. 1989.

Vol. 363: A.R. Meyer, M.A. Taitslin (Eds.), Logic at Botik '89. Proceedings, 1989. X, 289 pages. 1989.

Vol. 364: J. Demetrovics, B. Thalheim (Eds.), MFDBS 89. Proceedings, 1989. VI, 428 pages. 1989.

Vol. 365: E. Odijk, M. Rem, J.-C. Syre (Eds.), PARLE '89. Parallel Architectures and Languages Europe. Volume I. Proceedings, 1989. XIII, 478 pages. 1989.

Vol. 366: E. Odijk, M. Rem, J.-C. Syre (Eds.), PARLE '89. Parallel Architectures and Languages Europe. Volume II. Proceedings, 1989. XIII, 442 pages. 1989.

Vol. 367: W. Litwin, H.-J. Schek (Eds.), Foundations of Data Organization and Algorithms. Proceedings, 1989. VIII, 531 pages. 1989.

Vol. 368: H. Boral, P. Faudemay (Eds.), IWDM '89, Database Machines. Proceedings, 1989. VI, 387 pages. 1989.

Vol. 369: D. Taubner, Finite Representations of CCS and TCSP Programs by Automata and Petri Nets. X. 168 pages. 1989.

Vol. 370: Ch. Meinel, Modified Branching Programs and Their Computational Power. VI, 132 pages. 1989.

Vol. 371: D. Hammer (Ed.), Compiler Compilers and High Speed Compilation. Proceedings, 1988. VI, 242 pages. 1989.

Vol. 372: G. Ausiello, M. Dezani-Ciancaglini, S. Ronchi Della Rocca (Eds.), Automata, Languages and Programming. Proceedings, 1989. XI, 788 pages. 1989.

Vol. 373: T. Theoharis, Algorithms for Parallel Polygon Rendering. VIII, 147 pages. 1989.

Vol. 374: K.A. Robbins, S. Robbins, The Cray X-MP/Model 24. VI, 165 pages. 1989.

Vol. 375: J.L.A. van de Snepscheut (Ed.), Mathematics of Program Construction. Proceedings, 1989. VI, 421 pages. 1989.

Vol. 376: N.E. Gibbs (Ed.), Software Engineering Education. Proceedings, 1989. VII, 312 pages. 1989.

Vol. 377: M. Gross, D. Perrin (Eds.), Electronic Dictionaries and Automata in Computational Linguistics. Proceedings, 1987. V, 110 pages. 1989.

Vol. 378: J.H. Davenport (Ed.), EUROCAL '87. Proceedings, 1987. VIII, 499 pages. 1989.

Vol. 379: A. Kreczmar, G. Mirkowska (Eds.), Mathematical Foundations of Computer Science 1989. Proceedings, 1989. VIII, 605 pages. 1989.

Vol. 380: J. Csirik, J. Demetrovics, F. Gécseg (Eds.), Fundamentals of Computation Theory. Proceedings, 1989. XI, 493 pages. 1989.

Vol. 381: J. Dassow, J. Kelemen (Eds.), Machines, Languages, and Complexity. Proceedings, 1988. VI, 244 pages. 1989.